Red Years/Black Years

Red Years / Black Years

A Political History of Spanish Anarchism, 1911–1937

Robert W. Kern

ISHI *A Publication of the Institute for the Study of Human Issues Philadelphia*

Manufactured in the United States of America

Library of Congress Cataloging in Publication Data:

Kern, Robert W
    Red years/black years.

    Bibliography: p.
    Includes index.
    1. Anarchism and anarchists—Spain—History. 2. Confederación Na-
cional del Trabajo (Spain). 3. Federación Anarquista Ibérica. 4. Spain—
Politics and government—20th Century. I. Title.
HX925.K47   335'.83'0946   77–13595
ISBN 0–915980–54–1
ISBN 0–915980–83–5 pbk.

For information, write:

Director of Publications
ISHI
3401 Science Center
Philadelphia, Pennsylvania 19104
U.S.A.

To Jon and Josh

Acknowledgments

A grant from the American Philosophical Society and several faculty research fellowships from the University of New Mexico helped to finance the research on which this book is based.

My thanks go to the International Institute of Social History in Amsterdam and its curator of anarchist materials, Rudolf de Jong. I developed leads there which took me to Toulouse, Barcelona, Madrid, and a score of villages in Aragon. Many of the people I met would consent to be interviewed only "off the record"; hence the occasional "anonymous interview" cited in the footnotes.

A particular expression of gratitude goes to Alain Klarer of Paris, who provided many of the pictures; some of these came from the Centre International de Recherches sur l'Anarchisme in Lausanne, Switzerland. The other photos are of published or unpublished anarchist materials. I am also grateful for the work of Professor John Pawling, who served as map editor and cartographer.

A former student of mine, Shirley Fredricks, did some excellent research on Federica Montseny, and many people assisted in reading the manuscript, particularly David Holtby, Howard Rabinowitz, and Steven Kramer. Special thanks go to Meredith Dodge, who gave a great deal of time, encouragement, and assistance. Let me also thank my friends Lawrence Pitkethley and Linda Gutíerrez, who listened to the original idea and encouraged me to continue. And, finally, my gratitude and affection to my wife, Elizabeth.

Contents

Illustrations

Abbreviations and Definitions

AIT Asociación Internacional de los Trabajadores
CEML Comité Ejecutivo del Movimiento Libertario
CGT Confederação Geral do Travalho
CNT Confederación Nacional del Trabajo
FAI Federación Anarquista Ibérica
FIJL Federación Ibérica de Juventudes Libertarias
FNAE Federación Nacional de Agricultores de España
FSL Federación Sindicalista Libertaria
GIS German Information Service (Deutschen Informationsdienst)
JSU Juventudes Socialistas Unificadas
MLE Movimiento Libertario Español
POUM Partido Obrero de Unificación Marxista
PSUC Partit Socialista Unificat de Catalunya
UGT Unión General de Trabajadores

cenetista Member of the CNT
faísta Member of the FAI
treintista Member of a dissident faction of the CNT

A Note on Spanish Place Names

Some Spanish place names, including Andalusia, Catalonia, Cordoba, Castile, Corunna, Estremadura, Majorca, Navarre, and Saragossa, have been anglicized. In place names that have been left unchanged, most accents are omitted for simplicity.

Introduction

Anarchism . . . stands for the liberation of the human mind
from the domination of religion; the liberation of the human body from the domination of property; liberation
from the shackles and restraint of government. Anarchism
stands for a social order based on the free groupings of
wealth; an order that will guarantee to every human being
free access to the earth and full enjoyment of the necessities
of life, according to individual desires, tastes, and inclinations. [Emma Goldman, *Anarchism and Other Essays,* 1910]

Histories of the Spanish Civil War usually deal with military or diplomatic themes. Very few works have concentrated upon the participants themselves, especially if they happen to have been anarchists.
Thus, although almost forty years have passed since the outbreak of
fighting, the main figures of the Confederación Nacional del Trabajo (CNT) and the Federación Anarquista Ibérica (FAI) remain
indistinct, clouded by the confusion of war and the contradictions of
political movements struggling for survival.

The CNT in 1936 constituted the largest syndicalist union in the
world. Syndicalism at its simplest stood for mass unionism, the "one
big union" concept of the American Industrial Workers of the
World. It is no longer an important labor theory, and with its passing we have lost an understanding of the psychology of labor in the
early part of the twentieth century and of the political power that
these crude amalgamations possessed. By channeling the outrage
workers felt at poor working conditions and the insecurity of labor
into radical outlets, organizations like the CNT created a new type of
social institution—part political party, part union, and part guerrilla
band. The syndicalists acknowledged a debt to anarchism, but the

1

alliance between the two represents one of the unexplored aspects of modern European history. In Spain, the CNT was torn between continuing anarchist terrorism and seeking a political role for Spanish labor. During the civil war, when the CNT was confronted simultaneously by fascism and communism, these issues finally disappeared in the complications of the Popular Front coalition.

Still, the relationship of syndicalism to anarchism remains important because of what might have happened if the FAI, as the anarchist cadre of the CNT, had succeeded in controlling republican politics during the civil war. At the time, the anarchist revolution was criticized in Great Britain and France and ignored as an embarrassment by the democratic, anti-fascist propaganda of the communist-dominated Popular Front. In the postwar period, anarchist accomplishments were forgotten until an exchange of polemics between Noam Chomsky and Gabriel Jackson occurred in 1969. The debate centered on Chomsky's charges that Jackson, with liberal bias, systematically ignored the role of the anarchists.[1] Chomsky argued the proposition that the FAI was the heart of the resistance to fascism and communism alike.[2] After communists succeeded in destroying the anarchist movement in Barcelona during the May crisis of 1937 (so admirably described in George Orwell's *Homage to Catalonia*), the USSR ignored revolutionary demands and used the war as a propaganda showcase until its own defense needs led to a total withdrawal from the civil war.

This aspect of a political war within the civil war has attracted considerable attention. Burnett Bolloten's *The Grand Camouflage* documents the struggle between communists and anarchists from September 1936 to May 1937.[3] Bolloten makes a case that the war within the war, intensely waged at that time, was the true cause of republican defeat. If so, anarchists must have occupied a position of crucial political importance in Spain, but in pursuing the subject, the inquisitive reader finds only a limited selection of studies.

José Peirats is the official historian of the Spanish anarchists, and some of his writings have recently been republished.[4] Editions du Cercle and Editions de la Tête de Feuilles in Paris have issued works by Gaston Leval and Abel Paz dealing with various aspects of the movement.[5] César Lorenzo published a general history of Spanish anarchism, and there is John Brademas' Oxford dissertation (now a book) on relations between the CNT and the FAI.[6] Two Spanish historians, Maximiano García Venero and Eduardo Comín Colomer, have contributed studies of syndicalists and anarchists.[7] In English, besides Brademas, there is Murray Bookchin's recent work, as well as general studies on anarchism, with chapters about Spain, by George Woodcock, James Joll, and Daniel Guérin.[8]

So many parts of Spanish anarchist history bear upon republican society and the outcome of the civil war that a new and detailed study of Spanish anarchism seemed to be a useful undertaking. The FAI, particularly, was involved in aspects of modern politics that have rarely been discussed. The FAI's theory of anarcho-Bolshevism, its development of affinity groups (party cells), and its use of workers' councils and agricultural communes have captured the imagination of many students. The reason is not hard to understand: after thirty years of Cold War, politically interested persons who are searching for alternatives to the politics of capitalism and communism find the idealism and revolutionary dedication of the *faístas* refreshing. And no *faísta* has become more symbolic of revolutionary dedication than Buenaventura Durruti, already the subject of a novel and a biography, and now, in part, of this study.[9] There was something so incredibly compelling about Durruti and the rest of the *faístas* that Emma Goldman commented, "There are no other people so worthy of living and dying with."[10]

Whether this reputation was deserved I shall leave to the reader, although it is not a purpose of this book to further romanticize Durruti and his comrades. My major historical interest in the CNT and FAI has been to cover the last vestiges of the old anarchist movement. The postwar period in Europe finished the process of industrialization and urbanization and thus prevented emergence of additional utopian and anti-state protest from pre-modern agrarian sources. To find the equivalent of Spanish anarchism today, one must look to the non-Western world. Primitive rebels abound in South America, Africa, and the Middle East. But the terrorist groups of these areas are motivated by strong nationalist, religious, or anti-imperialist pressures, and this was not the case in Spain. The CNT and FAI were squarely in the tradition of libertarian anarchist thought begun in the nineteenth century by Pierre-Joseph Proudhon and particularly by Michael Bakunin.

Eric Hobsbawm pictured the Spanish anarchists as social bandits who cried for "vengeance on the rich and the oppressors, a vague dream of some curb upon them, a righting of individual wrongs."[11] Joaquín Maurín, a radical Spanish writer, saw them as a product of Spain's failure to develop modern institutions in the wake of its imperial collapse; to him, they were often as crude in their opposition to society as society was in its administration of justice.[12] Lenin characterized the movement as petit bourgeois, while Leon Trotsky

3

derisively called the CNT and FAI "a fifth wheel on the cart of bourgeois democracy."[13]

These interpretations contrast dramatically with Daniel Guérin's assertion that the Spanish anarchists "constantly sought to divert the people from a bourgeois democratic revolution in order to lead them to the social revolution through direct action."[14] George Woodcock has written that the CNT and FAI, despite some serious mistakes, "discovered a way to live in peaceful and free community."[15] Noam Chomsky mentions their "concern for human relations and the ideal of a just society."[16]

This divided opinion invites the historian to investigate the wreckage of a once-large political movement with a eye towards a postmortem. I believe, with Stanley Payne, that the Spanish anarchists were a part of the "disasters of twentieth-century revolutionary maximalism," participants in the unrestrained and confused political battles of our time.[17] Their excessive zeal, however, is not so hard to understand. The Spanish militants lived through an undeclared social civil war that existed long before the outbreak of the actual civil war in 1936. Lockouts, gun battles, and severe repression were the rule rather than the exception, and one can only conclude that the entire society assumed a high degree of tension, confusion, and violence. Slow economic growth had condemned Spain to live with the worst of both the old agrarian and the new industrial worlds—never totally in the one, never quite in the other.

What results from this kind of situation, according to David Rapoport, is a society with a deeply divided set of institutions populated by openly hostile classes with unequal shares of wealth.[18] In Spain, anarchists directed their early antagonism against the monarchy and the Church. Both had, in different ways, abandoned the people, leaving the field to the anarchists and other groups. Fifteen or more attempts were made on the life of Alfonso XIII during his rule from 1902 to 1931, and churches were damaged by the hundreds. This was primitive rebellion at its most violent.

But Alfonso abdicated in 1931, and the Second Republic disestablished the Church soon after. With its original targets thus removed, the anarchist movement was left without precise goals. Only very slowly did its intellectual horizons expand to encompass new ideas and a more consistent socialism. Even this evolution was interrupted by severe factional division. Although the issue of unionism versus terrorism had existed within the CNT since 1919, after the founding of the FAI in 1927 the controversy frequently diverted attention from more intelligent policy-making.

Terrorism, of course, was a well-established habit in a violent society. The Spanish state was not strong, and violence had always been its chief weapon. Its nominal liberalism declined in the face of a vigorous army, its own use of military justice, and a drive for revolution from above, as we shall see. Until 1931, anarchism survived as the only radical philosophy in Spain because it alone was sufficiently decentralized, militant, and violent to cope with governmental abuses.

But despite such terroristic predilections an end to primitive rebellion did occur, and the anarchists began to make solid political contributions. They were among the first to see serious flaws in republican policies on land and labor. Only recently have such scholars as Stanley Payne, Richard Robinson, and Edward Malefakis challenged the somewhat idyllic account of the Second Republic given by Gerald Brenan in *The Spanish Labyrinth*.[19] The anarchists saw these problems while on their first expedition into normal politics, and although they were still too unsophisticated to avoid the use of violence altogether, the movement did come of age between 1931 and 1936.

All to no avail, as it turned out, for the rightists capitalized upon a number of issues to come back into power in 1933 and begin an attack upon republican principles that upset the entire political scene. The anarchists hung back, partly from exhaustion but partly too out of a dawning understanding of political reality. Between 1933 and 1936 they used their time to develop new ideas of collectivization and worker organization. Internal wounds healed, and the movement modernized itself in a number of ways. Primitive rebellion was now a thing of the past.

Finally, the last stage, the civil war: revolution, exaltation, defeat from an unexpected source, and despair—all experienced in less than a year. Critics both in and outside the movement have faulted anarchist policies as weak, inadequate, or simply wrong—but I do not wholly share that view.[20] Anarchists in government (an anomaly if there ever was one) provided one of the most interesting moments in Spanish political history. Durruti's militia provided another high point.

Buenaventura Durruti weaves his way through much of this narrative, as do Federica Montseny, Francisco Ascaso, and Diego Abad de Santillán. In a sense, the book is a group biography of the major Spanish anarchists, for I felt that this biographical technique might capture nuances of the movement that would otherwise be lost. Out of the lives of the activists come details of the anarchist subculture—perhaps the richest and most interesting aspect of the movement. The main topic, nevertheless, remains the anarchists' politics and political behavior.

PART ONE

Origins, 1911–1930

CHAPTER ONE

Organizing the CNT

One may ask . . . if the proletariat is to be the ruling class, over whom will it rule? The answer is that there will remain another proletariat which will be subjected to this new domination, this new state. It may be, for example, the peasant "rabble" which, as we know, does not stand in great favor with the Marxists. [Michael Bakunin, *Statism and Anarchy,* 1873]

I. The Peasants

In 1900, while the rest of Europe was becoming increasingly bourgeois, the peasantry clearly comprised a large majority in Spanish society. This agrarian predominance in the midst of continental industrialism was almost unique. To the east the peasant masses of Russia remained submerged until the revolution of 1917, when they emerged briefly before disappearing again under Stalinism. Europeans at the turn of the century were accustomed to characterizing Spain, not Eastern Europe, as the archetypal peasant society; travellers' reports cast the country south of the Pyrenees almost as a new species. The term "third world" or "underdeveloped world" might have been applied if the words in their current senses had been available. As it was, the same thing was said in different ways.[1] "In no European country today," wrote one English traveller, "is there such a distinction between rulers and ruled as in Spain."[2] A Spaniard took the same view:

We see a Spain in the true style of Potemkin. Two historical accidents, the discovery of the New World by Columbus and the marriage of Doña Juana to the greatest family of Central Europe, have encouraged the view of Spain as grandiose and imperial. . . . But we are one of the

9

most ruined and troublesome outskirts of the planet. With a semi-African climate and a medieval population, we can produce only *caciques*.[3]

The *caciques* symbolized Spanish backwardness. These rural bosses controlled land and local political life as the result of nineteenth-century confiscations of ecclesiastical property—confiscations which, ironically, had been designed originally to eliminate aristocratic and clerical absentee landownership.[4] What might have afforded liberal reform ended by intensifying a major social crisis. Between 1837 and 1856, liberal governments succeeded in concentrating 33 percent of all agricultural property into the hands of 0.1 percent of the population, while the 10 million smallest agricultural proprietors owned less than 15 percent of all arable lands.[5] These changes in landownership slightly broadened control of political power, but only by extending it from the upper classes to middle-class *caciques,* who particularly dominated the twelve southern provinces throughout the last quarter of the nineteenth century.

Andalusia, the region most affected, had some 547,548 landless laborers who, according to a radical economist, earned less than one peseta a day.[6] A typical Andalusian village, averaging several thousand in population, might have no more than two or three families above the poverty line. The estate supervisor, the store manager, and perhaps a notary or lawyer made up a crude gentry class of sorts, subservient to the absentee landowner or, more likely, to a political boss of the leading provincial town. A village would have no school or at best three grades of religious education. Roads were so primitive that the towns, lying in medieval isolation, were places where the arrival of strangers was a real event.[7]

Two events stood out in the recent history of Andalusia: the cantonal revolution of 1873 and the Mano Negro conspiracy of the 1880s. The first came during the chaotic interregnum caused by the abdication of King Amadeo in 1873. Francisco Pi y Margall, an intellectual from Catalonia, adapted the federalist ideas of Pierre-Joseph Proudhon, a French anarchist, as the philosophy of an anti-centralist cabinet that held office briefly in the spring of 1873.[8] These principles failed miserably at the national level, but in Andalusia and the Valencia area thousands of peasants participated in the revolt of the "cantons." The Church was attacked for having failed to protect the people from liberal land confiscations, while attempts were made to return land to peasant ownership. A host of almost puritan prohibitions against smoking, drunkenness, and conspicuous use of money were issued by the cantons, and proclamations in favor of free love,

10

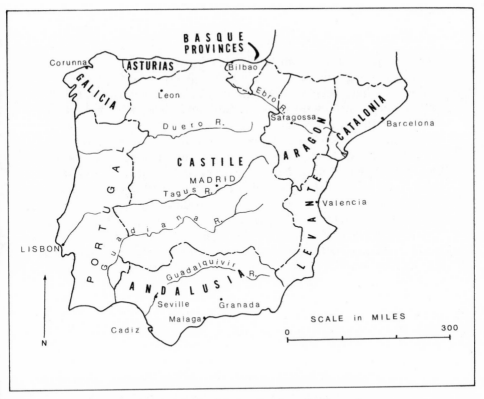

Spain, with the Major Regions Indicated

public education, and divorce demonstrated the utopian nature of the rebellion.[9] In Cadiz, in the provinces of Seville and Cordoba, in the villages of El Bosque, Benaocaz, Arahal, Bornos, Villamartin, Medina Sidonia, Pozoblanco, Iznajar, Fuenteovejuna, and scores of other places, federalism suddenly transformed itself into anarchism, although, as Eric Hobsbawm notes, perhaps its most prominent characteristic was an exaggerated sense of individualism.[10]

The Mano Negro, or Black Hand, continued the *jacquerie* tendency until the 1890s. A military campaign to crush the cantons in 1873–1874 was followed by strenuous police vigilance. The Civil Guard (a national constabulary) ruled the South like a conquered country, a procedure that caused frequent provocations by both sides. The actual Black Hand scare of 1883–1884 consisted largely of spasmodic strikes and attacks upon authority. Although these may have been fabricated in part by the Andalusian authorities, the general strikes in Jerez and Cadiz in 1892 and again in 1901 and 1904 were real enough, affecting thousands of peasants and fanning the

11

fires of discontent.[11] Only the power of the Civil Guard and the *caciques* kept the movement in check.

Already legends and leaders had appeared. Perhaps the most famous southern rebel was Fermín Salvochea, born in Cadiz in 1842, an exile in Great Britain at age fifteen, and exiled a second time in 1866 after the uprising against the monarchy at San Gil. His triumphant return in 1871 led to his election as a representative to the national Cortes. Two years later, in the cantonal uprising, he was elected mayor of Cadiz. No one worked harder than Salvochea to keep the revolt going; he travelled throughout Andalusia preaching a message of libertarian federalism. When the cantons were crushed, Salvochea was jailed until 1880 and then sent into exile again for another six years, after which he returned to Cadiz and founded a major radical newspaper of the South, *El Socialismo*. His fervent campaign for the eight-hour day, better working conditions, and land reform for the peasants led him into a deep involvement with the Jerez strikers. Fermín Salvochea was arrested for a fourth time in 1893. Although his term was commuted in 1899, his renewed support for the peasant movement forced him to flee in 1906 to Morocco, where he died.

For most Andalusian peasants, the experiences of Fermín Salvochea would have been exceptional. Yet often, so many factors in their own lives contributed to acute personal discomfort that even the most passive were not satisfied with their social condition. A yearly birth rate of 28.8 per thousand and a death rate of 17.8 per thousand, far above the national averages (although not high in themselves for such an area), meant a steady increase in population where land was already in desperately short supply.[12] In 1900 Andalusia accounted for 28.7 percent of the national population.[13] Laborers in the South, often seasonally unemployed, earned an average of less than a peseta a day for the 130–150 days a year they worked.[14] Underemployment was increased by the fact that industrial development existed only in the North. Under these circumstances, the political clashes between the peasants and Civil Guard provided a final element of misery and, in many cases, the motive for migration.

The movement of peasants north after the turn of the century was quite large. In 1900, country dwellers still outnumbered the urban population by 10 percent, but by 1921 the figures were almost equal. Agriculture continued to account for 37 percent of the work force, but industrial employment rose to 21 percent. One writer estimated that a million agricultural workers left the countryside for the city in the 1920s alone.[15] This rapid increase made itself felt in the industrial North, where the population of Barcelona rose from 721,869 in 1921 to 1,148,129 in 1934.[16] As many as 20,000 peasants left Andalusia annually to make the trek north, taking their grievances with them. The daily express of the Sudeste railroad, running from Cadiz to Seville, Cordoba, Valencia, and Barcelona, became a pipeline for migrants moving north.

Peasants also came to the northern cities from rural areas outside the South. Those from Galicia migrated internally (or emigrated to South America) to escape subleasing practices which frequently left the peasant cultivator with little or nothing to live on.[17] Exploitative rental practices also affected small farmers in Catalonia, the *rabassaires,* who sometimes quit their lands rather than put up with the marked favoritism shown landlords by the government.[18] Overpopulation was a chief cause of peasant migration from the Levante to Valencia and Madrid. All over Spain, as the shortage of land caused subdivision of acreages and the mechanization of agriculture reduced the demand for day laborers, peasants drifted to the cities to seek their livelihood.[19] Change finally had come to Spain, and its impact was felt in thousands of the smallest villages.

II. The Cities

The only industrial cities of Spain in the early twentieth century were Barcelona and, in the Basque provinces, Bilbao. Valencia, which offered longshoreman jobs at the harbor, had few other industrial opportunities. Madrid, over a million in population, was nevertheless in many respects a pre-industrial city, depending upon government jobs for much of its prosperity, although by 1931 small manufacture and construction had expanded significantly. Seville, the chief city of Andalusia, seemed sunk in its colonial glory, a center for the gentry and for religious activity. Cadiz and Malaga challenged Seville economically but were themselves too far away from the center of the nation to attract major industry.

Bilbao became the main site of the Spanish steel and iron industry and a center for shipbuilding and other heavy industries. Except for the British-owned Rio Tinto mines near Huelva in southwestern Spain, Bilbao's hinterland contained most of Spain's mineral resources. Belgians mined zinc, the French ran the railways, and European corporate giants like Schneider-Creusot, Krupp, and Armstrong-Vickers made substantial investments in the region.[20] But laborers from Galicia so filled the job market that Andalusians did not migrate to Bilbao in large numbers. Galicia suffered from its own poverty, and the Bilbao labor market was close at hand.

Catalonia and its capital, Barcelona, soon became the main destination for Andalusians. There they joined large numbers of migrants from other regions to serve as manpower for the flourishing industry and manufacturing of the Northeast.[21] Wool milling and metallurgical enterprises had already developed in the late nineteenth century, and during World War I foreign firms flocked to Barcelona to take economic advantage of Spanish neutrality. By 1918 more than eighty foreign companies had opened subsidiaries in Catalonia.[22] Canadians owned the electrical utilities, Americans and British the telephone system, and Basques a large new steel company, Siderúrgica Mediterránea, while General Motors began the production of trucks.

Part of the attractiveness of Barcelona for new commercial enterprise was the availability and cheapness of labor. More than five thousand new workers moved to the city every six months, and in 1910 their wages averaged 4.92 pesetas a day.[23] Crammed into the tenement districts of Atarazanas, Barceloneta, and Pueblo Nuevo near the harbor, in outlying *barrios* north and south of the city, and on the hills overlooking Barcelona, the newly arrived workers did not have the skills or education to move out of the vast unskilled labor pool that kept wages down and forced them to live in conditions very little better—and often worse—than those in the villages they had left. Public education did not exist; the Church controlled the schools and did not press for a widespread extension of education. There was a government-sponsored Institute of Social Reform, but its function was advisory rather than regulatory, and, as a consequence, working conditions and public health were almost always bad. Even public relief was controlled by the Church, whose parsimony made the lack of unemployment compensation and industrial accident insurance even more sorely felt in times of need.

Workers had no choice but to compete frantically for jobs, and the competition often encouraged employers to reduce wages. Membership in labor organizations routinely meant blacklisting for the most militant. When the Spanish-American War cut off cotton from Spain's colonies and caused a textile depression, crude new labor syndicates managed to attract enough support to call Barcelona's first general strike in 1902.[24] But even with the aid of the socialist Unión General de Trabajadores, the sole Spanish labor confederation, the syndicates could not prevent mass firings and

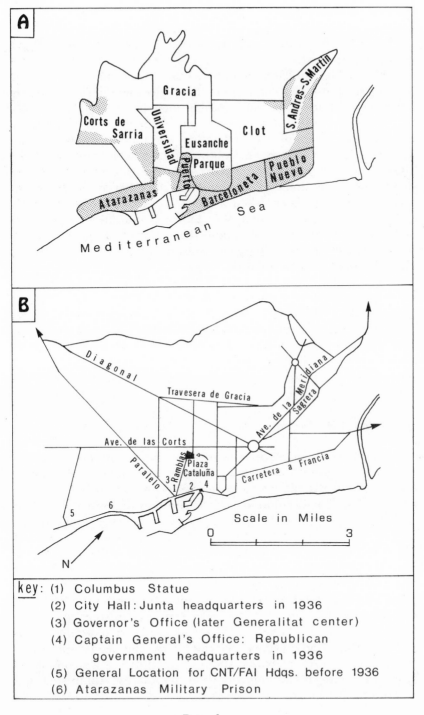

Barcelona

(A) Districts of the town, with workers' neighborhoods marked by dotted
pattern. (B) General street plan, with some important locations.

other anti-labor activities once the strike had been declared illegal by the government.

This failure probably encouraged the growth of violence which had begun to dominate Barcelona. For a decade, the city witnessed increasing conflict as peasants brought their frustrations into an urban environment that was ill-suited to help them. Employers fought back through an Employers Federation, and the result was a continuation of the *jacquerie* tendency of the countryside in a new setting. In 1892, protests linked with the Jerez strike led to two bombing incidents, one at the home of a general and the other at the Teatro de Liceo. Four years later, when a bomb was thrown into a Corpus Christi procession, more than four hundred radicals were arrested, and five were executed. Allegations that many of the prisoners had been tortured raised the charge of *"la Espagne inquisitorial"* and hardened the lines of separation which divided Barcelona into a city of warring camps.[25] The Montjuich fortress, built on a high hill to the south of the downtown areas—and just above Atarazanas, the largest worker district—became a symbol of the brutality of the Spanish government. Failure of the general strike further increased social tension, but even though the peasant influx continued unabated during the next few years and membership in the syndicates reached 45,000, political uncertainties soon began to overshadow labor violence.[26]

III. Political Background

Spain's political weaknesses after her defeat in the Spanish-American "disaster," as many called the war, were chiefly transitional. Loss of the last colonies coincided with the deaths of the two architects of the Restoration period, Antonio Cánovas del Castillo and Práxedes Mateo Sagasta. Their Conservative and Liberal parties, accustomed to a cooperative alternation in office, continued that practice only with greater difficulty until 1923. Seeking to quiet the strong demands for change now being heard, new leaders like Antonio Maura and José Canalejas tried to develop a moderate reform program in the face of opposition from Alfonso XIII. The new king, crowned in 1902 after seventeen years of regency following the death of his father in 1885, had a military education, clerical sympathies, and a grudge that the throne had been displaced by politicians. Unfortunately for Alfonso, the return of a strong monarch, far from rekindling Bourbon popularity, stimulated the spread of a passionate republicanism.

During the elections of 1901 in Catalonia, for example, Alejandro Lerroux, a radical republican, used anticlericalism and hostility towards the army to appeal to republicans and so win a seat in the parliament by a big margin over several other candidates. Styling himself the "tribune of the people," the antithesis of Alfonso, Lerroux with his radical demagoguery eclipsed even Nicolás Salmerón, the national head of the Unión Republicana. Part of his success came from the failure of Catalan strikes, for Alejandro Lerroux's promise to confiscate religious properties at least suggested a vague kind of social revolution. Over the next six years Lerroux dominated Barcelona politics, sometimes even winning support from national parties that preferred his street oratory to the more substantial threat of regionalism or labor politics.

The regionalists, the newest and most startling force in Catalan society, began their activity in 1886 by petitioning Madrid to allow Catalonia greater regional autonomy. Linguistic and cultural differences were important factors behind the request, but the persistence of Castilian free-trade policies was the crucial element. Industrial Catalonia resented the desire of rural Castile to import finished products cheaply at the expense of Catalan manufactured goods, which might otherwise have dominated the Spanish market at a higher cost to the consumer. In 1905, after giving up hope that autonomy would be freely granted, the overwhelmingly bourgeois Lliga Regionalista elected twelve members to the Barcelona city council and sent seven deputies to parliament. The national parties used Alejandro Lerroux as a counterforce to oppose the League, but an alliance of regionalists and republicans nevertheless elected forty-one candidates to the Catalan parliament in 1907. The potential breakaway of the second richest area in Spain was foreshadowed by these events, dramatizing the national crisis that now saw middle-class politics badly divided.

The first explosion of tension came in July 1909 after the various blocs had jockeyed endlessly in an increasingly volatile situation. Antonio Maura, the Conservative Premier and a sympathizer with administrative reform, loosely allied himself with another Catalan regionalist group, Solidaridad Catalana, much to the anger of Liberals like Segismundo Moret and José Canalejas, who attacked both the regionalists and Maura's pro-clerical efforts. Nevertheless, the Conservative Premier introduced in the national parliament a local government reform bill that placated Catalan regionalists, particularly because it was accompanied by anti-terrorist proposals to assure middle-class regionalists that workers would face heavy sanctions if unions attempted political action on their behalf.

Debate on the local government reform bill continued to July 1909 and stirred up a new wave of labor unrest that remained unappeased by passage of another bill giving workers a limited right to strike. This balancing of demands among sectors of society continued—disastrously, as it turned out—when the Premier gave in to military and economic pressure and sent an expedition to Morocco, where tribesmen in the Riff area threatened construction of a railroad outside the Spanish enclave of Melilla. Antonio Maura's hope was that this foreign adventure might unify Spain and reduce objections to his domestic program, but he had not counted on resistance to the mobilization of Catalan reserves or a general anti-war protest mounted by workers' groups and Lerroux's followers. Everyone had a grievance: the proletariat, for its unimportance in Premier Maura's program; Alejandro Lerroux's party, for its slow loss of political power; and even the Catalan regionalists, who could not agree to cooperate with the government in Madrid and so joined the protest.

Out of this odd compound and the fragility of the reform program came the Tragic Week—*la Semana Trágica*—which saw, from July 26 to 31, 1909, an unleashing of rioting and destruction throughout Barcelona by regionalists, anarchists, and other radicals.[27] Eight policemen and soldiers died, and 124 received injuries; 104 civilians were killed and 296 wounded. A dozen churches and convents were burned, and three priests were killed. In the wake of this tragedy, the government rapidly repressed the outbreak of public violence. Martial law lasted for months; public gatherings were banned; and civil liberties ceased to exist in Catalonia for some time. But the biggest consequence of the Tragic Week was Antonio Maura's fall from power on October 21, 1909, since with him went the opportunity to obtain reasonable change and reconciliation. Henceforth, the Conservative party, citing the Tragic Week, remained intransigently opposed to alterations of state policies designed mainly for a rural society. But radicals and regionalists rejected ecclesiastical and military institutions that had close associations with traditional society; and others, including the anarchists, went even further, seeking new forms of organization and solidarity to prevent the kind of persecution that had followed the Tragic Week and to bring into being a completely different society.*

*Of the 1,725 indictments handed down after the Tragic Week, 672 resulted in convictions. Fifty-nine of those convicted were sentenced to life imprisonment and five to execution.

18

IV. The Anarchists

The first result of radical alienation in the aftermath of the Tragic Week was the creation of the Confederación Nacional de Trabajo (CNT). While the CNT eventually became one of the world's most revolutionary trade unions, it began inauspiciously in 1911 with efforts by syndicalists and anarchists to regroup and to expand their earlier activities. Spanish anarchism had originated in 1868 with the arrival of the Italian anarchist Giuseppe Fanelli, an emissary of Michael Bakunin, the premier anarchist of the time. Out of Fanelli's proselytizing came the Alianza de la Democracia Social, which published the newspaper *La Federación* and preached anarchism at regional meetings at Valencia, Saragossa, and Cordoba. A nucleus of militants emerged who dominated the movement until the end of the century.[28] Loose ties existed with Michael Bakunin's own International Alliance of Social Democracy, and these acted as a conduit for his influence to infiltrate many regions of the country.[29] In 1873 the Bakuninists cooperated with the Proudhon-inspired federalists in their futile attempt at revolution, much to the disgust of Friedrich Engels and other Marxists, who did not believe Spain was ready for revolution.[30] After the collapse of the cantonal movement, the Alianza was banned and membership declined.

The basic ideas of Michael Bakunin, however, were well suited to Spain. The Russian anarchist stressed that revolutionaries should use all means at their disposal to end separation of the rural and urban proletariats and to unite and organize these two groups into one.[31] *Statism and Anarchy,* which Bakunin published in 1873, argued against Karl Marx's "dictatorship of the proletariat" by insisting that in reality it would create a dictatorship not of the working class but of intellectuals and technicians, whose power could be offset only by including in the dictatorship the peasant masses, with their inherently antagonistic attitude towards authority. Bakunin had a very simple platform: the use of "human reason as the only criterion of truth, human conscience as the basis of justice, individual and collective freedom as the only source of order in society."[32] Achievement of these ideals entailed absolute rejection of every authority that acted to restrict freedom, whether it was the state, which restricted the realization of individual liberty, or the economy, which imposed centralization at the expense of free association and federation, or Marx's dictatorship of the proletariat, which would afford freedom only to a few. In Bakunin's new society, state religion, monarchy, classes, and the state itself would be abolished. In their place, he

19

proposed an elected judiciary and "the internal reorganization of each country on the basis of the absolute freedom of individuals, of productive associations, and of the communes"; he also proclaimed a long list of individual rights—"the right of every man and woman, from birth to adulthood, to complete upkeep, clothes, food, shelter, care, guidance, education . . . , all at the expense of the society."[33]

Few other political philosophers ever made so total a claim for the rights of humanity, but Bakunin believed that only individual freedom could defend social liberty: the "public and private morality falls or rises to the extent that individual liberty is restricted or enlarged."[34] He buttressed this claim by an equal insistence upon work as the basis of all political rights. The very essence of his libertarian grant to the individual depended upon an equal sharing of labor and its responsibilities. Abolition of the right of inheritance, for example, would ensure that labor provided the sole source of wealth, with land and all other natural resources as the common property of all, to be worked collectively, since "association marvelously multiplies the productive capacity of each worker. . . ."[35] Encouragement would be given to formation of free communes as the basic unit of this new society, in order to utilize the social traditions of each particular district. In Spain, this meant that the collective agrarian and social practices of the medieval *fueros* (grants of autonomy), which had regulated local life long before the development of a strong monarchy, might be reincorporated into political thought.[36] But peasant collectivism had no validity if it was not tied to a philosophy of autonomy and self-government or if it did not allow the society to function efficiently.

Bakunin tried to spell out this philosophy in considerable detail. Without the moral controls of face-to-face relationships, "the world of politics has always been and continues to be the stage for unlimited rascality and brigandage . . . , which, by the way, are held in high esteem, since they are sanctified by patriotism, by the transcendent morality and the supreme interest of the State."[37] Against these conventional values, Bakunin held out a belief that, given a humane environment, human beings had a life-long capacity to develop the fullest use of their faculties. The best way to achieve this goal was by total change rather than through piecemeal reform or the granting of simple political liberty. Only through such total change would urban workers join in common cause with the peasants against the property-owners.[38] Both groups would come to understand that their only chance to obtain a humane environment lay in a collective effort.

20

If this union of urban workers and peasants was accomplished, civil war became almost inevitable, and Bakunin's celebration of civil war is an overlooked aspect of his thought. Civil war provided the best example of the state destroying itself and the greatest opportunity for spontaneous action of the masses. It was a chief agent, in his eyes, of progress—particularly if revolutionaries, taking care to remain sensitive to peasant feelings, prepared the way for civil war and its anarchist conclusion by developing the concept of solidarity between peasants and workers as fully as possible. In a sense, the revolutionaries formed a vanguard or, in his words, "a sort of revolutionary general staff" to assist in giving expression to the instincts of the people.[39] In other works, Bakunin went further and discussed these professional revolutionaries as an "invisible collective dictatorship" or International Brotherhood, usually with the qualification that they should not take office or otherwise abandon the apolitical principles of anarchism.[40] How binding this prohibition was has remained the subject of criticism ever since.[41]

For Spaniards, the International Brotherhood retained its vitality even after the death of Bakunin in 1876, the same year the Bourbon monarchy returned to Spain. Restoration politicians cracked down on what they called "illegal parties." However, at its high point in 1882, there were almost fifty thousand affiliates of the movement, which was now called the Federación de Trabajadores de la Region Española.[42] The Jerez strike and more limited actions like the demonstrations of 1903 and 1904 in the upper Guadalquivir valley kept the name of anarchism alive. Leaders like Fermín Salvochea continued to propagate Bakuninist doctrines, but after 1885 the Black Hand prosecutions, the rise of the socialist Unión General de Trabajadores (UGT), and new syndicalist concepts eroded the strength of the Federation.[43]

Spanish anarchism finally split in 1888 over whether to move towards syndicalism and cooperate with labor syndicates or remain purely anarchist. Anselmo Lorenzo, the best-known Spanish libertarian and new head of the Federation, favored the latter policy.[44] He was joined by Peter Kropotkin and Errico Malatesta, Bakunin's successors, who urged formation of small autonomous groups to pursue independent action. "Propaganda of the deed," a euphemism for assassination and terrorism, dominated anarchism during the following decade. The tactic was based upon the assumption that if the libertarian anarchist philosophy ("from each according to his means, to each according to need") could not be realized peacefully, anarchists should attack possessors of power in a new war against society.[45]

Daniel Guérin has argued that this tactic isolated anarchists from the working class. This was particularly true in Spain, where police surveillance forced even the most active into exile or hiding.[46] When anarchists were expelled from the Second International in 1896, disillusionment caused one Spanish militant, Federico (Urales) Montseny, to advocate a new form of libertarian anarchism, purged of foreign influences and adapted to Iberian circumstances.[47] But nothing of the sort happened; the movement was too out-of-touch to alter its philosophy. Propaganda of the deed remained a part of the Spanish anarchist outlook, even while Peter Kropotkin, the Russian anarchist (then in exile in Great Britain), was moving libertarian philosophy in another direction.

Peter Kropotkin's early life as the son of a Russian military noble and his work as a geographer and field naturalist in Siberia from 1862 to 1866 contrasted with his later political career. Between 1874 and 1876 he was jailed for acts of revolutionary propaganda. After his escape he resided in Western Europe until the Russian revolution. At first he accepted Bakunin's legacy of violent revolution, but in the 1880s he sought a different position. In *Mutual Aid,* which began to appear in article form at this time, Kropotkin examined the cooperative elements of human survival.[48] While not entirely a critique of the "struggle for survival" in Darwinian evolutionary theory, it nevertheless stressed a greater role for the social instincts of a species. *Mutual Aid* made it seem possible to envelop society in a web of communes and collectives until the state was no longer necessary. In later years this institutional approach was emphasized in writings such as *Fields, Factories and Workshops* (1899), *Memoirs of a Revolutionist* (1899), and *The Great French Revolution* (1909). Violence was increasingly replaced in Kropotkin's work by a new social voluntarism based on collectivist economics. Bakuninism, with its rudimentary economic emphasis, became outmoded, except in Spain.

The reasons Bakuninism survived there lay largely in the Spaniards' lack of education and their isolation from the mainstream of European life. Anselmo Lorenzo made some effort to propagate Kropotkin's ideas, but they remained unknown to the vast majority of Spanish anarchists. The Spaniards did share collectivist ideals with the Russian anarchist and often intuited some of the more communal aspects of his thought; but Kropotkinism on a major scale remained alien to them until much later.

Despite this failure to widen its intellectual horizons, the Iberian anarchist movement was saved by the Spanish-American War in

1898. The "disaster" caused intellectuals to show new interest in change. "Regeneration" become a momentary vogue. Azorín, one of the best-known Spanish writers, translated Peter Kropotkin; Anselmo Lorenzo worked with a French anarchist, Elisée Reclus, to produce several popular books on geography; and in Barcelona an anarchist named Francisco Ferrer opened up the Escuela Moderna (Modern School) for working-class children in 1901.

Francisco Ferrer's personal life, and even the depth of his anarchism, was controversial, but he had the flair of a radical popularizer. In 1906, for instance, he led his schoolchildren to demonstrate on Good Friday in favor of secular education.[49] Through the bequest of a wealthy admirer, Ferrer expanded his schools until he ran more than thirty in Catalonia, with a curriculum centered around simplified political thought and rationalist philosophy. His success made him hated by public officials in Catalonia, and he was arrested and jailed for a year after an abortive assassination attempt (of which he was not a part) upon Alfonso XIII in 1906. Afterwards he returned to Barcelona and worked with anarcho-syndicalists who found labor open to organization in the wake of the failure of the earlier general strike.

The syndicalists Ferrer joined were part of a growing movement that stressed labor organization as the main route to revolution. For many anarchists the motives of syndicalism were suspect, since "laborism" did not automatically lead to revolution and syndicate leaders were often unsympathetic to other libertarian ideas. Yet some cooperation between anarchists and syndicalists was inevitable: labor syndicates provided a weapon in the social struggle and were, at least to a degree, a companion organization to the free rural communes the anarchists admired. In any case, "propaganda of the deed" placed libertarians so far outside the normal boundaries of society that many, unable to live as criminals, had left the movement altogether.[50]

After the Confédération Générale de Travail was founded by French workers in 1895, syndicalism achieved greater revolutionary potential. The Amsterdam anarchist congress of 1907 accepted syndicalism as a branch of anarchism, even though misgivings lingered that syndicalism represented only a narrow materialism. Some anarchists objected to the class consciousness implicit in syndicalism, the concentration of its organizational efforts among factory workers, and the difficulty of modifying industrial unions to accommodate peasant agricultural workers. Others took exception to the assertion of Georges Sorel in *Reflections on Violence* that the social myth of worker solidarity brought about by the general strike (a favorite syndicalist tactic) was sufficiently strong to frighten the capitalist world into surrender.

23

The syndicalist movement in Catalonia began in the summer of 1907 when various municipal unions joined together under the title Solidaridad Obrera. No organization of this scope had operated in Barcelona since 1904, and the new group obviously benefited from the publicity surrounding the Charter of Amiens, a French syndicalist manifesto that circulated in Catalonia during this period.[51] The organization soon founded a newspaper using the same name, which appeared for the first time on October 19, 1907. Francisco Ferrer worked on the staff of the newspaper *Solidaridad Obrera,* along with Anselmo Lorenzo, who provided anarchist news from his wide circle of friends in Northern Europe, and Ricardo Mella, an Asturian anarchist since 1880, who was a friend of Fermín Salvochea and had been an organizer of the general strike in 1903. Other assistants included José Prat, an anarchist journalist and co-author with Ricardo Mella of a recent exposé of Catalan politics, and Federico Montseny, who, with Mella's help, founded a major anarchist journal (*La Revista Blanca*) in 1923.[52] Even the Catalan Socialist Federation and Alejandro Lerroux's party initially cooperated to produce the newspaper. The same group was active in strikes by teamsters, typesetters, and textile workers during the next year and had scheduled a general strike in July 1909 to protest unemployment and salary cuts caused by a recession in Catalonia when the Moroccan crisis struck.[53] *Solidaridad Obrera* quickly planned an anti-war rally for July 23, only to have it cancelled by the government. Tension mounted throughout Barcelona soon afterwards, and on July 26 the general strike suddenly became a reality.

Leadership during the Tragic Week came overwhelmingly from socialists and radicals. The rioting which took place was, in fact, curiously devoid of anarcho-syndicalist domination, largely because of the newness of that collaboration. Other than a revolutionary pamphlet by Francisco Ferrer, little evidence appeared to link violence in the streets with collective anarchist militancy. Catalan regionalism, political frustration, the opportunism of Lerroux, and labor unrest played more important roles. But when order was restored and arrests made, the anarchists suffered most severely. Ferrer and several others were executed for alleged provocation of the riots.

Reaction to the execution of Francisco Ferrer was widespread and indignant.[54] Demonstrations in Paris, Brussels, and London condemned the Spanish government, and during the following year in Spain, membership in syndicalist organizations increased to forty thousand, many of them short-term sympathizers.[55] One participant in the growth of the CNT reported that the mood at the time was "as if class war had just been declared. . . . "[56] Military occupation of Barcelona and the repression of Alejandro Lerroux's party probably contributed more to this mood than the identification of Francisco Ferrer with anarchism or a feeling that anarchists had led the insurrection, but clearly the Tragic Week and the execution of Ferrer handed the anarcho-syndicalists an opportunity to benefit from the situation. The Solidaridad Obrera group led the way by convening a small meeting of labor leaders and political activists from the Catalan region in September 1910. This body called for the creation of a new national labor confederation.

V. The CNT Emerges

The founding congress of the Confederación Nacional del Trabajo opened on September 8, 1911, and over the next two days fewer than a hundred delegates drew up the framework for a new anarcho-syndicalist labor movement. Andalusian participation was much less than might have been expected, but the death of Fermín Salvochea and the failure of the Andalusians to organize a syndicate of peasant laborers diminished their representation. Representatives from Asturias, Leon, and Galicia, where radical manifestations had not been as common, were more numerous.[57] The same areas also provided much of the leadership at the congress. Angel Pestaña, a native of Asturias and a veteran of several bitter strikes at the large Alto Hornos metallurgy complex, Eusebio Carbó, another organizer from Asturias, who had been founder of a workers' school in Vallodolid and was now active in Valencia, and Juan Peiró, a steel worker from Barcelona who had quickly become one of the most popular syndicalists, challenged the pure anarchism of Anselmo Lorenzo, Manuel Buenacasa, and Federico Montseny.[58] Syndicalists profited from their relative lack of notoriety, while the anarchists continued to be hunted down by police. Anarchist publications were shut down, and membership of the few anarchists in the CNT caused it to be declared illegal immediately.[59]

The only real power behind the CNT came from crude national associations of workers in the iron industry and transportation, such as the teamsters, who since 1909 had been calling for a CNT-type of organization. Their strength was greatest in Corunna, Saragossa, and Gijon. They were joined by several Barcelona textile syndicates,

25

a number of unaffiliated workers from a variety of industries, and peasant groups representing Jaen, Cordoba, and Cadiz.[60] A great disparity in outlooks was to be expected, and the founding congress failed to adopt more than a bare framework of confederation. Tactics proved to be a major stumbling block, with delegates divided between an openly revolutionary policy of provoking lockouts and a more evolutionary program of recruitment and development of locals. In the end, these alternatives were left to regional committees of the CNT, set up in accordance with the strong anti-centralist views of the delegates—although the very existence of regional committees assured a slower pace of growth and development than the revolutionaries wished. This was probably just as well, since the movement in Barcelona remained under strong restraints. The slightest sign of open labor activity remained a prosecutable offense until 1918.

For the next few years, the size of the CNT remained minimal, somewhere between 45,000 and 50,000, a far cry from the 500,000 it would have in 1919.[61] CNT-sponsored strikes by stevedores, teamsters, and metallurgical workers failed during 1912 in Barcelona, and the syndicates were closed by the government. In the South the Federación Nacional de Agricultores de España (FNAE), an affiliate of the CNT created in 1913, managed to attract only about two thousand members in its attempt to mobilize small tenant farmers and agricultural day laborers.[62] Militancy dissolved in the years immediately before World War I. The economy remained sluggish, and the expectations of the people stayed low. Anarchists also were discredited by several assassinations, including that of the Liberal party Premier, José Canalejas, by Francisco Pardiñas, an Argentine claiming to be an anarchist but unknown to the movement. In another case, a hanger-on, Chata Cuqueta, murdered a judge who had presided over the Tragic Week trials. All of this kept the Civil Guard busy searching out new anarchist conspiracies.

Government willingness to suspend constitutional guarantees, censor the press, and call up workers in essential industries as military reserves (as was done with railway employees in 1912 when they threatened to strike) added to CNT difficulties. No group that had anarchists in it could hope to succeed. Government officials blamed the anarchists for destruction of the Maura and Canalejas cabinets and refused to allow them to have legal contact with Spanish workers. As a consequence, syndicalists assumed most responsibilities in the CNT and stressed the bread-and-butter issues of unionism. On this level, they could not hope to compete with the socialists,

26

who were better organized and already operating a functional national union, the UGT. As a final blow, anarchists lost the inspirational leadership of Anselmo Lorenzo, their most responsible theorist, who died in 1914. Had it not been for national confusion during the next four years, Spanish anarchism, left alone, might have disappeared forever.

VI. The CNT and the War

The outbreak of war in August 1914 did not involve Spain directly, for the government understood that various national problems dictated a course of neutrality. Nevertheless, the impact of the war had a revolutionary effect as new economic growth exploded from the war-created demand for goods and commodities of all types. One observer noted that wages rose accordingly: "pay in the countryside, or at least in the dry-farming regions where on most days of the year it was impossible to work, remained as low as 1 or 1.50 pesetas a day, while in the towns the same people could earn 15, 20 or even 30 pesetas a day."[63] Exports to the European nations at war rose dramatically from 355 million pesetas in 1914 to 723 million in 1917. Large surpluses of exports over imports, rising from 184 million pesetas in 1914 to 577 million in 1917, began to create capital for industrial expansion. Family income increased from 4.71 pesetas a day to 9.42 or, on an annual basis, from 1,720 to 3,443.[64] At the same time, inflation ate into this temporary prosperity, especially in 1917–1918, when the food cost index rose from 126 to 179.[65] Strikes increased by almost 15 percent in 1915 and another 25 percent the next year.[66]

Pressure from these rapid developments worsened the already shaky political situation. The cabinets of Eduardo Dato and Count Romanones, saddled by a pre-industrial outlook and often preoccupied by the need to maintain neutrality in the war, ruled by decree and sought to maximize war profits without giving much thought to solid economic development. As a result, the jerry-built railroad system almost collapsed under its new traffic. Prices, affected by high transportation costs, jumped again. For those with fixed incomes, like the military, inflation in 1917 seemed intolerable. Many officers, already angered by the political confusion, joined *juntas de defensa* to press new claims against the government. In turn, once the military's restlessness became known, every other dissenting sector of Spanish society—Catalans, republicans, radicals, socialists, and anarcho-syndicalists—took the cue to make their own demands.

During this crisis, the CNT made up for its lack of size by cooperating with the larger, socialist UGT. Manuel Buenacasa, a mechanic and typesetter, became the national secretary of the CNT. While keeping many ideas of Fermín Salvochea and Anselmo Lorenzo, he was eager to revitalize the CNT by any means necessary so that it might survive the coming crisis. Many UGT members accepted the CNT only with hostility, but socialists also were mindful of a need for numbers. The two groups worked together warily to organize the first national general strike on December 18, 1916. Although it lasted for only a few hours, the failure of the government to oppose it strongly led to a second strike on March 27, 1917, caused in good part by the electrifying news of the Russian revolution. A Belgian living in Barcelona observed that the mood of the Catalan working class was transformed by a feeling that the monarchy of Alfonso XIII was no more popular or stable than that of the deposed Nicolas II of Russia.[67]

News of the Russian revolution gave anarcho-syndicalists new millenarian expectations. *Tierra y Libertad,* an anarchist newspaper that had been published in Madrid, revived and moved its operations to Barcelona, where *Solidaridad Obrera* also began publishing four or five times a week. A workers' committee, formed to coordinate revolutionary activity, was led by Manuel Buenacasa and Salvador Seguí, the latter a young textile worker of considerable energy and intelligence, the first of a new generation of anarcho-syndicalists.[68]

Seguí and Buenacasa used the committee as a liaison with Catalan regionalists to develop a joint revolutionary approach. Salvador Seguí, whose policy this was, did not expect miracles from the alliance with the Catalan regionalists, but there seemed to be, he was quoted as saying, no other course: "[The Catalans] would like to use us and then do us dirt. For the moment, we are useful in their game of political blackmail. Without us they can do nothing: we have the streets, the shock-troops, the brave hearts among the people."[69] Even so, cooperation quickly broke down. In June the committee published a list of radical demands which called for price controls, the right of open labor association, and destruction of the monarchy.[70] Catalan regionalists objected to the demand for price controls and socialists to the precipitate revolutionary call that ended the manifesto. Both soon dropped away, with the Catalans concentrating on the regionalist side of their work. Socialists moved towards closer cooperation with a new party, the Reformist Republicans, a faction that contained men of present and future importance such as the philosopher José Ortega y Gasset and Manuel Azaña, the future Premier of the Second Republic. In many ways, this group presented a more attractive form of radicalism; it drew, however, from a middle-class clientele. Unlike the CNT, the Reformist Republicans stood for election, and by 1920 they had picked up more than twenty seats.

This phenomenon of a vigorous and successful radical opposition, coming on the heels of other national difficulties, became so alarming to the government that a major crisis began in the early summer of 1917. It started when the Prime Minister, Eduardo Dato, sensing the strength of the anti-monarchical coalition, suspended constitutional guarantees and closed down the national parliament. Catalans, military officers, UGT officials, and republicans joined together in an *ad hoc* Constituent Cortes, scheduled to assemble in Barcelona on July 19, 1917. The prospect of a new parliament raised the excitement of the city to fever pitch. The very existence of an alternative government hinted at civil war and jolted the anarchists, who knew their Bakunin, into taking to the streets behind Seguí. While the *ad hoc* Cortes raced around the city in a vain attempt to elude the Civil Guard on July 19, anarcho-syndicalists fought a pitched battle against army troops near the Catalan parliament building. Salvador Seguí and Victor Serge (a Belgian syndicalist and later a leading European Trotskyist) were arrested, along with several hundred rioters.

Martial law was imposed upon Barcelona, but on July 22, after a chaotic meeting of CNT elements at Vallvidrera, Manuel Buenacasa hurriedly called another revolutionary general strike. Although exhaustion prevented much more than a series of wildcat strikes, among railway workers on the MZA line and the Compañía de Ferrocarriles del Norte, where recent wage negotiations and the firing of workers had produced embittered relations, the strike movement increased syndicalist strength.[71] This alarmed the UGT, whose preserve it was, and a young socialist leader, Francisco Largo Caballero, responded by maneuvering the UGT towards another general strike, over the objections of Pablo Iglesias, one of the founders of Spanish socialism.[72] Whether Largo Caballero's motives derived from an over-optimistic evaluation of revolutionary possibilities or a fear of CNT victory is not clear, but on August 10, 1917, when the strike began, the CNT again joined in.

The work stoppage lasted three days and left more than seventy dead, hundreds wounded, and thousands in jail. Although its scope was the biggest yet, in the end the strike failed to topple Eduardo Dato's cabinet or bring an improvement in the condition of Spanish labor. Madrid had no alternative but to resist with every measure of its strength. In the aftermath, relations between the two confederations cooled considerably, with the CNT criticizing the UGT's quick capitulation in ending the strike and socialists describing syndicalist efforts as half-hearted. After the rampage of July 19, the anarchists obviously were not at their strongest, and the socialists remained divided as to which path to take. The general strike became the first of many conflicts between the CNT and UGT.

The "August Rebellion" did not confine itself entirely to Catalonia and the North. Construction workers and unskilled, unemployed peasant migrants in Madrid fought with the police intermittently for the next three months, sometimes aided by students.[73] One of the latter, Diego Abad de Santillán, a Spaniard raised in Argentina who was a law student at the University of Madrid, threw over his liberal commitments and belief in reform to join the anarchists.[74] Although he soon went back to Argentina, where he became an activist in the anarcho-syndicalist Federación Obrera Regional Argentina, he returned to Spain in 1931 to play a major role in anarchist affairs.[75]

Diego Abad de Santillán was not alone in rushing to join the CNT during the August rebellion. Anarchists in Valencia, led by Eusebio Carbó, claimed to have gained almost ten thousand sympathizers and organized a dozen or so strikes and demonstrations, and Carbó created a Centro Obrero which published a newspaper entitled *La Guerra Social*. Elsewhere, the Spanish Agricultural Federation (FNAE) accelerated its activity in Andalusia; it led twenty strikes during August 1917 alone. The failure of agricultural incomes to rise in the face of inflation fanned strong resentment, and the number of strikers rose from 8,587 in 1917 to 27,514 in 1920.[76] This startling increase indicated that the August rebellion was only a foreshadowing of events to come.

In October 1917 the groundswell of violence convinced moderate politicians in the Constituent Cortes that prudence was the wisest course. When they finally reconvened, their only strong recommendation was a demand for greater electoral democracy. In the meantime, the king raised military salaries to offset the spread of the junta movement to noncommissioned officers. Antonio Maura formed a new Conservative cabinet in March 1918, but his return to office was disappointing after the heady expectations of the previous summer. Salvador Seguí characterized Maura's premiership as an expression of the contempt that official Spain felt towards the aspirations of the people.[77] The CNT used the general disillusionment as an effective argument against regenerationists and Reformist Republicans who still believed that some elements of the system could be saved.

In fact, the new national parliament elected in March 1918 actually broke the old Liberal-Conservative pattern: six socialists, seventeen Reformist Republicans, and twenty-five Catalan nationalists won seats. But Salvador Seguí brushed aside any suggestion that this in itself represented a permanent change. The dissenters in parliament would not have been there at all if the CNT had not fought in the streets for their rights. The CNT, Seguí believed, had a claim upon them: they should work for legalization of labor activity, improved working conditions, and higher wages. Seguí styled this new parliamentary direction as "possibilism." He justified his position to anarchists on the grounds that since revolution could not be realized immediately, the CNT had to take advantage of liberal sympathies in order to gain a legal, open position in society. Syndicalism might then be made into an instrument of moral and material liberation to give the proletariat an ability to rule themselves.[78]

Again, lukewarm cooperation with parliamentary radicals continued off and on, but it did not accomplish very much. A more important step was taken in June 1918 at the Congress of Sans, a preliminary national conference of the CNT, where the principle of industrial unionism was adopted. Skilled and unskilled workers now belonged to the same syndicates, a common syndicalist practice that the CNT had been too weak to implement until now.

While the creation of the industrial unions *(sindicatos únicos)* represented a victory for the syndicalists, anarchists were able to obtain a promise that the industrial unions would never exclude workers, peasants, or anarchists from their membership. Control over the industrial unions rested with regional committees, which decentralized many of their executive functions. In any case, there was little prospect that industrial unions could cooperate with each other without strong CNT assistance, and the large number of anarchists in the textile, transportation, and longshoreman syndicates assured them of a voice in industrial union affairs.

Other decisions made at the congress favored an anarchist point of view. Salvador Seguí was able to get Ricardo and José Mella, two brothers from Asturias with activist reputations, to introduce a long list of libertarian proposals as part of the CNT bylaws. Women were admitted to membership, and the principle of sexual equality was recognized. Secular education, abolition of child labor, and realiza-

31

tion of the eight-hour day became a part of the program Seguí called "neo-syndicalism." He described the new syndicalism as a commitment to adopt the best of anarchism and syndicalism in the struggle to achieve a proletarian state.[79] The program was an effort to create a positive response to the Russian revolution. Some delegates even tried to convert the syndicates into primitive "soviets."[80]

In the months after the congress, CNT activity flourished all over the country much as in the previous summer. Eusebio Carbó worked with followers of Errico Malatesta in Valencia.[81] The ideas of the Italian, once a radical anarchist, now matched those of Seguí, since Malatesta did not believe an anarchist revolution was likely. The most anarchists could do was work closely with other social revolutionaries to overthrow capitalism and to prepare for their own revolution sometime in the future.[82] Yet in the South revolutionary expectations had already reached such a level that the Spanish Agricultural Federation found itself leading sixty-eight strikes in 1918. The province of Cordoba, as the epicenter of this disturbance, daily witnessed serious violence.[83] Even northern agrarian regions like Aragon formed chapters of the FNAE.

The intellectual José Ortega y Gasset noted to the British Ambassador at this time that there was not much connection between urban syndicalism and rural protest, because peasants were now demanding land whereas city workers wanted only an improvement of labor conditions and political freedom.[84] The civil war in the countryside, more than any other factor, kept alive a fervor for revolution after the CNT pulled back from an expectation of immediate revolt. Salvador Seguí wanted more time to build an organization, but the FNAE pressed for membership in the CNT, and in the fall of 1918 the two bodies united. In December the CNT merged the FNAE with the recently formed Federación Obreros Andaluz as a full regional branch of the Confederation.[85]

In November 1918, while agricultural strikes continued to keep militancy high in Spain, the war in Europe came to a close. The temporary prosperity of the war years suddenly halted, and any certainty that industrial workers would continue to receive current rates of pay or even be able to hold onto their jobs disappeared. For the CNT, the war ended before its national organization was completely built. The Congress of Sans represented only a few of the regional groups, and since June 1918 the entire South had come into the CNT. Even Salvador Seguí's position was unclear: he led the Catalan militants and had a considerable degree of authority, but only Manuel Buenacasa was well known to the CNT as a whole.

Some anarchists, like Eusebio Carbó, had secure working-class constituencies; but others, like Manuel Buenacasa, preferred the classic clandestine role of the nineteenth-century anarchist.

The rank-and-file anarchists were a mixed lot. While Victor Serge, on the eve of his departure for Russia in 1917 to join the Bolshevik revolution, called the Barcelona militants "great big children" and "surly proletarians," a majority might have been better described as low-skilled workers only a few years removed from close village relationships.[86] Their anxieties, in a time of collapsing liberal politics, regionalism, and belated modernization, made them feel isolated and vulnerable. The movement as a whole was afflicted by a strong millenarian sense, the traditional and passionate loyalty of Spaniards to their group or "family" (no matter how abstract), and a tenacious commitment to the ideas that anarchists had taught to an educationally deprived people.[87] And now the strength of the CNT was about to be tested as the anarcho-syndicalist movement entered a new period of difficulty.

CHAPTER TWO

The Postwar Struggle

We are not in the least afraid of ruins. We are going to
inherit the earth; there is not the slightest doubt about
that. The bourgeoisie might blast and ruin its own world
before it leaves the stage of history. We carry a new world
here in our hearts. That world is growing this minute.
[Buenaventura Durruti, Toronto *Star*, September 21,
1936]

I. La Canadiense

The first trouble in the immediate postwar period began at the electric plants of Riegos y Fuerza, popularly known as La Canadiense
because the predecessor company, Barcelona Light and Traction,
had been incorporated in Canada. As the very model of an early
multinational enterprise, Riegos y Fuerza was held by Ebro Irrigation and Power, a creation of Canadian and General Finance Company Limited and, as minority stockholders, Société International
d'Énergie Hydroélectrique (SIDRO), a Belgian company with strong
English backing.[1] Since its founding in 1911, La Canadiense had
been the largest of the three electric companies in Catalonia and the
most influential. Because of its foreign ownership, the company cul-
tivated Catalan friends like Francisco Cambó, a well-known conservative regionalist leader, who sat on the board of another enterprise
linked with SIDRO.[2] Until the end of the war, La Canadiense
proved to be a good investment, since the expansion of manufacturing in Catalonia greatly enlarged the need for electricity. However,
in early January 1919 the company was forced to cut back its electric
production by as much as a quarter. In turn, La Canadiense asked
its personnel to accept wage cuts as high as 35 percent.[3]

34

The timing of this cutback could hardly have been worse. Perhaps most important, the CNT was in the midst of an organizational drive, seeking to pick up the numerical strength to make employers afraid to cut wages or lay off personnel. The Sindicato Único de Agua, Gas y Electricidad, involved in the process of organizing La Canadiense, stood ready to fight the company strenuously, but what made the situation particularly violent was, once again, the Catalan regionalist free-for-all. A plebiscite in November 1918 had registered 98 percent of Catalonia as in favor of autonomy, and the sentiment for independence ran so high that most Catalan deputies walked out of the national parliament in December 1918. Count Romanones, the Spanish Premier, responded by suspending the constitutional guarantees of Catalonia in January 1919 and declaring a state of seige.

Catalan tempers flared almost at once. Francesco Macià, an ex-army officer now rapidly becoming the most forceful and radical Catalan regionalist leader, announced that he was taking Catalonia's case for independence to the Versailles Peace Conference. The Allies would not hear his arguments, but it was a highly dramatic ploy since it allowed Macià to call for armed resistance to the national government until the Allies "freed" Catalonia. Count Romanones responded by ordering preventive arrests which put hundreds of regionalists and syndicalists on board the prison ship *Pelayo* in the middle of Barcelona harbor. Salvador Seguí, Manuel Buenacasa, and other high-ranking CNT leaders spent most of January and February in jail, out of touch with the rest of the organization.

Violence soon became a daily occurrence at La Canadiense. After a company director, Joaquín Baró, was assassinated on January 12, 1919, the management refused to bargain. The civil governor of Catalonia, Antonio Ossorio y Gallardo, tried to get the two sides together but failed, and on February 5 the strike officially began. More than 140 workers were arrested during the first days, and on February 8 La Canadiense locked out the remaining workers in the hope of crippling union activity and ending demands that the wage cuts be nullified. Instead, the decision widened the strike by politicizing it. The CNT began calling for a general strike, but before other CNT groups could be notified, the tram drivers of La Fraternal syndicate went out on a sympathy strike. They were followed on February 17 by the Catalan textile workers.[4] The strikers' demands had a paradoxical quality that revealed either a lack of leadership caused by the preventive arrests or a new hardening of

CNT attitudes. An eight-hour day, union recognition, a half-day off on Saturday, industrial insurance, and a ban on hiring workers under the age of fourteen had never been granted during the period of wartime prosperity. Now, during a recession, they were totally unacceptable. Unemployment in Catalonia was up by about 25,000 since the end of the war, and gross production figures had fallen by more than 20 percent.[5] The CNT was on a collision course with trouble, pushed by militancy from below rather than from above. Manuel Buenacasa and other officials, including Angel Pestaña, commented bitterly about the pressure by militants, referring to them as "the ambitious, the hot-heads, the criminal. . . ."[6]

The strike movement, driven by the massive insecurity felt throughout the working class, peaked on February 21, when the electrical workers of the other Catalan companies joined the workers at La Canadiense on strike. Public transportation halted and the city went dark despite Count Romanones' use of army engineers to restore services. The Captain-General of the province, General Lorenzo Milans del Bosch, urged Romanones to issue a limited state-of-war proclamation which would temporarily draft strikers into the army. When this was done on February 27, more syndicates struck. In effect, Barcelona was in the throes of a general strike. Even the Sindicato Único de Artes Gráficas struck, temporarily shutting down the newspapers for printing government notices.

New negotiations began on March 1, 1919, but demands for a union shop, amnesty for jailed strikers, abolition of militarization decrees, and the right to negotiate directly with the government proved to be unacceptable to the cabinet. Exasperated Barcelona businessmen issued an ultimatum through their Employers Federation (Confederación Patronal): all workers not back on the job by March 6 would be fired. The Premier, Count Romanones, trying to avert a total breach, stepped back into the situation and forceably inducted essential workers in gas, water, transport, and power into the army to prevent employers from carrying out their threat. Neither side, unfortunately, agreed with his action. Nonessential workers continued to be fired by management, while workers on the Sarria-Barcelona line and other Catalan railways now joined the walkout and paralyzed the city again.

The failure of employers to stop the strike convinced the government that some other approach had to be found. Thus, on March 13, Count Romanones announced that Barcelona was under a state of seige. Workers of all kinds again faced military discipline. Although the anarchists called for civil disobedience, essential services were restored the next day.[7] A new civil governor, Carlos Montañes, reopened labor negotiations on March 17, and a week later a solution was reached. No action would be taken against the arrested strikers, wage increases were guaranteed, and the eight-hour day would become, at long last, a reality.

The strikers, some twenty thousand strong, met at a bullring to ratify the agreement. While Salvador Seguí, speaking for the CNT, and Simón Piera, head of the construction syndicates, argued for acceptance, a majority favored holding out until all those jailed during the forty-four-day-old strike were actually freed. Members of an ultra-Left faction acknowledged sometime later that this condition was actually a pretext for defeating reformism and continuing the "revolution." Their rhetoric swayed the audience, which rejected the government's terms.[8]

A new general strike thus began on March 24, but as workers walked off their jobs at noon, use of the state-of-war and state-of-siege proclamations brought the army back onto the streets. The next day all legal guarantees were again suspended. In wealthy districts fear of social revolution brought droves of volunteers to the informal militia units that roamed the wide sidewalks of the Ramblas like vigilantes.[9] On Monday, March 26, minor violence flared on both sides. The scale on which strikers were now being arrested finally convinced the strike committee that an amnesty was necessary. When the committee met with Carlos Montañes, the civil governor took a hard line by refusing to pardon imprisoned workers, adding that the syndicates could expect no leniency since they had already rejected the best possible offer.

This impasse encouraged the Employers Federation to urge its members to fire all workers still on strike by March 29. Some companies gave their workers a forty-eight-hour period of grace, but most stores and factories forced employees to return the next day. At the same time, certain labor leaders were placed under arrest. Miguel Burgos, head of the tanners syndicate, was shot and killed by the police. His death provided the CNT with another strong issue, and locals in Gerona and Palafrugell now joined the Barcelona unions on the picket line. Altogether, approximately 125,000 workers remained out on strike.

Ominously, militants used the death of Burgos to recruit the most adventuresome workers for new ultra-Left groups. These nameless bands, often with no ideology but class war, came into being to protect the lives of labor leaders and guard strike lines. Some who joined were already anarchists or quickly became libertarians; others, easily frightened, dropped out, but not before getting some sort of exposure to the social civil war going on around them—the start, no doubt, of an increasing Spanish sectarianism that would not end until the outbreak of general civil war in 1936. A few participants in the ultra-Left bands began calling themselves anarcho-Bolsheviks and criticizing Seguí's reformist tactics. Others, in the tradition of Louis Blanqui's nineteenth-century insurrectionism, were simply *pistoleros*. [10] Many fervently wanted to duplicate the Russian revolution in Spain, a desire that was expressed again and again. Not since the Paris commune had a foreign event made such an impact upon the Spanish working class.[11]

As revolutionary expectations continued to grow, the government decided that stronger action was required. On April 2, syndicates were outlawed in even stricter terms, and a massive roundup of all anarchists and syndicate activists began. Armed soldiers closed down *Solidaridad Obrera* and arrested its editor, Angel Pestaña. Then, on April 3, the eight-hour day was finally ratified by the national parliament, although it would not go into effect until October. This combination of the mailed fist and moderate reform broke the back of continued Catalan resistance, and workers began returning to work. While the state-of-war was dropped, the state-of-siege proclamation was not rescinded until August 12, more than four months later, and wages were not raised as promised. These omissions were obviously mistakes. Martial law drove labor activity underground and strengthened the ultra-Left, which could point to the broken promises as good examples of why the fight should be continued.[12] However, the middle class felt that the strikers were getting off too lightly, and this backlash forced the Romanones cabinet out of office on April 15. General Milans del Bosch, Catalan labor's most determined opponent, orchestrated a similar downfall of Carlos Montañes in Barcelona.* Antonio Maura, considered to be an enemy of Catalonia, replaced Count Romanones, and for the next few months the two sides watched each other warily.

*Part of the difficulties encountered by Montañes and Romanones lay with the army's unhappiness over the restricted nature of the duties they had performed during the strike. The military juntas promised more trouble over salaries if shoot-on-sight orders were not given, and Milans del Bosch conveyed these feelings to Juan La Cierva, a "stern unbending Tory" in the Romanones cabinet, who undermined the Premier in Madrid. See the letter of Dayrell Crackan-Thorpe to the Foreign Office, April 22, 1919, British Record Office, *Calendar of State Papers Relating to Western and Southern Europe*, FO 371, file 873.

II. Rio Tinto and the South

As the Northeast subsided, the South jumped back into prominence. Violence became a part of daily life in the winter of 1919. The Russian revolution stirred protesters to demand reform in Andalusia, and the congress of the Spanish Agricultural Federation, meeting at Castro in November 1918, called for syndicate recognition, regional wage negotiations, and the abolition of piecework in the fields. In subsequent months, tenant farmers and proprietors of small farms (who had more freedom than landless field laborers) strongly backed a drive for agricultural unionism and sometimes organized whole villages into a single syndicate.[13]

In some cases, sudden growth had an adverse effect upon the syndicates. Large landowners joined for political purposes.[14] In Cordoba, where syndicates controlled sixty-one of the seventy-five townships, moderates wanted to form a new political party, much to the disgust of the anarchists.[15] Some new members defended private property and tried to develop a reform program that would distribute land to individuals instead of collectives.[16] The agricultural syndicates themselves wavered between demanding state land reform or seizing land at once.

This confusion only increased the violence. Salvador Seguí spent much of his time in the spring of 1919 trying to calm tempers in the South. He saw agricultural syndicates as intermediate institutions which would encourage collectivism in rural areas through "use in common." The term was not synonymous with communal agriculture. By forming equipment cooperatives, joint marketing boards, and redistribution commissions (for the free exchange of land), the syndicates might initiate the first tentative aspects of communalism.[17] But Seguí did not spell out his ideas very clearly, and hereafter the agrarian theories of anarcho-syndicalism remained confused and without much content. The southerners fought their battles alone.

A more tangible area of CNT operations in the South proved to be among foreign-owned businesses. As southern radicalism became more pronounced, a kind of xenophobia towards foreign companies swept through the region. British firms like United Alkali, Peña Copper Mines, Esperanza Copper and Sulphur Company, Cartegena and Herrerias Tramway, and Almeria British Mining found themselves struck with increasing frequency. The British business community accused the Spanish government of providing little protection.[18]

The Rio Tinto Copper Company (owned by the Rothschilds)

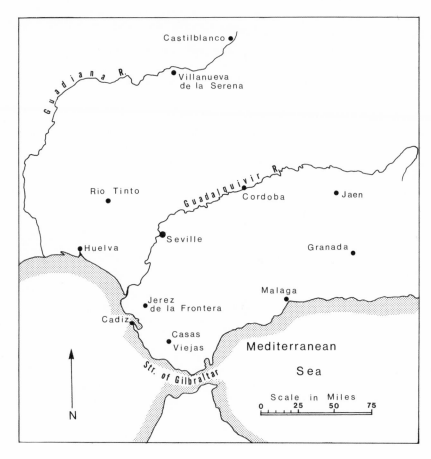

Revolutionary Centers in and near Andalusia, 1919–1933

was the biggest British firm in the South, and its mines were the largest copper mines in all of Europe. It began to experience serious labor troubles during 1918. Management blamed the difficulties upon German provocations, but in the spring of 1919, walkouts over wage cuts, demands for the eight-hour day, and other familiar contentions dispelled this myth.[19] Though some workers returned to the mines in late May 1919, a fairly large contingent stayed out indefinitely. Portuguese and Canary Islanders were brought in to replace long-term strikers, who were evicted from company housing and occasionally driven out of the area by the Civil Guard.[20] Even a British legation official sent to report on the situation called it "the

40

most unfortunate strike from every point of view that has happened here in Spain," with the employees justified in their demands, the English managers "absolutely obdurate" in their attitude towards the workers, and the outlook for a resumption of normal operations hopeless.[21] All of Huelva province, where Rio Tinto operated, was, according to a Spanish newspaper, "a kingdom of hell."[22]

The basic problem in Rio Tinto's labor relations began with the arrival of a new British manager in 1913 and his transfer of skilled workers to unskilled jobs as punishment for their political activities. This provoked both the CNT and the UGT to step up their recruiting, but as more workers joined unions, the management retaliated by cutting wages from ninety pesetas a month to seventy-five. In April 1919 the restoration of prewar wage scales became a chief issue of the strike, with strikers pointing out that they were one of the few groups of skilled workers to have their pay decrease in wartime. Improved housing and food allotments were other issues, but when Rio Tinto refused to negotiate, the UGT and CNT stepped in and assisted the strikers by boarding their children elsewhere in Spain. This act dramatized the Rio Tinto situation and made it an affair of honor for many Spaniards, whether radical or not. Manuel Buenacasa made a much-publicized trip to Huelva in July 1919 and returned to give a graphic description of the miners' suffering. Much later, in November 1920, Salvador Seguí also journeyed south and was harassed by the Civil Guard and prevented from speaking to a rally of miners near Rio Tinto property. These links with the much stronger northern labor movement helped keep the strike alive until early 1922 and encouraged the CNT to expand its operations outside the confines of Barcelona.*

The strike at the neighboring copper mines had a strong effect upon the Andalusian agrarian situation. Agricultural day laborers in the Jerez de le Frontera area refused to harvest wheat and grapes without large wage increases. When raises were denied, they went out on one of the most massive local strikes of the period. Even though the peasants were forced back into the fields by military intervention, their slogan, "Solidarity with Rio Tinto!," was heard all over Spain during the summer of 1919. In Aragon landless peasants also struck the big farms in record numbers. In the coal fields the Asturian Miners Syndicate strongly empathized with the Rio Tinto

---

*In fact the Rio Tinto strike was as big an expansion for the UGT as for the CNT. The UGT made considerable gains during 1920, in particular, when the strike reached even greater proportions than in 1919. The southern miners remained socialist during the Second Republic, largely because of CNT organizational difficulties.

workers and so began their own process of radicalization, which finally made them, by 1934, one of the best-organized groups of militant workers in the country.[23]

Many individuals were permanently radicalized by the Rio Tinto strike. In Leon the most important of these new recruits was a twenty-three-year-old terrorist, Buenaventura Durruti, who supported the strike by engaging in acts of sabotage and violence.[24] Durruti had been born in 1896, the second of eight children of Santiago Durruti and Anastasia Domínguez, a peasant couple that had moved to Leon to find work. His father, a radical UGT member, was often active in labor disputes. Buenaventura Durruti received only a few years of education before he went to work for a mechanic, Melchor Martínez, who was called "El Socialista" by the townspeople. After serving his apprenticeship in this radical environment, the young mechanic left to take a job in the coal mines close by. Involvement in labor activities at the mine forced him to leave in 1914. His father, who worked for the Compañía de Ferrocarriles del Norte, got him a job on the same railway. He lost this job for his activities in the general strike of August 1917, when he led sabotage squads. A gun battle with army troops brought him to the notice of the Civil Guard.

During the next several years, Durruti moved through the North, often just ahead of the police. He would emerge from hiding briefly to join strike lines or to attack factories and banks, then go back into hiding when security became tight. He associated with a number of anarchists during these travels. In this way he met Manuel Buenacasa on two occasions. Through him Durruti came into contact with Francisco Ascaso, who was to become his closest friend and political associate. Francisco Ascaso, a man of many talents, had been a carpenter, teamster, and textile syndicate member. His parents had migrated to Barcelona from the South. He had seen members of his family arrested, dispossessed of their land, and locked out of factory jobs in Barcelona. Like Buenaventura Durruti, Ascaso had a strong urge for vengeance and a willingness to fight for his crude concepts of social justice.

Rio Tinto struck both men as a symbol of the injustice that had dominated their lives. They formed a small group to attack Rio Tinto copper trains and to rob banks that did business with the company. Participants included Ricardo Sanz, a casual laborer, and Juan García Oliver, a nineteen-year-old waiter from Barcelona. They were all terrorists first and anarchists only a distant second, but they would soon have a much greater identification with the libertarian movement.

The deep involvement in radical activities of Buenaventura Durruti and Francisco Ascaso was not unusual in this era. Rio Tinto drew wider sympathy from the Spanish working class than had the strike at La Canadiense. Perhaps the most important aspect of the difficulties at Rio Tinto was that they did not take place in Catalonia and therefore could not be confused with the regionalist agitation going on in the Northeast. A strong sense of Spanish chauvinism spread rapidly during the long months of the conflict.

III. Lockout

As Rio Tinto problems mounted, political complications began to multiply again. In Madrid the cabinet of Antonia Maura clashed with the king over solutions to the strike and to the Catalan regional question. Maura, who had tried vainly to stage a political comeback, resigned in favor of the more conservative Joaquín Sánchez de Toca. A few days later, however, on July 23, 1919, the Catalan leader Francisco Cambó placed this new cabinet in jeopardy by attacking the government's continuation of the Catalan state-of-siege orders. Approximately three thousand Catalans had been imprisoned since April on a variety of political charges.[25] A rising toll of assassinations, which claimed six unionists, three employers, and two Civil Guards as victims, alarmed Cambó, as did the gunfights between paid assassins of the Employers Federation and gunmen of the CNT. The leader of the auxiliary police force involved in so many of these activities, the Baron de Koenig, was a friend of General Lorenzo Milans del Bosch and the former Barcelona police chief, Manuel Bravo Portillo. Rumors that Koenig had been a German spy in Spain during the war circulated constantly during this period, but by 1919 he may have been in the pay of British intelligence.[26] Much of his following came from the Federación de Sindicatos Católicos Libres (usually called Sindicatos Libres) and from demobilized foreign soldiers.[27] Court records show that several Frenchmen, an Italian, and a Yugoslav—all presumably in Koenig's employ—were arrested for attacking union headquarters or syndicate leaders. This violence kept the ultra-Left alive as a paramilitary branch of the CNT, although their organization still remained crude.

Not long after Cambó's tirade, in August 1919, the government in Madrid made a serious attempt to end this incipient social war by appointing a moderate governor in Catalonia, Julio Amado, who was given wide-ranging powers to find some solution. He at once proposed to pardon jailed syndicate members if the CNT would agree to participate in labor arbitration boards—"mixed juries"—with the Employers Federation. Although this meant cooperation with political authority, the CNT tentatively agreed. In early September more than seventy thousand workers, most of them locked out since the March strike, returned to work. Almost simultaneously, the Employers Federation encouraged formation of Sindicatos de los Patrones (company unions) to give management additional power in the mixed juries. The CNT protested to the press and the government without success. Bitter at having its first significant political concession offset by the rising power of the company unions, the CNT began collecting contributions for another general strike fund. At the same time, new violence began altering the relationship of the anarchists to the government, especially when the Barcelona police chief, Manuel Bravo Portillo, was assassinated on October 15, 1919, by the Claramonte gang, which called itself "anarcho-Bolshevik."[28] Pedro Claramonte, Joaquín Blanco y Alcodori, and José Pellejero belonged to the painters' syndicate, whose leader, Pablo Sabater, had been killed by Koenig's gunmen several months earlier. Bravo Portillo and Augustin Serra, a painting contractor, were rumored to have been responsible for Sabater's death. When talks between the CNT and the government broke down, this old score was settled. Even though the killing had little directly to do with the relations between anarchists and the government, it signalled a new period of increasing difficulty.

Worse violence soon occurred. The victims of October 1919 were usually workers who had refused to join the syndicates or support the strike fund; some forty or fifty were killed or wounded, and a number of workers were killed by the police as well. Many Barcelona laborers remained uninvolved in the political struggle going on around them, more concerned about declining living conditions and the growing insecurity of life in Barcelona than about political principles. But if the CNT, struggling for its existence, harassed them from the Left, the Employers Federation soon began to attack them from the Right.[29] The assassination of Bravo Portillo accelerated the development of company unions and the use of gunmen dedicated to exterminating the CNT.

Many companies refused to implement the eight-hour-day legislation when it went into effect in October. The national meeting of the Spanish Employers Federation, convened in Barcelona in mid-October, rejected all social legislation and resolved that Spain was in the process of social disorganization. By secret resolution, employers decided to use the lockout to break all future strikes.[30] Their chance came on November 2 when Salvador Seguí, who had worked closely with the civil governor, Julio Amado, in setting up industrial arbitration (mainly so the CNT might obtain more influence), rejected limitations upon the right to strike. Given the position of the Employers Federation, he had no other choice, but almost as soon as the CNT balked, the employers announced a lockout in Catalonia and several other regions.

The civil governor worked desperately to get Seguí back to the bargaining table. By recognizing the CNT as a national bargaining agent, he removed some of the worst obstacles between government and labor. The recognition document, signed on November 12, 1919, created a model contract to be used in all future labor negotiations, with detailed obligations and responsibilities binding both sides.* A labor commission made up of labor, government, and management representatives would adjudicate all future disputes within Barcelona. However, if management met half the union demands in a particular conflict, the strike would be considered automatically settled.

The cabinet hailed Seguí as a far-sighted labor leader for his part in the settlement, but such national recognition did little to persuade businessmen to cancel the lockout. In fact, the Employers Federation continued the lockout for ten weeks amid increasingly confused national politics. The moderate Conservative, Joaquín Sánchez de Toca, resigned the premiership under fire on December 10. He was followed by an anti-labor Conservative, Eduardo Dato, who immediately dismissed Julio Amado and replaced him as civil governor of Barcelona with Count Salvatierra, a very reactionary member of the Conservative party. The Employers Federation played a major role in this series of events to penalize Joaquín Sánchez de Toca and Julio Amado for their conciliatory attitude towards the CNT. Count Salvatierra had close personal ties with various business groups and frequently spoke out against the peril of a strong labor movement. He was also friendly with the former Premier, Antonio Maura, and his chief assistant, Juan de la Cierva; the anti-Catalanism of these two, rooted in the Tragic Week of 1909 (and often confused with their hostility to anarchism), further antagonized the syndicates.[31]

*No management decisions could be made by the syndicates, no industrial sabotage could be committed by workers, and sympathetic boycotts or strikes were prohibited. Management had the obligation to provide adequate work conditions and modern tools or machinery. *Heraldo de Madrid,* November 13, 1919, p. 4.

To make matters worse, Alfonso was growing tired of the perpetual labor battle. Rumors circulated that the king had approached General Miguel Primo de Rivera, an eccentric, strong-willed army man, about the possibility of forming a military government.[32] Alejandro Lerroux, the discredited radical republican from Catalonia, was also moving towards an ultra-conservative position and strongly supported the idea of a military dictatorship.

Clearly the mood of the major national political leaders now undermined any equitable approach to the CNT. The members of the Employers Federation went so far as to announce that they would not be satisfied until syndicalism was destroyed forever.[33] Many of their subsequent statements excoriated political weakness and demanded strong military rule.[34]

Nevertheless, despite the new reactionary national mood, the CNT broadened its strike. About fifty thousand workers had been out in November and December 1919. In January 1920 the number increased to approximately a hundred thousand. New strikes were declared in other areas. Rio Tinto experienced more violence than at any time since the previous summer. More than five thousand laborers walked off their jobs in Seville. Miners in Oviedo began a long strike to increase wages for pit workers. The dock workers in Alicante and Valencia closed down those ports, and a bakers' strike in Madrid kept bread in short supply for several weeks. But Barcelona remained the most seriously affected city. Construction workers had been on strike since November 25, 1919, and stevedores since December 2. Although in terms of participation this strike did not reach the magnitude of the August rebellion two years previously, in violence it surpassed any earlier labor conflict. At least twenty (and probably more) deaths were recorded during the lockout, among them that of Fernando Pintado, a journalist sympathetic to the CNT. Jaime Graupera, head of the Barcelona Employers Federation, was wounded but survived to order his gunmen to attack the CNT even more openly than before.[35]

While the battle in the streets raged on, the British consul in Barcelona reported that "the working class has been reduced to begging and it is impossible to walk the streets without being molested by beggars, mostly women—carrying infants in their arms—who appear to be half starved."[36] Barcelona employers occasionally offered to take back workers individually, but adamantly refused to rehire known syndicate members. The strikers, through the CNT, demanded back pay for the weeks lost in the lockout. When this was refused, they formed new groups like El Soviet Metalúrgico and Los

Jovenes Bárbaros.[37] Rumors of Soviet involvement and the presence of Russian spies and agitators were very common and alarmed the government more than the violence and suffering going on in Barcelona. Negotiations between Premier Dato and the Employers Federation put pressure on employers to end the lockout, much to the displeasure of General Milans del Bosch, who openly demanded a military solution to the disturbances.

By January 24, 1920, the government had won, and the lockout was lifted. Milans del Bosch was soon replaced by General Valeriano Weyler, the so-called "butcher of Havana," whose reputation for severity in the Spanish-American War made him a natural candidate to control the city on his own without help from the Employers Federation. The CNT immediately extended its own general strike in protest, but strike funds were depleted. Most workers had to return to work on the terms of the employers or continue to starve.

IV. Development of the CNT

While the lockout was going on, the CNT itself underwent a series of formative changes. The most important were adopted by the first national congress of the CNT, held in Madrid on December 10–18, 1919. More than 420 delegates, representing approximately 649,000 CNT members, met at the Teatro de la Comedia, thanks to Premier Sánchez de Toca's permission, another act instrumental in bringing about the downfall of his cabinet.[38] The crucial question in everyone's mind concerned the ability of the CNT to withstand the lockout. The UGT, meeting in Madrid at the same moment, found itself so seriously handicapped by management's animosity towards the labor movement that it proposed creation of a united front with the anarcho-syndicalists.[39] Eleuterio Quintanilla, representing the Asturian Miners Syndicate, argued in favor of a temporary merger with the UGT; revolution could not succeed unless the Spanish proletariat was united and autonomy of the regional branches forsaken in favor of greater executive power.[40] However, many others, believing that such a move would mean the absorption of the CNT by the UGT, rallied behind Angel Pestaña's defense of autonomy. Salvador Seguí sided with Quintanilla, but the proposal of a merger lost. Instead, the congress adopted a substitute motion that rejected any unity with the socialists.[41] Because of this obstinacy, some of the Asturian miners left the meeting, and the CNT was never again quite so powerful in Asturias.

47

Salvador Seguí's leadership was also challenged in the debate over industrial unions. Since the Congress of Sans, industrial unionism had been the stated policy of the CNT. Yet regional executives of the CNT had not even begun to establish industrial unions. Seguí believed this was a serious error and, again backed by Eleuterio Quintanilla, asked for the immediate development of national industrial federations to organize workers of each sector. The effort would be made from above and anticipated greater CNT centralization. Unrestricted autonomy for regional anarcho-syndicalist groups could only lead to premature uprisings and a lack of understanding of general labor problems. Seguí doubted that the conspiratorial nature and revolutionary elitism of the CNT would foster the leadership necessary to educate Spaniards for an eventual seizure of the state.[42]

On this, there was dogged anarchist resistance. According to Manuel Buenacasa, national industrial federations would place a special emphasis upon labor problems and elevate skilled workers into special political groups. The unity of the CNT could be maintained only by resisting all schemes of organization which would thus segregate workers in hierarchies.[43] The congress overwhelmingly voted down the motion to push industrial unionism into the forefront of CNT policy, although it was kept as a future goal.

Organizational matters clearly took second place to more emotional concerns. The Russian revolution dominated the attention of many delegates. Younger anarchists such as Andrés Nín, a Catalan journalist of strong ultra-Left tendencies, Joaquín Maurín, an Aragonese journalist and sometime schoolteacher, and Hilario Arlandis, a Valencian carpenter and the Spanish political figure most enthusiastic about Lenin's "anarchist" work, *State and Revolution*, joined older militants like Manuel Buenacasa and Eusebio Carbó in praising the dictatorship of the proletariat established in the USSR and in urging the CNT to join the Third International.[44] Insurrection rather than organization (as in the preceding debates) became a central issue. Salvador Seguí and Eleuterio Quintanilla again took an unpopular stand. The two moderates argued that the October revolution had been led by a political party. Russion unions gained very little from the Bolsheviks. Lenin, despite his revolutionary qualities, used centralism in all aspects of creating a post-revolutionary society. The dictatorship of the proletariat, which existed in name only, had little to do with anarchist or syndicalist principles.

Once again, on the other side, Manuel Buenacasa insisted that it was too early to condemn Lenin's new regime. The civil war imposed

a heavy obligation to defend the revolution against foreign intervention. What mattered most was that the Russian people had destroyed
an oppressive regime to organize a radically new society—a process
that had not yet been completed.

The congress compromised by provisionally adhering to the
Third International while maintaining loyalty to the Bakuninist
principles of the First International. If the Third International
proved to be a true international of workers, CNT membership
would become final. Delegates to a forthcoming meeting in Moscow
(the second Comintern congress) were chosen carefully.

As the final act of the congress, the CNT proclaimed "libertarian communism" as its basic ideology. No one was sure what the
term meant, but the CNT was desperate for a motto that might
inspire continued resistance to the lockout.[45] In the euphoria that
followed the Russian revolution, any strong term had its value. Salvador Seguí, who disliked the motto, was repudiated for a final time.

When the CNT delegation arrived in Moscow on July 14, 1920,
Angel Pestaña, chief Spanish delegate to the second congress of the
Comintern, immediately objected to Lenin's strong stress on the role
of the communist party in Third International activities. The Spaniard became a leader of dissatisfied European unionists who called
for the creation of a Red Trade Union International to democratize
communist labor organization.[46] Victor Serge, still interested in
Spain and already dissenting from Bolshevik policy, briefed Pestaña
on the anti-libertarian aspects of the Bolshevik dictatorship.[47] Unlike
Andrés Nín and Joaquín Maurín, CNT delegates who did accept
Bolshevik leadership, Angel Pestaña associated primarily with foreign anarchists like the German Augustin Souchy, the exiled Americans Emma Goldman and Alexander Berkman, and a Russian-born
anarchist, Alexander Shapiro, who had spent a long exile in London
with Peter Kropotkin.[48] Soviet destruction of Nestor Makhno's
anarchist regime in the Ukraine, one of the conflicts which drove
communists and anarchists apart at the Comintern meeting, occupied much of their attention. Pestaña so impressed his comrades that
Emma Goldman called him "one of the ablest labor men of Europe."[49] Undoubtedly his enhanced status forced the CNT, upon his
return to Spain, to abandon plans to enter the Third International.

During this interval, Salvador Seguí, who had remained in
Spain, struggled to moderate the CNT's call for "libertarian communism." He convinced Ricardo Mella that he should oppose the
confederation's confused politicization of labor problems. Seguí visu-
alized the labor movement and its political arm as two different

49

organizations, fraternally related under the broad doctrines of anarcho-syndicalism but performing such totally different functions that their paths would not often cross until a political crisis demanded a united front. This vague plan, developed in the months after the 1919 CNT congress, found some support in the regional congress at Saragossa in May 1922.[50] Angel Pestaña accepted the plan since it took political activity out of syndicate life; it "de-bolshevized" the CNT.[51] Ironically, Seguí's formula provided a basis for the split of the anarcho-syndicalists in 1927 into the CNT and the Federación Anarquista Ibérica (FAI). The FAI became the action arm of the CNT and later, during the Second Republic, a source of considerable radical pressure.

Yet the original intent was not to pursue greater radicalism or a more sectarian base. Far from it: Salvador Seguí sought to hold a moderate line against the ultra-Left, which had consistently voted down his points in 1919. In a sense, his position represented orthodox Bakuninism being raised against terroristic voluntarism, a return in spirit to the International Revolutionary Association within the earlier Social Democratic Alliance. In this case Seguí's main interest was in the larger organization rather than the smaller one, unlike Michael Bakunin and the First International. Labor progress was necessary before libertarian communism could be implemented. If progress was not achieved, Seguí feared, anarchists would return to a simplistic "propaganda of the deed" philosophy and block development of the labor movement indefinitely.

To achieve broader unity, the CNT established a temporary alliance with the UGT on September 3, 1920, in the wake of anarcho-syndicalist disillusionment with the Third International. The two confederations agreed to bargain and lobby jointly for progressive labor legislation. Although a jurisdictional dispute over Rio Tinto soon nullified the importance of this alliance, the CNT did not break off relations with the UGT or follow the new directions that had been called for in December 1919.

Crucial to this new reasonableness was the fading emotional power of the Russian revolution. "What mainly attracted anarcho-syndicalist elements to the Bolshevik revolution was agrarian reform and the promise to end the war. . . . The Bolshevik slogan 'peace, bread, land' seemed to have been borrowed from the anarcho-syndicalists."[52] However, with the rise of a workers' opposition movement in the Soviet Union which culminated with the Kronstadt rebellion in February and March 1921 (when sailors, libertarians, and anarchists unsuccessfully battled against the Soviet dictatorship), anarcho-

Bolshevism became a relatively isolated ideology within the CNT. Union solidarity, threatened by Lenin's insistence that it was the duty of all communists to seize control of trade unions in order to subordinate syndicates to the party, now became stronger. Lenin's position clashed with the anarcho-syndicalists' strong preference for individual freedom.[53] The CNT refused to send official delegates to the first congress of the Red Trade Union International (Profintern) in July 1921 despite the role of Angel Pestaña in creating this organization, and although Andrés Nín did attend, he was now calling himself a communist.

More and more, the international ties sought by anarcho-syndicalists were with anarchists. This development culminated in the revival of a new anarchist international. No large anarchist congresses had been held since the 1907 Amsterdam congress, although a tiny International Syndicalist Federation had existed until it was taken over by communists in 1919 as a part of their expansion into trade union activities. In December 1920, anarcho-syndicalists from Switzerland, France, Germany, Holland, Great Britain, and Argentina met in Berlin and rejected full participation in the Red Trade Union International's convention the following summer. Salvador Seguí and Angel Pestaña agreed by letter with this decision.[54] A few syndicalist groups did go to Moscow in July 1921, but their hostility towards party control of union affairs was great enough to stimulate a breakaway meeting in Dusseldorf in October to plan an international anarchist congress to be held later in Berlin. After several postponements, the congress finally met from December 25, 1922, to January 2, 1923—a fitting anarchist touch, to begin on Christmas day.

The Asociación Internacional de los Trabajadores (AIT), or the International Workingmen's Association, claimed more than 2,068,100 members and 209,250 affiliates from thirteen countries.[55] The CNT, with two workers, Avelino González and José Galo Díez, as representatives, was the largest syndicalist movement in the new International; but because getting out of Spain had become difficult for radicals, the arrival of the two Spanish delegates was delayed five days. Diego Abad de Santillán, representing the Argentine FORA movement, unofficially spoke for Spanish interests throughout the meetings.

Despite limited input from the CNT, the AIT stuck closely to the line Seguí had been urging since the CNT congress of 1919. The AIT was to be an association of labor unions, not political parties. Syndicalist unions would attempt to organize agricultural workers as intensively as industrial labor and otherwise follow the principles of

51

the First International (by which the AIT meant Bakunin's Social Democratic Alliance). Most anarchists reacted strongly against the policies of the Third International and the Red Trade Union International. Syndicalists, torn between a hatred of conservative society and a growing dislike for the new Soviet state, now found as many enemies on the Left as on the Right. The prospect was so discouraging that the AIT sought mainly to develop some strength from its numbers (although the figures cited for each member organization were wildly distorted). The AIT established an International Bureau to propagandize for anarcho-syndicalism. One aspect of its activities was the publication of the AIT's *Bulletin of Information*, issued monthly in French, German, Spanish, and, with more anarchist eccentricity, Esperanto. Editors of the *Bulletin* included Augustin Souchy, an organizer with strong syndicalist interests, Rudolf Rocker, a German follower of Peter Kropotkin, and Alexander Shapiro, one of the disillusioned participants in early Soviet rule.[56]

For the Spaniards, just as the 1919 CNT congress in Madrid had put anarchists from different regions in touch with one another (sometimes for the first time), the Berlin meeting broke an isolation that the CNT had felt since its creation. Spanish anarcho-syndicalists were put into a larger, more European context. Strong international ties developed in the next decade as members went into exile and the visits of foreign anarcho-syndicalists to Spain united AIT activists. This discovery of new comrades, as much as any other factor, encouraged the CNT to continue struggling for a labor constituency without fully following its most radical inclinations. At the same time, European anarcho-syndicalists were particularly helpful in providing anticommunist materials. Rudolf Rocker's anti-Soviet writings, *¿Soviet o dictadura?* (1920) and *Bolchevismo y anarchismo* (1921), were quickly translated and had a considerable impact, as did, somewhat later, Emma Goldman's *My Disillusionment with Russia.*

Unfortunately, the positive experiences derived from the AIT had a limited impact upon the CNT, touching only the upper echelons. The rank and file of the anarcho-syndicalists rarely heard of the AIT or knew anything about anarchism abroad, radical or conservative. Their own radicalism continued unabated, still inspired by the Russian revolution and their hope of duplicating it in Spain. CNT militants saw only that their lives were subject to worsening social conditions and new antagonism from their employers, the government, and the Civil Guard. In a Spain still locked into an incipient civil war, their instincts were to fight back with whatever weapons they possessed.

V. Incipient Civil War

The lockout was called off on January 25, 1920, but violence lingered on. Strikes in Madrid continued until February 3; at Rio Tinto more miners were dismissed; and the port of Valencia remained shut down until March. The government refused to support the CNT's demand that employers pay back wages lost in the lockout. Candidates of the liberal parties, preparing for the February municipal elections, increasingly demanded harsh treatment for the CNT if it did not drop that issue. The military, in fact, prepared for a new crackdown, but the parliamentary situation prevented its start.[57] Count Romanones, now out of office, remarked that if he were an insurance agent, he would not insure the life of the government for more than fifteen days at a time.[58] Some liberals did oppose the behavior of General Milans del Bosch and the Employers Federation, but the majority did not and used the old regional and political issues to continue the attack upon the CNT. In any case, Dato soon fell and was replaced by Manuel Allendesalazar, a caretaker Premier who tried unsuccessfully to minimize the social war now consuming Spanish society.

In March 1920 the numbers of workers on strike steadily increased as few wage increases or back-pay settlements were received. Protests by Andalusian railway workers led to a national rail strike on March 22–23, and miners in Asturias and at Penarroya, near Cordoba, went out at the same time. Barbers in many towns, CNT militants to a man, staged a national strike a few weeks later, and bakers followed them in April 1920. Railway strikes continued to plague the country in May and led to bitter parliamentary debates over the use of strikes by management to force the government to raise rates and fares.[59] Allendesalazar, faced by some unpleasant choices, desperately sought to develop a plan of social reconciliation to end the lockout and strikes. New labor legislation was introduced, dealing with working conditions and the right to bargain collectively, but the inevitable reaction to this moderately enlightened policy forced Manuel Allendesalazar to resign on May 4, 1920. Eduardo Dato returned once again to the premiership.

The new cabinet did not continue Allendesalazar's labor initiatives, but it did at least withdraw implied government support from the Baron de Koenig and his gunmen. The German adventurer was deported in June, and a new civil governor of Barcelona, Carlos Bas, released more than a hundred syndicate members from jail. Momentarily it seemed possible that social tension might abate, but the

CNT, still not decided between revolution and peaceful labor evolution, took this opportunity to expand its own operations. Several mass rallies for the Rio Tinto strikers were held. The Catalan textile industry shut down when more than fifty thousand workers walked out over rejection of new pay demands, and the organization of anarcho-Bolshevik "action groups" accelerated.

Since the lockout, some Catalan syndicates had used these action groups to guard executive committees and union offices.[60] Manuel Buenacasa, now growing impatient with Salvador Seguí's "labor diplomacy," worked with the action groups and put them in touch with one another. The assassins of Bravo Portillo, the Claramonte gang, merged with a group from San Sebastian called Los Justicieros, and on August 4, 1920, this band assassinated Count Salvatierra, who had been the civil governor during the Canadiense strike. The Dato cabinet threw off all restraint and declared war against the CNT. Chaos descended again, this time entirely the fault of the CNT.

The first step in Dato's counteroffensive was suspension on August 10 of the industrial arbitration machinery, which had been operative for less than a year. The arrest of Salvador Seguí and Juan Peiró on conspiracy charges came almost simultaneously, removing the moderate wing of the CNT and thereby leaving the radicals in charge. They began another strike at La Canadiense, this time with even more violence than in 1919. As in the first strike, the anarcho-syndicalists received support from Catalan regionalists, who took an anti-foreign position and called the wages paid by the firm a "mockery" to all Spaniards.[61] As they pointed out, Spanish law prohibited foreign ownership of public utilities, a fact that had been overlooked when La Canadiense was founded in 1911.[62] However, when the CNT learned that the Catalan regionalist funds in this campaign were being subsidized by Emilio Riu, a wealthy friend of Francisco Cambó and an entrepreneur who hoped to purchase stock in the company cheaply, the alliance was broken off.[63]

Once released from jail, Salvador Seguí travelled to Rio Tinto and Madrid to develop support for a national general strike in conjunction with the UGT. He planned to call a general strike each time a new cabinet took office, thus forcing a choice between military rule and revolution. The socialists, initially interested, hesitated and then rejected the idea as irresponsible. Seguí may have worked out this stillborn scheme in anger at mistreatment he received while in jail. It was a prominent and marked exception to his usual caution and common sense.

The cabinet, responding to rumors that the CNT planned revolution and not knowing that it stood alone, counterattacked on November 8, 1920, with the appointment of Severiano Martínez Anido as the new civil governor of Barcelona. Martínez Anido, an army general and previously a local garrison commander, represented the greatest political success of the military to date. His rise to power came for a very good reason: the Moroccan war, lingering since the Tragic Week in 1909, had taken on political dimensions with the persistence of fighting in the Riff between tribesmen and Spanish troops. To forestall new growth of an anti-war mood, the army demanded full control of Barcelona, the most volatile spot in the nation. When this was granted with the appointment of Martínez Anido, repression of the CNT became the first order of business.

An intimation of things to come took place on November 20 when sixty-four CNT members were arrested on charges of conspiracy. The next day Ramón Arín, president of the Catalan Metal Workers syndicate, was jailed while on his way to a CNT conference in Reus, forcing cancellation of the meeting and leaving the executive committee in confusion and disarray. Soon after, José Canela, a friend of Seguí's, was assassinated. On November 29, Luis Companys, a lawyer for the CNT and future Catalan Premier, found himself under detention, while a colleague, Francisco Layret, was shot and killed in the Plaza Cataluña, one of the busiest places in Barcelona. Altogether, twenty-one other confederation members died in battles with police and gunmen in the first three weeks of Martínez Anido's regime.

Throughout December 1920, several thousand additional CNT members went to jail on vague charges. When both Premier Dato and Count Bugallal, the Minister of Justice, refused to control Martínez Anido or his police chief, Colonel Arleguí, the situation deteriorated drastically. The *ley de fugas*, a "shoot-on-sight" application of the court-martial law of 1905 (the first concession of Alfonso to the army), was ordered in January 1921. Forty-nine CNT members died in 1921, and twenty-one were wounded.[64] Thousands of others, including Seguí and more than twenty syndicate executives, were deported to Mahón in the Balearic Islands, where they remained under house arrest pending charges.[65]

Anarcho-syndicalism almost disappeared during the next few months. *Solidaridad Obrera* ceased publication and its presses were smashed. CNT national offices closed, and workers whose membership in the Confederation could be proved lost their jobs. Others saved themselves only by joining company or Catholic unions on

55

orders of the *somatén*, the vigilantes.[66] The ultra-Left threatened to call another general strike to protest the government's tactics, but before this step could be taken, Martínez Anido and Jaime Graupera, president of the Employers Federation, met with cabinet officials at the Ritz Hotel in Madrid. The cabinet asked for a general wage hike as a way of keeping the peace, but the Employers Federation rejected this proposal unless it was accompanied by tax concessions or preferential tariffs. Dato acquiesced, choosing the alternative of increased wages combined with tax concessions, and he began using government gunmen against the CNT. Soon, too, striking syndicates found the jobs of their members taken away by scabs. Soldiers sometimes arrested skilled workers and interned them in their factories. Company unions collected more dues than the CNT, supposedly to establish labor exchanges as a means of reducing unemployment, though this was never done. Company unions also promised to bargain fairly for labor with management, but they were usually controlled by agents of business or government, making such negotiation as took place a one-sided process. The very fact that company or Catholic unions were the only legal labor associations between 1920 and 1922 created an explosive situation.

Reduced to complete disorganization and illegality, the CNT was represented best during this period by "action groups" who considered themselves to be in a war and acted accordingly. Saragossa in particular teemed with young militants still enthusiastic about communism or syndicalism and willing to fight for their beliefs. One young anarchist murdered the editor of *El Heraldo de Aragón* (a major Saragossa newspaper) for supporting the crackdown.[67] Most, indeed, believed that they belonged to a communist CNT. Evelio Boal, a printer friend of Buenacasa who was the new secretary-general of the CNT, failed to inform anarcho-syndicalists of Angel Pestaña's hostility to the Third International. Pestaña had gone almost directly from Moscow to a Spanish prison and so could not argue his own case. Boal sympathized with Manuel Buenacasa and opposed a total breach with the communists, perhaps out of fear that Andrés Nín and Joaquín Maurín would then lead the most radical militants into a Spanish communist party, which was still in the process of formation.[68]

The militants lived in an ideological vacuum, with violence as the only clear-cut aspect of their lives. Members of Los Justicieros and other gangs flocked to Saragossa and inspired other young men and women in Barcelona and Madrid to organize themselves along similar lines. Exotic names like Vía Libre, Impulso, and Voluntad abounded among the groups, which began to collect arms and to develop alliances sometimes reaching as far afield as the Basque provinces and Seville.[69] Probably fewer than two hundred persons actually belonged to action groups, but with most of the CNT leadership in prison, this was enough to control public activities of the Confederation.

First target for assassination in this anarchic counteroffensive by the ultra-Left was Count Bugallal, the Minister of Justice who had refused to intervene in Catalonia against General Martínez Anido.[70] To kill him, a group of Catalan metal workers—Pedro Mateu, Luis Nicolau, and Ramón Casanellas—travelled to Madrid in early March of 1921. They quickly discovered that security was less strict around Premier Eduardo Dato than around Count Bugallal. After following the Premier for several days, they decided upon March 8 as the day of assassination. Trailing Dato after he had left a night session of the Senate, the assassins drew even with his limousine as it passed through the Plaza de la Independencia and shot him from the side-car of their Indian motorcycle. Mateu and Nicolau were soon picked up, tortured, and sentenced to life terms. Alfonso walked in Dato's funeral procession down the Avenida Castellaña and won an emotional outpouring of sympathy and support. Militants also celebrated : the assassination was a triumph which advertised their existence. As soon as they had smuggled the third assassin, Casanellas, out of the country to the Soviet Union, they redoubled their efforts to find another victim.[71]

The most natural target was General Martínez Anido. For more than a year, the action groups had dogged his footsteps. After the Dato assassination, however, the security net around public officials was almost impossible to penetrate. The Claramonte gang tried to bomb the general at the Teatro Barcelona as he arrived to attend a benefit theatrical performance. As Joaquín Blanco y Alcodori began the attack, another member of the group, José Pellejero—the lookout and, in reality, a secret police agent—shouted "There they are!" to forewarn waiting Civil Guards. The bomb was thrown at the police instead, and the terrorists managed to get away, although the next day Claramonte was killed in a gun battle with the Civil Guard and four other members of the group were subsequently killed.[72]

Then in August 1921 three young activist workers from Barcelona, Ricardo Torres Escartín, Francisco Ascaso, and Aurelio Fernández, went to San Sebastian, where Martínez Anido was vacationing. Leaving their pistols and bombs in a hotel room, they were dining in a cafe when the civil governor walked past. The three rushed to get their weapons, only to find that his bodyguards had noticed their presence and persuaded Martínez Anido to move on immediately to Corunna. When the anarchists followed the general there, police were waiting. Two were arrested on contrived charges of drug smuggling.[73] As it turned out, Martínez Anido lived on to serve as a vice-president of the Council of Ministers with General Primo de Rivera during the dictatorship and to fight under General Franco in the Spanish Civil War. However, other targets, less well known, did not fare so well. At least thirty-three company union members, police, and employers died in 1921, and sixty-three were wounded.

Obviously this new rash of violence did not improve the situation of the CNT. Evelio Boal and Juan Peiró were arrested in the aftermath of the Dato assassination. This left the CNT without any of its top officials. Someone like Juan Peiró, a Barcelona syndicate leader with considerable influence and very moderate views, was needed to help negotiate a truce between the CNT and the government. But in the bitterness of the conflict, moderates were swept up with radicals. Allendesalazar, Dato's successor, could placate public opinion only by continuing the repression. A few socialist and republican deputies in the national parliament did demand on April 15, 1921, that the suspension of the constitution be lifted, the company unions abolished, and the CNT legalized once again; but no one supported their motion, and the number of CNT members arrested continued to rise during the summer of 1921.

At this point, a sudden new national development intruded into the labor situation. On July 21, 1921, a division of the Spanish army was wiped out by Riff tribesmen at Annual, Morocco. In time Annual was seen as the most humiliating defeat in Spanish history—a defeat, moreover, accomplished by the same Berber irregulars who had been the enemy in 1909 when the Tragic Week first stirred anti-military and radical sentiments. The political significance of this loss sent shock waves through Spanish society, since it demonstrated how badly the army was managed by the government. The king was particularly implicated; rumors soon spread that he had advocated the ill-advised campaign but would not accept responsibility for its failure.

The CNT could not immediately take advantage of this new turn of events. The government used intensive measures to insure that nothing disturbed the public order.[74] The executive committee of the CNT, now severely depleted, met secretly at Logrono in August and voted to send a delegation to the Soviet Union to see what aid might be forthcoming in the aftermath of the Annual disaster. Only one delegate at Logrono was an anarchist—and he was French—so little came of the trip. The Frenchman, Gaston Leval, a syndicalist and resident of Toulouse, returned from Russia to support Angel Pestaña's thesis that the CNT should have nothing to do with the Soviets.[75] The fact that this issue could be debated again showed how out of touch and fragmented the movement had become.

The inability of the CNT to recover its footing allowed action groups to develop at a faster pace in late 1921 and 1922. These clandestine factions, usually composed of workers too young to have police records, possessed some slight freedom of operation, but they usually were only a step ahead of the Civil Guard or military officials. In Catalonia the action groups occasionally received some aid from Francesco Macià, who believed that the suspension of the constitution hurt regionalism as much as anarchism. Some of the Saragossa militants drifted to Barcelona, attracted by Macià's aid and happy to escape police pressure and the competition of the Catholic trade unions organized by Archbishop Juan Soldevila Romero. In October 1922 these elements formed a new group, the Solidarios, or Collective, which irregularly published its own newspaper *Cristol,* the "Crucible."[76] Buenaventura Durruti, Francisco Ascaso, and Juan García Oliver were very much a part of the founding Solidarios cadre.

Perhaps the most important aspect of the Solidarios was its revival of Bakuninism. The practice of forming cells within larger labor or political organizations, originally a tactic of Bakunin's, now was readapted to meet the competition of similar Bolshevik ideas. *Cristol* cited Bakunin again and again as a man of action, an activist, the only political philosopher whose ideas might be useful in the struggle against military dictatorship—a possibility which *Cristol* saw looming on the horizon, bringing with it the final repression of the Spanish labor movement.[77]

The Solidarios, seeking to increase its influence, began by calling together the first Comité Regional de Relaciones Anarquistas de Cataluña in December 1922 to link youth groups and the action cells in a common front against the military and the government.[78] Little in the way of formal resolutions or policies was adopted by the secret conference, but most participants recognized the Solidarios as the leading action group in Barcelona. The meeting also fostered a strong sense of collective unity—the motto adopted was *"ir a por el todo"* (literally, "to act for all")—and a belief in the usefulness of revolutionary committees working as informal soviets. A dictatorship of the proletariat was possible: just how it might be achieved, they

59

were not sure, but Spain had to follow Russia. The success of the Bolsheviks gave the Solidarios a hope and a model. This vision appealed to young workers as the ideal way to combine skilled and unskilled workers, thus destroying the old artificial divisions within the syndicates. In any case, *Cristol* advised, unskilled workers did not need unions so much as a cause to fight for.[79]

Yet much of the activity at this point was simply rhetoric. The Solidarios could do no more than irritate the government by using terrorist methods on a very limited basis. A more sophisticated program would not be developed until after the founding of the Federación Anarquista Ibérica (FAI) in 1927.

In the meantime, *Cristol* mounted a campaign against King Alfonso, calling him *el rey felón* and Alfonso *el africano,* both slurs on his involvement in the Moroccan war. The Solidarios as a group initially worked hard to create a committee of workers and soldiers to fight the growing importance of the army in Spanish life, but the campaign won few recruits. Increasingly the members turned to assassination as their chief activity, beginning with the plot—involving Durruti, Ascaso, and García Oliver—to kill Ramón Leguía, a leader of an employers' group in Manresa. Leguía was slightly wounded, but in the aftermath, while the plotters got away, all CNT activity in the town was prohibited.[80]

The most celebrated assassination of the time came soon after, on June 4, 1923, with the death of Juan Soldevila Romero, the Archbishop of Saragossa. Hated because he had dared to found Catholic trade unions in competition with the CNT and UGT, Soldevila had been followed by Solidarios members off and on for months before Francisco Ascaso and Torres Escartín, with the help of Buenaventura Durruti, managed to shoot and kill him at the door of a religious establishment. Ascaso and two lesser Solidarios conspirators were immediately arrested, but Durruti managed to get as far as Madrid before being captured.[81] He hid his identity, was mistakenly freed the next day, and soon joined Torres Escartín in a hideout in the northern Pyrenees, where they plotted to free Francisco Ascaso. A series of bank robberies (including robbery of the Bank of Spain in Gijon, where the first Solidarios militant, Eusebio Brau, was killed) provided money to bribe the guards, but before a prison break could be staged, Torres Escartín was captured in Saragossa and charged with the assassination of Archbishop Soldevila. Hundreds of other anarcho-syndicalists, including Angel Pestaña, were rounded up in a series of mass arrests.[82] Temporarily, Ascaso stayed in jail.

VI. The Final Agony

The notoriety of the Solidarios in the summer of 1923 contrasted strongly with the inactivity and disorganization of the CNT over the past year. After all the persecution, when leaders of the CNT had been imprisoned, exiled, and routinely subjected to house arrest, not even the reestablishment of constitutional guarantees in April 1922 made much difference. Strikes continued throughout 1922–1923 of course, but they lacked coordination or purpose. Miners in Asturias were more active than most syndicates, going out on several major strikes in 1922. Metal workers, members of one of the best organized industrial unions, pressed for unemployment insurance, public works, and a restrictive tariff policy to keep out foreign goods.[83] But such open political activity was very rare, for the anti-labor tide still ran high. Striking gas workers and electricians in Granada were deported to the Spanish Sahara when they refused to abandon their demands.[84] Many employers continued to ignore the eight-hour-day legislation, and a general strike in Bilbao broke out over this issue in March 1922.

Count Romanones revealed in the national parliament that more than a thousand labor officials and workers, not charged with any crime, still were being sent from jail to jail.[85] In the spring of 1922 a scandal over the protection money demanded by gunmen working for the Employers Federation caused a public outcry, as did charges that the Barcelona police chief, Miguel Arleguí, was continuing to sanction scores of secret arrests and preventive arrests. A new Premier, Rafael Sánchez Guerra, began to argue that these excesses could be stopped only by a strong defense of civil liberties. Then, on August 25, 1922, Angel Pestaña, while on a visit in Manresa, was wounded by assassins probably in the employ of the police. Martínez Anido and Arleguí, implicated in the crime, fought to remain as Captain-General and police chief, but they were forced to resign in October 1922.

The new civil governor of Catalonia, Julio Ardanaz, a moderate, resisted alliance with the Employers Federation. Through patient negotiation he managed to bring some calm to the social crisis by January 1923, aided considerably by exhaustion on both sides. But complete normalization was impossible. Rumors circulated of a planned uprising by a combined force of anarcho-syndicalists and Catalan regionalists and of the army's near rebellion over public ridicule of their unsuccessful efforts in Morocco.[86]

King Alfonso, sure that he could control the military through

61

personal diplomacy, continued to see the CNT as his chief enemy. In January 1923 he had the cabinet draw up an emergency labor code. Syndicates were legalized in shops where there were a hundred syndicate members or more. No national organization of syndicalists would be permitted, and no individual syndicate could adopt a political ideology. Many of the rights granted to syndicates concerned apprenticeship programs, educational self-improvement, or savings banks for workers. Collective bargaining was limited narrowly to an executive committee which would present employee demands to management. Both the government and management nominated members to this committee, thus always outnumbering labor two to one. The government received power to supervise the syndicates, and all union membership lists went to the Ministry of Labor, the civil governors, and appropriate police officials.[87]

The CNT, stymied by this empty grant of labor respectability, suffered an even greater loss on March 10, 1923, when Salvador Seguí, along with a friend, Francisco Comas, was assassinated in Barcelona. His murderer never was apprehended, and while Seguí's enemies on the Right were legion, rumors soon spread that the assassin had been an anarchist disgusted with the CNT leader's moderation.[88] Although the charge arose from sensational journalism, the death of Seguí did strengthen the position of the Solidarios, whose members saw no reason to accept social pacification. But in all fairness, Seguí had no intention of accepting Alfonso's labor code, and the Solidarios undoubtedly knew that he would not. In any case, Seguí's role had declined precipitously since the lockout. It would have been very difficult for him to recapture control of the anarcho-syndicalist movement.

Though Seguí's assassination aided the Solidarios, it did not come at a time when a struggle for leadership was possible, since the CNT and anarcho-syndicalism were still under attack. To assume a leadership role meant accepting burdens that would have destroyed the fragile Solidarios structure.[89] The entire labor movement took the lead in calling a one-day general strike on March 13 in Barcelona to honor Salvador Seguí. Later, Solidarios members worked with Catalan regionalists in an unsuccessful attempt to bomb Alfonso's train as he was travelling north to visit Barcelona. In its propaganda, the Solidarios, already predisposed to associate anti-labor bias and military favoritism with Alfonso, argued that Seguí's assassination had all the earmarks of a royal plot to cover up the king's implication in the Annual disaster. The authorities fought back by taking more than nine hundred suspects into custody, while anarchists retaliated by shooting and wounding José Pons, vice-president of the Employers Federation in Barcelona. The social war grew hotter, and as it did, the circumstances surrounding the assassination of Seguí faded into obscurity.

By the summer of 1923 the Moroccan crisis upstaged whatever else was happening. Parliamentary inquiries had reached the point where both the generals and Alfonso faced a possibility of public exposure. Only the summer recess of the parliament averted an immediate hearing. In the interim Alfonso sought first a royal dictatorship and then, failing that, a military regime.[90] On September 23, 1923, General Primo de Rivera, a bombastic, energetic officer, presently the Captain-General of Catalonia and a man rash enough to believe in the king's integrity, responded by pronouncing against the political parties and parliamentary rule. The Liberal era in Spain, which dated back to 1833, ended with the general's *pronunciamiento*. The constant tension between constitutionalism and extra-legal government that had plagued Spain for so long now was resolved in favor of military dictatorship. Hereafter the anarcho-syndicalists could expect even harsher treatment—treatment that would make their earlier battles seem like minor skirmishes. They were the visible malcontents, the protestors of injustice, the organizers of the opposition in a society drifting towards bitter times.

CHAPTER THREE

Exile and Dictatorship

When a revolutionary situation arises in a country, before the spirit of revolt is sufficiently awakened in the masses to express itself in violent demonstrations in the streets or by rebellions and uprisings, it is through *action* that minorities succeed in awakening that feeling of independence and that spirit of audacity without which no revolution can come to a head. [Peter Kropotkin, *The Spirit of Revolt,* 1880]

I. Dictatorship and Destruction

General Miguel Primo de Rivera, assuming power in September 1923, presented a simple but powerful program to the nation. Speaking for the monarchy and military, he demanded an end to the threat of violence presented by Catalan regionalists and the CNT. A key to attaining domestic peace, he believed, was the destruction of anarcho-syndicalism. Once the CNT disappeared, Catalan regionalists would lose the movement they hid behind and so might themselves subside. Primo distinguished between the CNT and the rest of the labor movement. He was clever enough to divide and rule by giving the UGT a favored place in the military regime; Francisco Largo Caballero eventually became Minister of Labor. Anarcho-syndicalists were left isolated and exposed, without labor allies or mass support, reduced to the anarcho-Bolshevik cadres of the northern cities, which did not even have the good will of more old-fashioned syndicalists.

Formal destruction of the CNT began on September 19, 1923, when streetcar workers and other transport groups called a general strike in reaction to rumors of a *coup*. They failed to shut down

Barcelona, and troops quickly mobilized to patrol the avenues in order to prevent further walkouts. More than a hundred strikers and demonstrators died in the next few days of fighting, and on September 23 the CNT was outlawed.[1] *Solidaridad Obrera,* which had resumed publication in the spring of 1922 with restitution of the constitutional guarantees, closed down again in November. Soon after, in early December 1923, a regional conference of the CNT in Granollers dissolved the formal existence of all CNT institutions. The organization began to go underground, and its remaining centers were closed by military authorities in May 1924, leaving most syndicates without offices or headquarters. Former CNT members drifted into the UGT or other "free" unions, except where a few locally autonomous *cuadros sindicales,* or CNT cells, came into existence. The entire CNT structure now resembled the anarcho-Bolshevik groups.

The initial reaction of the Solidarios to the dictatorship had been for its members to arm themselves. During October 1923 they bought or stole a thousand rifles, twelve machine guns, and 200,000 bullets. When the police discovered this arsenal cached in Pueblo Nuevo, new shipments were brought across the French border by Antonio Martín, a notorious Spanish smuggler.[2] The rearmed Solidarios groups began using lone gunmen or quick terrorist attacks upon police stations and banks. Civil Guard forces retaliated by shooting down two young Solidarios members, Gregorio Suberviela and Manuel Campos, in a Barcelona cafe. By the end of December 1923, Barcelona was under secure police control, and the terrorists were forced to take to the mountains or go into exile in France.

Buenaventura Durruti, still free despite a series of dramatic brushes with the law, slipped over the border into France without difficulty. His friend Francisco Ascaso, still in prison in Burgos when the dictatorship began, was the chief participant in an escape that utilized bribery, diversions by other prisoners, and assistance by a number of Saragossa radicals outside the jail. Ascaso then posed as a train conductor while en route to France. Even the staff of the Solidarios newspaper *Cristol* (including Romona Berni, Pepita Not, and Gregorio Jover) managed to flee *en masse* across the border to join the growing exile communities in Toulouse and Paris. But many were not so lucky: Aurelio and Ceferino Fernández and Adolfo Ballano stumbled into a police trap on February 24, 1924, and were charged with the Gijon bank robbery. Aurelio Fernández later escaped from jail, but the others remained incarcerated throughout the dictatorship.

Once the Solidarios had sufficient strength in France, its members began joint activities with comrades still in Spain. The group's most important act in 1924 was the Vera del Bidosa raid. The first stage began on November 6 with a diversionary attack upon the Atarazanas prison in Barcelona to free six or seven Solidarios members held prisoner there. Then, on November 7, 1924, a band of about thirty exiles and sympathizers attacked the *carabineros* (border guard) headquarters at Vera del Bidosa, the largest government installation near the border. Both attacks failed: the Atarazanas prisoners either committed suicide or were executed, while in the other battle three border raiders and two *carabineros* died.[3] The setback crushed the revolutionary expectations of the Paris committee (Durruti, Ascaso, and several Macià followers) that had staged the raid. To these activists the motto "the revolution must continue" now seemed impossible to fulfill.[4]

As the Solidarios subsided, the CNT vainly tried to pick up the pieces. Juan Peiró, new secretary of the CNT's national committee, was a thirty-six-year-old Catalan, the former president of a glaziers' syndicate and a convinced syndicalist. He resented usurpation of CNT power by action groups and blamed many current problems upon the anarcho-Bolsheviks. In 1924 he sought the friendship of Macià in order to obtain aid from radical Catalan sources. A June meeting of the national committee in Saragossa approved a policy of collaboration. Macià, with Peiró's help, founded the Confederación Catalaña de los Trabajadores, a labor organization with regionalist overtones. This step raised the question of how much support the syndicalists were willing to give Macià's statist, but radical, aims. Juan Peiró argued that it was the best alliance the CNT could find in the dictatorship, but actually this cooperation with Catalan regionalists widened the split already present within the CNT.[5]

More confusion developed when the UGT refused to have anything to do with such an alliance, since socialists supported Primo's new policies of providing low-cost housing, low-cost medical programs, and state arbitration of labor conflicts. The new labor legislation revived Alfonso's emergency labor act of 1924 by creating mixed juries of labor, management, and government delegates to negotiate labor issues. Francisco Largo Caballero led socialist acceptance of this compromise. On the anarcho-syndicalist side, Angel Pestaña maintained that the CNT should follow the UGT in not fighting the government.[6] Peiró, caught between Largo Caballero and Pestaña, continued to cooperate fitfully with Macià, who, in the absence of the Solidarios, represented the most implacable opposition to Primo, especially after the partial autonomy of Catalonia was abolished in April 1925.[7]

Finally, the CNT, meeting in Blanes, accepted the informal alliance between Peiró and Macià. The CNT would work with anyone who was willing to overthrow the monarchy and dictatorship.[8] Hereafter, despite considerable feeling that Macià was a lukewarm revolutionary, the CNT committed itself to support Catalan demands for a federal republic.[9] But nothing was really settled; the CNT simply divided even further into polarized factions despite Peiró's efforts. Little could be done to heal the breach, for it became increasingly difficult to hold meetings. After disruption of the national committee's Sabadell meeting in May 1924, a decision was made to replace the CNT congress with a national assembly of regional representatives, further decentralizing the CNT until only local and regional groups had any power. No national CNT congresses were held again until 1931.

The anarcho-Bolsheviks continued to go their own way. Manuel Buenacasa won the backing of a syndicate still operating in Blanes, near Gerona, to finance publication of a newspaper entitled *El Productor,* which was edited and published in Barcelona.[10] The paper followed the old line of *Cristol* in excluding the CNT from anarchist support and proposing instead that a Comité Regional de Relaciones Anarquistas provide a loose party structure. An enthusiastic response came from individuals and groups in Madrid, Valencia, Seville, and Malaga. Anarchist exiles in France also supported the proposal, and a new generation of militants like Bernardo Bou, José Magriña, José Vázquez, and Vidal Jiménez travelled clandestinely in Spain rallying additional converts. But there were few experienced revolutionaries left to work with them. Ricardo Sanz was the highest-ranking member of the Solidarios left behind. He worked vainly in Saragossa to free the three comrades on trial for the Soldevila assassination, but finally he too was jailed before Buenacasa could contact him.

In the meantime, the Soldevila defendants were found guilty: Ricardo Torres Escartín received life imprisonment and was sent to San Fernando Island, while José Salamero received nine years.[11] Durruti and Ascaso, still in France, were given life terms *in absentia.* The dictatorship used the case to stage a publicity attack upon the anarcho-syndicalists. In its wake, Buenacasa was unable to win an audience for his new ideas. Temporarily, at least, anarcho-Bolshevism was as dead in Spain as anarcho-syndicalism.

The efficiency of General Primo de Rivera's military intelligence contributed to the collapse of opposition. Spies were everywhere, checking and reporting all activities on the Left, often infiltrating groups as double agents. The man in charge of this system was General Martínez Anido, now Minister of the Interior in the military government. As one of the oldest and most ferocious enemies of anarchism, the general gave military courts jurisdiction over civil and political crimes. He also was instrumental in establishing the Military Directorate of Inspection to maintain public order in a way that allowed anarchists no opportunity for action. In addition, Martínez Anido actively encouraged various middle-class groups, especially the Employers Federation, to work closely with the Directorate on a vigilante basis.[12] *Delegados militares gubernativos* (military subgovernors) kept watch over civilian bureaucrats (now purged of *caciques*) to insure that the Left did not take advantage of corruption to stage a revival. Officers often became mayors or civil governors.[13] The military influence obviously ran deep, and Martínez Anido's system gave dissenters little freedom. Exile was the only alternative to imprisonment.

II. The Exiles

Spanish exiles of this period came in all descriptions: young and old, important and rank-and-file, middle-class and proletarian. Jaime Balius, who left for Paris in 1924, never had been identified previously as a militant. He attended medical school and had a bourgeois family to protect him. But even medical students could get into political difficulty, and Balius had to flee after leading a demonstration. In Paris he quickly found an anarchist circle of friends and became a fledgling revolutionary. During the Second Republic and the civil war he counted himself among the ultra-radicals.[14] Another student who fled was Valeriano Orobón Fernández, a twenty-three-year-old Asturian. After leading several early protests against the dictatorship, he too travelled to Paris, where he helped publish the anarchist newspaper *Acción* until he ran afoul of the French police in 1926 and was deported. German syndicalists helped him get established in Berlin as a Spanish teacher at the Berlitz school. Rudolf Rocker took a special interest in the young man, whom he soon called the most capable in the Spanish movement. As a result, Orobón Fernández worked closely with the AIT International Bureau and wrote often for the *Bulletin of Information*.[15] He drew upon this background of experience during the Second Republic to become a talented labor specialist, perhaps the most suitable successor to Salvador Seguí.

Few other Spanish anarcho-syndicalists had the personal resources of Jaime Balius or the leadership abilities of Valeriano Orobón Fernández to allow them to make use of their new freedom. Many of the five or six thousand exiles took low-paying jobs in France, Germany, or Belgium. Through the introductions of Gaston Leval, a lucky few flocked around Sébastien Faure, a leading French anarchist, or the exiled Russian anarchist celebrity, Nestor Makhno. Sébastien Faure did not stress solid labor organization like the Germans of the AIT Bureau. Instead, his ideas were strongly anti-nationalist and pacifist. The anti-militarism of his thought greatly attracted Spaniards fighting a military dictatorship. Faure believed that organizing masses of everyday people into a Gandhi-like campaign of public non-violence would render military power useless.[16] Spanish anarchists who listened to this message hoped his ideas would be useful in reviving popular action against the dictatorship.

Nestor Makhno, who spent a good deal of time at Faure's headquarters at 14 Rue La Petite in Paris, where the anarchist *Revista Internacional* was published, had become the patriarch and hero of the radical Russian exile community abroad. Makhno had participated in the Russian revolution of 1905, robbed banks, presided over a Workers' and Peasants' Soviet in 1917, and created a Ukrainian anarchist republic, which he led between 1918 and 1920. He was a man out of the pages of Bakunin—an activist, as *Cristol* had once demanded that all anarchists should be.[17] In light of his experience fighting both the Red and White armies during the Russian civil war, Nestor Makhno spread the gospel that a revolutionary army was the only sure means of destroying the state—not a professional army, by any means, but rather a fully political body composed of militant cadres prepared to fight a guerrilla campaign. They would work primarily with peasants in rural areas to communalize agriculture and to create a secure base for the guerrillas. When these tasks were accomplished, occasional attacks upon the cities, aided by the cooperation of urban guerrillas to distract public authorities, would accelerate into a full-scale war.[18] The anticipation of Mao Tse-tung and other guerrilla theorists of later days was remarkable (just as Sébastien Faure, to a lesser degree, anticipated some of Gandhi's ideas). Nestor Makhno might have joined the attack on Vera del Bidosa if he had not become seriously ill a short time before the border raid took place.

Even though French and Spanish libertarian philosophies were dissimilar, Sébastien Faure and Nestor Makhno had a great impact upon the Spanish anarchists. Buenaventura Durruti and Francisco Ascaso spent a great deal of time with both men, discussing new ideas and political strategy in unaccustomed freedom. The idea of a political army proposed by Makhno was later used in organizing the FAI and the militia army of Aragon during the Spanish Civil War. Faure's pacifism soon was discarded, but his ideas on the use of public protest campaigns inspired anarchist publicity in 1931 and 1933.

Durruti later remarked that this period of his life in France was like a university education. For the first time he had an opportunity to read and learn. Faure and Makhno were "masters in the art of revolution," and Durruti used them to help plan further assaults upon the Spanish dictatorship. If he had remained longer in France, new border raids would have been made. But the Spanish embassy in Paris, on orders from Madrid, protested the presence of Durruti and Ascaso in French territory. The police soon closed in, and in December 1924, using false passports, Durruti and Ascaso fled France from Marseilles on a Dutch ship bound for Cuba.

The epic experiences of the two anarchists over the next several years created a romantic legend certainly rivaling and perhaps even surpassing that of their tutors, Makhno and Faure.[19] The two Spaniards stayed in Havana for a few weeks. Durruti made a number of public speeches while trying to organize anarchist cells. When the results proved disappointing, they moved on to a sugar plantation between Cruce and Palmira. Within a short time they had organized a union of cane workers. A confrontation over wage demands ensued, and when the plantation owner called the rural guards, Durruti and Ascaso were again forced to flee. Three workers caught by the guards on the plantation were killed.[20]

After pausing to rob a bank to obtain travel funds, the fugitives signed on a small boat in Havana harbor and sailed to Veracruz, on the east coast of Mexico. In Mexico City they were joined by Ascaso's younger brother, Alejandro, and a close Solidarios friend, Gregorio Jover, both veterans of the Vera del Bidosa raid. The four Spaniards, calling themselves Los Errantes, did some organizing for the Mexican Confederación General del Trabajadores. Durruti, under the name "Miguel," even lectured to petroleum workers in Tampico on the educational ideas of Francisco Ferrer.[21] But bank robbery was more profitable, and various members of the gang took turns posing as a rich Peruvian mine owner to gain access to bank vaults, which they would loot. In the late spring of 1925 the Mexican police discovered their identity and applied such pressure that Ascaso, Durruti, and Jover (leaving behind the younger Ascaso who had been wounded) set sail for South America.

Their itinerary until they reached Chile is difficult to trace. The trio may have spent some time in Venezuela or Peru, but there is nothing definite until June 9, 1925, when they landed at Valparaiso, Chile. On July 11 the trio held up a bank in Santiago, Chile, and escaped by train to Argentina.[22] Arriving in Buenos Aires was like coming home again, for during the Twenties the city was, in many respects, the capital of South American anarchism. The Federación Obrera Regional Argentina constituted one of the largest AIT sections, and some of its Spanish or Italian members knew the three fugitives from Barcelona or Paris. Activities of the FORA included the Editorial La Protesta, a publishing house run by Diego Abad de Santillán, who had represented the FORA and the CNT at the AIT founding and was, as we have seen, an expatriate Spanish revolutionary.[23]

Durruti and Ascaso grew close to Abad de Santillán and to Donato Antonio Rizzo, editor of the anarchist newspaper *La Antorcha*. Although forced to adopt a variety of aliases to avoid arrest by the Marcello de Alvear government, the two Spaniards reached a large audience and were soon well known to Argentine militants. But, as in Mexico, Durruti and Ascaso found it necessary to rob in order to survive. After several attempts, they attacked a bank on November 7, killing a policeman in the process. There was considerable confusion as to the identity of the bandits until Spanish authorities, alerted by their embassy, sent "wanted" posters on Durruti and Ascaso to the Buenos Aires police. Another manhunt ensued, and the trio had to rob a bank at nearby San Martin to obtain funds for their getaway from Montevideo in February 1926. They shipped out to the Canary Islands, where they impersonated Spanish policemen for a brief time until they could take a British boat to Southampton and cross over again into France.[24]

Their adventures were far from being finished. Anarchists hailed them as heroes, but the French police took a dimmer view of their return, particularly since Alfonso XIII planned a state visit. On June 25, 1926, the three were arrested on charges of plotting to assassinate the king.[25] Almost at once the Spanish government demanded extradition of Buenaventura Durruti and Gregorio Jover for the Vera del Bidosa raid and Francisco Ascaso for the Soldevila assassination. Argentina also asked for custody of the three so that

71

they might be tried for the murder of the policeman, but during the summer of 1926 Sébastien Faure organized a massive protest movement which attacked the presumption that possession of firearms by the three anarchists created a *prima facie* case of conspiracy. The protest ridiculed the cooperation of the French and Spanish police and asked if the French government, lately embarrassed by dictator Benito Mussolini's rampant Italian nationalism, planned to make it a policy to cooperate with fascists.

An even larger sample of public opinion believed that the charges had been trumped up to ease international relations between Spain and France, strained by the earlier attack upon Vera del Bidosa. Several Paris newspapers opposed an accommodation and began to print unflattering accounts of Primo's alleged misdeeds. Considerable space was given to a language decree of March 1926 that inflicted fines of up to 25,000 pesetas upon Catalans who did not use Castillian in public.[26] The French public, sympathetic to the Catalan cause, took note that Alfonso was so unpopular in Catalonia that recently he had been forced to cancel a state visit. Nevertheless, the cabinet of Raymond Poincaré brushed aside accusations of pro-fascist sympathies. A raid by French police had uncovered a plot by José Carillo, a Macià follower, to attack several Spanish installations in Catalonia from French territory. Premier Poincaré was determined to bring such conspiracies to a halt, but when Francesco Macià was arrested in Toulouse, another torrent of propaganda hostile to Primo and Alfonso was unleashed by Sébastien Faure, this time with much greater impact.[27]

Faure accused Premier Poincaré of blocking the operations of all Spanish opposition parties: democratic, socialist, and anarchist. His propaganda anticipated the Popular Front line of 1936 that all anti-fascists were friends of France. Put in these terms, the argument overrode all other considerations, and the trial of Durruti, Ascaso, and Jover was postponed six months to allow more time for additional depositions to be made. During this lull the French Right and Left frequently battled over the case, with almost daily headlines and much excited comment.[28] The FORA, in Argentina, found itself under strong attack by the government for its association with the three and began a decline which continued until it was outlawed entirely by the Irigoyen dictatorship in 1930. But in Europe, as the case dragged on, publicity spotlighted Buenaventura Durruti and made him into a romantic, mysterious, and almost idealistic revolutionary. It was as if Europeans longed for the simpler days of primitive rebels instead of the confusion caused by the Stalin-Trotsky struggle going on in the Soviet Union. Spanish anarchism emerged from the shadows as a major political movement—the antithesis, Sébastien Faure wrote, of communist or capitalist parties, and ultimately far more powerful than Primo and Alfonso.[29] Durruti believed that Spanish anarchism never could have found such an opportunity on its own to try the dictatorship in the public press, especially since Primo had just succeeded in ending the war in Morocco, thus achieving his greatest triumph.[30]

In April 1927, rumors circulated that France was about to extradite the prisoners to Argentina, thus avoiding criticism for cooperating with Spanish authorities. The matter immediately went to the Chamber of Deputies, where it was debated by such important French politicians as Édouard Herriot and Pierre Renaudel. Socialist and communist party deputies defended the anarchists, and the cabinet finally washed its hands of the whole affair by deporting the three to Belgium on July 29, 1928.

Once the three anarchists were released, Belgian police refused to allow them to cross the border. The French solved this problem pragmatically by helping them cross illegally the next night. Hem Day, an anarchist writer, provided a hideaway in Brussels while various possibilities were explored, including a refuge in the USSR.[31] After the Russians declined to grant sanctuary, a half dozen other countries followed suit, and in October 1928, when their presence in Belgium had become known, they moved clandestinely to Berlin. Rudolf Rocker, Alexander Shapiro, and Erich Mühsam, an anarchist playwright who had been in the Russian revolution, befriended the three comrades, and it was through Shapiro and Mühsam that the Spaniards learned more about Eastern European politics.[32] Life in Berlin was quiet, and several months passed before Catholic spokesmen in Berlin brought the three Spanish exiles to the attention of the Prussian government. The Soldevila assassination prejudiced their case, and an expulsion order came through in January 1929. Once again Durruti, Ascaso, and Jover found themselves on the Belgian frontier, but this time friends in Brussels guaranteed their behavior. For the next two years the three disappeared from the European headlines and worked quietly in Belgium.

Their example motivated other young Spaniards to oppose General Primo de Rivera. One was Juan García Oliver, a twenty-four-year-old in 1925. A Catalan and a minor member of the Solidarios, he had first been jailed in the dragnet that followed Vera del Bidosa. Once released, he returned to his job as a waiter but quickly became a courier between exiles and the few remaining Spanish activists. In 1926 he was arrested on a minor charge near Burgos. Imprisoned for six months, he left immediately afterwards for Paris, where he joined the demonstrations to free Durruti, Ascaso, and Jover. He too worked closely with Faure and Makhno, even finding time to help edit an anarchist encyclopedia. He also assisted Aurelio Fernández in smuggling pamphlets and fugitives in and out of Catalonia.[33] One of these expeditions implicated Ricardo Sanz, who remained in jail for nearly two years. García Oliver also ran into trouble with the French police over his political activities. He left Paris to join Durruti and Ascaso in Brussels, where he worked on a small newspaper, *La Voz de Libertaria,* that Durruti and Hem Day had started.[34] Juan García Oliver was lucky to have a political job at all, for by September 1929 there was little open activity among the other exiled anarchists.

III. La Revista Blanca

While the exiles struggled on, one outlet in Spain continued to provide an encouraging forum for libertarian opinion. *La Revista Blanca* (*The Blank Journal*) had been publishing since July 1923 in the face of enormous odds. The journal's title referred to its censorship problems. There was no freedom of the press in Primo's Spain, and the publication of each issue was a battle. On numerous occasions the Civil Guard raided the print shop and broke the plates. More frequently, copies of *La Revista Blanca* simply disappeared in the mail or were seized, making it necessary to deliver the journal by hand. Some exiles wondered at the time how it could continue to exist at all without government protection, raising questions about its loyalties. In all likelihood its publishers did have some agreement with government officials not to print any specific material on domestic politics, because none ever appeared.[35] *La Revista Blanca* remained a theoretical publication and did this very well, its loyalties clearly on the anarchist side. A whole generation received a remarkable education in libertarian philosophy, preserving continuity with the past. Whatever arrangement kept the journal publishing did not interfere with its usefulness.

The articles published in *La Revista Blanca* were of a rhetorical and theoretical nature, inspirational but not revolutionary. Perhaps the best example were Elisée Reclus' essays on nature and mankind, which appeared in serialized form in 1926–1927.[36] Other contributors opened a window on the world for Spanish readers: Arthur Douglas Smith wrote a regular column from London, Jacques Descleuze reviewed French literature, and there was frequent coverage of Latin American affairs.[37] Jean Gravé wrote often on French syndicalist topics, and one of the most prolific contributors, the anarchist historian Max Nettlau, sketched a history of North American anarchism before and after World War I.[38] The latter also made a notable contribution with his series on libertarian communism, which led to a long, many-part discussion, albeit veiled and often obscure, of the political future.[39] With these last articles the journal sometimes found itself in trouble with the authorities, but the abstract tone probably convinced them that the number of readers for this kind of journalism was limited. Nevertheless, *La Revista Blanca* kept alive the ideals of anarchism at a very bad time.

The force behind the journal came from Federico (Urales) Montseny and his daughter, Federica Montseny. They published, edited, and hand-set the type and usually contributed many of the articles, while also finding time to print fifty or so short novels that Federica Montseny wrote, many of them on feminist themes, between 1923 and 1936.[40] Urales had been an associate of Anselmo Lorenzo and had participated in the Tragic Week and the founding of the CNT. But as an extreme individualist and something of a mystic, he moved away from anarcho-syndicalism when Salvador Seguí and Manuel Buenacasa led the CNT into battle during and after World War I, preferring to live on his farm north of Barcelona and pursue his studies and writing. Federica was the only child he had with Soledad Gustavo, his "life-long companion" (an anarchist phrase for describing a common-law marriage not registered with the state). Federica came of age when the members of the Solidarios were on the rampage in Barcelona, but she continued to live at home, reading and educating herself. When *La Revista Blanca* moved into the vacuum of radical politics caused by the dictatorship, the Montsenys soon made up for their previous lack of activism.

From the very beginning Federica Montseny concentrated upon women's rights and the feminist movement.[41] These were new themes in Spanish libertarian thought, although the movement had supported both since the Congress of Sans in 1918. In a society where, as Emma Goldman later observed, women still appeared to be cloistered, the policy of the CNT barely scratched the surface of sexism.[42] All the more reason, Federica Montseny wrote, why the emancipation of women would lead to a quicker realization of the social revolution.[43] Spanish women, kept as semi-slaves and brutalized by society, perpetuated ignorance and social inequity.[44] There could be no hope for social progress as long as society entrusted the education of each generation to these home-bound persons, chained by the conventions of church and state (both male institutions) to religiosity and conservatism.

The revolution against sexism would have to come from intellectual and militant "future-women." According to this Nietzschean concept of Federica Montseny's, women could realize through art and literature the need to revise their own roles.[45] Change would not come automatically through enfranchisement or an equalization of rights and privileges but through a much deeper phenomenon, a humanistic revolution "allowing unlimited freedom and independence to both sexes."[46] It might best be accomplished by utilizing the more idealistic nature of women, "an epic and legendary element, . . . a lyrical and emotional force necessary in order to convert itself into an invincible movement of opinion, atmosphere and consciousness."[47] Men and women were not interchangeable—they each possessed basic and individual differences—and women certainly could not win their freedom simply by masculinizing themselves.[48]

This sense of individualism marked the thought of both the Montsenys and the pages of *La Revista Blanca* as well. It applied to other areas Federica Montseny wrote about and contrasted strongly with the more collectivist ideas of Salvador Seguí and the Solidarios. The works of Nietzsche, Stirner, Ibsen, and Reclus were her acknowledged favorites, and the latter particularly influenced her anarchism.[49] Here was the concept of a "vital dynamic" in every individual, responsible for his or her particular uniqueness and sociability. The potential of this will and ideal allowed an individual to develop a life and a mode of action independent of the group, "a life that lives" all by itself within the person and is unaffected by social pressure or normal societal conventions.[50]

What united the individual with society was an excess of love and will that each person possessed. This gregarious spirit caused individuals to struggle for attainment or search for creativity. Yet almost as soon as individuals grasped for creativity, they learned that, without true social freedom, personal fulfillment could not be obtained. As a consequence, when the excess of will in each person met obstacles, the individual was forced to reach out for solidarity with others to surmount these restrictions on his or her liberty.

Anarchism recognized this solidarity of individuals in expanding their freedom, for there was no other way to recognize individual accomplishments than to fight jointly for liberty. As a movement, the anarchists had little interest in forcing people to accept uniformity. Anarchism sought to promote liberty and increase the individual's potentially unlimited freedom of development. Much of Montseny's own writing thus concentrated on the exposition of great lives that illustrated their own search for freedom: Lenin, Ibsen, Shelley, Goethe—all part of the heroic sense of life.[51] To live otherwise made one into a "present-man or woman," unable to progress, isolated, gregarious without a purpose. The heroic rebel, on the other hand, fought for progress, the future, and for herself or himself, violently if that was the only possibility. The guideline to be used was whether or not the society seemed static, unable to provide individuals with the freedom to achieve their own personal goals or make the vital dynamic of each person into something socially useful and progressive. If this condition did not exist, then the right of revolt was present, and for the future-person, revolution was almost an obligation.

Unlike members of the Solidarios and other anarcho-Bolsheviks, Federica Montseny at first shied away from elitist, cadre-type political behavior and the imposition of political leadership over the revolutionary process. Although she never criticized her anarchist comrades in print, at least up to 1931, she and her father did quarrel with Durruti, Ascaso, and other anarcho-syndicalists like Rudolf Rocker in Berlin at an AIT conference in 1928 or 1929.[52] This question of elite political action versus spontaneous mass revolution had remained a persistent irritant in anarchist theory since Michael Bakunin's time. The Solidarios followed the program of the International Brotherhood implicitly, and there had been a few earlier examples of small anarchist groups struggling to lead the masses to revolution in Europe without constituting themselves as political parties or trade unions.[53] The Montsenys opposed conscious elite formation in the style of the Solidarios group, because each individual's road to self-awareness was different. But, like most anarchists, they could not turn their backs on the need for some kind of leadership. What they urged was "propaganda through conduct . . . which makes each militant anarchist a model man in all concepts; an "exemplary man capable of inspiring the masses."[54] Buenaventura Durruti, for all his criminal acts, must have struck the Montsenys as a perfect prototype of the supreme militant, an exemplary man capable of inspiring the masses with the vision of a society produced by anarchist individualism and social justice. He possessed Bakunin's "revolutionary instinct" for seizing every possible opportunity to revolt.[55]

Behind individuals of this type, "future" persons might begin "a period of permanent agitation" against bourgeois society.[56] How long this transitional stage might last depended upon how ineptly authorities misread the demand for progress from the people. In Spain particularly, the complaints of peasants had been ignored for so long that no solution could be expected from the dictatorship or any other non-revolutionary regime; the movement thus should concentrate its efforts in the rural regions. Urban militants made easy targets for government repression, but the countryside had hiding places and a guerrilla tradition that might shelter anarchist agitators. Here the revolution, long fermenting, would begin. Peasants still possessed empathy with individualism, and once they destroyed the forces that repressed them, they would converge slowly on the cities and join forces with the urban proletariat.[57] The old state-dominated world would be destroyed, and in the post-revolutionary period, "the right of individual liberty after the revolution" would become the focal point for reestablishing a functional society.[58] A new federalist structure would propagate the widest possible individualism by de-structuring society and abolishing the central state.

Federica Montseny joined the Solidarios in condemning syndicalism as an expression of "atavistic social tendencies, based upon the consideration of life in a bourgeois society."[59] She was willing to support syndicalist union activities until the successful end of the revolution, but she also warned against the power of labor leaders, who would *not,* as Salvador Seguí had believed, educate the masses to emancipate their own lives so much as use labor power to become political *caudillos.*[60] Syndicalism was too technocratic and bureaucracy-prone, without any real socialist content. It remained silent on matters of crucial importance such as "the redistribution of land, the tools of labor, and all production," which would have to be socialized in any future society.[61]

On the other hand, the socialism of Federica Montseny was also at great variance with social democracy or communism. The first, she wrote, mitigated social problems through participation in governance; the second imposed collectivizing solutions from above.[62] Her socialism, which she called libertarian communism, stressed the intrinsic, collective patterns that would naturally revive after the collapse of the capitalist state (although more effort would have to be made in the cities to develop factory councils as an approximation of rural communalism). But a balance would be reached slowly as society learned to live without the restrictions of property. It would be the task of anarchists to fight against the imposition of collectivization from above. Unlike the anarcho-Bolsheviks, she did not approve of Lenin's objectives and condemned his tactics.[63] The revolution would be destroyed if it took Lenin's path. Communists and social democrats alike ignored the individualistic impulses of the people to lead their lives in their own way.

Very few of the Spanish anarcho-syndicalists had the philosophic sophistication of the Montsenys. Their writings, strongly influenced by French philosophy of the will and German individualist thought, displayed considerable syncretic talent and intellectual ability. Their own journal gave them an outlet and a purpose which others did not have. Even more important, the Montsenys became close friends with the Austrian anarchist Max Nettlau, one of the most respected scholars and theorists of the movement in the twentieth century. By this time, Nettlau was hard at work on his history of the First International, a project that brought him to Barcelona in 1928.[64] He remained in Spain for two years and during that time gave the Montsenys a certain cachet. Whatever resentment the exiles might have felt towards them disappeared in the aura cast by Nettlau. In any case, Federica Montseny's participation in the Federación Anarquista Ibérica, founded in 1927, ended any further doubts about her militancy.

IV. The FAI

The founding of the FAI took place at a time when the Left in Spain had grown desperate. General Primo de Rivera's successes in ending the war in Morocco and shifting the make-up of his cabinet from military men to civilian politicians raised the specter of an on-going dictatorship as powerful as Benito Mussolini's in Italy. "Wild West justice and a soldier's contempt for lawyers," to quote Raymond Carr, seemed to have won the day.[65] A slight restiveness was noticeable on university campuses over the arrest and muzzling of intellectuals like Miguel de Unamuno, but students did not rise against General Primo de Rivera until April 1928. The UGT, enjoying the official blessing of the dictatorship, caused even fewer problems with Francisco Largo Caballero in the cabinet. Catalan regionalists, after an abortive rising at Prats-de-Molló in November 1926, were left leaderless and exhausted. Almost every identifiable anarchist was in hiding, jail, or exile.[66]

Yet anarchism still was very much in the news. An attempt to bomb Alfonso's train in 1925 led to the arrest of a number of alleged Catalan regionalists and anarchists who did not come to trial until

May 1926, amid rumors that they were actually *agents provocateurs*.[67] A Canadiense worker alleged to be an anarchist, Domingo Masachs, attempted unsuccessfully to knife General Primo de Rivera while he was on tour in Barcelona soon after this trial. During the summer of 1926 a bomb explosion in the Civil Guard barracks at Garaaf was blamed upon anarchists. In October 1927 the police announced the discovery of an anarchist plot to blow up the National Assembly. Often any protest against the regime was simply labeled "anarchist" by the authorities, who used scare psychology much of the time. In the few cases where anarchists were involved, the use of violence kept opposition alive and attracted new members to the ranks.

The leaderless and discouraged Catalan regionalists now threw in their lot with the anarchists, as did a few radical students. Another source of militants was the Confederação Geral do Travalho, an anarcho-syndicalist organization in Lisbon with AIT affiliations.[68] The size of the CGT was estimated at about 150,000. It was strong in the Portuguese merchant marine and among stevedores, commercial fishermen, and farm workers. The latter often worked in the Andalusian harvests, where they came into contact with the Spanish Agricultural Federation and, more rarely, the CNT.[69]

Closer ties between the two Iberian groups arose in 1926 after a military *coup d'état* against the Portuguese republic of President Bernardino Machado. Generals Gomes da Costa and Carmona (a good friend of General Primo de Rivera) aimed to reestablish order after sixteen years of republican uncertainty.[70] General Carmona assumed the acting presidency in November 1926, intent upon achieving state capitalism, tight political control, and the extermination of radicalism. His model was the Spain of Primo de Rivera or the fascist Italy of Benito Mussolini. The rationale for dictatorship was provided by Portuguese debts to Great Britain, incurred during Portugal's fruitless participation in World War I, which were now causing a ruinous inflation. The Portuguese syndicalists, singled out as the chief enemy of the new military regime, immediately sought an alliance with the CNT. Germinal de Sousa, a Portuguese exile living in Barcelona, was able to obtain pamphlets, books, a few guns, and some money for the Confederação Geral do Travalho. Portuguese anarchist cells operated in Valencia, Seville, Bilbao, and Barcelona. *La Revista Blanca* often discussed Portuguese problems.

Some Spanish anarchists began to consider formation of a new organization better adapted to the changing circumstances. Their mood in 1927, one of them recalls, was so troubled and pessimistic that the purpose of the new group was to be defensive—a last-ditch stand against dictatorship and the destruction of political liberty.[71] A few had more sectarian reasons for joining; Angel Pestaña's approval of CNT participation in the mixed juries revived fears that CNT reformism might again dominate anarcho-syndicalism. Anarchist exiles in France were particularly upset at this possibility; they had not risked everything just to create a trade-union state.[72]

These fears led to a revival in 1926 of efforts to link the small regional anarchist groups. Manuel Buenacasa, who led a charmed life during this period—arrested only once (and then to serve a short sentence)—finally decided to call a new conference in 1927. In his view, the reformism of the Congress of Blanes in 1925 no longer had any meaning. The military regimes in Iberia were too dictatorial and reactionary ever to cooperate with the labor movement, and anarchists risked political contamination by remaining a part of the larger syndicalist organizations.[73]

The Valencian beach resort of Cabañal was chosen as the site of the meeting. The Federación Anarquista Ibérica, as the new group was called, met there on July 24 and 25, 1927, using the huge crowds that came to the fiesta of Valencia to hide their activities.[74] Fewer than fifty militants, including two Portuguese, were present at the creation of the FAI, representing three large groups: the Federación Nacional de Grupos de Anarquistas en España, Buenacasa's Catalan organization; the Unión Anarquista Portuguesa, representing the Left wing of the Confederação Geral do Travalho; and the Federación de Grupos Anarquistas en Francia, the exile organization in France.[75] Smaller factions in attendance, mainly Valencian workers' clubs like Sol y Vida, Los Forjadores de la Idea, and Paso a la Verdad, sat with the Federación Nacional de Grupos Anarquistas, as did local Comités de Relaciones from Seville, Malaga, Rubi, and other towns.

No exiles attended the conference. As a result, most of the delegates were relatively unknown villagers from Aragon, Valencia, and Catalonia. The more intellectual, urban, and volatile anarchists remained in exile, jail, or hiding. This made the FAI, at the very beginning, an organization with surprisingly deep roots in local society. In part they tapped a kind of pure anarchism that neither the CNT nor the Solidarios had possessed. Such diverse topics as vegetarianism, the use of Esperanto, and the prohibition of tobacco and hard liquor were debated seriously by the Cabañal assembly. The form of basic organization adopted by the FIA (affinity groups rather than cells or syndicates, so that village assemblies, interest groups, or other revolutionary groups could be consulted by local chapters) opened the possibility of a very broad federation, particularly in the rural areas. This dedication to representing peasant society was reinforced by separation of rural and urban federations to keep urban viewpoints from dominating the FAI.[76] Finally, discussion of agricultural cooperatives and rural communes took up a great deal of time at the first meeting and pushed the *faístas* (FAI members) far beyond earlier agrarian positions taken by the CNT or the Solidarios. For the moment, peasants had a secure place in Spanish anarchism.

Continuity with the past was retained in other ways, largely through the importance of Manuel Buenacasa and his *El Productor* comrades. They had been connected with older anarcho-syndicalist or anarcho-Bolshevik groups, and most felt the CNT ought not be abandoned to Angel Pestaña or Juan Peiró, whom they considered labor politicians.[77] Now that the FAI had united anarchists into one organization, could it take over the CNT without succumbing to political activity or reformism? Most members of the FAI also belonged to the CNT, so the question was an important one, although many founders of the FAI refused to discuss union matters at all. Time ran out before any decision could be made.

The role of Manuel Buenacasa in the founding of the FAI is worth noting. He was as sectarian in 1927 as he had been in 1919 at the first congress of the CNT, when he had opposed Salvador Seguí. His pure Bakuninist philosophy endowed the FAI with a clandestine character and an intransigent, bitter hatred for "all authority, hierarchy, the state, all legal action, and temporization."[78] The dictatorship made these qualities even more extreme; the fact that a Spaniard could be a Bakuninist at all in 1927 says a great deal about the pressures of life in Spain under Primo's rule. The FAI thus embodied Buenacasa's own classical nineteenth-century anarchism, a new version of the propaganda of the deed. Workers had to create their own "state within a state" by destroying all social control over them so that they could stand alone, able to take over their own governance.[79]

V. The Dictatorship's Fall

The first several years of the FAI were inauspicious. Its French branch could not supply much in the way of arms or funds, and tentative plans to establish affinity groups in France and fascist Italy did not materialize.[80] Expectations that Portuguese anarchists would contribute measurably to a united front also had to be abandoned, despite the work of José Quental as sub-secretary in Portugal, largely because the military regime understood the threat presented by the CGT-FAI and arrested or exiled thousands of Portuguese activists.[81] At home, General Primo de Rivera's government faced serious trouble in 1928 from university students and other dissatisfied blocs. Conservative party politician Rafael Sánchez Guerra finally coordinated these various factions in staging an uprising in Valencia during July 1929. The first coordinated attack against the dictatorship for some time, it failed to dislodge the general; but almost simultaneously the peseta fell on the international money markets, and suddenly the regime found itself in difficulty.

The FAI was not able to take advantage of these opportunities to do its own work. *Faístas* played almost no role in the attack upon the Spanish government; the Solidarios had been more potent at the start of the regime than the FAI was at its conclusion. The reason for this failure lay in the small size of the FAI, its inexperience in organizing (some anarchists did not know of its existence until 1930 or 1931), and the exile of so many potential members.[82] Buenaventura Durruti learned of the FAI in Belgium because *Voz de Libertaria* mentioned it several times. Federica Montseny joined early in 1928 to protest her father's arrest in one of the periodic dragnets which swept up thousands of suspected subversives. But for many sympathizers, the FAI seemed more like a debating society than an action group. As a result, membership barely exceeded several thousand until 1931.

In an effort at publicity, the *faístas* started two new papers, *¡Despertad!* in Vigo, and *Acción Social Obrera* in Barcelona. They also contributed much of the material in *El Productor* until it was closed by police in late 1928. All of this material stressed the differences between the CNT and FAI. The next several years were spent in rancorous debate. The FAI sought, through its journalism, to create a favorable situation to take over—or at least attain parity on—various national committees of the CNT. Since this was almost the only activity of the Confederation during the period, the issue had more importance than it might seem. The FAI scored its first victory on January 15, 1928, when joint CNT-FAI representation on the Comité Pro Presos, a prisoner-relief organization very similar to the modern-day Northern Irish Civil Rights group, was approved by Juan Peiró in hopes that the *faístas* would moderate their criticism of the CNT.[83] Quite the opposite took place: the *faístas* rapidly domi-

83

nated the committee and began to exclude CNT officials. Soon after, when liberal action committees began to protest declining standards of living and the continued police-state tactics of the dictatorship, the FAI rushed to control these, too.[84]

What angered Juan Peiró and Angel Pestaña most was the *faístas'* constant depreciation of the CNT. They felt that the FAI, almost from its inception, had attempted to bypass them in order to take away control of the Confederation. Increasingly the *faístas* joined the CNT and worked against it from within, and Peiró and Pestaña saw this as a communist tactic. The anarcho-Bolshevik label was revived and applied to the FAI with more precision than it had been when it was used earlier.[85] But in many respects the quarrel was academic. Peiró and Pestaña, constantly harassed by the dictatorship, did not feel any less revolutionary than the *faístas,* and they knew that the CNT lay in ruins.[86] The FNAE, the peasant branch of the movement, had not operated since 1923, leaving the rural sector almost totally unrepresented. Most syndicates had been reduced to skeleton size or did not operate at all. There was no anarcho-syndicalist youth movement of any kind.

On the other hand, the socialists remained intact. Their locals were larger than ever before, and they had created the Juventudes Socialista Unida as a junior branch of the organization. Even their cooperation with the dictatorship was not particularly embarrassing, since they justified collaboration on the grounds that the parliamentary system had not been worth keeping.[87] Juan Peiró and Angel Pestaña pointed to socialist successes in defending their own policy of keeping the CNT open and flexible, able to move freely to recapture its once large constituency. The FAI, representing the old maximalist position, stood against them, determined to break with compromise in order to move towards revolution. Each waited, slowly marshalling strength, aware that their time might soon be at hand.

These sectarian issues were momentarily eclipsed by the resignation of General Miguel Primo de Rivera on January 26, 1930. His fall was caused as much by the weakened value of the peseta and the Depression as by the slow revival of civil politics. The "man of tomorrow," as his supporters had once styled the general, possessed too great a reputation for indiscipline and flamboyance to be trusted to deal soberly with the international economic crisis.

As Primo de Rivera's popularity declined, the monarchy and generals backed away to protect themselves. Their support went to another general, Dámaso Berenguer. Conservative continuity was kept by this selection, although General Berenguer had practically no popular support and none of the charismatic *machismo* of his predecessor. The new cabinet presided over the collapse of the monarchy. General Berenguer spoke often of the dangers of "anarchy" and "anarchism," and used the martial law statutes to shore up his slipping regime, but there was little latitude for the government to take positions hostile to labor or to the radicals. Unlike 1919 or 1923, the question now was not the behavior of anarcho-syndicalists but the performance of the military dictatorship itself.

This fact became particularly apparent on April 30, 1930, when a broad amnesty granted the CNT and other labor organizations the right to operate legally again. Spokesmen for the regime claimed that this act would open a new era of social harmony, but the CNT/FAI disagreed. In a national executive meeting called by Juan Peiró and Angel Pestaña and held in Blanes on April 17–18 (the first since the CNT had broken down into regional executives in 1924), the anarcho-syndicalists had shown that they were in no mood to compromise. A majority held a euphoric belief that the Berenguer cabinet was stopgap and destined shortly to fall.[88] Legalization would prove only that labor, after its long ostracism, had the strength to prevail over its opposition. Many felt that the CNT was about to begin another era of great success.

A minority at Blanes accepted this optimistic outlook only with the proviso that the future success of Spanish labor depended upon adoption of an intelligent philosophy more open and less sectarian than past policies. Angel Pestaña, for instance, argued that the CNT should accept a wide range of social ideas and must use anything which benefited the working class, including official participation in politics.[89] Juan Peiró went further by accepting principles contained in the *Inteligencia republicana*, a manifesto put out by Catalan republicans who sought to emphasize the usefulness of a normal legal regime.[90] *¡Despertad!* and *Acción Social Obrera* both supported this position, and so did Angel Pestaña in a speech during the summer of 1930.[91] The pages of *Solidaridad Obrera*, edited by Juan Peiró after August 1930, often discussed the value of a moderate response to political freedom when the dictatorship ended. But Manuel Buenacasa and Eusebio Carbó disagreed: the CNT, they insisted, survived the dictatorship only because it had been a center of resistance against the Right. Its principles of anti-parliamentarianism, direct action, and collectivism would remain valid even in a more liberal environment. After all, anarchism had begun in the liberal era of Antonio Cánovas del Castillo in the late nineteenth century.

The Blanes conference concluded by attacking government intervention in labor arbitration through continued use of mixed juries. The conferees believed that workers had every right to reject the illegal power the state claimed in this area. Direct action by strikes received wholehearted CNT approval, but the meaning of direct action differed among the various factions.[92] Some *faístas* like Ramón Arín, syndicalist leader in Barcelona, interpreted CNT endorsement of direct action as an invitation to stage wildcat strikes and street demonstrations. The weakness of CNT groups involved in these manifestations quickly forced him to accept a moderate position, and this later led to his expulsion from the FAI.[93] Most *faístas* believed that anarcho-syndicalism could not afford to play a quiet role in labor matters. The Berenguer cabinet continued to prohibit the reappearance of industrial unionism and this left the UGT's legal craft unions free to resume recruitment. The CNT stood to lose many of its former members if it did not take a leading role in the political opposition. Still other anarcho-syndicalists adopted a fatalistic attitude. A new wave of strikes to raise wages, which had been held down by the dictatorship for almost six years, inevitably would bring new labor violence and a strong government reaction. They supported new controls on action groups.[94]

Trouble was not long in coming. Dozens of wildcat strikes broke out over wage demands, as the FAI had predicted. The miners of Alto Llobregat, Cardoner, Suria, Sallet, and Figols were briefly locked out of the mines.[95] General Berenguer flatly refused to permit the operations of the Sindicato de la Industria del Transporte, one of the first industrial unions to reactivate. Barcelona stevedores also ran into difficulty in reviving the Sindicato de Servicios Públicos Urbanos and went out on a long strike. Military troops unloaded ships themselves or rounded up stevedores at gun point and forced them to work.

General Emilio Mola, National Director of Security (and later an important military figure in the Spanish Civil War), personally intervened in the stevedores' strike, but discontent continued to spread in Barcelona. During the summer of 1930 it affected the construction industry, La Canadiense and other utilities, Pirelli Tires, the Phillips Electric plants, and many other firms.[96] Antagonism reached a high point in September 1930 when an FAI member was found to have a large cache of arms and ammunition. Fearing a new plot, officials had leading anarcho-syndicalists and Catalan regionalists arrested.

This repression meant more moderate policies were forced into the background. The quick return to an open social struggle angered liberals, who had hoped for a more stable political order. Their anger explained why neither the CNT nor the FAI received an invitation to the clandestine meeting of socialists, radical liberals, and regionalists in San Sebastian on August 27, 1930, which created a republican coalition dedicated to the overthrow of monarchy and military rule. When Rafael Sánchez Guerra met with anarcho-syndicalist leaders in October, the movement refused to be drawn into a political compact and asked pointedly for arms to bring on the revolution.[97]

Behind this bravado were real uncertainties about many things: the divisions that had existed for years between anarchists and syndicalists, the unresolved (or undeveloped) nature of the FAI, the absence of leaders like Buenaventura Durruti, and the lack of a basic institutional structure. There were no real anarchist or anarcho-syndicalist movements in 1930, merely a jumble of groups trying to speak for a tradition of rebellion that was instinctive but long repressed. Nothing was fixed or certain, and the reflexes of the CNT were dull from years of enforced inactivity.

But public unrest did not wait for the CNT to catch up. Strikes began in September in Malaga, Seville, Saragossa, Granada, Cordoba, and Barcelona and soon spread to smaller towns. On September 15, 1930, the entire workforce of the Barcelona construction industry walked out; shutdowns later affected Reus, Igualada, Sabadell, and Comarca del Vich as well. CNT or FAI leadership of these strikes was badly organized or almost nonexistent. When two liberal politicians, Miguel Maura and Angel Galarza of the Comité Revolucionario Nacional Político (the coordinating agency of the San Sebastian coalition), tried to unite all these strikes into a national day of protest, no one knew whom to contact. Finally several minor CNT officials were located, but they refused to cooperate with the UGT. The national day of protest took place without major anarchist participation.

But the strike movement continued to grow. On November 14, 1930, construction workers walked off the job and for two days attacked government buildings and police headquarters. Two workers died and scores were wounded in the rioting. On November 17 the CNT convened a special meeting to coordinate labor strategy. Some sense of panic crept into their deliberations; events were moving too quickly for the resources of the organization to meet. No real solution could be found, although various regional officials did promise to cooperate more closely. A number of moderates begged for caution in the vain hope that the Berenguer cabinet might grant amnesty to the nine thousand anarcho-syndicalists in prison.[98] No amnesty was granted, and the CNT found it impossible to give adequate leadership to any of the new strikes.

National events did not wait for anarcho-syndicalist leadership. On December 12, 1930, a rising of liberal military officers at Jaca, an Aragonese garrison town, proclaimed the unreliability of the army to the Berenguer regime.[99] The general resigned in early February 1931. Municipal elections, to be held in April, were announced on February 8, and many believed that the elections could be used to vote out the monarchy of Alfonso XIII.

The CNT and FAI derived little satisfaction from these changes. Even strident calls in *Solidaridad Obrera* and *Tierra y Libertad* (which began publishing again in August 1930) did not produce a quickening of revolutionary activity. Except in a few strikes, the militants stayed out of public view. On April 12, 1931, Spain rejected military candidates in the municipal elections; the lack of anarchist provocations, which might have pushed moderates towards the military, contributed to a massive republican-socialist victory. Two days later Alfonso XIII, without formally abdicating his crown, hurriedly left the country.

PART TWO

The Second Republic, 1931–1936

CHAPTER FOUR

Reorganization and Discord

Spain is different. Capitalism has persistently failed in that country and so has social revolution. [Eric Hobsbawm, *Revolutionaries*]

Spain is the country of revolution without any peer in Europe. [*Solidaridad Obrera*, May 1, 1932]

I. Return of the Exiles

A trickle of anarchists returned to Spain in 1930. Valeriano Orobón Fernández was one of the first, arriving in the spring from Berlin as a representative of the AIT. Only thirty, attractive and articulate, he was serious in his search for a positive political philosophy that might prevent a reversion to the terrorism and violence of the pre-dictatorship period.[1] Orobón Fernández believed in organization and cadres more than in spontaneity; in the following months he travelled to Barcelona, Saragossa, and his home in Valladolid, reactivating contacts and preaching a message of organization.[2] Half a generation had passed since Spanish labor had been free to develop and express itself politically. New groundwork had to be laid if labor was to compete with bourgeois groups for the allegiance of Spaniards. To that end, Orobón Fernández slowly began developing the Juventudes Libertarias (FIJL), a libertarian youth federation that provided the CNT with a recruiting ground. Formation of other special bodies became a high-priority task, although some militants characterized his activities as busy work.[3] The AIT, unprepared to deal with the criticism, took a neutral position which left Orobón Fernández without support. The Montsenys were his only real

91

friends, but the new possibilities opened up by the lifting of censorship, which included publication of a new paper, *El Luchador*, took
much of their time. Federica Montseny's writings, tentative and un-
sure of revolutionary priorities, did not place great stress upon reorganization of CNT institutions. Instead, she demanded immediate
freedom for jailed members of the CNT/FAI, full rights for labor,
and full political liberty under the new regime.[4]

The number of anarchists returning to Spain increased early in
1931 when the Berenguer cabinet resigned. For the first time since
his student days, Diego Abad de Santillán returned to Madrid from
Argentina, where the Uriburu dictatorship had outlawed the FORA.
Almost at once he began to gather economic material in preparation
for a journalistic career. He was not alone; many of the other six
thousand exiles now returned to Spain.[5] Those on the most-wanted
list stayed away until April 14, 1931, when the monarchy was finally
overthrown, because General Martínez Anido, that durable specialist
in anti-terrorism, had been Interior Secretary under Berenguer and
kept his influence to the very last. Thus, both Buenaventura Durruti
and Francisco Ascaso remained in Brussels, where they had lived
since 1929, waiting for a general pardon which a new regime—now
daily growing more inevitable—would bring. In the meantime they
continued their domestic pursuits. For Durruti this meant time to
spend with Emilienne Morín, his new "life-long companion," and
their infant daughter Colette.[6]

By April 14 the waiting was over. After the local elections and
Alfonso's flight, Niceto Alcalá-Zamora, a moderate leader in the San
Sebastian coalition, formed a cabinet of republicans and socialists as
the new provisional government.[7] The socialist Minister of Justice,
Fernando de los Ríos y Urruti, made it clear that those indicted by
the dictatorship might return to civil life without fear of new prose-
cution by the republican cabinet.[8] Durruti, Ascaso, Jover, and García
Oliver all travelled back together and entered Spain on April 15.

The situation they returned to was chaotic. Even while the new
government was organizing itself (with elections scheduled in July
for a Constituent Cortes to write a republican constitution), the
CNT/FAI was warning Premier Alcalá-Zamora that continuation of
old anti-labor policies or repressive political limitations would put
anarcho-syndicalists back into the opposition.[9] On April 19 a regional committee of the Barcelona CNT sponsored a series of rallies
where more demands were made. Buenaventura Durruti, ill at ease
as the chief speaker, called for liberation of all political prisoners,
abolition of the Civil Guard, an end to army meddling in civil affairs,

92

and immediate secularization of the state.[10] A crowd at Montjuich park, on the edge of the working-class districts, received the returned exile enthusiastically, and FAI Sunday rallies in the park became a tradition that lasted until 1937.

Almost two weeks later, on May Day, Durruti spoke to an even larger crowd, this time at the Palacio de Bellas Artes in Barcelona. In his speech, he showed bitter contempt for politicians, characterizing Francisco Largo Caballero, the Labor Minister, as a "fool" and an "ass" for seeking to continue the mixed juries. Durruti charged that the labor arbitration boards had never once made an unbiased decision.[11] Francisco Ascaso and several other speakers supported Durruti's emotional plea to the republican coalition to abandon the mixed juries.

Nevertheless, on May 7, Francisco Largo Caballero announced the retention of mandatory labor arbitration. Anarchists opposed it because chaos served their revolutionary purposes, but the Second Republic was not willing to give up a weapon against prolonged social disorganization.[12]

Faístas moved up and down the northeast coast for weeks afterwards, denouncing Largo Caballero's perfidy. Buenaventura Durruti was finally arrested in Gerona on old charges stemming from the Soldevila assassination. Although he soon was released through the intervention of higher Catalan officials, the message of the government was clear. They intended to defend compulsory labor arbitration strongly.

Up to this moment, the attitude of the anarcho-syndicalist movement towards the Second Republic had been ambivalent. On the negative side, three members of the republican cabinet were actively disliked by the CNT/FAI. Santiago Casares Quiroga, the Interior Minister, represented moderate liberal hostility to the libertarian ideas of the anarchists. Two others, Indalecio Prieto, the Finance Minister, and Francisco Largo Caballero, the Labor Minister, were both high socialist party officials and representatives of the UGT. They were known to feel that the CNT presented a threat to the socialist confederation as well as a challenge to the stability of the Second Republic. Francisco Largo Caballero's decision to continue the mixed juries was prompted largely by these suspicions.

On a more positive note, some syndicalists (though certainly not all) had voted for republican or socialist candidates in the recent local elections.[13] High-level contacts existed between republican leaders and the moderate syndicalists. And while both Juan Peiró and Angel Pestaña refused any direct involvement with the coalition cabinet, they opposed violence and wanted to cooperate in stabilizing the new government—if only to gain time to rebuild the CNT.[14] Their commitment to the principles of the *Inteligencia republicana* manifesto still stood.

The militants saw these acts as reformist threats. Buenaventura Durruti's speech on May Day was filled with veiled references to the "politicians" in the movement and the threat of reformism to a "total victory" of revolution.[15] But the radicals were themselves confused by the activity of the Catalan regionalists. While the republicans had promised autonomy for Catalonia, regionalists continued to demonstrate and campaign. Colonel Macià, the most radical regionalist, had even gone so far as to contact Durruti and Ascaso in Belgium to seek their support.[16] They refused, suspicious of the consequences, and shortly after their arrival in Barcelona, *Solidaridad Obrera* (with Ascaso as one of its editors) warned Colonel Macià not to take any action hostile to anarchism or anarcho-syndicalism.[17]

This possibility increased somewhat when, in early May 1931, the conservative regionalist leader Francisco Cambó fled to France to escape charges of collaboration with the dictatorship.[18] Colonel Macià's Esquerra party now dominated the Catalan regionalist movement. Its philosophy changed rapidly from subversion to support for the Second Republic. Luis Companys, Macià's second-in-command and a former CNT lawyer, played a major role in discussions with the CNT and FAI. "My friends," he told the two groups, "if you feel strong enough to bring off the revolution, proceed. But if you understand that the only revolution possible is a radical, evolutionist policy that will give you ample freedom for your propaganda, help me."[19]

After slight deliberation, the FAI rejected the Esquerra offer. Francisco Ascaso was adamant that Catalan regionalists could not be trusted to ignore middle-class fears of the anarchist revolution. Any movement that put autonomy above social revolution was not suitable as an ally.[20] He backed up this position by negotiating to buy arms for the FAI; only in this way could workers "conquer economic power."[21] Soon after, the FAI began to move in new revolutionary directions.

II. The FAI Prepares to Seize Power

In May and June 1931 the FAI established itself as a new force in Spanish politics. Its first major gathering on April 19 at the Teatro del Bosque del Barriado de Gracia heard Juan García Oliver, the best orator among the *faístas,* demand major wage increases for workers of all categories to make up for losses suffered under the dictatorship.[22] This meeting and others that followed in successive weeks saw thousands flock to join the FAI. One observer called them the Bolshevik party of the early Second Republic.[23] The popularity of the *faístas* came from an expectation that the Second Republic would follow patterns of the First Republic and recreate another Revolution of 1873, this time successfully.[24] "Seize power!" became the motto of the FAI, and it was quickly put into practice.

Scattered street fighting (the first to involve the FAI) broke out on May Day against the Civil Guard. Demonstrations for higher wages led to a new violence on May 11 in Barcelona, and small cells of *faístas* staged similiar strikes in Basque fishing villages on June 13.[25] The biggest strike came on June 6 with the beginning of a lingering telephone dispute in Barcelona, a strike against a subsidiary of Standard Eléctrica Ibérica, itself a part of International Telephone and Telegraph. The Compañía Telefónica de España held a monopoly granted by General Primo de Rivera, apart from the existing telephone systems he had previously nationalized. Its high rates, ruthless international business methods, and support for the old regime made it a prime target, very much as La Canadiense had been in 1919.* The FAI worked hard in May and June to build support among telephone workers, campaigning for a 25 percent wage increase. Their demands were rejected, and a strike began— only to be declared illegal by the Labor Minister, Francisco Largo Caballero. He believed that the Second Republic could ill afford to antagonize international business so early in its existence. In any case, arbitration through the mixed juries had not yet been attempted.[26] When the Sindicato Nacional de Teléfonos set up strike lines, police moved in and, during the latter part of June and early July, arrested more than two thousand strikers. Many non-CNT workers were frightened into returning to work, but CNT/FAI members remained out, now as angry at the government as at the telephone company. They felt that the republicans had reverted to the policies of Milans del Bosch and Martínez Anido during the lockout of 1919–1920 and later troubles.

*According to Anthony Sampson, *The Sovereign State of ITT* (New York: Stein and Day, 1973), pp. 24–25, Sosthenes Behn, the founder of ITT, was able to gain the Spanish monopoly with lavish bribes. The Duke of Alba became the figurehead for the Compañía Telefónica de España, but in 1925 it was merged into a new acquisition of ITT, Standard Electric, Great Britain's largest electrical company. The Telefónica became a part of International Standard Electric, which in turn spawned Standard Eléctrica Ibérica to produce telephone equipment for Spain.

Part of their anger may have been justified. While Indalecio Prieto, on April 25, had promised to end the immunity from taxation that the telephone company enjoyed, the issue was never pressed very forcefully. Negotiations on this point eventually proved futile, as did attempts to get the company to rehire workers who had been fired for political activity. Miguel Maura, the Assistant Interior Minister, was openly saying that the CNT/FAI would not come into line except under extreme pressure. The cabinet, adopting an antagonistic position, subsequently refused to bargain and finally declared the strike illegal. The UGT, urged on by Indalecio Prieto and Francisco Largo Caballero, created its own telephone syndicate and began organizing the telephone workers in direct competition with the CNT.[27]

Anarchists fought back with similar methods. Buenaventura Durruti and Francisco Ascaso took a prominent role in the strike, often addressing strikers from a speakers' platform set up in the Plaza Cataluña, close to the telephone building in Barcelona. *Faístas* raided UGT syndicates to sign up new members. There was strong competition between the CNT and UGT in the stevedores' union. Even the mediation of Francesco Macià could not prevent violent scenes between the two confederations.

In the meantime, the FAI won new popularity in the fabric and textile unions and, with the aid of Antonio Ortíz Carpintero, president of the woodworkers' syndicate, took over the woodworkers almost totally.[28] It was also successful in the mining district of Alto Llobregat and among Barcelona metal workers. These new recruits helped stage brief but violent demonstrations against republican labor policy in Barcelona, Saragossa, and Santander and as far south as Granada, where agrarian unrest once again affected Andalusia, causing the cabinet to reactivate shoot-to-kill orders against peasant rioters.[29]

Many new groups began to take part in these challenges to the republican order. The Solidarios name had been adopted by an FAI youth group in Catalonia, and so Buenaventura Durruti and his circle began to style themselves the Nosotros. This organization attracted several hundred members and thousands of sympathizers.[30] Other new ultra-Left clubs included Group A, the "Action Group" (Grupo Nervio), and Group Z.[31] Group A combined elements of anarchism and Trotskyism. The "Action Group," led by Diego Abad de Santillán, who now lived in Barcelona, contained a number of communists, since there was no Catalan communist party in 1931. Group Z was created by another Catalan youth group that had split off from the Solidarios.[32]

96

The one common denominator that united these groups was the FAI, now suddenly more important than at any time previously, since disillusionment over CNT and republican policies made many workers seek a new allegiance. Perhaps the most significant boost for the FAI came from Federica Montseny, who had not played much of a role until now. She began using her oratorical talents on the platform at street demonstrations to praise the FAI, and she published a number of articles in *La Revista Blanca, Tierra y Libertad* (now edited by Diego Abad de Santillán), and *El Luchador,* all anarchist publications. Federica Montseny saw the FAI as the only viable alternative to further labor oppression by the Second Republic.[33] She attacked the republican cabinet for using the international economic depression as an excuse for not developing adequate social reforms.

This publicity played upon the insecurity of workers caught in a major economic crisis and uncertain as to the intentions of the new government. Many workers had heard capitalism denounced by the Left for years. Now it did seem that the system was actually failing. Foreign investment dropped 40 percent, while European produce markets, adopting protectionism, accepted fewer Spanish oranges and vegetables. Unemployment rose 9 percent in 1931 alone. The Second Republic, like most governments, was unprepared for an international economic crisis. It looked inept, and this appearance of official chaos sent thousands of Spanish workers to the FAI. At assemblies held in the North and the South during the summer of 1931, the FAI emerged into the open for the first time since its clandestine birth to write a constitution for the movement.

The new bylaws of the FAI stated that the aim of the body was the "nullification of the exploitation of man by man, by the socialization of all means of production and distribution."[34] The FAI stood for federalism as the only organizational solution possible for Spain. Membership would be composed of all "manual and intellectual workers" who wished to join, but each applicant needed two recommendations from *faístas*. This requirement might be waived for those who could prove that they were anarchists or syndicalist militants before August 1931.

The structure of the Federation began with an affinity group of from six to fifty people organized as a cell or a series of cells. These were never very secret and no procedures to maintain secrecy were ever adopted after 1931. Expansion of *faísta* membership and propaganda activities were delegated to these affinity groups, of which two varieties were recognized: the district group, for cities of more than 60,000, and the local group for villages.

97

Above the various groups were regional federations, made up of all local units of the region, whose major task was to create technical advisory commissions to develop positions on fundamental socio-political problems of the area.[35] These commissions might study agricultural or industrial problems, do research into educational needs, or investigate social questions. And while their recommendations could not bind the entire organization, all local groups of the region were obligated to discuss the recommendations of the commissions and attempt to develop common tactics for their solution.

At the head of the FAI was the peninsular association, composed of representatives of regional bodies and the national officials. The latter acted as a permanent secretariat of the peninsular association and was composed of a secretary, treasurer, and auditor named by the association. Policy was made by the national body upon recommendations of the regional associations, and it was carried out as a part of the secretariat's function. No one could hold a position on the national committee for more than a year.

Regional meetings were obligated by the bylaws to meet every six months, while the national plenum of the FAI met annually. The national committee had the power to take action in the name of the entire organization if time prevented a consultation with national or regional plenums, and it could demand the obedience of all local chapters if a crisis was important enough. These actions would have to be defended at each national plenum, and provisions for removing the responsible officials from office were included if the FAI was wrongfully involved in some matter outside its scope.

Most of these ideas and procedures were developed and codified during the summer months of 1931, after the first open congress of the FAI met simultaneously with the CNT. The aspirations of the *faístas,* as can be seen from the bylaws (Appendix I), were to normalize the movement, even at the expense of burdening its membership with a set of dull, standard procedures. Henceforth the FAI would try mightily to push itself into the forefront of revolutionary leadership. If it took rules and a hierarchy to do it, then the organization was willing to create them.

This fact contrasts sharply with the usual interpretation of the FAI as an *ad hoc* group, mercurial and strictly spontaneous. Instead, the FAI began to see itself as *the* government of the future. The writing of the statutes was only the first step towards the establishment of an anarchist society.

III. The CNT Opposes the FAI

In the summer of 1931 the social atmosphere surrounding the FAI quickly became poisonous as scandalous stories spread about the criminality of Buenaventura Durruti and the other *faístas,* largely through stories in the liberal press.[36] Everyone was startled at the rapidity with which tension and polarization spread. Francisco Ascaso was anxious to delay any major confrontation with the CNT, the UGT, or the cabinet until the *faístas* obtained a larger following.[37] Buenaventura Durruti and Federica Montseny occupied a middle ground; they were alarmed by the odds against the FAI but were eager to take the offensive if conditions were right. Without a doubt, Juan García Oliver occupied the most extreme position. He used his oratorical ability to stress the ineffectiveness of republican initiatives for the working class. Unless the FAI provided leadership, he insisted, neither the Second Republic nor the CNT would be able to prevent fascists or communists from taking advantage of Spanish unrest.[38]

To outsiders the FAI appeared to be acting irresponsibly—upsetting the political balance by playing at terrorism in the summer of 1931 and by openly talking of an anarchist regime.[39] This theme was repeated in almost every liberal newspaper and in dozens of speeches by republican politicians. Such unanimity of opinion startled *faístas* and, in the end, drove them towards Juan García Oliver's position. Anarchists had many grudges to settle and too much pent-up antagonism towards the political system to live easily with the Second Republic.

CNT leaders like Juan Peiró and Angel Pestaña, though certainly not unaware of FAI hostility, were partially misled by the conversion of Manuel Buenacasa to the moderate position.[40] The old anarchist militant and anti-syndicalist now spoke out harshly against prolongation of the phone strike and a possibility of renewed terrorism. The CNT leadership felt that his opinions represented the radical attitude, but in fact Buenacasa was in his sixties and had had little contact with the Solidarios or the FAI since the start of the dictatorship. The exile group deeply resented his criticism of *faísta* radicalism and tended to dismiss his service to anarchism while Buenacasa himself was sincere in his desire to build a mass movement before committing the CNT/FAI to a program of open revolutionary activity. Unfortunately, his former comrades took this cautiousness as a dangerous vacillation on Buenacasa's part.

99

The CNT, unaware of this conflict, accepted Manuel Buenacasa wholeheartedly and followed him in charting a moderate course. In May 1931 they refused to sanction blanket opposition to the Republic and in fact hinted that their basic attitude was one of sympathy with the government.[41] The freedom to organize, granted by the cabinet in April, precluded open disloyalty. Even more pro-government sentiment became apparent in June 1931 at the second national CNT congress, the first since 1919. More than four hundred delegates representing 511 syndicates and 535,565 members of the CNT participated.[42]

The German anarchist Rudolf Rocker gave the opening address. Somewhat to the discomfort of moderate CNT leaders, he warned against close cooperation with the democratic republicans. In an era of economic crisis, he said, such collaboration would end in a republican defense of capitalism against the strongest efforts of anarcho-syndicalists to change the economic system.[43] FAI members in attendance gave Rocker a standing ovation.

The main order of business was a debate on the policies of anarchism in relation to the Constituent Cortes (due to convene in July) and the republican coalition. A young moderate, José Villaverde, spoke for the CNT leadership in establishing minimum demands that the cabinet was expected to recognize.[44] These included the right of association, freedom to strike, public programs to guarantee employment, and secure civil liberties. Anarchists immediately protested that even the most idealized formulation of principles carried with it a *de facto* recognition of the state.[45] But a majority agreed that the republicans had earned some measure of trust by their destruction of the dictatorship. Until the CNT was strong enough to lead a second revolution, it would have to deal with the state on a nearly normal basis.[46]

The leadership of the CNT, seeking to develop new economic policies, proposed the concept of the "Federación Nacional de Industria" as a step beyond the old industrial unions. Whereas the latter had facilitated maximum organizational effort and strike action, National Federations of Industry would provide additional economic, technical, and professional assistance to the individual syndicates. They might constitute a bloc of shadow institutions that someday would replace individual management of industry.[47] Some saw the National Federation idea as implying a series of high-level industrial councils to handle planning, developmental, and managerial functions—a kind of libertarian corporation designed to compete with capitalism, an alternative to the republican system of free enterprise.[48]

Faístas at the congress emphatically opposed the proposal. Juan García Oliver, their principal spokesman, called the federations "centralist, elitist, and anti-revolutionary."[49] He blamed the origin of the concept on the AIT and the influence of German syndicalist thought. Realization of the scheme would substitute a labor bureaucracy for the republican capitalist order and rob the anarchist movement of the spontaneity necessary to mobilize the masses. Spaniards could not work dispassionately in some evolutionary fashion to change the political system; the depth of abuse created by the Spanish state over the last three centuries demanded a purer revolution. In any case, *faístas* suspected the creation of formal institutions. By their very nature they were open to compromise, and the movement had learned that compromise inevitably worked in favor of the state. Ironically, the FAI adopted a modified form of the National Federations of Industry concept during the Spanish Civil War, but in 1931 it was clearly on the other side. The FAI was outvoted four to one when the proposal was brought to a vote.[50]

The same measure had been defeated in 1919. Its passage in 1931 showed how much stronger moderates had become in the CNT. Angel Pestaña was elected General Secretary despite his moderation and his cooperation with republican officials.[51] Juan Peiró continued as editor of *Solidaridad Obrera,* and other conservative syndicalists were appointed to the National Committee.

Thus the congress concluded its work, aware of the *faístas'* anger but optimistic that the new program strengthened the CNT. Organizational matters now took precedence over ideological disputes. Only the construction syndicate had grown during the dictatorship, and time was needed to build up the syndicates that had fallen into disrepair.[52] When time could be taken from recruitment, the National Committee of the CNT and its staff reshuffled the basic structure of the CNT, which in the summer of 1931 looked as shown in the table on page 102.

The National Secretary obviously occupied a position in the CNT hierarchy that influenced all other levels. Angel Pestaña's political views were offset slightly by those assistants like Mariano Vázquez (a young militant who headed the CNT during the civil war), but other moderate assistants like Horacio Prieto ensured that the National Committee remained conservative.[53] Organization, development, and evolution became the "motto" of the CNT leadership in the summer of 1931. Angel Pestaña was impressed by numbers, and as the ranks of the Confederation grew, he bragged that before long the CNT would be the most important force in republican society.[54] Juan

101

The Structure of the CNT

National Congress	Composed of representatives of each syndicate; responsible for the selection of basic organizational policy.
National Plenum	Composed of one representative of each Regional Committee: drew up program for congresses and passed upon the acts of the National Committee. Acted in times of labor crisis as an expanded National Committee.
National Committee	A General Secretary elected by the congress and seven Assistant Secretaries (part-time) representing the seven Regional Committees. Functions of the National Committee included propaganda, organizational matters, and coordination.
National Federations of Industry	Staff appointed by each of the three levels above or by regional congresses from below. Tasks included forming wage policies for various industries, general strike planning, studying working conditions, negotiating with employers on an industry-wide basis, and making general socio-economic studies.
Regional Congress	Composed of representatives of each syndicate in the region. Regional congresses often discussed matters of special interest, debated general policies to be brought before the national congress, and developed plans to meet the special needs of their areas.
Regional Plenum	Usually run by two secretaries appointed from Local and Regional Federations within the region. Their principal job was to make sure CNT national policy was understood and followed by the local syndicates. They also arbitrated disputes between locals or local leaders and ran general strikes when these were called.
Regional Committee	Selected by Local Federations of several provinces at the regional congress. Primary function was to facilitate communications between Local Federations and to handle administrative details of the National Committee.
Provincial Committee	Mainly concerned with wage negotiations, although the Catalan committee remained an independent power, often acting in the name of more important levels of the organization.
Local Federation	A coordinating board for the syndicates of large towns. In areas where CNT membership was scattered among a number of villages, or in rural areas, the work of the Local Federation was performed by the Provincial Federation.
Syndicates	Each syndicate had two parts: the general assembly of its membership and the administrative committee of three or four members who handled executive functions and represented the syndicate at the higher levels.

Adapted from Alexander Shapiro, "Rapport sur l'activité de la Confédération National du Travail d'Espagne, 16 décembre 1932–26 février 1933," Internationaal Instituut voor Sociale Geschiedenis (Amsterdam), AIT Collection, file 9, *passim*.

Peiró, the only other moderate with a big following, did not have the authority, as editor of *Solidaridad Obrera,* to challenge this view, even if he had disagreed. In fact, judging from his editorial policy, he seemed to have shared, perhaps more briefly, this same sanguine notion that the CNT faced few difficulties ahead.

Unfortunately there was not as much time for peaceful growth as Pestaña and Peiró thought. During May and June 1931, wildcat strikes increased dramatically as CNT syndicates in most major industrial sectors began to follow the *faístas'* lead in demanding large wage increases to compensate for the absence of free bargaining during the dictatorship. General strikes in San Sebastian and Gijon affected the Northwest most seriously in May. Chemical workers in Saragossa also struck, more as a refusal to accept the mixed juries than anything else. Miners syndicates in outlying districts of Catalonia and Alto Aragon went out in June while the CNT Congress was meeting.[55] The dramatic and lingering phone strike was followed in July and August by walkouts in every sector—rubber workers, nurses, miners, taxi drivers, fishermen—and then, on August 4, by a major strike in the metallurgical industry.

But it was the telephone strike that dominated the situation. The FAI denounced Francisco Largo Caballero for his policies as Labor Minister, while the republican cabinet in Madrid grew increasingly exasperated at the confusion and antagonism surrounding the strike.[56] Commissions of the Constituent Cortes were already meeting to prepare the new constitution, and ministers had little time to deal with the FAI, which now was causing more trouble than any other group in Spanish society, including the Right. Indalecio Prieto and Francisco Largo Caballero, the two most important socialists in the cabinet, contacted Juan Peiró and Angel Pestaña on the FAI problem many times during July and August. Any threat to limit the rights of labor constitutionally brought panic to the moderates in the CNT, who, only a short time previously, had been overly optimistic about the prospects of anarcho-syndicalism. Now they were prodded into action against the FAI at a very awkward moment, and this precipitate breach left the movement in a shambles.

IV. The Treintista Declaration

The first indication of a split between the CNT and FAI came on August 16, when the National Committee of the CNT criticized both

103

the telephone and metallurgical strikes. Unless strikers moderated their militant behavior, the strikes would deprive workers of the general moral support earned through opposition to the dictatorship. The National Committee placed specific blame upon elements in the FAI, who were, against CNT advice, resorting to terrorism and ultra-militancy.[57] A day later, a spokesman for the FAI replied that the CNT's evolutionary tactics meant nothing if labor did not fight capitalism strenuously. "Is it the economy," he asked, "which determines events, or is it the will of men?"[58] The telephone strike finally did come to an end on August 28, largely due to the CNT criticism, but radical elements in the FAI were furious. *Faístas* accused the CNT of permitting Francisco Largo Caballero to interfere in labor relations with impunity.[59]

Moderates replied on September 1, 1931, with the *treintista* declaration, so named because it was signed by thirty moderates of the CNT. The document denounced *faísta* radicalism and proclaimed a virtual CNT independence from policies supported by the FAI. Signers like Juan Peiró, Angel Pestaña, Ramón Arín (once a *faísta* himself), Sebastián Clará, Augustin Gibanel, and Ricardo Fornells (the latter three important CNT officials in Catalonia and the Levante) warned that a premature and simplistic revolution led by the FAI "would lead to republican fascism."[60] Unless the FAI adopted a more conservative and evolutionary position, the CNT could not organize and lead Spanish workers towards an eventual triumph of labor democracy. The manifesto also spoke out in favor of better education, coherent organization, realism, prudence, and greater political sophistication, rejecting dogmatism as an ideological quality.[61] It ended by reiterating the threat to sever relations altogether between syndicalism and anarchism.[62]

The FAI counterattacked with a vengeance. *Solidaridad Obrera,* which supported the *treintistas,* was seized in a surprise attack by *faístas* on September 21. Felipe Aláiz became the new editor in place of Juan Peiró, and the full strength of the paper was shifted against the *treintistas*. Many of them found it prudent to relocate in Valencia, where a hastily printed newspaper entitled *Sindicalismo,* representing a moderate point of view, continued to defend the *treintista* declaration vigorously. Elsewhere *El Combate Sindicalista* and *Vertical* in Sabadell rallied around the moderate CNT bloc. Through their example many syndicates (particularly outside the city of Barcelona) went so far as to exclude *faístas* from membership or, in several other cases, to attack FAI members physically on the streets and in union meetings.[63] *Treintistas* in Valencia accused the FAI of being a communist organization.[64]

The FAI had most success in Barcelona, where the labor situation exploded when the CNT and FAI split apart. A new telephone strike began on September 3 despite warnings from the civil governor of Catalonia, Miguel Anguera de Sojo (a close ally of Miguel Maura and Francisco Largo Caballero), that he would initiate a campaign of repression worse than the postwar lockouts and martial law. Police did attack headquarters of the construction syndicate on September 5, injuring a number of workers and arresting more than three hundred syndicate members. Protests over police activity spread throughout the city, and in early October similar FAI-led demonstrations took place in Granada, Cadiz, and a number of smaller railway centers in the North. Labor walkouts protesting the "treason" of the CNT and republican labor policies also increased in Catalonia.

According to Luis Companys, the regionalist leader and aide to Francesco Macià, these strikes only hurt the cause of labor and delayed passage of important constitutional provisions.[65] The FAI immediately attacked this statement and took Catalan regionalists to task for placing reasons of state ahead of labor issues. Informal cooperation between anarchists and Catalan regionalists thus ended acrimoniously; and the new cabinet of Manuel Azaña had no difficulty imposing martial law upon Barcelona with regionalist support. Azaña, the intellectual essayist and journalist who had been a major force in the republican cabinet since April 1931, could find no time for fratricidal anarcho-syndicalist quarrels. He had replaced Niceto Alcalá-Zamora as Premier of Spain in the midst of constitutional debate over article 26 on relations between church and state. Alcalá-Zamora objected to the anticlericalism of the majority and resigned in October 1931. Manuel Azaña devoted all of his time to keeping the republican majority in the Constituent Cortes from disintegrating.

The FAI thus did not find a national audience for their grievances. Their meetings were prohibited and their other activities curtailed. But FAI-inspired strikes and street demonstrations increased, and on December 17, 1931, shoot-on-sight orders were given to the Civil Guard by the Azaña cabinet. Ironically, this security act was the first issued by Manuel Azaña as regular Premier of the Second Republic. The constitution had been approved on December 9 almost unbeknown to the feuding anarchists and syndicalists.

Looking back at this period, it is clear that the breach between anarchists and republicans sadly frustrated the great expectations of the spring. The new constitution, while hardly revolutionary, pro-

105

vided for the social use of property and recognized Spain as a "republic of workers of all categories," certainly a step forward in the constitutional history of Spain.[66] Of signal importance was the grant of partial autonomy to Catalonia through creation of a new regional government, the Generalitat, which handled matters of finance, social legislation, and public order for the Northeast. Article 44 made land subject to indemnified expropriation for purposes of social utility, while article 26 created a secular state, disestablishing the Church even further than liberals had done in the nineteenth century. Catholics and conservatives disagreed with these innovations, but republicans and radicals had enough votes to overrule opposition. The moderate faction within the CNT saw enough promise in the new constitution to give the republican coalition passive support.

But the FAI chafed over one particular provision. The mixed juries now encouraged by the constitution were the only major institutional holdover from the dictatorship. Their inclusion was surprising, since labor relations had been sensitive for a long time. Critics of a national arbitration system could point to Mussolini's Italy and, in 1933, to Salazar's Portugal as examples of similar programs, designed to repress the power of labor organizations; or to Salvador Seguí's earlier (if temporary) acceptance of it for the CNT in 1919.[67] Militant anarchists never understood why mixed juries were allowed to continue. They refused to accept Manuel Azaña's assurances that the Second Republic was simply seeking a device to insure social stability. Their most common suspicion was that Francisco Largo Caballero used the mixed juries to assure republican aid for the UGT, thus compensating for the numerical differences between the CNT and UGT.

There were other irritants, such as the reluctance of the Republic to permit immediate land confiscations in Andalusia, where the crisis over land once more dominated politics.[68] The FAI attacked the republican coalition for only pretending to seek reform while in fact trying to maintain the *status quo* for all their grandiloquent talk of democracy. To a movement that had already suffered under the worst aspects of liberalism, democracy had no meaning. At best, the anarchists believed, democracy and private property were synonymous. After all, it had been the democratic United States that had executed the anarchists Sacco and Vanzetti in 1927 for being anarchists.[69] The USA was a "great desert," or a "yankee abyss," and there was no reason to expect a democratic Spanish republic to be any different.[70] This was the basic gulf, and it was one that could never be entirely closed.

CHAPTER FIVE

Black January
to Red October

Two things militate against gradual revolution: vested in-
terests and the pride of the government. [Pierre-Joseph
Proudhon, *The General Idea of Revolution in the Nineteenth
Century*]

I. Black January, 1932

The outlook of the FAI became increasingly gloomy late in 1931.
Having twice failed to crush the *treintistas,* the *faístas* now faced
incipient rebellion by more moderate CNT members and ostracism
by politicians in Barcelona and Madrid. During a CNT regional
plenum on November 18, the FAI failed to obtain a retraction of
the *treintista* declaration. Some delegates went so far as to threaten
to organize "syndicates of opposition" if the *faístas* did not end their
revolutionary activity.[1] While FAI militants managed to pass a motion calling the *treintista* declaration an illegal change of confedera-
tional policy and another stigmatizing the Second Republic as a
"regime of oppressors," the sense of the meeting was far less favorable to the FAI than passage of these motions indicated. Opinion
divided: some did not have the heart to return to opposition so
quickly, others favored a gradual build-up of the labor movement,
and a few did not see the Second Republic in a bad light. Barcelona delegates were particularly disappointed at the apparent break
with the Catalan regionalists, since the anarcho-syndicalists and the
regionalists had travelled a long way together. Now their paths
diverged.

This divergence shocked everyone. The Esquerra threatened to organize its own labor union if the FAI did not accept the Second Republic and moderate its criticism of the new Catalan regional government. Regionalists voted with the majority in the Constituent Cortes to approve a Law for the Defense of the Republic, which gave the national government extraordinary powers to suppress political, social, or religious turmoil.[2] A prison ship, the *Buenos Aires,* was readied as a floating jail in the harbor of Barcelona.[3] *Faístas* reacted predictably by opposing these acts, and in November and December 1931, wildcat strikes protested the Defense of the Republic act and publicized *faísta* rejection of mixed juries. Nevertheless, on December 17, 1931, the parliament passed a preliminary version of the mixed juries, and on December 24, Manuel Azaña's cabinet went one step further by asserting a right to control labor-management relations.[4] Many new and progressive labor reforms accompanied these stricter measures, but introduction of industrial-accident compensation, paid vacations, minimum-wage guarantees, and the eight-hour day (at long last) did not counterbalance, for the FAI, interference in the freedom of labor by mixed juries.

The mood of the FAI became more and more desperate. Federica Montseny wrote: "The immediate result of the [*treintista* declaration] has been the start of a violent repression against all the outstanding individuals of the FAI, and the beginning of an internal crisis within the Confederation, for which the anarchists will be blamed. . . ."[5] Catalan regionalists and the Madrid cabinet were alike in following a social policy that was "tolerant of the 'good little boys' of the CNT [while] 'tightening the screws on the FAI.'. . . "[6] Juan García Oliver added that the Defense of the Republic law gave the government extraordinary powers similar to those claimed by dictatorships. What was to prevent a new fascist group from seizing control of the Republic and making use of these powers after Azaña destroyed the anarchists? Republicans did not realize that anarchists stood as a bulwark against fascism or understand that the law could be used against republicans as easily as against the FAI.[7]

While these arguments raged, the social battlefront grew more violent. FAI meetings were suspended in Barcelona by the civil governor, Miguel Anguera de Sojo, but this did not deter a spread of labor trouble. The phone strike continued without surcease, and on the Barcelona docks, police and strikers frequently engaged in gun battles: one striker was shot and killed on December 17. Saragossa witnessed a bloody general strike in mid-December 1931. At Castilblanco, in southwestern Estremadura, a strike of agricultural day laborers caused such violence that four Civil Guards were literally butchered by rioters.[8] Resentment against the Civil Guard was particularly strong because of the outspoken conservatism of its commander, General José Sanjurjo, who was rumored to be sympathetic to a military *coup d'état* against the Second Republic. It infuriated the FAI that Manuel Azaña could keep him as head of the Civil Guard. Fighting between militants and guardsmen, in any case, spread rapidly. Arnedo, in Logrono province, witnessed new atrocities on January 5, 1932.[9]

A major FAI outburst in Catalonia might have come in late December 1931, but Buenaventura Durruti, distracted by a death in his family, spent several weeks in Leon, where he took part in demonstrations over working conditions in the mines. The Civil Guard threatened to arrest him on old charges stemming from the Gijon bank robbery. Until the investigation was settled, he could not leave the province. In his stead, Francisco Ascaso worked hard organizing the Alto Llobregot district of Catalonia, another mining district. When Durruti returned in early January 1932, the workers were prepared to revolt against the rising unemployment that plagued the area. Arms were secured, gunmen and militants arrived from Barcelona, and on January 19, 1932, the entire district FAI organization, proclaiming libertarian communism, seized mines and government buildings. The villages of Manresa, Cardona, Berga, Figols, and Sallent were heavily defended by the anarchists, and for five days Durruti and his followers withstood government attempts to restore order.

The rising was a major embarrassment to Manuel Azaña, who had ordered Catalan officials to seize Alto Llobregot "in fifteen minutes"—a way of expressing his contempt for what was occurring there.[10] Fortunately for the rebels, the general in charge, realizing the volatility of the situation, moved slowly to put down the disturbances. Buenaventura Durruti exhorted miners to dismiss notions of bourgeois democracy; the anarchist revolution had finally arrived.[11] However, it became apparent that Barcelona could not join the rising since the Republic had the military strength to keep the city quiet.

When government troops seized Figols, the insurrection collapsed. Durruti and Ascaso were arrested and transported to the prison ship *Buenos Aires*. An extraordinary tribunal sentenced 110 of the 600 prisoners to exile in Spanish Guinea on the west coast of Equatorial Africa. The departure of the *Buenos Aires* on February 10, 1932, prompted elements of the FAI, meeting in the suburb of Tarrasa, to call a general strike protesting the deportations. Snipers attacked barracks of the Civil Guard on the night of February 16,

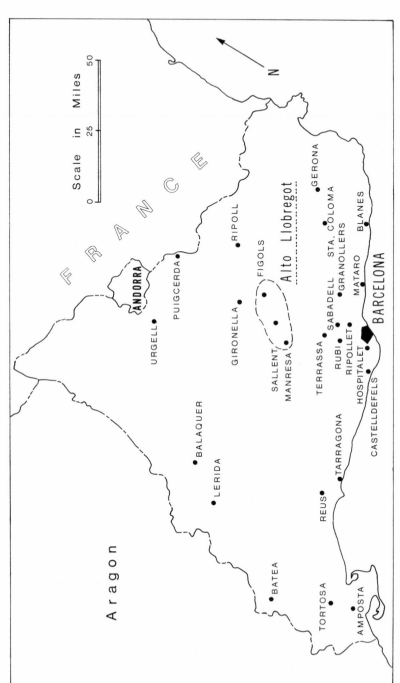

Revolutionary Centers in Catalonia, 1917–1937

and shots were also fired at the Barcelona city hall. Police reinforcements, arriving at the last moment, made it impossible for the CNT/FAI to carry out a general strike. The government was prepared for trouble and saw the situation through successfully. Outbreaks of violence in Andalusia, Saragossa, and Valencia likewise were suppressed without much difficulty.

With the departure of Buenaventura Durruti and Francisco Ascaso, the crisis precipitated by the anarchists collapsed. The two leaders were lost to the movement until October 1932. Yet their deportation added to the legends that later made them so important. In this respect it was similar to their fantastic Latin American trip in 1924–1925. They arrived in Spanish Guinea with their reputations preceding them, and prison officials refused to accept them into custody. In the end, Durruti and Ascaso were incarcerated in Rio de Oro, a Spanish possession in southern Morocco, where they were put in loose isolation at Puerto Cabras de Fuerteventura, a strip of land on the coast. Conditions of life here, it was rumored in Spain, would have killed normal men, but according to the legend the two anarchists thrived.[12] In fact, Durruti's health worsened from bouts with malaria and from a hernia he developed while constructing a rock hut. His followers on the peninsula, determined to create a demigod, knew nothing of these problems.

II. Land Reform

In the meantime, republican forces took the opportunity presented by the failure of the Alto Llobregot insurrection to press on with their legislative program. Dissolution of the Jesuit Order began in January 1932, and by April a new secular education program appeared. Army reform reduced the officer corps, already cut in 1931, to about a third its usual size. All in all, the period was one of the most productive the Republic would know, but anarchists took little comfort from it. They felt the attacks upon the Church and the army were simply republican self-defense measures and did not represent any strong commitment to libertarian ideas.[13] Instead, the true nature of the Republic was revealed by final passage of the mixed-juries legislation on April 8, 1932. *Solidaridad Obrera* called the new legislation a reactionary victory for capitalism, a prelude to the liquidation of the Spanish Left by "bourgeois socialists and republicans."[14]

Fortified by this self-induced pessimism, a number of the most

111

militant anarchists plotted desperately to assassinate Manuel Azaña
or one of the cabinet ministers in retribution. In late May 1932
Madrid was so shaken that members of the cabinet rarely appeared
in public and often remained overnight in their offices. Security
precautions were strengthened, but aside from minor bombings in
Madrid, Seville, and Manresa, none of the threats were carried
out.[15] Wildcat strikes in Seville, Valencia, Bilbao, and Barcelona ended
quickly, and only the strike at the Constructora Naval Company in
El Ferrol lasted more than a week. Anarchists increasingly felt the
pressure of being outnumbered and outmaneuvered. Vigilante groups
formed again throughout Catalonia, and the Esquerra succeeded in
organizing a union as a minor threat to the CNT. Its cooperation
with various proto-communist groups in Barcelona portended even
worse difficulties in the future.[16]

In other parts of Spain, the CNT/FAI was treated like an illegal
organization, and its members were hunted down and jailed.[17] Wildcat strikes drew such heavy fines that most syndicates could not risk
a walkout without imperiling what little their treasuries contained.
Thus, even this traditional means of protest was no longer available
to the movement.

Throughout these troubles, the *treintista* controversy continued.
Anti-FAI feeling surfaced alarmingly when Gilberto Gilabert, an ultra-Left FAI member, was elected secretary of the Catalan regional
plenum, causing a number of representatives to walk out in protest.
The *treintista* publication *Cultura Libertaria* kept up a running criticism of leading *faístas* until finally its editor, Juan López, was expelled from the CNT by FAI activists. They did this through FAI
control of the Catalan regional apparatus of the CNT, but use of
CNT institutions for FAI purposes caused an outcry against the FAI
stranglehold on the CNT.

In September 1932 this issue surfaced among various syndicates
in Sabadell, which pointedly refused to accept *faísta* tutelage over
their operations and declined to pay dues to the national confederation.[18] Provincial and Regional Committees quickly expelled the
Sabadell syndicates, although the action was strongly protested at
each level. Moderates contended that such expulsion should be carried out only by the National Committee or the full congress of the
CNT. In the end, the Sabadell syndicates were declared only in a
state of temporary suspension, and the issue was left for debate at a
future national conference.

New internal difficulties also arose in Valencia, where the Regional Committee, heavily infiltrated by *faístas*, proposed a plan to

112

create a new board to develop a coordinating agency for the CNT and FAI. Many moderate syndicates protested that this step could be taken only by a national congress, but objectors quickly found themselves under threat of suspension for having spoken out—a situation very much like that of the Sabadell syndicates. Again, the crisis continued for some time while issues were debated. Relations between the CNT and FAI deteriorated, and the final decision of the National Committee not to create the agency greatly antagonized *faístas*. News that moderates had received new backing from local syndicates in Huelva (including Rio Tinto), Asturias, and Galicia made matters appear even worse.[19] After the mixed-juries legislation and the Alto Llobregot defeat, continued spread of the *trientista* heresy was difficult for the FAI to accept.

Yet not everything turned out badly for the FAI. In early August 1932 the FAI and the Juventudes Libertarias, both disgusted with CNT moderation, signed a pact of unity that gave *faístas* a youth movement of some strength.[20] Then, on August 10, 1932, an abortive right-wing *coup d'état* by General José Sanjurjo suddenly validated the FAI assertion that the Second Republic had more to fear from the Right than from the Left. This situation was ready-made for the FAI, since the rising frightened the republican coalition so deeply that it was soon making overtures to the Left. Some observers assumed that the Right could overthrow the Second Republic without difficulty. Great areas of Catholic traditionalism and conservative political attitudes remained underrepresented in parliament, and reactionaries considered the new constitution an affront to old Spanish values. The Madrid politicians, shocked by the uprising, thus sought additional popular support by passing a new land reform act on September 19, 1932.

The exceedingly complex act expropriated land that had been badly farmed, was continually leased, or was part of the great estates.[21] These three categories faced gradual confiscation, with title remaining with the government. An Institute of Agrarian Reform was created to supervise the entire process, and a National Credit Bank was promised to finance purchases of land. Well-meaning as the reform was, it had been passed without thorough preparation. Occupation of confiscated land by peasant cultivators was so complicated that the reform caused very little rural improvement. Reforms in the period April 28–July 14, 1931, had already instituted the eight-hour day, tenant and sharecropper protection, and the right of agrarian syndicates to organize. The new legislation raised expectations without delivering land to the peasants.

The moderate nature of the reform and the red tape involved in implementing it ran counter to any simple occupation of land as advocated by the FAI.[22] The CNT had only a minimal policy on agrarian matters and, since the start of the Second Republic, had failed to establish functional rural syndicates like those of the period 1917–1920.[23] Even the FAI, founded to attract peasants, overlooked the rural sector in its preoccupation with militant activity in the industrial North after 1927. Despite frequent manifestations of rural revolutionary spirit, the only labor organization that attempted to organize the countryside was an independent union, the Federación Nacional de Trabajadores de la Tierra.[24]

Nevertheless, the FAI situation was improved, since the generally unworkable nature of land reform created discontent which benefited all groups advocating revolutionary solutions. But, more important, the social peace of the earlier republican period had been fractured. The FAI no longer stood alone in opposing the republican *status quo*. Socialists accepted the FAI's revolutionary activity as a way of protesting Manuel Azaña's land reform failure. Even a few republicans saw the FAI as a safeguard against military plotting or the sudden upheaval of a fascist regime. *Rapprochement* was in the air.[25]

What allowed the FAI to take action so emphatically in the wake of land reform frustrations was the absence, with the dismissal and arrest of General Sanjurjo, of a Martínez Anido prototype in higher police administration. The Civil Guard stood by in November and December 1932 while FAI demonstrations first raised the idea of a new revolution.[26] Few members of the socialist party or the UGT listened to *treintistas* or other CNT moderates who warned of what the FAI was planning. Many moderates feared that a renewal of revolutionary activity would make the Second Republic forget about General Sanjurjo and crack down again on labor activity. Horacio Prieto, a textile worker from Barcelona and a rising new labor spokesman, voiced the opinion of moderates on the CNT National Committee in saying that Alto Llobregot had represented a "putsch against the Republic" which would not be permitted a second time.[27] In fear of repeating earlier mistakes, the CNT lost all momentum and became inert.

This slowdown aided the *faístas*, who were handicapped by the loss of many anarchists, still in jail for their involvement in "Black January."[28] Juan García Oliver remained in hiding because of his part in the Alto Llobregot insurrection, and other militants were still lodged in African prisons. One of the few known anarchists with any degree of freedom was Valeriano Orobón Fernández, not a member of either faction, whose enthusiasm for the Federations of Industry and championship of a workers' alliance that would run across ideological lines—a kind of premature popular front—was, in the words of a foreign observer, "too sophisticated for the climate of Spain."[29] Even FAI journalists like Federica Montseny and Diego Abad de Santillán had to be careful not to violate provisions of the Defense of the Republic act. Little was accomplished until December 1932, when the FAI again opted for action.

III. Casas Viejas

Buenaventura Durruti and Francisco Ascaso reached Barcelona on October 25, 1932. Their sentences had been commuted in reaction to the Sanjurjo *coup d'état,* but the grant of clemency gained republican politicians very little favor. Throughout November, in Montjuich park, large crowds turned out to hear the two militants speak, a direct result of the deportation legends. This new organizing effort culminated on December 1, 1932, at the Palacio de Artes near the Plaza Cataluña, when Durruti reaffirmed his expectations of a new revolution. Many Catalans chose to take his prediction seriously, and so did the regional government. *Solidaridad Obrera* was closed on December 5, railway workers were threatened with conscription when they struck, and armed police occupied strategic areas of Barcelona. The rail strike continued throughout December 1932 after Indalecio Prieto, on behalf of the government, refused to raise wages. The FAI worked closely with the strikers and found itself coming under strong attack.[30] Leading *faístas* were often harassed. Juan García Oliver came out of hiding only to be briefly arrested, since his anti-regionalist ideas made him a special target.

A Committee of Defense was formed to push plans for a revolt. Although the committee had been created originally in 1931 as a liaison between the CNT and FAI, its roster now read like a "who's who" of the Nosotros group: Buenaventura Durruti, Francisco Ascaso, Aurelio Fernández, Gregorio Jover, and, after his release from police custody, Juan García Oliver.[31] Even some less militant *faístas* found themselves excluded, while all CNT members were forced out. The Nosotros believed the time had come to challenge the Esquerra party, now particularly handicapped by the serious illness of Francesco Macià, its founder. The Second Republic also had been

115

weakened by the recent land reform backlash aɪɪd the use of mixed juries by Santiago Casares Quiroga, the new Minister of Agriculture, to solve Andalusian agricultural strikes. This wholesale extension of arbitration by Casares Quiroga, an implacable foe of anarchism, enraged Nosotros members.

The insurrection was scheduled for early January 1933, but from the very beginning, FAI plans were confused and often haphazard. A store of explosives at the house of Hilario Esteban y Meler blew up on January 5, 1933, alerting police several weeks before the rising was scheduled to begin.[32] The insurrection in Barcelona was thus moved up to January 8, and when the call to arms went out, some syndicates were caught unaware. Others hurriedly proclaimed a general strike in the name of libertarian communism, influenced by an earlier directive of Manuel Rivas, a member of the CNT National Committee, which argued that if one section of the movement rose, the rest were morally bound to follow.

Almost as soon as the streets of Barcelona began to fill with strikers and would-be revolutionaries, police began to stage preventive raids on the headquarters of the CNT and FAI. Juan García Oliver was arrested at the very outset, charged with carrying a concealed weapon, and so seriously beaten in prison that he had to be hospitalized for several months. At least twenty *faístas* were shot in the street fighting, and one of García Oliver's friends, José Guillamón, allegedly died of a police beating in prison. So many others were mishandled in the same way that Federica Montseny began protesting these incidents to the press.[33] Buenaventura Durruti and Francisco Ascaso led a retaliatory raid on police headquarters on January 9 but were also captured. Rumors that they too had been assassinated circulated widely for several days afterwards until a delegation of lawyers went to the authorities on January 13, 1933, and found out that they were unharmed. But fighting had diminished, and even though the rumors proved to be false, it was too late to revive the struggle.

Fighting spread widely outside Barcelona. Tarrasa saw six days of rioting, with three deaths and thirty-five arrests. In Sardanola and Ripollet, suburbs of Barcelona, a number of factories were occupied, and two militants died in an attack upon the Uralita plant. The Lerida uprising lasted three days and saw four killed and thirty-one arrested.[34] In the Levante, where the rising was delayed, violence continued through January and early February, with the towns of Ribarroja, Bugarra, Betera (where there were four deaths), and Pedralba most seriously affected.[35]

Further south, in Andalusia, the government had time to prepare for the worst, and major demonstrations in Seville and Arcos
de la Frontera were put down promptly.[36] Undaunted, a dozen or
more other towns exploded into anti-government activity.[37] The
most publicized revolt of all occurred in the small village of Casas
Viejas on January 11. Here the villagers reacted to stepped-up police
activity by declaring themselves in favor of *comunismo libertario* and
marching on the Civil Guard post, where one of their number, Manuel Quijada Pino, had been incarcerated. After an exchange of
gunfire, he was freed, and the rebels attempted, without much success, to rouse the peasants of nearby Benalup de Sidonia. However,
upon seeing the arrival of Guard reinforcements, the peasants took
refuge in the house of "Seisdedos," or Six Fingers (traditionally the
nickname for a thief), Antonio Barberan Castellet. The seige lasted
only until the morning of January 12, but when it was over, eleven
anarchists in the house and another thirteen victims from the village
were dead—most of them shot after they had surrendered.[38]

Casas Viejas poisoned the atmosphere of Spain in the following
months. It had been a futile exercise for anarchists and government
alike, but the latter had much more prestige to lose. Durruti, Ascaso,
García Oliver, and the activists of Casas Viejas were sentenced only
to a few months imprisonment. García Oliver could not be moved
from Barcelona, but Durruti and Ascaso were sent to prison first in
Cadiz and then in Burgos. Anarchists benefited from an outraged
public opinion that censured the Azaña cabinet for overreacting to
the point of commiting an atrocity. This embarrassment lingered on
as many members of parliament, including the well-known intellectual José Ortega y Gasset, took the opportunity to condemn the
Azaña government for use of excessive force.[39] A formal hearing on
the Casas Viejas incident ran through March and April 1933. Manuel Azaña seemed to feel no remorse himself, but Francisco Largo
Caballero expressed shock at the incident and was clearly uncomfortable, perhaps for the first time publicly, about his association
with the republicans.[40]

Casas Viejas witnessed a culmination of the duel between socialists and anarchists that had begun in 1931.[41] Largo Caballero realized that he could not use political power without risking embarrassment. The findings of the investigation, which placed culpability on
the Civil Guard commander, were essentially a condemnation of
Manuel Azaña, who, at the end of a long chain of intermediaries,
bore responsibility for the atrocity.[42] A number of socialist deputies
henceforth found it increasingly difficult to give him their support.

Conservatives, of course, gleefully celebrated Azaña's "conversion" to law and order. The public reaction, particularly through the local elections of April 1933, was to turn towards the Right as a way of rebuking republicans for the incident. On June 8, 1933, Azaña's majority in the parliament disappeared, and he was replaced, first by several interim premiers, and then, on September 10, by Alejandro Lerroux, a politician altogether outside the San Sebastian bloc.

IV. Syndicates of Opposition

Moderate syndicalists unanimously interpreted the events of January and February 1933 as entirely the responsibility of the FAI, characterizing *faístas* as reckless and harmful.[43] Rudolf Rocker, Manuel Buenacasa, and the AIT felt that the uprising had been a dreadful mistake, a "tragic week" prejudicial to the anarcho-syndicalist movement, despite the apparent injuries inflicted upon socialists and republicans.[44] As Buenacasa wrote: "The conduct of some militants, wanting to exercise a moral hegemony over the workers' syndicates, has not been very good for the morale of the syndicalist organizations or for anarchist thought."[45] The impact of this criticism stopped the strike movement altogether from January to April 1933. Worse yet, from the FAI's point of view, the Sabadell syndicates presented a new and more difficult problem. The FAI, by placing its members on important local and regional CNT committees, had been able to manipulate the Catalan CNT since January 1932, when a number of moderate syndicalists were removed by threat or force. The Catalan CNT then demanded that the Sabadell syndicates dismiss all officials hostile to the FAI and repudiate their support of the *treintista* declaration.[46] The Sabadell syndicates refused, and FAI members of the CNT were able to begin proceedings that would lead to the expulsion of the conservative syndicates.

The *treintistas*, of course, were bitterly disappointed that the fiasco of the Barcelona rising had not weakened FAI control of the CNT. The time seemed right to lead a vigorous campaign against the *faístas*, and so the Sabadell syndicates sent out a call for the creation of a new national organization to unite the syndicates of opposition, as the dissenting unions were now called.[47] More than fifty groups from Catalonia, Valencia, and Huelva responded, some of them large and extremely successful unions which the CNT could ill afford to lose.[48] In May this Federación Sindicalista Libertaria (FSL) began opera-

tions, and on June 4, 1933, a national conference was held in Barcelona representing 26,000 members.[49] All agreed that the influence of
the FAI in the CNT would have to be purged before they would
rejoin the Confederation. In Juan Peiró's words, "the facts have
shown that the old theory of the action of audacious minorities . . .
has a very relative, not to say absolutely worthless, value."[50]

Unfortunately for the dissidents, the FSL itself remained a minority body throughout its short life. The strength of the organization
never reached very far beyond the original founding syndicates; few
unions came over to its side in the subsequent period. On policy
matters its members were too imbued with the general principles of
anarcho-syndicalism to accept a labor party nomenclature, although
Angel Pestaña pushed hard in this direction.[51] Eventually he left to
start a syndicalist party of his own (which in the election of November
1933 won one seat), but a vast majority of the Federación Sindicalista
Libertaria considered this heretical.[52] The main tactic adopted by the
FSL was advocacy of a "united front," an Alianza Obrera that might
unite all of the Left against the increasing power of anti-republican
parties.[53] Such a maneuver reached out to absorb CNT members like
Valeriano Orobón Fernández, who had been a proponent of the
united front for some time. It contrasted nicely, too, with the more
restricted and elitist revolutionary activity that the FAI used. The
workers' alliance emphasized a gradualist approach favored by the
FSL. It accepted the progressivism of the republican coalition, refo-
cusing revolutionary activity away from the Second Republic, and
attacked conservative and reactionary forces in Spanish society.

The FAI and its captive, the CNT, refused to embrace the
united front concept. After the wounds of January had healed, the
strike movement revived and gained new strength in April 1933,
when construction workers in Barcelona and miners in Cardona,
Gijon, Figols, La Felguera, Sallent, and Suria walked off their jobs.
Unemployment, rather than wages, now provided the main issue,
and in industries employing unskilled labor, such as stevedoring and
transportation, demands for a shorter work week as a means of
alleviating unemployment became common. Dockers and construction workers stayed out through April and May, largely with FAI
support, a fact that was not missed by the FSL, which accused *faístas*
of further weakening the CNT by supporting strikes at a time when
the Second Republic was rapidly losing strength.[54] Undaunted, the
FAI called a general strike for May 10, 1933, to focus attention upon
the half million workers currently unemployed.[55] Violence broke out
in a few places, but many CNT syndicates did not join the general

119

strike, either from weak coordination or from strong employer pressure. The poor showing gave critics of the CNT/FAI more ammunition: Juan Peiró called it the "most shameful defeat suffered by the CNT," and other *treintistas* attacked the FAI for striking without a chance of victory.[56]

Such criticism only increased a feeling of isolation in the FAI. This feeling was accentuated by destruction of the anarchist movement in Portugal by the Salazar regime.[57] The hoped-for unity between Iberian anarchists had never really occurred, and now, with the arrest, exile, or imprisonment of many Portuguese anarchists, the *faístas* had a foretaste of the coming struggle with fascism.[58] The strength of Premier Antonio Salazar, and the ease with which he forced adoption of a fascist constitution in 1933, convinced some members of the FAI that Alejandro Lerroux—the new Spanish Premier in September and October, 1933, and a politician of dubious antecedents stretching back to the original "Tragic Week"—would follow a similar path in Spain.[59] Among the many anarchist study groups in the prison system, a feeling of impending fascism became very real as rumors magnified the importance of outside events; letters smuggled out of jail by militants called upon the movement to resist by every possible means.[60]

Interim cabinets after the fall of Azaña faced this potential violence by obtaining a stronger law of public order which gave the Interior Minister more independence from the parliament in matters of public safety.[61] Thus in August 1933, when construction workers stepped up their strike activity by calling a nationwide walkout, the government retaliated by arresting more than nine thousand workers under the new act. So many members of the CNT/FAI were incarcerated that the Comité Pro Presos was reactivated and enlarged in order to propagandize for an amnesty. The prisoner committee worked hard in the summer of 1933 to attack the government and to block the *treintistas'* Alianza Obrera. In the fall, however, its activities declined when the political balance of the Second Republic grew instable. Alejandro Lerroux fell on October 2, and the cabinet of Diego Martínez Barrio called national elections for November. Electoral policy quickly replaced all other topics of importance.

Debate on the elections within the anarcho-syndicalist movement was predictably divided. *Treintistas,* through the Alianza Obrera, urged their members to support the socialist ticket.[62] The Asturian CNT had already signed a pact of cooperation with the UGT, which Valeriano Orobón Fernández enthusiastically supported.[63] The benefits of this new arrangement seemed to outweigh the disadvantages of involvement in political affairs that accompanied it. A joint socialist-syndicalist front reestablished the power of syndicates by giving them a major new political role in the fight against fascism. The simple act of voting socialist, in a moment of crisis, was not a major violation of anarchist principle, the FSL argued, taking this position because thus far intransigence had resulted in nothing more than a series of defeats, from "Black January" to Casas Viejas. Larger objectives were at stake. Anarcho-syndicalism could be declared illegal if the Right won the elections and took control of the Second Republic. Only the unity of socialists and syndicalists might prevent this possibility. FSL propaganda concluded by pointing to Germany as a recent example of a divided Left unable to stem the rise of fascism.[64] *Faístas* could not have disagreed more. The Right was weak, and revolution was close at hand, so "no voting" and "the social revolution instead of the election" became FAI mottoes. Together with the sections of the CNT it controlled, the FAI staged a series of demonstrations and rallies across the northern provinces which culminated at the Barcelona bullring on November 5, 1933, when Buenaventura Durruti, free once again, castigated the Second Republic for jailing construction workers. The FAI was a vanguard of workers, he said, and an alliance of the moderate CNT and UGT was a step backward from vanguard action, now on the verge of bringing down the government.[65]

In the days after the rally, Durruti and his followers continued a campaign of provocation at every opportunity, often with bloody results. During a demonstration of Barcelona construction workers, *faístas* went on a rampage through downtown streets. Many demonstrators were arrested, and two—José Bruno and "El Sentín," a young gunman—were killed, allegedly while in police custody.[66] A meeting between officials of the Catalan regional government and representatives of the FAI did very little to ease the tension, and the FAI remained on the offensive in Catalonia until the election on November 19, 1933. No one could possibly claim that anarchist violence drastically weakened the Left in the elections, but *faístas* no doubt did frighten some voters, while factions on the Right worked together closely to attract new adherents.

V. *Revolt in Aragon*

The result of the election, to which the FAI's refusal to support the socialists contributed, was a clear victory for a Center-Right coalition.[67] The Confederation of Autonomous Right Parties (CEDA), led by the Catholic conservative José María Gil Robles, won 110 seats, while Alejandro Lerroux's Radical party gained a hundred places in the new parliament. Lerroux, minimally acceptable to the republicans, stood ready to inherit the premiership, since Gil Robles, who in September 1933 had travelled to Austria to study Chancellor Engelbert Dollfuss' techniques of clerical conservatism (stopping on the way back at a Nazi party rally in Nuremberg), chose to remain ominously in the background.[68] Gil Robles was aware that his assumption of the premiership would cause a civil war, and he was willing to wait for the growth of such fascist movements as the Falange Española, which was far more action-prone than the CEDA. The Falange, led by José Antonio Primo de Rivera, son of the former dictator, believed implicitly that conservative ideals had to be defended by force, and it quickly evolved into a paramilitary organization hostile to all groups on the Left.[69]

Suddenly the FAI no longer held a monopoly on violence; and the socialists, jolted by the election results, began to place a new value upon friendship with the FAI. The abortive land reform legislation and the incident at Casas Viejas had alienated the UGT from the republican coalition. Moreover, a socialist intellectual, Luis Araquistaín, had returned to Spain from his diplomatic post in Berlin full of first-hand information about Adolf Hitler and the German Nazi regime. Francisco Largo Caballero, shaken by the failure of his efforts on behalf of the Second Republic, listened to Araquistaín and became apprehensive about the potential rise of fascism within the Spanish Right. Almost as therapy, one observer noted, Largo Caballero read Marx seriously for the first time in many years and launched a more radical phase of his career.[70]

But if the socialists were startled by the election results, the anarchists were convulsed. Faístas cast around for a decisive new revolutionary strategy, convinced that they had been right about the Republic all along. Buenaventura Durruti, speaking to a huge crowd in Barcelona late in November, demanded that Casas Viejas be avenged.[71] Surprisingly, however, the Nosotros was divided on this issue, since Juan García Oliver opposed the notion of revenge. The revolutionary coalition had to be broadened; few, after all, would fight simply to overcome the previous defeats of the anarchists. Instead, García Oliver favored greater cooperation with the socialists, but Durruti attacked the moderation of Indalecio Prieto as proof that socialists were still so divided on strategy that they would not accept an alliance with the anarchists.[72] The large number of people who had not voted in the recent elections, Durruti said, justified a repudiation of the election results.[73]

In early December 1933, Durruti broke away from his former associates and convened a national committee of defense which included two relative newcomers. Cipriano Mera came from Madrid and was one of the most important new leaders in the construction syndicate of Castile. Isaac Puente was a doctor who had practiced much of his life in rural Aragon. In 1931 he had become secretary of the regional FAI and had led numerous rural strikes throughout the area.[74] Puente had a strong following in Saragossa, which once again had become a place of considerable support for the CNT/FAI. Durruti, of course, knew Saragossa well from the Soldevila assassination, and his personal popularity there was of almost legendary proportions. Police vigilance in Aragon was not nearly as sophisticated as in Catalonia, and the syndicates of chemical, metallurgical, and transport workers provided a fresh labor movement. Moreover, recruitment had been strong among the peasants who flocked into Saragossa looking for work. A rising here might penetrate rural areas of Aragon and even rekindle the flagging militancy of the Barcelona workers. It would also challenge Catholic labor unions, which continued to experience some success among the Aragonese workers, and the UGT, another powerful organization in Saragossa.

The Saragossa revolt was launched on December 8, 1933, the day the new conservative parliament began its sessions. Proclamation of a general strike spread through all major CNT/FAI strongholds and caused the caretaker government to declare a "state of prevention."[75] Durruti had hoped that the strike might prevent Alejandro Lerroux, who was sure to become the next Premier, from taking office, but the alert made this almost impossible. Fighting began on the evening of the general strike announcement. It broke out in several places in Barcelona, which Durruti had not expected to rise. At Prat de Hospitalet, on the road to Madrid, anarchists seized the town hall, hoisted a red and black flag, and barricaded a road. A Catholic center was set on fire to draw in Civil Guards, while the rest of the FAI force dispersed through the orchards, setting the stage for an ambush in which three Civil Guards were killed. Fighting continued furiously the next day and spread through the Barcelona suburbs.[76] Meanwhile, a major disturbance had erupted at Prat de Llobregat, where Civil Guard barracks were attacked on December 9. Reinforcements quickly arrived, and one rioter was killed and twenty-four arrested. None of these groups managed to make contact with the others, and guerrilla bands within Barcelona itself were

123

left to fend for themselves. By Tuesday, December 12, the city was again quiet.

It was a different story in Saragossa. Municipal authorities, anticipating violence, closed all cafes and places of amusement on December 8, 1933. During the night several major Civil Guard posts came under attack and by Saturday morning the center of the city was under seige. The target was the office of the civil governor. When this attack failed, demonstrators fanned out, attacking churches and government property at random. Three churches and a convent were seriously damaged, and five fatalities occurred among the demonstrators, while forty-five or more were arrested. On Sunday, Durruti and his aides were arrested. When factories opened normally on Monday, many socialist workers decided to go back to work. This caused renewed fighting, but it died down by Tuesday under pressure of additional Civil Guard and military reinforcements.

Briefly the focus shifted to the countryside. All of the country to the north and west of Saragossa was radicalized by the rising, with Logrono and Huesca becoming new centers of insurrection. Anarchists in Logrono attacked Civil Guard headquarters early on Saturday, December 16, and cut communications. A heavy raid was made on the offices of the civil governor, and when this attack was quelled, the rioters spread out to neighboring villages. Resistance remained high well into the next week, and in some villages, like Briones, insurrectionists for a time gained complete control. In Huesca the entire province rebelled, with Barbastro and Alcampel the two towns hardest hit. Revolutionaries seized the town halls, burned notary archives, and killed government employees, only to suffer losses themselves when Civil Guards arrived. In San Vicente de Sonsierra the Guard was trapped in its barracks until reinforcements arrived from Vitoria.

Other disturbances of lesser importance occurred in Burgos, Vitoria, Gijon, and Oviedo. A general strike in the Asturian coal fields was narrowly averted, although miners in Corunna raised a small rebellion. San Sebastian, Bilbao, and the Basque country generally remained quiet except for a few bomb explosions in Bilbao and an attempt to derail a train near Irun. The syndicates of opposition kept Valencia from joining the revolt, but a train was derailed here, too, killing sixteen passengers. Andalusia was forceably kept quiet, except for church burnings in Granada, through use of the army. Finally, in Madrid, the UGT flatly refused to have anything to do with the general strike.

Far from greeting Durruti as a liberator, the public soon expressed exasperation. President Macià of the Catalan government probably was typical when, on December 10, he called on all citizens to reject the anarchist cause and told workers to ignore orders of the revolutionary committee for a renewed general strike.[77] His appeal was not entirely successful. Riegos y Fuerza del Ebro, the old La Canadiense company, reported considerable sabotage soon afterwards; but such activities did not long continue. On December 15, Buenaventura Durruti, Isaac Puente, and Cipriano Mera were ordered by a special tribunal to be held indefinitely under a state-of-war provision.

After the leaders were detained in Burgos prison, the rising abated quickly. In the wake of the revolt recriminations spread, with the UGT accusing the anarchists and anarcho-syndicalists of utter stupidity for having staged the insurrection.[78] Far from overthrowing the Right, they charged, the violence prepared the way for Alejandro Lerroux to pander to middle-class fears of disorder. Buenaventura Durruti had consulted no one and depended entirely upon outnumbered cadres of troublemakers who had no chance of defeating the Civil Guard, thus playing into the hands of the very forces he had set out to destroy. In the words of a *treintista,* the revolt had been counterrevolutionary.[79]

VI. *The Bienio Negro*

The aftermath of the revolt in Aragon saw the fortunes of the anarchists at a low ebb. Alejandro Lerroux formed his cabinet on December 19, 1933, ushering in the Bienio Negro—the two black years. Earlier republican reforms were suspended or annulled by the Center-Right coalition as concessions to the monarchists or Catholics. Lerroux called himself a "historic republican," and indeed he had practiced his odd republicanism for more than thirty years. Originally hostile to clericalism and the regionalists, he was now reconciled to the political role of the Church, although his dislike of regionalism remained.[80] The real danger of the Bienio Negro lay in the Premier's need for support from the CEDA, and, indirectly, in the war against the Left that the Falange might conduct in the streets. A merger with another right-wing group, the Juntas de Ofensiva Nacional Sindicalista (JONS), on February 11, 1934, had greatly expanded the size and power of the Falange.[81] José Antonio

125

Primo de Rivera, with his "dialectic of fists and pistols" and his newly won parliamentary seat, symbolized the sudden turn of events that saw Durruti reviled and the son of a former dictator become a successful parliamentary deputy. Throughout the first half of 1934, CNT meetings were broken up, speakers shouted down, and attacks made upon syndicate headquarters and strike lines.

The Falange was not the only active force. Unhappy with Center-Right opposition to Catalan autonomy, an opposition they blamed in part upon the social agitation of anarcho-syndicalists, regionalists in the Esquerra frequently fought anarchists. Political interference in a number of local Catalan strikes increased, and use of lockouts reappeared. In March and April 1934 more than 40,000 workers were laid off by the textile industry. Labor difficulties hit potash mines in Sallent, coal fields in Asturias, the chemical industry in Saragossa, and steel plants in Alcoy.[82] Remnants of the FAI tried to instill a strong sense of militancy by commissioning Nestor Makhno to analyze Spanish anarchist mistakes and provide suggestions for a new paramilitary movement.[83] In addition, a new secret Portuguese branch of the FAI, Pro Agro, was created as a part of this desperate effort to shore up the organization.[84] Neither act had much effect.

The reason lay with the stance of increasing independence adopted by syndicates of opposition. The revolt in Aragon had caused an almost irreparable breach, and not even the mediation attempted by Eleuterio Quintanilla and the Asturian miners healed the schism.[85] Led by a reformed Comité Regional de Oposición Confederal, the FSL was actively negotiating with the UGT for common participation in the Alianza Obrera. Valeriano Orobón Fernández wrote the basic proposal and made it quite radical. He excluded any collaboration with the bourgeois regime, pushed hard for "revolutionary workers' democracy," and urged immediate socialization of production, transport, communications, housing, and finance.[86] Above all, anarchists should work within syndicates and abandon the small groups they had favored; otherwise they risked losing contact with the working class. A return to the "propaganda of the deed" served no one's best interests except the fascists'. Strong syndicalist participation might offset the executive-style government of the socialists and create a workers' government of unusually strong proportions. On March 28, 1934, the CNT and UGT of Asturias became the first branches to sign the pact. They called jointly for a regime of economic equality based upon principles of socialist federalism, with nationalized ownership of the land, abolition of land rent, ownership by possession, development of cooperatives in areas of latifundia, creation of irrigation projects and credit banks, disbandment of the regular army in favor of militias, and a number of other reforms.[87]

Elsewhere, consideration of the pact ran into many delays. On the CNT/FAI side, energy was consumed by another general strike in Saragossa. The shutdown was almost total for thirty-six days in March and April 1934. Government forces were remarkably unsuccessful in coercing Aragonese workers to return to their jobs. As in the Rio Tinto strike so many years before, children of the strikers were sent away for the duration. This stirred sympathy for the strikers and admiration for their steadfastness in having walked out twice in four months.

At the same time, socialists found themselves under attack by the government for the first time since World War I. *Grupos de choque* run by the socialist youth clashed frequently with the Falange, and UGT aid to rural syndicates led to a strike among Andalusian peasants in June.[88] Alejandro Lerroux fought back by censoring socialist newspapers and arresting the leaders of the youth groups. All of this delayed final formation of the Alianza Obrera.

Sectarian difficulties added another level of problems. The CNT and UGT quarreled in Malaga over jurisdictional boundaries and in Madrid over a strike in June that the UGT failed to back. While Francisco Largo Caballero continued to argue that there were no fundamental disagreements between the two confederations, Indalecio Prieto nonetheless used his influence to prevent many locals from embracing full cooperation.[89] Once Buenaventura Durruti was released from preventive detention, he denounced the Asturian CNT leader, José María Martínez, for signing the pact without having consulted the CNT's national organization. Francisco Ascaso popularized the maxim that anarchists could find revolutionary support only by going to the people—and not by allying themselves with other political groups.[90] The *faísta* Jaime Balius wrote glowingly of rural southerners and the vital assistance they could provide the CNT/FAI in raising a new revolution.[91] Other voices spoke out against Trotskyists, who had recently played an important role in supporting development of the Alianza Obrera.[92] All this amounted to a solid counteroffensive by the FAI, and on June 23, 1934, a national meeting of FAI regional groups censured the Asturians for their cooperation with the socialists. *Solidaridad Obrera* called Francisco Largo Caballero "a lucky plasterer with more cleverness than brains."[93]

127

Before matters went any further, the attention of both sides was distracted by a new political crisis erupting in Catalonia. The old regionalist leader Francesco Macià had died in January 1934. Luis Companys, his successor, concerned by conservative inroads, pressed for a new *ley de cultivos* to support a populist peasant organization, the Unió de Rabassaires. This law, passed in April, nullified long leases in the Catalan vineyards. Peasant tenants, unable to pay stipulated rents because of the Depression, obtained an arbitration tribunal to renegotiate the leases. Rents were cut in half and the expulsion of renters forbidden. By June the owners' appeal reached the Supreme Tribunal in Madrid and the law was annulled. The Esquerra led passage of a virtually identical bill in the Catalan parliament a few days later, and this act raised the most serious constitutional question in republican history.

The unexpected radicalization of the Northeast by the *rabassaires'* controversy made any further discussion of the CNT-UGT pact moot. Now, suddenly, the Alianza Obrera was overshadowed by the struggles of middle-class Catalan regionalists and, at the end of the summer, by Basque regionalists as well. The Basque National Action Association demanded a boycott of the national parliament as a result of setbacks suffered by a proposal of Basque autonomy in Madrid. Since the CNT and UGT had thousands of members in the industrial centers of Barcelona and Bilbao, it was inevitable that regionalist politics soon dominated everything else. Throughout the summer of 1934 the Alianza Obrera collapsed despite a spread of militancy, ironically more general than at any time since April 1931.

VII. Red October

The outburst of opposition caught the government by surprise. Ricardo Samper, premier since the *rabassaire* controversy of the early spring, lost his usefulness to the Right and was replaced by Alejandro Lerroux on October 2, 1934. Rumors circulated of a CEDA cabinet takeover and when Lerroux appointed three CEDA members to his cabinet, it was assumed that this maneuver prepared the way for the premiership of José María Gil Robles. Whatever might have been planned, Lerroux never did step aside for the CEDA leader, largely because of opposition from the President of the Republic, Niceto Alcalá-Zamora. It did not matter: the rumors had an incendiary effect upon the Left, particularly in the North, and not just among socialists (who called a rising on October 5) or anarchists. The Catalan regionalists, still enraged by the *rabassaire* issue, reacted most emphatically by declaring a Catalan republic within a federal Spain on October 6—a signal for risings to erupt all over the peninsula.

From the anarchist point of view, this sudden outbreak of violence came at an inopportune moment, when they had no real policy or plans for action. Alexander Shapiro of the AIT may have been responsible in part for this de-escalation of activity, since he saw the impossibility of reaching a consensus and so had counseled strongly for a reexamination of the divisions within the CNT/FAI as a last-ditch attempt to save the Alianza Obrera pact.[94] Pressure was exerted upon the Asturian CNT to revoke its agreement with the UGT. By October 5 this had been only partly accomplished, since the rank and file supported the Alianza Obrera and refused to destroy it. Rebellion was too far along in Asturias to break ranks now.

In Catalonia there was very little unity The regional government solicited the CNT an hour before the general strike went into effect and never did announce Luis Companys' decision to declare a republic.[95] The CNT received no arms or financial aid from the regional government, and even its plea for release of anarchists still incarcerated went unheeded.[96] Without such concessions, it was impossible to expect the CNT/FAI to end its long quarrel with the Esquerra. *Solidaridad Obrera* had been allowed to publish for only two months in 1934, and union halls and cultural centers (*ateneos sindicalistas*) had been closed altogether.[97] Negotiations between the CNT and regionalists were handled through the office of the Catalan Minister of the Interior, Dr. Josep Dencàs, one of the most committed regionalists in Luis Companys' circle.[98] His use of the Esquerra's Worker Alliance as the parent body of the general strike guaranteed a CNT refusal.

As a result, the number of CNT members who joined the rising was small. Only in La Felguera did a revolutionary committee of anarchists rise to seize the Duro-Felguera steelworks, the second largest in the country.[99] Elsewhere, anarchists would have nothing to do with the regionalists, and the Nosotros was particularly hostile. Juan García Oliver accused Luis Companys of embarking upon an insurrection as badly planned as the revolt in Aragon had been in December 1933.[100] Durruti, only recently out on bail, was caught in Saragossa, still working among the Aragonese; Civil Guards placed him under preventive arrest on October 6. Francisco Ascaso was arrested the next day, and the Montsenys had their publishing

129

center ransacked. But none of the anarchist leaders could have saved the situation, since the revolt of the Catalan regional government had ended almost before it began. Luis Companys and his followers did little except retreat into their offices and wait for the army to arrest them.

Austurias was another matter entirely. The general strike of October 5 found a united working class waiting for the call to arms. Mieres and Oviedo became centers of the Alianza Obrera, now an impromptu organization made up of workers of all political persuasions, largely under socialist direction. Alliance forces mobilized more than 30,000 armed workers and quickly seized the Aller and Nalón river valleys. They confidently waited for battle, sure that if the Left won here, the country would rise to overthrow Alejandro Lerroux and José María Gil Robles. As one anarchist described the optimistic mood, the movement had seized "large factories of arms, munitions and explosives. The mountains offer an excellent natural defense. And the mining population is essentially rebellious. ... . [They] are a rebel multitude, familiar with danger and with the actual struggle."[101]

Alejandro Lerroux responded by sending Moorish troops from North Africa into Asturias, since the loyalty of the other Spanish regiments was suspect. The Moroccans landed at Aviles and Gijon on October 8. Anarchist-led workers attempted to repel the invasion, but the effort was frustrated by lack of communist or socialist aid, or so the anarchists charged.[102] Oviedo fell on October 12, and Mieres on October 18, 1934, after very bitter fighting, much of it house to house. The two weeks of insurrection cost the lives of approximately twelve hundred, including forty captives of the Left, executed before the fall of Oviedo to government troops.[103] Among the rebels killed were a brother of Durruti, and José María Martínez, the CNT leader in Asturias.

Red October, as it subsided, was the last of the putsches against the Second Republic. Its importance stemmed not from the role of the anarchists but rather from the spread of their psychology and tactics to other republican groups. The anarchists themselves were too exhausted or too suspicious of other groups in join in. While Asturian anarchists fought and died in large numbers for the sake of the insurrection, they did so because they were caught up in a local *jacquerie*. But now the socialists and communists were filled with the same kind of anger that once had motivated the CNT and FAI. Other sections of the Spanish Left began behaving as if they too were anarchists.

130

CHAPTER SIX

The Popular Front

The revolution is a thing of the people, a popular creation; the counterrevolution is a thing of the State. [*Tierra
y Libertad,* July 3, 1936]

I. *Hard Times*

Red October's aftermath was milder than might have been expected.
Alejandro Lerroux, elated that victory freed him from the threat of
José María Gil Robles' taking power, used some slight degree of
moderation in strengthening the power of his cabinet.[1] As a result,
no radical or regionalist organization was declared illegal. However,
more than twenty thousand socialists and anarchists were jailed
briefly on a variety of serious charges or simply held in military
detention without being formally charged.[2] There was anger at the
frequency with which anarchists were detained. Buenaventura Durruti spent four months in a Valencia prison and remained in temporary custody or under surveillance thereafter. The same was true
of other major anarchist leaders.

Prison-camp justice, moreover, was uncertain and erratic and
often focused upon militants of the CNT and FAI. Military courts-
martial decreed death penalties a few days after the insurrection,
and many executions followed.[3] Some of those shot were anarchists,
and even Catalan anarchists, despite their unimportant role during
Red October, received harsh treatment.[4]

Although the CNT and FAI were not proscribed, it was not easy
for either organization to resume operations against strong government pressure. *Solidaridad Obrera* and *Tierra y Libertad* did not publish
from October 1934 to April 1935, and between November and Febru-

ary raids on anarchist centers came frequently. Public meetings were outlawed until April 1935, when the Comité Pro Presos, as it had so many times before, began to use the prisoner issue as a way of opening up public discussion of anarchism. Demonstrations were held in Pamplona, Bilbao, and several smaller towns, but the government always made major security preparations which severely limited the mobilization of public opinion. Francisco Ascaso despaired of ever overthrowing bourgeois Spain and its "abject, repugnant" state.[5] Time was running out, he believed, in the struggle to rid the "real Spain" (peasant Spain) of the false European values that had dominated the country for so long.[6] The impotence of the CNT/FAI in the wake of Red October only confirmed Ascaso's gloomy prediction.

While anarchists waited, the national government moved to consolidate its recent gains. The imprisonment of Manuel Azaña, his trial by the Supreme Tribunal (which found him innocent of any complicity in Red October), and a parliamentary investigation (which dropped the matter in the fall) kept opposition to the Center-Right coalition off balance for half a year while Lerroux and Gil Robles abolished many earlier republican measures. Education again became parochial, and investment in new facilities almost disappeared. Landowners regained the right to expel tenants from their property. Land reform and the work of the Institute of Agrarian Reform were hopelessly confused.[7] In the Northeast transfer of sovereign power from Madrid to the Catalan federal government ceased on December 18, 1934, when responsibility for those areas that had come under regionalist control in April 1934—education, justice, and the police—passed back to the national government. For the moment, autonomy was dead, a stunning blow to the hopes of the Catalan middle class; this was perhaps the lowest point in the history of the movement since the beginning of the dictatorship more than a decade previously. Francesco Macià's death in 1934 deprived the Catalans of their most important leader at a very difficult moment.

But the Spanish Left was much too large to collapse entirely in face of Center-Right triumphs. Threat of further reaction slowly began to intensify a new drive for revolution. Two small groups merged to form the Partido Obrero de Unificación Marxista (POUM) to do battle under a Trotskyist banner. Leadership of POUM fell to Andrés Nín and Joaquín Maurín, both former syndicalists.[8] Angel Pestaña's own syndicalist party attracted fourteen thousand members by February 1935, six thousand of them ex-CNT members.[9]

Communist membership grew at an even faster rate, and communism attracted sympathizers like socialist deputy Carlos Lamondeda, the writer and politician Julio Álvarez del Vayo, and socialist youth leader Santiago Carrillo.[10] In Catalonia, communists and socialists flocked to join the Partit Socialista Unificat de Cataluñya (PSUC), headed by Juan Comorera, which was in the process of formation.

By May 1935, the communists were strong enough to issue a manifesto entitled "To All Socialist, Communist, Anarchist and Syndicalist Workers of Spain: To All the Workers of Spain, Catalonia, the Basque Country, and Morocco." It demanded confiscation of land without indemnification, nationalization of major industries, dissolution of the armed forces, creation of a Red Guard, and close association with the USSR.[11] This maximalist manifesto found support from the socialist party, whose rapid evolution towards the ultra-Left continued. The government, sure that Red October had ended the revolutionary threat and now distracted by factional quarreling among its own supporters, did little to stop this growing militancy. They were satisfied that suppression of the anarchists (dictated by the previous putsches against the Second Republic) was sufficient to control the situation, even though socialists and communists now presented a greater threat to public security.

This belated effect of earlier anarchist insurrectionism severely hampered the CNT/FAI while allowing freedom for the PSUC and UGT just at a moment when revolutionary ideas were spreading more widely than ever before. FAI activity almost entirely disappeared; it was the worst moment in the organization's history, according to one observer.[12] Many CNT members, fighting old battles, went on record once again as opposing the Alianza Obrera, still the main weapon of the *treintistas*. They also refused to join the communists' united proletarian front. Eventually the strength of the Right and fear of fascism reunited anarcho-syndicalists, but in 1935 there was as much hostility within the CNT as before. The CNT did not grow significantly but remained a bitter, feuding organization, totally negative in its approach to changing political circumstances.

Some of this failure can be blamed on the AIT in Paris. As part of the AIT's annual meeting in March 1935, Alexander Shapiro prepared a report on Spain based on material sent him by a German exile, Helmut Rüdiger. Both men were strong syndicalists, with a bias against the FAI. Shapiro and Rüdiger believed that Spanish labor was in a better position to organize than ever before, if the FAI could be kept from using "propaganda of the deed." The "putschism" of the *faístas* developed from a failure to evolve politically away from nineteenth-century anarchism.[13] Their stance brought opprobrium upon the FAI because fascism, particularly in Germany, was causing a wave of revulsion against all violence. A diligent organization of labor provided the only true defense against fascism. Detracting from this effort, the FAI's putsches against the Second Republic were all the more tragic because that government had been the only one sympathetic to the free association of labor in twentieth-century Spain. The use of revolutionary terrorism against it clearly had been inappropriate.

The *treintista* position was viewed favorably in the AIT report, although Alexander Shapiro stopped short of outright identification with the moderates. Just as he condemned useless violence, the AIT secretary criticized the *treintista* program for lacking a thorough infrastructure or a clear theoretical basis. Moderates divided their allegiance among the industrial unions, the National Federation of Industry, and the Alianza Obrera. They also flirted with the notion of launching their own syndicalist party that would be openly involved in national politics, yet nowhere was there evidence of consistent organizational support for any of these commitments. The CNT/FAI, while possessing the largest membership of any AIT chapter, had failed to take advantage of its strength and plunged from crisis to crisis until its adherents were so seriously divided that revolutionary opportunities slipped away.[14]

The report was the most serious criticism ever made against the CNT/FAI, but it was not entirely fair. The AIT suffered from some of these same problems itself. Officials in Paris had never acquainted themselves with the special problems of their Spanish affiliate. Moreover, Alexander Shapiro was known to be unhappy that Valeriano Orobón Fernández had never risen to high rank in the CNT. His lack of popular appeal, however, was hardly a failure of the CNT's.

Fair or unfair, AIT criticism hurt the morale of the Spanish anarcho-syndicalist movement. It followed major political setbacks and seemed to cap a particular ineffective period in the life of the CNT/FAI. There appeared to be no end to difficulty in 1935, but, in fact, the nadir had been reached.

II. Revival

The Spaniard who responded most seriously to the criticisms in Shapiro's report was Diego Abad de Santillán. Since his return to Spain in 1931, the former Argentine syndicalist leader had risen in anarchist circles by attracting young disciples to his Nervio group. Older CNT members criticized this faction as crypto-communist, while others felt uncomfortable with Abad de Santillán's old ties to the liberal "regenerationist" school of reform or with his university and law school background.[15] He had long since abandoned these earlier stages of his political career, but his 1934 entry into radical journalism in Barcelona as the editor of *Tierra y Libertad* angered some, who felt that *La Revista Blanca* and *Solidaridad Obrera* were sufficient for the needs of the Left. But Federica Montseny had turned to writing feminist works, and in 1935 *Solidaridad Obrera* was suppressed by the regime. To fill the vacuum, Abad de Santillán moved boldly, despite censorship, to edit still another new periodical, *Tiempos Nuevos*, which specialized in economic theory. Because of government pressure very few editions appeared in 1935, and in early October Abad de Santillán was arrested and detained for a few weeks on charges of revolutionary activity.[16]

Despite these setbacks, Diego Abad de Santillán was able to write a short book on anarchist economic theory, which appeared in late 1935. *El organismo económico de la revolución: cómo vivimos y como podríamos vivir en España* went through several editions and appeared definitively only in 1937, but the first edition contained enough of the basic argument to constitute a serious attempt to meet Alexander Shapiro's charges.

Diego Abad de Santillán had very strong views about the history of the Spanish crisis. He believed that in early modern times loyalty to the Crown, "God and Spain above all," had been proverbial; but that after the death of Philip II the monarchy lost its grandeur and the Church took advantage of decay to construct a theocracy. The people, abandoned, went back to local laws and institutions first developed when monarchical control had been weak centuries before. Soon the state became a shell empty of authority, unwilling to recognize the individual as anything more than an obligated subject yet itself furnishing nothing in return. As a result, indolence, aversion to change, and eventually inability to resist local authoritarianism (*caciquismo*) became the usual norms of Spanish life. It was against these conditions that anarchists rebelled, recognizing that they had persisted under more recent governments.[17] Anarchists began seeking to develop a mixture of traditionalism and modernization based upon the popular sovereignty of the people, who could be the only real beneficiaries of change. Until now, unfortunately, the battle to overthrow state power had taken precedence over economic development, and it was this situation that Abad de Santillán set out to correct.

His economic philosophy came in part from Peter Kropotkin's theory of mutualism, which Kropotkin had developed in several of his works but particularly in *The Conquest of Bread*.[18] Abad de Santillán's work marked the first major inroad of Kropotkin's thought into the Bakuninist spirit of Spanish anarchism—the spirit that had kept the movement without an economic theory for so long. The major factors of production, according to the theory of mutualism, consisted of nature, human labor, and machinery. Capitalism added rent, interest, wages, profits, and government defense of private property to the cost of production. Consumer needs were often neglected, labor was devalued, and the demands of society were not served. Capitalism, often directed by the concerns of a few individuals, was interested in utilizing only an infinitesimal part of the social resources. This selfishness on the part of a few kept millions of Spaniards poor, despite their hard work and productivity. Such a system could be changed by recognizing work as the common denominator of the total social experience: "He who would eat, must work."[19] A collectivist economic system might lower the barriers of poor education, lack of material resources, and loss of initiative and thereby free Spaniards from centuries of bad government and economic exploitation. Collectivism would contrast vividly with parasitic capitalism, which stood in the way of maximum utilization of resources, creating a social crisis that caused half of the work force of ten million to remain unemployed at any given time.[20]

Diego Abad de Santillán spoke out repeatedly in favor of a "work" revolution that would furnish maximum employment by coordinating all the forces in the economic order.[21] The work revolution would diverge from the Russian revolution; social conformity, the Bolshevik ideal, was unimportant. "We have no wish for everyone to dance the same step; we even admit the possibility of different organisms, some more and some less revolutionary, some more and some less friendly to the new situation."[22] Absolute political liberty would flourish, since the purpose of the new revolution was chiefly to provide economic coordination. "Excessive generosity to workers," not vengeance upon the rich, would be the watchword of the revolution.

The means of obtaining this work revolution would be through mutualism, which Abad de Santillán saw as an expression of the popular will totally separate from any state action or factional activity. Mutualism was collective economic activity developed spontaneously by the people themselves, a revolution from below, sustained by a long history of Spanish collective practices which he took some care to emphasize.[23] Should an elaborate, centralized state apparatus arise to direct collectivization, the revolution would be destroyed.

136

The capitalist world could only be confronted by a new system emanating from popular sources. This did not mean a return to artisanship or some other utopian socialist scheme. Population growth, if nothing else, demanded development of public resources above a primitive economic level.

To propel mutualism into operation, Abad de Santillán relied upon a form of council communism. His format utilized factory councils and syndicates of trade and industry, linked together by federalized economic councils. On the first point, little description was provided, and it is unclear how familiar he was with the ideas of the Italian factory-council theorist, Antonio Gramsci.[24] All he mentioned was that the factory council should represent every section of an enterprise. The council had the responsibility of coordinating production of the factory in all of its operations. Then, at a higher level, coordination and planning for the entire industry would be provided by an industrial council, composed of representatives of each factory council, as well as of specialists and consumer groups.[25] There would be fourteen industrial councils altogether, representing foodstuffs, construction, clothing, agriculture, livestock, forestry, mining and fishing, public utilities, transport, communications, chemicals, sanitation, publishing and culture, and metallurgical industries. In many respects, these divisions followed the old pattern of syndicates that had developed forty or fifty years previously.

Parallel to industrial self-government Abad de Santillán constructed a three-tier system of local, regional, and federal councils of the economy. The local economic council would perform, through a direct democratic assembly, political and administrative tasks for the municipality. It would be responsible primarily for local production, price control, and economic development. Projects too large to accomplish at the local level would be delegated to the regional economic councils, which would provide expertise and technical assistance for local and regional productive activity and coordinate local production through evaluation of supply and demand, surveys of consumer need, and study of long-term necessities. The members of each regional board were to be elected local council representatives, who would vote by districts. Much of the work would be carried out in conjunction with regional sections of the industrial councils, which could provide expert first-hand information about the performances and capabilities of industry. Actual allocation of resources, however, would always remain in the hands of the local and regional economic councils.

At the top level a federal economic council would act as a liaison between regional councils and the various national industrial councils. When it did not coordinate regions and sectors of the economy, its work would involve serious planning functions. "It will know where the deficiencies and where the excesses of production are, it will know the requirements of transport and communications, and the needs for new roads, new cultivations, new factories. And where the regions do not have sufficient resources, it will provide national assistance for public works of recognized need."[26] Comprised of representatives from regional economic and national industrial councils, it would have as its main purpose the coordination of all aspects of the economy. This federal council would be led by the council of credit and exchange, a board of economists and experts, to whom would be delegated the quantitative task of maintaining exact statistics on production and consumption, supply and demand, reserves and deficits. From these statistics, the national economic council, in conjunction with its regional and local components, would direct the economy towards realization of a society of producers and consumers—the only socioeconomic lines recognized by the new society.

In developing the general structure of his council communism, Diego Abad de Santillán took his inspiration from syndicalism and, with anarchist overtones tried to follow former CNT organizational patterns. Syndical hierarchies were slightly expanded into national agencies, while syndicates and national federations of industries were converted into larger economic and industrial councils. When he discussed general reform, however, Abad de Santillán's tone became distinctly that of a nineteenth-century Spanish technocrat rather than an anarcho-syndicalist. Regeneration of productive capacity, improvement of productive resources, and social modernization had been discussed thoroughly by such reformers as Joaquín Costa, Gumersindo Azcárate, Damián Isern, Ricardo Macías Picavia, and Joaquín Lucas Mallada. All were members of an elitist, middle-class reform group inspired by Krausismo, a vague philosophical school that eventually moved towards a theory of practical reconstruction advocating adult education, technocracy, and, if necessary, an "iron surgeon" to dictate modernization.[27] Abad de Santillán knew the reform program from having spent the years 1910–1917 at Madrid's National University, a breeding ground for regeneration and reform. It was natural that he incorporated these ideas into his study.

The consequences of this mixture made Abad de Santillán's work more important than it would have been otherwise. Ideas of regeneration, reform, and utilization of ancient collectivist practices had circulated popularly for a half century or more. Anarchists were

138

not the only believers in the legend of a golden, cooperative, communal Spanish past. Reformers of the late nineteenth century publicized many of the medieval customary institutions and practices, and Abad de Santillán's use of this material obviously attracted a larger readership for his book.[28] Beyond this, however, he was the first Spanish anarchist to give a clear picture of a possible libertarian society. Most Spaniards had long wondered about the society the anarchists had struggled so long to produce. *El organismo económico*, for all its sketchiness and imprecision, provided them with an ambitious model, complete with a series of reformist ideas. Peasants, populists, and even corporativists found the book useful.

The timing of the book's appearance was also important. Land reform remained a hopelessly irritating controversy, with the *rabassaires* issue and national land reform as far from resolution as ever. Not only had the Agriculture Minister, Manuel Jiménez Fernández, failed to win approval for his scheme of strengthening small independent farmers, but in July 1935 a law revising the original agrarian reform act, passed by the Center-Right deputies in the national parliament, effectively rendered the original act meaningless.[29] Years of republican effort to improve the condition of rural Spain came to naught almost simultaneously with a series of scandals—particularly the *straperlo* affair, a gambling case with undertones of influence peddling—which seriously embarrassed the government.[30] Even for those not politically conscious, this conjunction of events tarnished the Center-Right coalition almost as badly as the Casas Viejas affair had undermined Manuel Azaña's bloc in 1933.

Among peasants caught in these shifting controversies, comfort could be found in Diego Abad de Santillán's ideas about the revolutionary transformation of agriculture, for he denounced economic enslavement of peasants by landlords and demanded immediate development of collective ownership.[31] Councils of production should be established to represent all the agricultural workers of an area. In addition, national councils in various sectors of agriculture would bring technical assistance to local communes and coordinate production. Further aid might be generated by cooperation with local economic councils, so that agricultural products could be bartered for industrial goods. Such a process circumvented the monetary system altogether and thus advanced the achievement of a society of producers and consumers. Where the output of an area was entirely agricultural, the council of production would merge with the local economic council, giving agricultural workers primary control of local government.

These ideas stood out in the difficult days of the Bienio Negro as an indefatigable defense of revolutionary goals, now put in a new theoretical context. Wandering speakers like Isaac Puente, the radical Aragonese doctor, popularized the message of *El organismo económico* and discussed Diego Abad de Santillán along with Peter Kropotkin. Attendance at anarchist meetings soon increased in Aragon, rural Catalonia, and the Levante. Slowly anarchism recovered momentum and began to rally its forces.

III. Popular Front

In the meantime, national political events were also changing rapidly. Disaffection struck Alejandro Lerroux's Radical party, and a new Republican Union party, led by Diego Martínez Barrio, challenged the Radicals. Another new group centered around Manuel Azaña, whose popularity, in the wake of his persecution by the government, rose dramatically again. He and Martínez Barrio were able to create the Left Republican party in July 1935, just at the moment when the Comintern, speaking for a wide range of international communist parties, adopted a "popular front" strategy of broad cooperation between all anti-fascist groups. Communist independence, never very great in Spain since the movement was still tiny, diminished even further when communists made overtures to the republicans and socialists for a joint program of opposition to the Center-Right coalition. *Rapprochement* developed further in meetings between the various Popular Front partners in August 1935, and from August to December 1935, the arrangement worked smoothly. The President of the Republic, Niceto Alcalá-Zamora, convinced that the scandals and tumult of the past year had destroyed the effectiveness of the Center-Right, dissolved the cabinet and appointed Manuel Portela Valladares, a moderate, as Premier on December 14, 1935. Three weeks later, on January 7, 1936, the parliament was dismissed, and new elections were scheduled for February 16, 1936.

During this period, leadership of the fledgling Popular Front came from the socialist Indalecio Prieto, whose exile in France since Red October had brought him into contact with Léon Blum and the French Popular Front. On January 15, 1936, he was able to enlist the republican parties of Azaña and Martínez Barrio, the Catalan Esquerra, the communists, and his own party in a new Center-Left alliance. Newspaper censorship disappeared, and election campaign-

140

ing began, freed by the sudden moderation presidential policies inspired. *Solidaridad Obrera* confidently predicted a new revolution in its late January editions, but beneath this optimism, anarcho-syndicalists felt unsettled by the rapid movement of events. Emergence of the Popular Front obviously promised better days ahead, but the events of the early Republic were not easy to forget. Moreover the UGT was pressuring the CNT and FAI for support, and this again raised the possibility of anarchists voting in a Spanish election.

Two meetings of CNT/FAI leaders, one in Saragossa January 9, 1936, and one in Barcelona two days later, considered the question. The great number of anarchists still in prison was an important point, because their terms would be commuted if the Popular Front was victorious. Another factor was the assassination of an Andalusian CNT official, Manuel Ballester, in Cadiz during December 1935 by the Falange, for this was an indication that anarchists were again coming under the guns of the Right, a situation the Popular Front might alter.[32] And there were also fears that the movement might be ostracized if it did not find some kind of political influence quickly. The assassination of Miguel Badia, a police official in Catalonia, had already been blamed upon anarchists by Catalan conservatives.[33]

These various reasons persuaded the leaders at the two meetings to vote in favor of electoral participation. The formula for CNT support demanded guarantees that the new Popular Front regime would be proletarian, committed to local government, and representative of a united working-class society.[34] Many syndicates, faced with heavy competition from the UGT, supported this formula strongly, as did the Catalan regional plenum on January 25. Even Buenaventura Durruti gave participation in the elections a lukewarm endorsement after the Popular Front promised to free all political prisoners. "We face a situation which could quickly turn into a revolution or a civil war," he said. "The worker who votes and then quietly returns home, will be a counterrevolutionary; so will the worker who does not vote but nonetheless refuses to fight."[35]

On election day, while a majority of anarchists and syndicalists did not go to the polls, enough of them voted for socialist candidates to provide the margin of victory for the Popular Front. *Solidaridad Obrera* placed their number at a million; 200,000 may be a more realistic figure.[36] Altogether the Popular Front held a 300,000 vote plurality over the Center-Right coalition, so that the "anarchist vote" proved to be crucial and at the same time clouded the outlook of the new government. The CNT/FAI did not formally belong to the Popular Front, but it nevertheless had a claim upon the Popular

Front's services, having managed to assert the importance of anarchism without seriously sacrificing apolitical ideals (since, after all, a majority of anarchists had remained immune to electoral appeals).[37] Somehow the CNT and FAI had managed to play a decisive role. Now, unexpectedly, they were closer to real power than at any other point in their history, but how or when the revolution would come remained as uncertain as ever. The February victory temporarily caused a tremendous euphoria, but the anarchists took no steps to utilize their power.

The new cabinet, led by Manuel Azaña as Premier and composed of Left Republicans, took office on February 18, well in advance of the convocation of parliament. Political unrest spread rapidly, partly as a result of demonstrable anarchist power but also because of the possible communist role in the Popular Front. In fact, the first post-election violence came as a result of victory parades staged by socialists. The Falange retaliated by attempting unsuccessfully to assassinate a socialist deputy; mobs reacted to this Falange violence by sacking two churches and burning the printing plant of a conservative newspaper, *La Nación*. The role of anarchists in these outbreaks was initially small. They called a brief one-day strike among iron workers in Catalonia and the Basque provinces to demand reduction of the longer working day introduced by the Center-Right two years previously. No doubt this also served as a warning to Manuel Azaña not to resume use of mixed juries in labor arbitration. If so, the walkouts achieved their purpose, for during the next few months the Popular Front allowed strikes to run their normal course without interference.

IV. Mobilization

Abandonment of mixed juries caused increasing turmoil between February and July 1936, when most business firms were disrupted by labor demands. There were thousands of requests for factory councils, profit sharing, and employee vetoes of managerial functions. Some small businessmen were able to band together to protect themselves, but even they added to the confusion by staging protests against the high prices charged by suppliers and objecting to competition from large chain stores. Other businesses were run by committees of workers in conjunction with the proprietors. Cobblers in large cities voluntarily formed a national syndicate of shoemakers to

142

enforce industry-wide regulation and cooperation. Foreign-owned businesses, attacked from all sides, were taken over by workers entirely or had to sell blocks of stock to Spaniards.[38] The largest plants in the North often experienced four or five strikes simultaneously, as departments or sections walked out over minor issues, usually concerning the orders of a foreman or conditions in one small part of the factory. Whenever possible, councils of workers were formed in anticipation of the revolution. Union leaders sought ties with technical personnel in order to assure the continuation of production when the time came to expel the higher administrators and owners.[39] The total number of work stoppages became inestimable; strikes occurred daily and in profusion. Workers of all political persuasions—communist, socialist, anarchist—believed the revolution had already begun.

This volume of discontent caught the political parties and the Popular Front by surprise. The Ministry of Labor tried to win the good will of the labor movement by decreeing that workers fired after January 1934 for their political views had to be rehired—an order many employers refused to accept, causing more turmoil. When government enforcement of the order proved to be weak, Buenaventura Durruti reminded the Popular Front of its obligations to the anarchists: "We . . . tell the men of the Left that we are the ones who decided your triumph. . . ."[40] Almost immediately, CNT strikes in the textile and transport industries were settled favorably through Manuel Azaña's pressure upon management.

Still, some moderate politicians did not take the same accommodating view of the anarchists. Santiago Casares Quiroga, former Minister of the Interior and a republican politician consistently hostile to the CNT, manifested his dislike by mounting a strenuous campaign against a CNT building trades strike in Madrid, charging that anarchists were taking advantage of the Popular Front's sympathy for labor.[41] More opposition was met in Catalonia, where the March elections returned the Esquerra strongly to power. The Esquerra worked closely with the PSUC's Unió Socialista de Catalunya, led by Juan Comorera, who appealed to Catalan workers on a basis of regionalism, not radicalism, and who sought to diminish the role of the CNT in the North.

All of this presented a very confusing picture to the anarchists. Did the Popular Front really represent their interests? Many suspected it did not; Casares Quiroga and Comorera resembled General Martínez Anido and other early opponents too closely to make anarchists comfortable. Besides, while both the UGT and the *treintis-*

143

tas now muted their criticism of the CNT/FAI, neither group made haste to collaborate with them. The possibility of further competition with the UGT began to upset some anarchists, who questioned the usefulness of further cooperation with the Popular Front.

That there was good reason for this attitude was seemingly confirmed on April 4, 1936, when Manuel Azaña presented the Popular Front program to the national parliament. The original republican reforms of 1931–1932 were restored, but few Popular Front measures received his endorsement. He made no provision for the socialization of banks, industry, or land. Anarchists had assumed, perhaps foolishly, that the opposition of the Falange, the CEDA, and the Radicals would force the Popular Front to take action on these neglected matters. Now it was clear that Manuel Azaña would not do so, despite prolonged street rioting by the Falange that *faístas* saw as grounds for beginning a full-fledged revolution of their own. CNT propagandists heatedly equated the Spanish Right with Fascist Italy or Germany and spoke eloquently about the murder of the German anarchist writer, Erich Mühsam, as an object lesson in the struggle against fascism.[42] On April 16, 1936, the CNT and FAI expressed their general exasperation by sponsoring a one-day general strike to protest activities of the Falange, although there seemed to be more bitterness against the government than against fascism. The strike may have been an attempt to propel the CNT/FAI into a leadership role in the growing conflict now consuming Spanish society. If so, it was a miserable failure which left anarchists no better off than before.

Even a general strike could not draw attention away from the dramatic events taking place in Madrid, where Manuel Azaña had decided to depose the President of the Republic, Niceto Alcalá-Zamora, on the dubious grounds that the President had waited too long in recalling the Left to power. Alcalá-Zamora was impeached through a provision in the constitution which allowed the parliament to examine presidential policy after a second dissolution of the legislature. Many deputies were not even agreed on the constitutionality of such a move, but President Alcalá-Zamora nevertheless was dismissed so that the Popular Front could realize its more radical objectives. Unfortunately, a successor could not immediately be found, and in late April, Manuel Azaña decided to take over the presidency himself. In doing so, a natural leader of the Popular Front moved to the dim and distant presidential office. And Azaña's appointment of his close friend Santiago Casares Quiroga, a long-time enemy of anarcho-syndicalism, as the new Premier enraged the anarchists.

V. The Civil War Approaches

Reaction to these high-level changes came at the national congress of the CNT, held in Saragossa in early May 1936, almost simultaneously with Casares Quiroga's assumption of office. The outraged conferees turned to the ultra-left for leadership. The Nosotros, which recruited for the first time during the Popular Front period, found more than two hundred converts.[43] But one did not have to belong to the Nosotros to believe the major assertion of the congress: that Santiago Casares Quiroga, in his hostility towards anarchism, would encourage, or at least do nothing to prevent, the formation of anti-republican conspiracies in the army. Thus, anarchists and anarcho-syndicalists decided to form an armed confederal militia to defend the movement at all costs. A few delegates, led by Cipriano Mera, opposed such a step on grounds that the CNT ought not violate its long-standing antimilitarism. But strong pressure from the Textile and Fabric syndicate and impassioned speeches by Francisco Ascaso and the head of the union, Ricardo Montserrat, proved decisive. A base near the town of Ebro was designated as the militia center, and all syndicates were requested to pay 10 percent of their treasuries into a special militia fund. A request for arms and ammunition was dispatched to comrades in Belgium and France.

Another radical success came in the discussion of land reform. Several speakers interpreted the shift from Manuel Azaña to Santiago Casares Quiroga as a sign that cooperation with the Popular Front was now a thing of the past. "Let each group find the revolution in its own way," one anarchist insisted, and thus the congress decided to move at once towards collectivization of land despite Popular Front policy to the contrary.[44] In response to powerful speeches by Diego Abad de Santillán and Isaac Puente and ringing quotes from Peter Kropotkin's *The Conquest of Bread*, the delegates to the congress were almost unanimous in adopting the proposal. Villages were urged to seize the property of absentee landowners as soon as possible. It was imperative, Diego Abad de Santillán told the congress, that local economic and producer councils be established to forestall the counterrevolution.

Unfortunately, many delegates seemed genuinely confused about the functions of the councils, while others debated the propriety of starting a rural revolution without making an equal effort to mobilize factory councils and national industrial groups. Here, however, the CNT had still not reattained its pre-1933 membership levels. If social revolution began immediately, likelihood of urban failure might be very high.[45] The congress hesitated briefly in the face of this prospect and then decided overwhelmingly to begin the revolution. As a consequence, in the weeks afterwards rural plans went one way and the logistics of urban insurrection another, with very little coordination attempted.

That such sweeping plans could be adopted testifies to the sense of crisis and impending civil war which pervaded the congress. Unity and reunion became watchwords, with the *treintistas* providing the latter. Alarmed by the great violence now engulfing the country, they abruptly returned to the fold and were received with an enthusiasm that belied earlier sectarian differences. Several factors lay behind their return. One was the sudden death of Valeriano Orobón Fernández, the victim of a heart attack. As a major force behind the *treintista*-supported Alianza Obrera, he was the only leader who could have won mass support for it. But, in addition, socialist pressure was already creating an informal CNT-UGT alliance on labor matters and in para-military opposition to the Right, something close to the old Alianza Obrera concept. This new reality made the separation of *cenetistas* and *treintistas* meaningless. Since the CNT was in fact entering the mainstream of labor politics, as the *treintistas* had wanted all along, the moderates rejoined the radicals, closing the CNT schism almost as rapidly as it had first opened.

The socialists, in seeking their new alliance with the anarchists, were strongly influenced by the new radicalism of Francisco Largo Caballero. His revolutionary Marxism grew out of the disappointments of the Popular Front, Manuel Azaña's puzzling strategy, and his own lack of a role within the coalition. Throughout June and early July 1936, Largo Caballero continued to express a strongly felt sense of unity with the anarchists, even approaching members of the Nosotros for support.[46] This created a minor split among other socialists, with a few, like Julio Álvarez del Vayo and Rafael Vidiella, branching off with the communists to form the Unified Socialist-Communist Youth (JSU) and the Unified Socialist-Communist party of Catalonia.[47] Anarchists who once had denounced the UGT's moderation now began to fear serious communist gains if the CNT and the Largo Caballero wing of the UGT did not amalgamate their operations.

At the same time the rural situation consumed great amounts of time and attention. Since March 1936 resumption of land confiscation and redistribution had been crippled by the slowness of title transfer. All too often, the deadline for spring planting came before ownership of the land had been established. The Popular Front did the best it could, but peasants poured onto the land and illegally took possession. The Saragossa congress supported these moves, but few anarchists had the time or the ability to coordinate the collectivization process. Villagers had no recourse but to take matters into their own hands. Class lines solidified overnight in many towns, and slogan battles dominated village political life. Conservatives would creep out in the middle of the night to paint "Long live Christ the King" near the homes of militants, while anarchists and socialists dabbed UGT and CNT/FAI acronyms everywhere.[48] Sloganeering was usually followed by gunfights and riots. By July 1936, on the eve of the civil war, a tremendous fund of ill will had built up in many localities. Some of the worst acts were committed in the name of anarchism, but among anarchists themselves, the feeling of being pursued by uncontrollable pressure from below caused a paralysis of decision-making.[49]

This mood of helplessness was increased by the absence of Buenaventura Durruti. He had been hospitalized for a double hernia in June and was still recuperating during the first weeks of July. Diego Abad de Santillán travelled as often as he could to the most militant rural districts, but he was also busy reorganizing labor syndicates in Barcelona and Valencia in preparation for urban revolution. More often out of touch than not, he was seldom available for serious planning. This task most frequently fell to Francisco Ascaso and Federica Montseny, both of whom tried to expand the revolutionary alliance with the UGT and to develop the confederal militia. Unfortunately, fewer than six hundred anarchists had enlisted in the militia, and plans were cut back to weekend training in small arms drill and the use of TNT and crude grenades.[50] Many were FAI members, but the bulk of the *faístas* were spread thin throughout Huesca and other parts of Aragon or in the Catalan factories, where anarchists usually played crucial roles. The UGT did not send anyone to the base, and neither did they find the time to ratify the Saragossa agreement.

UGT cooperation with the CNT also foundered in Madrid over a construction strike which had already erupted several times since February 1936. By June no settlement seemed obtainable. CNT officials were so upset that they advised strikers to engage in economic sabotage and disruption. Alarmed, the Popular Front warned that the strike threatened to bring down the government unless some progress was soon made. Enormous pressure was exerted on the unions. Finally, on July 6, 1936, the UGT agreed to participate in a mixed jury, a step the CNT adamantly refused to accept. Once again, the two labor confederations had broken over the principle of arbitration.

147

Francisco Largo Caballero's policy of CNT-UGT cooperation now lay in ruins, and it was unlikely that it could be revived in time to meet the counterrevolution. Cipriano Mera spoke for all anarchists when he accused the socialists of lacking revolutionary unity just at the time when the Right was preparing to attack.[51] The FAI realized that there was no chance to rise before the army or the Falange staged its own revolution.

In fact, such plans were already well under way. The Unión Militar Española, a circle of conservative officers, had been conspiring actively for months to overthrow the Second Republic. The Falange also stood ready even though José Antonio Primo de Rivera had been in prison since April 1936, jailed under the Defense of the Republic act. Nevertheless, with the Left in disarray, the conspiracy led by the Generals José Sanjurjo (who died before he could return to Spain), Francisco Franco, Emilio Mola, and Manuel Goded moved towards its final stages. Opportunity came on July 12, 1936, when a Falangist assassination of a pro-republican officer prompted the murder of a leading CEDA deputy and former official in the Primo dictatorship, José Calvo Sotelo, on the evening of July 12. Only five days later, on Friday, July 17, 1936, General Francisco Franco flew to Morocco and reunion with a disaffected Spanish army of the Protectorate. Within twenty-four hours the first battle of the Spanish Civil War began.

PART THREE

The Civil War

CHAPTER SEVEN

Civil War and Revolution

Anarchism is the most constructive social philosophy worth living, fighting and, if need be, dying for. [Emma Goldman, in a letter written in 1936]

Give an anarchist a box of matches and some petrol, and he is a happy man. [Jon Burmeister, *Someone Else's War*, 1973]

I. July Days

The terrible tension of the preceding weeks ended at 5 p.m. on July 17, 1936. At that moment, the army of Spanish Morocco rose to support General Franco and the anti-republican plans of the Unión Militar. All through the night the news spread, and on Saturday, July 18, a series of successful right-wing insurrections were staged in southern Andalusia, northern Castile, western Aragon, and Navarre. The cities of Pamplona, Saragossa, Seville, and Burgos fell quickly into the hands of the military rebels, although their hold on Saragossa was not secure. The situation elsewhere was confused by rumors, which circulated with great frequency. Perhaps the best description of this state of uncertainty can be found in the opening pages of André Malraux's *Man's Hope*. A republican officer tries to call a number of military bases, only to get a mixed response, profane and slogan-filled, as each locality proclaims its allegiance. By the end of July 17, probably more than 60 percent of the regular army had gone over to General Franco, although the navy, rising to assassinate its officers, remained loyal to the Second Republic.[1]

The loyalty of Barcelona remained in doubt during the early hours of the insurrection. The CNT and FAI tried to call a plenum

151

late Friday night. Not everyone could be found, but Buenaventura Durruti, still recuperating from his operation, appeared at FAI headquarters very quickly, accompanied by members of the Nosotros. Many were already armed, since the group had been on alert for a month. This nucleus convinced the transportation syndicate that it should call a general strike. Public transportation stopped running about 10 p.m. Many neighborhoods erected barricades, and a Nosotros command post was established in the house of an FAI member not far from the Ramblas.[2]

While the Left organized as best it could, the military prepared for action slowly. Manuel Goded, the rebel general responsible for Barcelona, established his forces on Saturday and early Sunday in the Balearic Islands. According to the conspirators' plan, Barcelona would be too difficult to seize immediately from within, and creation of a safe base in the islands had top priority. Small numbers of troops under Colonel Pedralbes and General Burriel took to the streets about 5 a.m. Saturday, July 18, to hold the main squares (Cataluña, España, and Universidad), the harbor, and the airport for the troops coming in from the Balearics. Unknown to the rebels, this plan had been betrayed by air force personnel at the Prat de Llobregat base and by soldiers from the barracks of Atarazanas and San Andres.[3] Bands of loyalists successfully harassed the initial wave of rebels with crude, homemade bombs and the ancient arms that had been stored away by anarchists.[4]

The main battle took place on Sunday, July 19, 1936. An ominous quiet hung over the city early in the morning; streets and plazas remained empty of all but small squads of soldiers and militiamen. Shooting broke out now and again at the telephone building and the Hotel Colón, both occupied by the rebels. Shortly before 11 a.m. a pitched battle began around the university, where CNT members (including Angel Pestaña) managed to take and hold the plaza. About the same time anarchist forces, led by Buenaventura Durruti and Francisco Ascaso and composed of Nosotros cadres, seized the upper Ramblas and then worked their way over to the Vía Layetana and the Paralelo.[5] A military barrack on the Avenida de Icario was overrun and its machine guns rushed to the much larger military installations of San Andres and Atarazanas, where troops were preparing to reinforce rebel soldiers fighting at the university. Both barracks came under a hail of gunfire from anarchist besiegers, and a furious counterattack along the Paralelo and the Calle de San Pablo was defeated after a number of buildings had been destroyed— the most bloody moment in the fighting.[6]

Once San Andres and Atarazanas were contained, the harbor fell into loyalist hands. Any chance the rebels had of taking Barcelona was lost, since both barracks dominated the lower city, with Atarazanas well located at the foot of the Ramblas. By mid-afternoon, elements of the CNT, FAI, UGT, and Esquerra had taken most of Barcelona. Rebels were defeated at the university, in the Plaza Cataluña, and at the telephone building, even though General Goded, who had arrived to take command personally, was now committing parts of seven regular army regiments to battle.[7] By 4 p.m. Sunday a loyalist force, mainly anarchist, took the Capitanía General and other buildings of the civil government after intercepting a small column of artillery troops moving into the city. Had it not been for this success, Barcelona might have seen considerably more fighting, but now the euphoria of actually holding a center of state power drove the anarchists on with a new fervor.

In fact, the attempted *coup d'état* was almost finished in Barcelona. While fighting still engulfed the government buildings, a pitched battle broke out in the Plaza España near General Goded's headquarters. His surrender, although it did not actually come until the next morning, July 20, was assured. Wild rejoicing broke out at the magnitude of the triumph. As bad news poured in from the rest of the country, it became apparent that anarchists had managed to win the most spectacular victory of the loyalist republican side.

The cabinet of Santiago Casares Quiroga, clearly unprepared for the uprising, resigned on July 18, 1936, and was replaced by one organized by José Giral, another friend of Azaña's, who was acceptable to the Popular Front only because he was such a nonentity. But a change of cabinet did little to stem the rebel nationalists. Within a few days air and sea lifts brought the Spanish Army of Morocco to the southern coast. Andalusian military commanders supported General Franco almost unanimously, with General Gonzalo Queipo de Llano seizing Seville on July 19 while loyalist revolts in Granada and Huelva were being put down. In the North, General Mola wiped out pockets of resistance around Burgos and in parts of Leon (where Durruti's mother and several other relatives were executed) and began a drive southward on Madrid.[8] The capital remained under republican control thanks to UGT strength and the work of Cipriano Mera, David Antona, and Teodoro Mora, three major anarchist leaders in the city.[9] Valencia, Oviedo, and Bilbao also remained in loyalist hands, but Vigo, Corunna, Vallodolid, and Saragossa were lost.

Back in Barcelona early on Monday morning, the revolutionary loyalists rushed to consolidate their gains. The expropriated Casa de Cambó, one of the most modern buildings on the Vía Layetana, was made the new headquarters of the anarchist movement, outraging moderate Catalan opinion. The central police station was occupied jointly by various political factions, and under the leadership of Juan García Oliver, militia patrols began to police the city.[10] Fort Montjuich rebelled and went over to the loyalists, and finally only Atarazanas was left fighting. Durruti and Ascaso, backed now with artillery, led the final few charges. The conquest should be, to their way of thinking, a crucible, a severe, searching test of martial ability, a way of seeking out men for the military campaigns ahead. As it turned out, the battle became a tragedy. Francisco Ascaso was killed in the final moments, dying at the head of the volunteers who took up arms against the rebels. Buenaventura Durruti narrowly avoided death and twice was slightly wounded.

The death of Francisco Ascaso was a severe blow to the anarchists. He and Durruti had one of the most remarkable friendships in radical history. Looking back at their exploits, it is difficult to separate the two men. In general, Francisco Ascaso appeared to be the more reflective of the two, perhaps better educated as a youth (although he had only four years of instruction), more able to express his feelings. Seen from our own age, which is cynical about such things, their friendship can only be summarized as a revolutionary partnership, an incredible voyage by a pair of Spanish peasants through the politics and crime of Latin America. Western Europe, Africa, and Spain. In many situations there was something of the *pícaro* about them, not in the sense of *Lazarello de Tormes*, but more in remaining what they were, of not craving publicity or seeking a large following, of constantly working for a goal while staying very much as they always had been. Peasant rebels in an urban, industrial century, as political individualists representing the collective revolutionary dream of the countryside, unfettered by vanguardism or any of the other rigorous dialectics of the modern Left, they had a certain roguish quality. One survivor who remembers Ascaso called him "one of the last of the nineteenth-century libertarians," a radical thrown up by the great upheavals of the early capitalist era when everything was much more black and white than in the 1930s.[11] Still, had Francisco Ascaso lived, the anarchists might have been greatly strengthened during the civil war, and Buenaventura Durruti might not have had to shoulder so many burdens alone.

II. The Militia Army

After the fall of Atarazanas, Barcelona was momentarily safe from nationalist attack. The loyalty of General Martínez Monje and the strong presence of radical sailors kept Valencia with the Second Republic.[12] Elsewhere, Lerida had fallen briefly to the rebels, but when General Goded failed in Barcelona, Lerida was abandoned, and the nationalists retreated into Aragon, executing Popular Front sympathizers along the way. In Saragossa the loyalists failed to dislodge General Miguel Cabanellas, who at the last moment joined the military uprising. The CNT called a general strike, and pitched battles between syndicalists and soldiers continued for a week. Miguel Chueca, head of the Aragonese CNT, hurriedly sent an appeal for help to his comrades in Barcelona. Almost as soon as fighting in the Catalan capital stopped, on Monday, July 20, plans were made to relieve Saragossa.

Many events intervened in the four days before help could be sent. Late on Sunday, July 19, Luis Companys called together representatives of the Catalans, Trotskyists, socialists, communists, and anarchists to shape what soon would become the Anti-Fascist Militia Committee. The meeting continued almost without interruption on Monday and Tuesday, with Juan García Oliver speaking for the Nosotros, Diego Abad de Santillán for the FAI, and Federica Montseny (among others) for the CNT. At first there was a great deal of bickering. Luis Companys blamed anarchists for doing needless damage to ecclesiastical property. Federica Montseny rejected the accusation emphatically and countercharged that the Catalans hoped to discredit anarchism for their own purposes. Why, she asked, had Luis Companys refused in the week before the revolt to release militants from jail while arresting others for carrying arms?[13] Another quarrel developed over whether the Trotskyist POUM had a large enough membership to qualify for representation on the committee.[14]

Finally these issues were put aside, since the crisis overshadowed old animosities. Anarchists were catapulted into political cooperation of a new kind by participating in a revolutionary committee that shared administrative power with Luis Company's regional government. Hereafter they were committed to assist in the running of the Catalan state, a controversial step no previous anarchist group, save possibly Nestor Makhno's, had ever taken.[15] Diego Abad de Santillán was typical of the majority who saw no other choice. Paralysis of the republican government in Madrid and continued advances by nationalist forces threatened to envelop Spain in fascism. It was up to the anarchists to transform the militia committee into a truly revolutionary body.[16] Max Nettlau expressed this attitude best when he told his Spanish comrades: "Today we revolt, tomorrow we criticize."[17] The movement had to make the best of existing circumstances and postpone difficult questions until later.

Once these political considerations were out of the way, the committee quickly got down to the business of fulfilling its military role. On Monday it decided to put a militia army into the field by Thursday, with Buenaventura Durruti as its political commander-in-chief. At first, however, Durruti remained closeted with Francisco Ascaso's family and their old comrades. The funeral took place on Tuesday, July 21, when Ascaso's body was carried through the streets of Barcelona as large crowds looked on. Durruti eulogized Ascaso as "the first victim of the civil war . . . but also the first martyr of the revolution," an undertaking that he vowed would end triumphantly.[18]

Late in the day Buenaventura Durruti plunged into the job of preparing his army, which was mired in a chaos of recruiting, finding supplies, and organizing the campaign. Diego Abad de Santillán administered requisitions, while Major José Salavera, a regular army officer, took charge of local defense. Even on Thursday the militia lacked significant amounts of arms and men, until whole syndicates began to volunteer.[19] Those who had received earlier training at the Ebro center provided a barely sufficient staff of military instructors and in order to obtain experienced men, the militia was reduced finally to advertising in *Solidaridad Obrera* for present or former regular army members. Still enlistments lagged, and Abad de Santillán had to appeal directly to the political parties for aid, quickly losing his hope that the militia might remain unfactionalized. Overnight, columns bearing the names of Lenin, Maurín (POUM), Macià and Companys (Esquerra), Caballero and Claridad (UGT), and Carlos Marx (PSUC) appeared to join the militia. Abad de Santillán commented: "What does Karl Marx have to do with our age or our struggle?"[20]

Finally, late Thursday afternoon, July 23, the first troops left Barcelona for the Aragon front. Command was slightly altered by the addition of a radical former army major, Antonio Pérez Farras, as military commander-in-chief, a change Buenaventura Durruti himself requested, doubting his own capacity for military command. An informal executive committee of the militia army came into being, composed primarily of Nosotros members such as Ricardo Sanz, Juan García Oliver, and several party representatives. Behind the lines, Diego Abad de Santillán became chief liaison officer of the militia in Barcelona, while Federica Montseny had the responsibility of forming a second army, called Tierra y Libertad, to be sent to the front later. Almost simultaneously, a smaller column, led by Pedro Jiménez de la Beraza, took up a position on the French frontier to forestall nationalist efforts to block communications with France. A final group began preparations to occupy the Balearics.

Approximately three thousand men, a majority of them anarchists, left Barcelona for Aragon by Friday evening, July 25. Most of those in the Aguiluchos (the Young Eagle group), about 500 in all, had been recruited by Juan García Oliver from the FAI. A smaller unit of anarchists, led by Juan Alvadetreco and Captain Manuel Tortosa, marched under Francisco Ascaso's name. These two militia groups reached Lerida by a variety of routes, stopping in villages along the way to recruit and to hold drumhead trials of priests, large landowners, and Civil Guards which usually ended in execution. No accurate count of these executions ever has been made. In many cases the villages already had been the scene of bitter fighting, and many of the atrocities that occurred had been performed by local groups (although the death of Isaac Puente in Aragon did provoke some atrocities by militiamen).[21] The columns paid more attention to propagandizing in favor of the revolution and encouraging the formation of communes than to seeking revolutionary justice.

Once the columns reached Lerida, militiamen provided by the political parties joined the advance units. But the expected reinforcements from Valencia did not arrive. In all, three columns had been raised: the Iron Column, all anarchist; the socialist "Ghost" column; and a mixed regiment. Most of the militia were destined for Madrid, the obvious target of the northward-bound nationalist armies. The Iron Column branched off towards Teruel, only to be attacked by Franco supporters. Teruel thus continued to exist as a nationalist enclave in republican territory. The other two columns reinforced Madrid.

The status of Valencia remained uncertain through July. The province was the object of a three-cornered struggle between the CNT/FAI, the republican government, and the Valencia garrison (a mixture of ideological factions), which was not disarmed until the Popular Front gained the upper hand in early August. The result of this struggle was that the militia army received little aid from the South. Urgent messages passed between Lerida and Valencia concerning reinforcements, but assistance could not be guaranteed. Supporters of Durruti had to redouble their efforts to recruit additional personnel in the North.

The advance into Aragon thus began without the expected manpower or supplies, although Lerida did provide an estimated 1,500 volunteers. On Monday, July 27, the militia divided its forces in two, with half moving along the Barbastro-Huesca highway and half on the main Lerida-Saragossa road. The reception by peasants along the Barbastro route was joyous. It was a real heartland of rural anarchism, and many local defense juntas had been formed. Rough terrain and lack of transport proved to be the only major obstacles, slowing the columns to a crawl and giving the nationalist general Cabanellas vitally necessary time to fortify Saragossa. His retreat from Lerida earlier had concentrated upon destruction of bridges and mountainous sections of the roads, which the militia army was not equipped to repair. Although a lack of motorized vehicles made it primarily a foot brigade, the state of the highways kept artillery at the rear and delayed the resupply process. The northern route could reprovision the militia from local produce, but there were few towns on the main highway to supply food. All these problems slowed down the advance upon Saragossa and placed serious strains upon the hastily put-together force.

Only a great groundswell of support for the militia in Barcelona, especially from foreign exiles, kept it going during the first difficult weeks. Camillo Berneri, an Italian anarchist who had been in and out of Mussolini's jails, was one of the volunteers. He had fled Italy the year before the outbreak of the Spanish Civil War and settled in Barcelona with other libertarian exiles, finally starting his own paper, *Guerra di Classes,* one of the loudest voices against fascism and Stalinism.[22] George Orwell, author of the famous *Homage to Catalonia,* joined one of the militia army's POUM units in December 1936.[23] Helmut Rüdiger, founder of the German Information Service (GIS), which often paid the fares of political exiles from distant European points to Spain, enlisted many German anti-fascist exiles. Under GIS auspices, men flocked to the army. Samuel Kaplan, a German-Jewish anarchist from Frankfort, Karl Brauner, an Austrian syndicalist, Georg Roth, a Viennese intellectual, and two Bulgarian anarchists, Nicolas Mladenoff and Kano Bratinof, were among the volunteers.[24] In the United States, Maximiliano Olay, founder of a Spanish-language newspaper, *Free Society,* sent money and several young volunteers.[25] Occasional Mexicans and Argentines could be found in the ranks, along with many volunteers from Leon, who were inspired by the example of their countryman, Buenaventura Durruti.

Initially, supplies for these men were obtained illegally. New trucks from the General Motors plant near Barcelona were simply driven away. Equipment to manufacture Mausers was smuggled on board freighters at Santander or flown in a Douglas transport to Barcelona for a new arms factory. This took time, and until production began, Durruti depended upon whatever he could confiscate. The guns from San Andres, Atarazanas, and Civil Guard storehouses armed the militia during the first months of the campaign. There was a similar shortage of planes since many of the aircraft of Prat de Llobregot were diverted to the Balearics or to Madrid.[26] Diego Abad de Santillán constantly complained about the supply situation at early meetings of the Anti-Fascist Militia Committee, but little could be done to regularize procurement or production.[27] In the midst of a revolution and a civil war, difficulties proved to be the rule rather than the exception.

Meantime, the militia army slowly headed west, harassed by the air attacks of the nationalists, who used a base at Logrono to excellent advantage.[28] Fraga and Bujaraloz fell on August 4, 1936, opening the road to the villages of Gelsa, Velilla, Pina y Osera, Almolda la Naja, Castejon de Nonegros, Monegrillo, and finally Alfajarin, thirty miles east of Saragossa. But by August 12 the army could move no further, having outrun its lines of supply without pausing to replace casualties or form itself into a more cohesive unit. Durruti feared that the nationalists might take advantage of these weaknesses to attack the southern flank, bordering the Ebro river, unless that sector was strengthened at once. So Alfajarin became the forward post of the militia army. Both sides settled down for a temporary seige of Saragossa which was still held by nationalist forces. General Emilio Mola began rushing Carlist militia (the ultra-Catholic Requetés) from Navarre to Saragossa, until that city looked like a permanent fortification.[29]

The Aragon line ran for six hundred kilometers from the Pyrenees to southern Aragon. Lerida was the rearguard center, with lesser areas of militia command at Sarinena and Barbastro in the north, Fraga, Bujaraloz, and Caspe in the center, and Alcaniz in the south. The conquered territory was also divided into political zones, with the POUM controlling Villaba, the FAI-dominated Aguiluchos and Ascaso columns holding the Huesca area, and the Trueba-Del Banio column, a mixed political regiment, administering Tardienta. In the mountains northeast of the line around Alcubierre (including

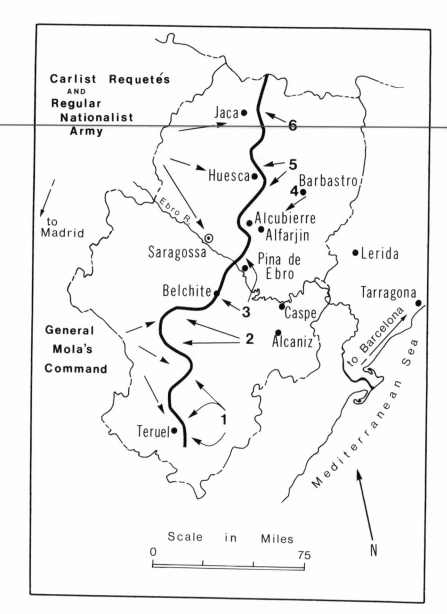

The Campaign in Aragon

The heavy line marks the front in September 1936. The nationalists moving east were countered by the republican forces identified as follows: (1) Tierra y Libertad, Iron Column, Pachín; (2) Commander Ortiz, POUM, various mixed brigades; (3) Durruti, Tierra y Libertad, Solidaridad Obrera, CNT and FAI brigades; (4) Pérez Farras, Nosotros, Metal Workers, Transport Syndicate, various foreign groups; (5) García Oliver, Aguiluchos, Alvade-treco and Tortosa (Ascaso Column); (6) POUM, Frontier Regiments.

La Naja, Alcubierre, and Lecinena), the POUM and UGT cadres were strong. The Durruti column held an area from Alcubierre to the left bank of the Ebro.

During the pause, the militia army developed its most noticeable characteristics. Buenaventura Durruti was a charismatic leader who commanded by inspiration. He was indefatigable, usually impatient with administrative details, sometimes fighting beside his own men. Despite his earlier reluctance to become a military planner, he participated in many planning sessions and showed a good strategic sense. Had he followed his inclination to continue past Huesca to cut off Saragossa, the later unsuccessful frontal attacks might not have been necessary. But his assistants felt that the militia forces were not strong enough to be permanently divided, and available transport was not mobilized to keep the approaches of Saragossa from being fortified.

Buenaventura Durruti depended upon inspiration to lead his army. He spoke of Nestor Makhno's Ukrainian guerrillas as the organizational precedent for the militia in Aragon, a "force of pure action" that would attract militant new participants into the anarchist ranks.[30] One combatant, caught in a firefight west of Bujaraloz, looked up to see Durruti at the head of the patrol throwing grenades; another remembers him accepting rejection of his advice on a particular strategy without pulling rank.[31] The war, at least for the moment, was another adventure to be relished, like so many of his earlier experiences. The depression caused by the deaths of his mother and Francisco Ascaso lifted somewhat. At least in public, he was his old self again.

Under Durruti, the militia army quickly became embued with anarchist principles. Rank had only minimal importance. All units elected their officers, most of whom were non-commissioned; few captains or lieutenants were deemed necessary. Representatives elected to the Council of Workers and Soldiers wielded the real power. Each unit elected one man to present its wishes to the army at large. The council thrashed out most of the militia plans, even down to where and when to advance, what units to use, and how to administer liberated territory. Commanders met with council members and considered them their staff. Within each unit, council members had few prerogatives to distinguish them from the average militiaman. They were not commissars in the Red Army sense (as under the system later adopted by the republican army), although occasionally Durruti's staff did appoint councillors who provided political instruction to companies filled with former servicemen or

161

peasants. But for the most part there was little need for ideological coercion, since the army was filled with true believers in the libertarian revolution.

In other ways the democratic structure of the militia army did cause difficult problems. Much was later made of the refusals of units to accept orders, of the chaos that a non-authoritarian army can cause, and the inefficiencies that often occurred.[32] Some of these criticisms were politically motivated, and a few were simply ridiculous. No army two or three weeks old could find the time to streamline its procedures while simultaneously fighting in the field. That supplies were wasted, the most common charge, was partly true, but it was used to explain away the more complex and political reasons why Madrid failed to furnish substantial aid. Chaos in Aragon was quite common, but Aragon was a war zone, after all. The refusal of units to fight grew out of the addition of non-anarchist forces to the army. In other situations, POUM and UGT or PSUC troops objected to anarchist leadership or found it difficult to cooperate in larger operations, sometimes not so much out of cowardice as out of conviction. But even here the overwhelming radicalism of most militia troops at the start of the civil war provided a common purpose and gave the army enthusiasm.

Among the various units within the militia army, Tierra y Libertad, official militia of the Catalan FAI under the leadership of Juan Ramos, compiled one of the best records among front-line groups. When the decision was made on August 23, 1936, to cross the Ebro river and strike south against nationalist forces at Belchite, the unit fought off far superior numbers despite the loss of Ramos and 360 other casualties. It retreated only when a shortage of gasoline crippled supply operations and dictated a pullback.[33] The Pachín group, a terrorist offshoot of the Nosotros formed in 1935 and led by Antonio Seba Amoros, showed similar tenacity in battle. The Nosotros itself went to war *en masse*. Ricardo Sanz assumed responsibility for militia training at Pedralbas. Juan García Oliver led the Aguiluchos group for a time, Gregorio Jover the Ascaso Column, Antonio Ortíz a mixed brigade holding the Ebro flank, Aurelio Fernández joined the Anti-Fascist Militia Committee in Barcelona.[34] The closeness of the group kept the situation from becoming one of competing *generalisimos*, with each autonomous in his own area, although Juan García Oliver's frustration on the reduced Huesca front occasionally did lead to minor friction.[35]

The basic problems of the militia army were supply shortages and a lack of support from Madrid. The civil war had started with too great a rush for all factions of the Second Republic to agree upon basic logistics. As a result, the supply situation remained critical almost from the very beginning. After the Belchite foray cost the militia dearly in soldiers and materials, headway was permanently lost. Buenaventura Durruti was reduced to having part of his forces make weapons at the front under the direction of "Braulio" (Valgirio Prieto Robles), the inventor of a simple hand grenade.[36] Loss of activists like Juan Ramos created a serious leadership problem and limited use of guerrilla bands (which depended heavily upon good leaders for effectiveness) in southern Aragon, where the topography favored such strategy. And as the battle turned in favor of the nationalists in this area, Durruti was forced to throw units together without consideration for military experience or skills. With plenty of front-line soldiers but few supply officers or logistical groups, the militia seemed to consist entirely of infantry or artillery men. Quartermasters were almost nonexistent; anarchists did not want to mind the store. These kinds of inconsistences could be found throughout Aragon; there was no basic structure to the militia except political sectarianism. Units fought together for political principle, not to serve particular military needs.

III. Revolution in the Rearguard

The revolution in Barcelona blanketed Catalonia with a revolutionary euphoria that converted the CNT and FAI into dominant factions almost overnight. Perhaps the best example of this transformation was the appearance on July 29, 1936, of "Radio CNT-FAI," a series of programs from 6 p.m. to midnight presenting anarchist news and talks. The station had been government-owned until July 25, when the Anti-Fascist Militia Committee took over.[37] Now it produced readings from Peter Kropotkin and Michael Bakunin, foreign-language commentaries aimed at exiles in the militia, recordings of speeches made by major European anarchists, and even on several occasions "kitchen hints," for the communal cooks who did not know how to stretch a recipe to feed a whole village. *Solidaridad Obrera*, suddenly the largest-selling newspaper in Barcelona, printed the program each day, and no doubt the station's offerings were an effective propaganda device, since radio was still a novelty in Spain.

Radio was just one of many new activities which anarchists organized. Femmes Libres and the anarchist youth emerged to become

163

large, active movements, sponsoring rallies, educational compaigns, and drives to collect money, scrap, and whatever else was necessary for the war effort.[38] The FAI gave them a considerable role, too, in the worker patrols that took over civil police work.[39]

Other new groups developed by the CNT/FAI included the *comité pro escuela nueva unificada*, a popular education group; *comités de abastos*, neighborhood food-supply committees; *comités de empresa de las colectivizaciones*, worker councils in the collectivized industries; and *comités de control de las industrias no colectivizadas*, worker councils in the smaller, still private businesses. And there was a host of other, less important groups.[40] Sometimes special councils emerged very rapidly to deal with special problems. At the Barcelona docks in early August, stevedores who felt that their wages and working conditions had not changed significantly demanded their own council to improve the waterfront's political representation.[41] It was part of the anarchists' philosophy to organize alternative, non-state-controlled institutions whenever possible. Their most creative period came in July and August 1936.

With all this activity, it was difficult not to notice how anarchist in appearance Barcelona had become. CNT/FAI armbands were worn, and CNT/FAI signs and banners were painted or plastered on every available wall and on buses, cars, and trains as well, usually courtesy of the painters' syndicate. Anarchist headquarters on Vía Layetana (later changed to Vía Durruti) had a mural several stories high, and so did the telephone building. Hundreds of open-air rallies and demonstrations were held in the parks, and the Barcelona bullring was a favored place for big meetings of the two organizations. Syndicates decorated factories with anti-fascist slogans of every description, happily proclaiming their allegiance. Other political factions also covered the city with their own signs and banners, but the anarchists had a special zest the others did not possess. In many respects the mood of Barcelona in the late summer of 1936 was festive.

Amid this euphoria, the CNT and FAI voted overwhelmingly to unite, creating the Movimiento Libertario Español (MLE) as the agency of their unity. Little changed, as both kept their organizational structures. Twelve representatives from each body met periodically to coordinate policy and activities. Most cooperation came on matters of publicity and fund raising, but youth groups merged into a new Juventudes Libertarias.[42] To everyone involved, the step was a great improvement over the sectarian spirit that had ruled only a few short months previously, though it is hard to judge how enthusiastic *faístas* were about the rehabilitation of former *treintistas* like Juan Peiró or the appearance of strong syndicalist propaganda in the published materials of the MLE.[43]

Still, this was not the moment to fight old battles again. Fascism loomed too large for internal disputes to have great impact. The quick victory of the revolution in Barcelona also pacified the normal combativeness of the *faístas*. "The CNT and FAI," Helmut Rüdiger wrote, "have made history."[44] But this "victory" led to another problem. Many anarchists and syndicalists, fooled by the triumph in Catalonia, felt that the civil war would soon be won. Anticipating revolutionary success, both the CNT and the FAI adopted a moderate tone designed to reassure Spaniards that anarchist rule would be just and tolerant. A joint plenum of the Catalan CNT/FAI rejected totalitarianism on July 28 and voted for collaboration with the Anti-Fascist Militia Committee.[45] The strongest advocate of this step was Horacio Prieto, the national CNT secretary, but others chimed in to support him. Federica Montseny argued that if the anarchists did not take a role in this *de facto* government, a dictatorship "worse than Stalin's" would result.[46] The movement had no choice but to collaborate; the alternative was fascism. Participation of bourgeois regionalists and other "statist" factions in the work of the committee and its consultations with Luis Companys' cabinet were conveniently overlooked, although they would eventually provoke bitter debate.

Even so, the anarchists did not rush into a partnership with the forces they had so long condemned. During early August 1936 the CNT/FAI prevented recognition of the Anti-Fascist Militia Committee as the official Catalan government, which for all practical purposes it was. Representatives of the POUM and the PSUC were forced to resign the government jobs they had taken in the days after July 18–19.

In the end, however, this non-political tone could not be maintained. After July 24, 1936, all government officeholders were forced to join parties of the Popular Front. The fiction that the CNT/FAI had been a member of the coalition allowed anarchists to become government employees. Others played important roles on behalf of the Catalan government. In August 1936, Emilio Santana, the national secretary of the CGT Portuguese syndicalist party-in-exile, was sent to Great Britain to raise money and buy arms.[47] Facundo Roca and Augustin Souchy negotiated with Moroccans on August 12, 1936, in Paris. The CNT/FAI promised to abandon all Spanish territory in Morocco if Berber soldiers in General Franco's nationalist army somehow could be lured away.[48] Other anarcho-

165

syndicalists were dispatched to Madrid to coordinate the Catalan war effort with that of the republican government. Diego Abad de Santillán and Aurelio Fernández played major roles on the Anti-Fascist Militia Committee.

But many anarchists still hung back from openly joining the Catalan government. An official explanation of this reluctance mentioned the possibly negative foreign reaction to anarchist participation.[49] In private, the CNT was having difficulty with FAI elements who did not think it proper to take a political role. Former *treintistas* argued that the situation created by the civil war justified the use of a "political" sense. They resurrected Salvador Seguí's scheme of neo-syndicalism to justify political participation as the preliminary organization of the masses prior to revolution. The *faísta* failure in the three putsches against the Republic underscored the need for a new policy. The advice of the *treintistas* carried some weight, particularly since most revolutionary anarchists now were away fighting in Aragon.

In any case, the CNT and FAI did not have the time or the perspective to weigh these arguments long or carefully. They knew that Madrid might be forced to accept aid from the USSR, thus increasing competition from the communists. In Catalonia, they faced in Luis Companys a regionalist leader who, while sympathetic to the anarchists, had won a big victory in the elections of March 1936 through the strength of his commitment to autonomy.[50] The fact that, as one writer had observed, "within every Catalan there is an anarchist" did not mean that Luis Companys was willing to subordinate regionalism to anarchism.[51]

This left two options open to the CNT/FAI. The most natural course would have been to sever Catalonia from the rest of Spain in order to develop a revolutionary republic. But this would have played into the hands of the Catalan regionalists, since secession had long been an Esquerra issue. At worst, it might have caused a civil war within the civil war.

The other option was to establish a Council of National Defense, composed of all factions, which would be guided by council communism as the philosophy that appealed best to workers, peasants, and regionalists.[52] In this way, the last vestiges of formal national government would be replaced by a broadly based defense council acceptable to anarchists. As the logical successor to the Popular Front, this council would expand anarchist influence outside Catalonia while containing regionalism and communism. Anarchism, of course, would stay pure of any collaborationist, "political" taint.

Who developed this latter approach remains a mystery. The

AIT did not, if Emma Goldman is to be believed. She noted that Alexander Shapiro and the secretariat in Paris gave no advice to their Spanish comrades in July or August 1936.[53] Horacio Prieto and Federica Montseny leaned towards a policy of cooperation with Madrid that left political questions unresolved until the end of the war.[54] Buenaventura Durruti, absorbed in his campaign, expected the military struggle to create a stronger revolutionary consciousness. Only Diego Abad de Santillán enthusiastically supported the concept of a Council of National Defense. The idea was consistent with his writings, and he discussed it on many occasions, but without mentioning its authorship.[55] Perhaps it was his idea that the proposal be sent to Madrid on August 16, 1936. There it joined many other projects that the Giral cabinet ignored. The republican government in Madrid lived in chaos, unable to manage the war. A serious proposal to alter the structure of government had little chance of consideration.

In the meantime, the pressure of daily crises forced a working relationship between anarchists and state institutions. The Basque CNT entered the Bilbao defense junta on August 13, 1936, pleading military necessity and the desirability of maintaining popular unity against fascism.[56] The Catalan CNT, meeting on September 15, stumbled upon a formula for participation in what they called a "de-politicized" government.[57] About all this seemed to mean was that the word "committee" would be substituted for the word "government."[58] An ill-defined and *ad hoc* relationship slowly grew and expanded, while the content of anarchism shrank. The war took up most of the CNT/FAI's energy, and the Anti-Fascist Militia Committee absorbed what was left. The problem was one of survival; theoretical issues were momentarily forgotten.

IV. Revolutionary Government

Revolutionary government in Catalonia started functioning on July 20, 1936, with the creation of the militia committee. Its functions paralleled and often overlapped those of Luis Companys' cabinet until August 2, when the Catalan parliament, in one of its infrequent meetings, granted the Premier the right to rule by decree. Two days later he agreed to share this power with the committee, thus yoking cabinet and committee together in a dyarchy. On August 20 the new government claimed the sole right to issue passports and collect customs fees in Catalonia. On August 30 it announced that Catalonia was no longer subject to laws made in Madrid.[59] In the tumult of war there was little the republican government could do about the independence being asserted in the Northeast.

On paper this dyarchy looked decidedly odd. The cabinet and regular departments of government continued to function, but revolutionary institutions were constructed alongside them and sometimes served the same functions. The two most important revolutionary instrumentalities were the Anti-Fascist Militia Committee, charged with mobilizing the war effort, and the Catalan Economic Council (Consejo de Económico de Cataluña), founded on August 11 as a fifteen-member board with specific control over the Catalan economy. At a lower level, somewhat like committees of public safety, control patrols (patrullas de control) developed into organs of revolutionary justice with quasi-police powers, controlling 700 (later expanded to 1,500) justices and security officers. At a still lower level, various groups and councils operated to solve specific problems: food committees, councils for collective industries, and small business councils.

Even the top two levels on the revolutionary side of the dyarchy often overlapped and duplicated functions. Heads of factory councils could receive orders from both the militia committee and the economic council. Orders might often be contradictory, although theoretically the needs of the former overrode those of the latter. The most significant aspect of the militia committee was its tenuous links with the control patrols and other lower-level committees and councils, more from similarity of politics than by delegated power. Sometimes patrols recruited for the militia committee or organized rudimentary military training among youth groups and older men. Food committees collected rations or clothing and shoes for soldiers. On other occasions, the cabinet did these same jobs; less frequently, so did various political parties. Lines of authority tended to become indistinct, as was perhaps only proper in an anarchist revolution.

Three places on the Anti-Fascist Militia Committee were allocated to the CNT, two to the FAI, four to the Esquerra, three to the UGT, and one apiece to the PSUC and the POUM. Jaime Miravittles of the Esquerra was general secretary of the committee, supervising a staff which grew to six hundred in a month. Most committee work was performed by a series of subcommittees. Two militia subcommittees operated as recruiting boards and general supervisors for the Barcelona militia (essentially training units) and the militia in the field. Buenaventura Durruti nominally headed the latter subcommittee, although he was almost always absent from its meetings because of his obligations in the field.

The second area was operations, where three subcommittees operated: investigation and vigilance, food, and transportation.[60] Juan García Oliver supervised all three areas, although he too was usually absent on military duty. Anarchist control of investigation and vigilance was almost total: Aurelio Fernández, José Asens, Rafael Vidiella, and Tomás Fábregas belonged to this subcommittee. It worked closely with control patrols and was responsible for the strong FAI make-up of these groups. Angel Samblancat, the Catalan Minister of Justice, often sat on the subcommittee and strongly supported its decisions. José Torrents and Diego Abad de Santillán led the food subcommittee and used its powers to collectivize food industries. The transportation subcommittee worked closely with CNT and UGT rail syndicates in taking control of that industry.

The Anti-Fascist Militia Committee also created another body almost as important as itself. This was the Council of Aragon, established on September 15, 1936, to administer territory seized by the militia army. It had twenty-five members representing various political factions and the communes, most elected by peasant and worker groups.[61] The council was responsible for development of public works, education, public health, and other matters too difficult for individual collectives to handle. Because of the war, most of its work lay in provisioning the army, organizing a rural constabulary, and developing cottage industries for the manufacture of small weapons. Self-government was an old Aragonese ideal, and council delegates participated with considerable enthusiasm.[62] But the war severely limited operations, and financial dependency upon Catalonia introduced a great deal of uncertainty.

The Catalan Economic Council was another new institution, first formed on August 11, 1936. Its fifteen members plunged into work at a feverish pace. Anarchists claimed that the council brought industrial peace, reduced unemployment from 65,000 to zero, and reduced the power of foreign companies in Catalonia—but these were, in fact, effects of the civil war rather than of the council's work.[63] Much of that work amplified what the cabinet and Anti-Fascist Militia Committee had done earlier. The principle of collectivization dated back to July 21, 1936. Revolutionary control of private banks began on July 25, and a day later the labor minister decreed a forty-hour week, a 15 percent wage increase, and full recognition of trade unions.[64] On July 31 all rents were cut by a quarter, and on August 6, labor courts gave workers quick and popular justice in cases of political discrimination, illegal labor practices, or hostile management decisions. The council embarked upon a program to increase collectivization by drawing upon funds from a Catalan Industrial Bank, the latter an institution created on July 30 by seizing the private accounts of fascist and nationalist supporters. But after the collectivization program was announced, the bank ran into difficulties, since only anarchists were on record as supporting full collectivization. Catalan regionalists, who made up half the council, showed considerably less enthusiasm.[65]

In the midst of this division, Diego Abad de Santillán had the most decisive influence among the anarchist councillors. He drew up a list of priorities which included supporting the war effort, developing industrial freedom, simplifying the economy, and ending rural exploitation as a means of obtaining cheap foodstuffs.[66] He fought particularly hard for adoption of *talleres confederales*, or socialized industries. All businesses in a particular field, even including suppliers, were collectivized, or at least placed under the same priorities and rules.[67] Railways and transport were the first industries to be reorganized, followed by the steel and automotive industries. Industries already nationalized by the dictatorship, like CAMPSA, the government oil monopoly, were placed under worker control. Syndicates and plant or store councils provided management of these industries under direction of the economic council. In September 1936 the economic council created its own agency, the Council of Collectivized Industries, and a counterpart, the Council of Uncollectivized Industries, to provide better coordination.[68] This step anticipated creation of the fourteen industrial councils outlined in *El organismo económico*, but time intervened before they came into being. However, local and regional councils did proliferate.

How well did these new arrangements work? Coal was always in critical undersupply, since the nationalist army in Saragossa blocked the rail lines from Asturias to Barcelona, and the German and Italian navies harassed maritime transportation. Steel production declined sharply in Catalonia because of the civil war. In other areas, anarchists claimed progress in the development of several electrical projects using confiscated property of La Canadiense and actually increased production in textiles and dairy products.[69] Most other industries held fairly steady or declined slightly. Between August 1936 and December 1937 military industries produced sixty million Mauser bullets, four thousand artillery shells a month, a thousand kilos of gunpowder a day, and some specialized military equipment.[70] On the deficit side, truck production at the General Motors plant dropped by about a quarter.[71] The problem of plant maintenance constantly plagued worker managers.

170

A chief problem was lack of capital. The Bank of Collectivized Industries estimated that the flight of capital from Catalonia in the two weeks prior to the generals' revolt emptied 75 percent of all accounts in the banks. To remedy the situation the Catalan regional government called for war loans on September 8 and made plans to float bond issues. But little money was raised, and Catalan industry remained without investment capital for the next few months.

National politics caused other problems. Madrid, increasingly communist-dominated, believed that the economic revolution should be postponed until the civil war was won. Anarchists disagreed and continued collectivization. When Madrid retaliated by refusing to allow CAMPSA to sell gasoline to the militia army, CNT members at the General Motors plant refused to allow their trucks to be sent to the capital.[72] This kind of internecine warfare was a daily occurrence that drastically limited the Catalan economic revolution. On the few occasions when entirely new plants were built, they were almost total failures because Madrid did not furnish sufficient capital resources.[73]

Justice, through the control patrols, was another partial failure. Revolutionary law depended upon rather arbitrary standards. Anarchists sometimes behaved with restraint but then exacted terrible vengeance when it was least expected. Occasionally a glint of humor surfaced, as when a former smuggler was appointed to become chief of the border patrol, but such occurrences were infrequent.[74] Priests were assassinated one moment and saved the next. A vague category of "social crimes" forced rich women to scrub the floors of CNT/FAI headquarters, while the desertion of militiamen went unpunished.[75] Perhaps a civil war always brings retribution and irrationality, but in general the control patrols provided simply another form of class justice, a problem Spain had suffered from long enough already. The patrols spent too much time settling old scores and waging war against bourgeois society. Justification came from the atrocities committed by nationalists behind their own lines, but in Catalonia the control patrols antagonized those who otherwise might have supported the Second Republic. A better administration of justice could have neutralized bourgeois Catalans and at the very least permitted the anarchists more time to consolidate their position.

Nothing contributed more to the difficulties encountered in maintaining a just legal system than the action taken on August 6, 1936, when the Catalan Attorney-General dismissed all cases pending from the revolutionary disorder of July 19–21, 1936. Many of these cases had less to do with resistance to the generals' revolt than

171

with theft and other petty crimes. The crime situation quickly became so bad that on August 10, 1936, the FAI actually demanded
continuation of some form of justice. Federica Montseny suggested
that the informal patrols already in the streets be formalized.[76] The
militia committee responded by recognizing the patrols as a major
agency for revolutionary law enforcement. For the first time since
1844, Civil Guards disappeared from the streets and highways in
Catalonia—loyalists among them being shipped off to the front,
while nationalists were jailed and often executed.

Diego Abad de Santillán and Federica Montseny built the control patrols, but neither stayed at their head for very long.[77] Angel
Samblancat assumed control, using his office of Attorney-General to
sanction the groups (the best example of close Catalan regionalist
cooperation in the revolution). The FAI provided judges, while the
CNT furnished police personnel; altogether 325 out of the first 700
enlistees in the patrols were anarchists or anarcho-syndicalists.[78]
Members of the investigation and vigilance board of the militia committee sometimes heard appeals, and they represented control patrols
in larger matters. Conflict with militiamen on leave in Barcelona was
one of the patrols' greatest difficulties. Angel Samblancat felt that the
riotous militia misconduct in Barcelona encouraged chaos. When he
tried to get patrols to crack down, the militia committee overruled his
action.[79] Eventually patrols were regularized and their authority
strengthened, with eleven districts linked by a Comité Central de
Patrullas that coordinated efforts to tighten justice.[80] The plan succeeded in bringing the militia under some degree of control.

Control patrols also played a major role in the social revolution.
Radicals supplied patrols with lists of suspects who had "fascist" lean-
ings. In this way a large number of people were arrested and interro-
gated. Many ended up in front of firing squads, although the exact
number is subject to dispute. One observer claimed that 25,000 were
executed in the two months following the generals' revolt.[81] Another
believed that more than a hundred executions took place each day
between July 20 and September 9, 1936, a total of about six thousand.[82] Some have doubted the responsibility of control patrols in
many cases, since a majority of the executions came in the first days of
revolution when property was expropriated—a matter which greatly
excited passions.[83] The British legation in Barcelona estimated that
eighty executions took place a day, a total of approximately 4,200 for
the same period.[84] The control patrols obviously meted out rough
justice, but the workers of Barcelona had frequently seen the law used
against them. Now they reversed the situation.

V. The Rural Revolution

While the urban situation held the attention of most observers, a more profound revolution was taking place in the countryside. Communes encompassing villages (sometimes six or seven neighboring population centers) and their surrounding lands developed in Aragon, Catalonia, the Levante, and Castile as a culmination of the long agrarian crisis.[85] Some came into being as an expression of a long-felt need to collectivize, a way to recapture earlier communal practices.[86] Others were prompted by the militia army, while the rest emerged simply for the sake of survival. Monetary devaluation, the collapse of banks, and the disappearance of many young men into the military created a mutual need that was best served by pooling labor and services.

Social motivation for radical action also was not lacking. Old class divisions in the backlands created the feeling of *cacicadas* (exploitation, unfair advantage), and this bitter mood was heightened by what one anthropologist has called the Spanish rural gentleman complex, the social brokerage role of village notables.[87] Severe restriction of land holdings created by the failure of reform also forced peasants in the North to make do with less land. The civil war finally allowed all of these old scores to be settled, since the high expectations of the republican years had prepared peasants for the millennium which the events of July brought. Land reform had been discussed for a century; now the time came to use direct action to seize what had been promised.

So much has been written about the rural revolution that a general work cannot hope to compete with more specialized studies.[88] The amount of land which came under collectivization was staggering: three quarters of all the land in Aragon, half of all the land in Catalonia and the Levante, altogether 5,692,202 hectares divided among 1,200–1,700 communes (see Appendix II).[89] Many communes affiliated with the CNT or FAI through the Federación Regional de Colectividades, an all-purpose body created in September 1936. In Catalonia small independent farmers, already beneficiaries of the *rabassaires'* revolt in 1934, remained uncollectivized in part and created their own Sindicato Agrícola. The militia committee decreed collectivization on September 3, 1936, to strike back at this group, but creation of communes took a long time and caused antagonism. "Individualists" were increasingly criticized by the radical news media for resisting collectivization. The issue became livelier when the UGT and PSUC sponsored their own communes in the Levante, Alicante, Albacete, and Murcia. The communist Federación Campesina, announced in mid-September 1936, obviously posed a major threat to the anarchists' near-monopoly on rural organization. Efforts were made to unify and coordinate rural activities, but the war effort and the political struggle claimed the anarchists' attention in August and September. Communes temporarily found their own way without much supervision or coordination.

VI. The Revolution Elsewhere

Aragon and Catalonia dominated the news in the first months of the civil war. The CNT/FAI were strongest there and could control events to their own advantage. But elsewhere they experienced more difficulty. In the Balearic Islands, Ibiza and Minorca supported anarchism, while Palma de Mallorca went fascist. An expeditionary force organized by the Sindicato Único del Transporte Marítimo de Barcelona fought to hold Minorca for the Republic, but the islands were quickly lost to the nationalists. Italian air and naval forces were too strong to overcome, especially when anarchist aid was going primarily to Aragon. The expedition turned into the first defeat suffered by the CNT/FAI.

In the South the anarchists were at a numerical disadvantage. They formed a relatively minor faction in Madrid, where Cipriano Mera and his assistants recruited militant cadres of construction workers into guerrilla bands that held the Guadarrama mountain passes against General Mola's forces in the early fighting. Many anarchist militiamen died before they had a strong impact upon revolutionary Madrid, and while elements of the Tierra y Libertad column from Barcelona soon increased militia ranks, the formation and growth of the communist Fifth Regiment and the determination of the republican government to ignore the anarchists quickly crippled the movement in Madrid. The UGT long had been stronger in the capital, and now communists provided new competition by proselytizing among bureaucrats and regular army officers. The communists placed anti-fascism before social revolution and found willing converts who soon formed a hostile bloc against further libertarian revolutionary developments.

Valencia was another trouble spot. Confused fighting continued in the city until August 1, 1936, when the garrison was finally disarmed. The republican government in Madrid initially rejected creation of a special cabinet for Valencia, but the CNT and UGT nevertheless formed the Popular Executive Committee in imitation of the Catalan Anti-Fascist Militia Committee. Almost from its start, the committee experienced problems. The defeat of the Iron Column, low anarchist militancy, the *treintista* presence, and dependence upon Madrid for military and industrial goods crippled its efforts. Lack of a sophisticated brand of separatism in the Levante also reduced the committee's mandate. Valencia remained attuned to Madrid, unable to go its own way. Even the departments established by the Popular Executive Committee were staffed largely with personnel furnished by the Second Republic.

Further south a number of defense juntas were created by the CNT/FAI, UGT, and communists to rule the larger towns like Alicante, Cartegena, and Malaga. In large part their power was reduced by the presence of regular republican military authorities. The proximity of nationalist forces led to strict military discipline and a larger role for Madrid than in Catalonia or even Valencia. Anarchists could not experiment with militias, and there was little opportunity to collectivize economic life because the Second Republic immediately nationalized industry and land.

The military situation in Andalusia also differed considerably from that in Aragon. Nominally anarchist leaders like El Campesino (Valentín González), caught squarely in the path of the nationalists, accepted communist aid and direction without reservation. Many units changed ideologies each time a different group gave them supplies. Andalusians had no secure bastion of anarchist power, no Barcelona with its Anti-Fascist Militia Committee or collectivized industries. But this was not the only explanation for weakness. The CNT ignored the South after 1931, while the FAI, which had initially dedicated itself to a defense of peasant society in 1927, also abandoned the region in favor of work in the North. As a consequence, both the CNT and FAI were dangerously weak in Andalusia when the civil war broke out.

Communists had no such failures on their record, which was a *tabula rasa* as far as the South was concerned. Their control of the Ministry of Defense in Madrid came from the growing friendship between the Soviet Union and the Second Republic and the possibility of Russian arms shipments—now a crucial issue since Great Britain and France had begun the discussions which led to creation of the Non-Intervention Committee, a device to preserve their neutrality. Bitter clashes between anarchists and communists began to dominate republican affairs. The impact of this struggle would be felt increasingly in the weeks and months ahead.

175

CHAPTER EIGHT

The Popular Front and the Civil War

I believe, as I have always believed, in liberty. Liberty understood in the sense of responsibility. I consider discipline indispensable, but it must be self-discipline moved by
a common ideal and a strong feeling of comradeship.
[Buenaventura Durruti, in an interview with Emma Goldman, *Spain and the World*, October 9, 1936]

I. Crisis in Aragon

Early September 1936 found the militia army bogged down on the
Aragon front. Saragossa remained an irresistible goal, unobtainable
yet impossible to overlook: its conquest would mean triumph in the
North, a successful conclusion to the anarchist revolution. But
nothing of the kind occurred; militia lines remained to the east of
Huesca and Saragossa. Buenaventura Durruti's army accomplished
less and less, even though its manpower increased. The militia
swelled to approximately thirty thousand, and more were on the
way. In the United States, Sam Romer, a Newspaper Guild journalist long associated with libertarian causes, worked to form a "Debs
Column" of American volunteers for the militia. It would be a
counterpart of the International Brigades organized by American
and Western European communist parties. Romer approached the
socialist Southern Tenant Farmers Union for aid, but eventually
most of the volunteers—about forty in all—came from New York
garment and textile unions.[1] French, British, Belgian, and Dutch
anarchists travelled to Spain in larger numbers, and a contingent of
former FORA members set sail from Buenos Aires. All were enthu-

siastic, even exultant at the thought of an anarchist victory, but few were militarily trained.

Lack of military experience hurt a great deal. Durruti depended upon no more than fifty-five former army officers and perhaps two thousand others with some military training.[2] This inexperience exacted a toll in guns improperly maintained, ammunition wasted, and mortars that could not be used for lack of trained crews. Discipline, even without anarchist political overtones, was chaotic. Squads sometimes vetoed support of other groups when they differed politically. Work with communes took up the time of some anarchists. In a few groups political debate consumed more effort than actual fighting, particularly if POUM units were involved.[3] Other units, especially the UGT members in Aragon, became progressively disenchanted with the CNT/FAI leadership of the campaign and drifted towards communism.

Shortage of military equipment and supplies also hurt the militia's fighting capacity. Large quantities of arms had to be left with the rearguard to meet Luis Companys' demand for the defense of Catalonia.[4] Yet anarchists were responsible for misuse of weapons themselves. Some Catalan and Aragonese peasants were of dubious loyalty, and loyal CNT/FAI committees armed militants to guard against rebellion. This policy bothered moderates like Juan Peiró:

> If today you should go to different parts of Catalonia to speak to the peasant of revolution, he will tell you that he does not trust you, he will tell you that the standard-bearers of the revolution have already passed through the countryside. In order to liberate it? No, they have passed through the countryside in order to rob those who throughout the years and throughout the centuries have been robbed by the very persons who have just been defeated by the revolution.[5]

All this caused the arming of forward areas to falter.

The supply problem soon became a national political controversy. In the French press, Jesús Hernández, a Spanish communist deputy and member of the party's central committee, brought charges of ineffectiveness against the militia army as justification for the laggard aid given Buenaventura Durruti by Madrid.[6] Protests immediately were sent to the communist party and to Premier José Giral, defending anarchist conduct of the campaign. Nonetheless, communists pressed their advocacy of a regular army. In late August 1936, they created the Fifth Regiment, nucleus of the disciplined Red Army that Jesús Hernández had called for. The failure of Premier Giral to obtain international assistance only accelerated the growth of Soviet-styled groups and initiated an inclination towards the USSR among republican officers. Obviously, aid could come only from the communists, and the time was propitious to introduce military reforms that might induce the Russians to intervene. Large supply shipments to the anarchist militia might be construed by the USSR as a breach of faith.

Anarchists, somewhat mistakenly, concentrated their criticism upon Santiago Casares Quiroga, Defense Minister in the Giral cabinet and an old enemy who as Premier had refused to arm workers shortly before the outbreak of the civil war. Buenaventura Durruti attacked him for attempting to restore the ties between state power and the professional officer corps that the revolution, in its greatest accomplishment, had severed.[7] In fact, Casares Quiroga was simply typical of liberal republicans who had lost their bearings in the wake of the Anglo-French decision to support a Non-Intervention Committee rather than the Second Republic.

When the Popular Front cabinet of Francisco Largo Caballero replaced that of José Giral on September 4, 1936, it took only a week for the new Premier (who was also Defense Minister) to create a People's Army. Actual implementation took longer, but the presence of two communists and six socialists in the reconstituted cabinet guaranteed that the move would have full support. It initiated a new period of hostility against anarchist militias.

This was not hard to do. Short memories caused the accomplishments of Durruti's August campaign to be forgotten, while the Fifth Regiment's activities around Madrid received considerable attention.[8] Regular army officers in the Ministry of Defense, heartened by the formation of a normal unit with hierarchical discipline, suddenly saw the militia in a new negative light. Defectors came forward who disagreed with the strategy used in Aragon or who had not been trusted. Jesús Pérez Salas, former Esquerra commander of the Macià-Companys column, was one of the latter. His book, *Guerra en España*, subsequently attacked the militia more violently than any other work.[9] He criticized such things as poor command structure, gross waste, lack of military knowledge, insubordination, and the sectarianism of many militiamen. One of the chief points Jesús Pérez Salas made was that the anarchists spent more time organizing communes than fighting.

On several occasions Buenaventura Durruti tried strenuously to defend the reputation of his army. Formal "militarization" of the militias would alienate peasants and limit their participation in the revolution, he insisted. The regular army always had been a counterrevolutionary force in the countryside; memories of Asturias were still fresh. The militia format, for all its alleged inefficiencies, permitted a citizen army to emerge for the first time since the War of Independence in 1808. Moreover, the regular army had amply demonstrated its lack of interest in the people by following General Franco into rebellion. What better argument in favor of a citizen army could be found? An attempt to create an orthodox military branch would end in a new disaster. Revolutionary Spain did not need another military elite.[10]

Nevertheless, Buenaventura Durruti did begin to make changes in the militia. As many as thirty militiamen convicted of theft or murder were executed at the front in September.[11] He also stepped up his exhortative role by making scores of speeches, mostly centered on the need to conserve weapons and ammunition or the necessity of placing military goals above political passions.[12] The command structure of the Aragon units was tightened up, with all *jefes de la columna* meeting regularly. Antonio Pérez Farras received the job of enforcing greater discipline, a role where he could use his regular military background with considerable effectiveness.[13]

On October 1, 1936, this strengthening of discipline was codified in stringent new rules adopted by the CNT/FAI. Militiamen were obliged to obey the rules of battalion committees or political delegates. They could not act alone on military matters or reject the duties assigned them. Infractions were subject to group-imposed punishments. Deserting, leaving one's post, pillaging, and spreading demoralizing talk constituted crimes punishable by death.[14] The militia adopted a new motto—"Obey and do one's duty"—a far cry from the libertarian watchwords of the early revolutionary period.

Unfortunately, only so much could be done internally. Victory remained the best stimulus, but Saragossa, Durruti's obsession, was too well fortified to be taken. Huesca became an alternative target, even though Juan García Oliver had failed to take it some weeks previously. On the northern flank, the town was surrounded by peasant anarchists who swelled militia ranks when Durruti attacked Huesca again on September 14, 1936. To feint nationalists out of position, Pina del Ebro was bombarded for several days. But at the last minute Huesca was reinforced with several thousand additional Navarese. Even so, the advance looked promising until the militia's supply lines broke down. Lack of ammunition ended progress in the rough terrain south of Huesca, and the delay turned the campaign into another siege, denying the militia a victory it desperately needed.

This disappointment convinced Durruti and his aides that no

179

campaign in Aragon would succeed without more substantial republican support. On how to best achieve this, anarchists split into several groups. Juan García Oliver led the "possibilists," who reluctantly felt that changes should be made in the militia to please Madrid. He proposed formation of new military schools as a sign of good faith to assuage critics of the militia.[15] Too much blood and effort had already gone into the war to lose now because of unwillingness to cooperate with other elements in the Popular Front. Nothing could stop the anarchists from running the military schools according to revolutionary principles, so little would be lost in the enterprise.

The FAI did not accept this approach, even though Juan García Oliver was one of their own. Younger *faístas* like Jaime Balius, and even more recent newcomers, caught up in the long terrorist tradition of the FAI, balked at concessions to the moderates. Some openly discussed using terrorist tactics against the Madrid government; perhaps a dramatic act of violence might revive anarchist fortunes.[16] Another faction advocated completely severing contact between Madrid and Barcelona. The export of war materials from the North did drop significantly in September, but this may have resulted from other factors.* If it was a deliberate policy, it quickly proved to be disastrous. Expansion of war industries stopped without capital grants; and the acquisition of foreign commodities, especially gasoline (now available only at a very high price because of the Non-Intervention Committee's blockade), became impossible without help from Madrid.

These problems caused the center of attention to shift to the disposition of the Bank of Spain's gold reserves, some $578,000,000 which could not be deposited abroad for fear of impoundment.[17] Rumors circulated that Francisco Largo Caballero might send the gold to the USSR in early October to pay for war goods. Almost at the same time, the first International Brigades began arriving in Albacete, led by the Italian Palmiro Togliatti and the Frenchman, André Marty, both well-known communists. This conjunction of events threw everyone into a panic. The Catalan Congress of Syndicates, meeting on September 24, 1936, in Barcelona, heard the Catalan economist Juan Fábregas open a campaign to have the gold reserves shared equally among Catalonia, Aragon, and Castile. According to his figures, the northern provinces had given Madrid 800 million pesetas in general credits, 30 million for materials of war,

---

*How much of this decrease was caused by the natural dislocations of the civil war, as opposed to deliberate policy not to furnish goods to Madrid, is an interesting question whose answer cannot be easily deduced from the few economic statistics available.

and 150 million for raw materials and had a billion pesetas deposited in the Bank of Spain.[18] Their contribution to the war effort, he concluded, had already been far greater than anything the Soviet Union could furnish.

Francisco Largo Caballero disagreed. Bank credits could not be converted into airplanes or tanks without Russian aid. Moreover, to have various provinces negotiating with international arms dealers or foreign powers would only dilute the power and credit of the Second Republic. He preferred to handle all foreign negotiations himself, and he said so in a sharp response which ignored the pride of the anarchists and the difficulty of their situation.

Buenaventura Durruti met on September 29, 1936, with Juan García Oliver, Diego Abad de Santillán, and a French representative of the AIT, Pierre Bresnard. The secret conference discussed ways of obtaining the gold in Madrid, since all agreed that Largo Caballero would not finance or supply the militia. The only account of the meeting credits Abad de Santillán with proposing to use anarchist militiamen in Madrid to make a daring attack on the Bank of Spain.[19] Over the objections of Garcá Oliver, who felt Largo Caballero might still side with the anarchists, the plan was hastily adopted. Abad de Santillán left on September 30, travelling openly to Madrid under the guise of official business. Durruti made the same trip incognito, flying to Madrid from Prat de Llobregat on a courier plane. The next day, October 1, scores of militiamen were briefed on the plan, and a few officials of the railway syndicates provided a special, secret train. The night of October 2 was chosen by the conspirators for the attack.

By the next morning, republican officials had learned of the plan, obviously from one of the participants. When the news reached Premier Largo Caballero, he arranged a meeting with Durruti, Bresnard, and ten representatives of the militia for the late afternoon. Largo Caballero's month in office had been frustrated by a complete lack of accord with the anarchists. Now the Premier had to resolve this crisis or face the consequences of a major split. Perhaps the crucial fact was that the USSR had as yet made no major arms deliveries, while the anarchists had been in the field against General Franco for two months. In any case, the Premier, after considerable bargaining, promised Durruti 1.6 billion gold pesetas.[20] CAMPSA would provide the militia in Aragon with large quantities of gasoline; Russian war materials would be divided equitably; and Madrid would not block reasonable purchases of foreign commodities by Catalonia and Aragon. In return, the anarchists

181

would cooperate with republican officials in every way possible and provide arms and men should Madrid come under attack by General Franco's southern armies.

Quietly, late in the afternoon, the great gold robbery was cancelled, a casualty of the accords. Buenaventura Durruti must have been relieved at his success with the Premier, since he knew that closer cooperation was a vital necessity. The Barcelona meeting of September 29 coincided with orders from Madrid creating a general staff and imposing normal military discipline and organization upon all republican forces, the anarchists included.[21] Juan García Oliver persuaded Durruti to accept the orders if the militia in Aragon would be supplied in the same manner as other units. The meeting on October 2 with Largo Caballero assured anarchist leaders that this would indeed be the case.

Throughout October the militia was slowly integrated with the republican military. The first step affected unit designations. The Durruti, Ascaso, Ortíz, Hilario-Zamora, Aguiluchos, Solidaridad Obrera, and Rojo y Negro groups joined the 25th, 26th, and 28th Divisions, while the 27th became PSUC, the 29th POUM, and the 30th Catalan regionalist.[22]

Buenaventura Durruti accepted this first step of militarization. In an interview with an anarchist publication on October 6, 1936, he stressed that the threat facing Madrid was too dangerous to ignore. Toledo's surrender on September 27 exposed the southern approaches of Madrid to attack at any moment. He steadfastly believed the city could be defended, but he warned that only a united effort—"the most important test facing the revolution"—might save it from nationalist conquest.[23] All supporters of the Second Republic had to join their efforts, even if this violated "certain principles"— clearly a reference to the changing status of the militia. Durruti was not sanguine about the implications of such action, particularly the irony of fighting to preserve a state—"any state." But he did accept the proposition that Madrid was the spot upon which everything depended, including a continuation of the revolution in the North.

Not all anarchists agreed with him. The Iron Column of Valencia, noted for its lack of discipline, revolted against militarization in mid-October. Bitter denunciations appeared in a few anarchist publications, particularly against the introduction of rank into the militia.[24] Buenaventura Durruti refused the high rank offered to him, but other anarchists, including Gregorio Jover and Juan García Oliver, became uncomfortable majors. Among hard-line militants, the act of formally commissioning officers seemed like utter heresy.

In their minds, militarization was akin to politicalization, a move towards abandonment of a society of equals. Relations within the CNT/FAI grew strained and difficult as nationalist forces continued to move towards Madrid. The long political crisis came to a head amid the military difficulties.

II. Political Crisis

The military crisis was symptomatic of larger political controversies agitating the Second Republic. Military necessity caused many aspects of political life to change. For instance, aid from fascist Italy and Germany made revolutionary republicans see their own struggle in a new international light. In the midst of an anti-fascist war, many old issues in domestic politics were depreciated. In another area, the CNT quarreled with the FAI over whether defense of democracy or revolution was the correct line of propaganda. A third bewildering issue arose from the uneasy alliance of anarchists with the Madrid government. Anarchism lost its old antagonist, the state. Any central focus to the movement had disappeared, just when thousands of Spaniards were being driven by anti-fascism towards revolution.

Of course, many of these radical Spaniards did join the CNT/FAI. The CNT claimed a membership of three million (up more than 500,000 from 1935), while the FAI had about 150,000. The FAI enrolled collectivized peasants in larger numbers (although new members technically joined both), but practically all the industrial workers in Catalonia went into the CNT as soon as their factories were collectivized in August and September 1936.

This influx predictably lowered the efficiency of both organizations. Observers noted the crude ideology of most new members and their lack of understanding of anarcho-syndicalism. Older anarchists complained about the uselessness of this huge flood of initiates.[25] Numerical success dwarfed coherence and intelligence. New members wrapped up their life frustrations inside the CNT/FAI package and often caused, as one observer noted, a grotesque gap between ideals and reality.[26]

Swamped by the gargantuan growth of their organizations, leaders of the CNT and FAI struggled to retain some measure of normal administration and direction. Joaquín Ascaso was elected chairman of the national CNT Congress, largely because of his late brother's name and his own power among Aragonese communes.

Horacio Prieto remained national secretary of the CNT until November 1936, when the rising young moderate Mariano Vázquez replaced him with the aid of Juan Peiró, still a power in the confederation and ever a conservative. Juan López ran the regional plenum in Valencia almost single-handed; *Fraga Social* and *Frente Libertario* were unquestionably his newspapers. Juan Fábregas, a newcomer with considerable economic ability, rose rapidly in Catalonia. On the FAI side, the national committee expanded to include Buenaventura Durruti and Federica Montseny. The only unusual addition was Augustin Souchy, a French syndicalist, who became the organization's international secretary in November. Federica Montseny filled in as acting national secretary during the fall, with Diego Abad de Santillán often performing these duties, too.

There was never enough time for these cadres to meet collectively. Problems seldom were discussed in detail. Consultation between the CNT and FAI became more infrequent as the business of the Anti-Fascist Militia Committee, the problems of the militia army, liaison with the central government, and international propaganda efforts loomed larger than daily procedure. All too often, the organizational work was left for junior members to do on an *ad hoc* basis. The unsatisfactory results of their efforts forced the CNT and FAI to merge activities to conserve organizational leadership. Joint district and regional committees were created in Aragon, Catalonia, and Valencia. Membership lists, social and economic functions, even newspapers were consolidated. Most routine administration ended up being handled by these joint efforts.

One time-consuming joint project was an attempt to create a strong anarcho-syndicalist youth movement to compete with the united communist-socialist group (JSU). Anarcho-syndicalism did not have the time, money, or suitable youth leaders. Even after another combined task force took over the project, little progress was made. Femmes Libres was handled the same way, but more ably, attracting women in Catalan textile mills and from the agricultural communes. For the latter, Femmes Libres provided their first taste of freedom and involvement, a development that imbued the group with militancy. The women became responsible for neighborhood anarchist programs and, more ominously, for political surveillance on behalf of control patrols. So many overzealous accusations accumulated that Femmes Libres did not progress very far in other directions. Emma Goldman criticized the group for confusing political sectarianism with the general emancipation of women.[27] Anarchist youth concentrated on the radicalization of school curricula, often with disastrous results, since public education already had gone through turmoil earlier.* Several national conferences of both groups unsuccessfully attempted to straighten matters out.

Besides CNT/FAI committees, a number of joint CNT-UGT committees were formed, particularly in Catalonia and to a lesser extent in Madrid and Valencia. They handled the administration of factories where both confederations had locals, a common situation in larger industries such as the railroads. The founding of a newspaper entitled simply *CNT-UGT* quickly attracted moderates more at home with labor issues than with militia operations or revolutionary activity. The paper took a laborite point of view in the tradition of Salvador Seguí and the *treintistas,* but diversity of opinion in wartime simply added to CNT/FAI problems. Only anarchist need of socialist help kept *Solidaridad Obrera* and other anarchist papers from provoking a serious quarrel. *CNT-UGT* was quietly dropped in March 1937.

In Catalonia, anarchists sought greater cooperation with old regionalist groups. Esquerra, Acción Catalana, and the Rabassaires party had begun to protest anarchist gains and the eclipse of Catalan regional government by the Anti-Fascist Militia Committee.[28] More ominously, the PSUC (the united socialist-communist party of Catalonia), attracted dissident regionalists and other opponents of anarchism. By the middle of September 1936, the CNT/FAI found itself under attack by the PSUC, accused of limiting revolutionary participation to unskilled workers while ignoring progressive sections of the bourgeoisie.[29] The PSUC sponsored a league of small businessmen as a way of attracting middle-class support.[30] Some UGT locals also went over to the PSUC, eventually giving the new group more than sixty thousand members.[31] Rafael Vidiella and Juan Comorera, two principal PSUC leaders, used demands for a restoration of Catalan regional government to spur a membership drive.

PSUC strategy mirrored Popular Front policy for Spain. All means were used to inflate Spanish communism by the inclusion of bourgeois elements, even if this meant playing upon a fear of anarchist revolution or stressing the advantages of a military pact with the USSR. As a result, Soviet importance grew during September 1936. Expectation of Russian war materials attracted left and

---

*Education had been a political issue since 1931. A guarantee of public, secular education was contained in article 48 of the constitution, but matters were complicated by the Ley de Congregaciones Religiosas and other political considerations. Cf. Rodolfo Llopis, *La revolución en la escuela: dos años en la dirección general de primera enseñanza* (Madrid: M. Aguilar, 1973).

liberal republicans whose pleas for support from France or Great Britain had been rebuffed. ". . . Army officers and officials who had never turned the pages of a Marxist leaflet became communists, some through calculation, others through moral weakness, others inspired by the enthusiasm which animated this organization."[32] Two communists, Vicente Uribe and Jesús Hernández, joined Largo Caballaro's cabinet, an act that anarchist newspapers criticized bitterly.[33] As one pointed out, the anti-revolutionary policies of communists jeopardized further cooperative initiatives and made anarchism susceptible to attack by its supposed allies.

A bitter anti-communism spread among anarchists during late August and early September. The Spanish Civil War as an anarchist revolution became a symbol that rallied CNT members and *faístas* alike. "No collaboration" was on everyone's lips. Most anarchists believed that their revolution had spread more widely than it had, uniting all regions behind the red and black banners. Only a few informed anarchist leaders knew otherwise. The Levante, Castile, Murcia, and southeastern Andalusia were much more open to socialist or communist influence than Aragon and Catalonia. The great size of General Franco's armies in the South demanded military action, not rhetoric. Even formation of agricultural communes and the collectivization of industry could not provide the weapons necessary to stop nationalist armies in time to save the South. So while the militia sat stalemated in the North, southerners accepted communism or socialism as a necessary expedient. Durruti knew of the problem and did nothing about it. Other anarchists advocated a policy of watchful collaboration with the Popular Front as a way of getting Russian supplies. Some wanted collaboration only to be able to veto the most drastic anti-revolutionary changes proposed by republicans. But their dilemma was unknown to the rest of the movement, and it remained unresolved in the leadership of the CNT/FAI.

These contradictions had their origin in the premiership of José Giral. Most anarchists regarded the Premier with contempt and were too involved with the initial stages of the Aragon campaign to give him much thought. By late August 1936 the barbs of the communists and their own inability to take Saragossa changed the situation drastically. On August 28 the Anti-Fascist Militia Committee asked Madrid to consider creating a National Council of Defense modelled upon itself.[34] Within two days representatives of the committee, Abad de Santillán included, met with Premier Giral to plead their case. A council form of government allowed anarchists to collaborate with other parties. Any other course would destroy the movement and deprive the Second Republic of the united anarchist support needed to link Aragon with the Basque provinces and Asturias. But the condition placed on this proposal was that the gold reserves should be equally divided. The Premier refused to consider this step, and when the delegation called upon Manuel Azaña, the President of the Republic, he refused to intervene in a cabinet decision, calling himself a prisoner of the constitution.[35]

José Giral's cabinet fell on September 3, and the next day Francisco Largo Caballero formed a Popular Front cabinet with socialist and communist members. The new government provoked anarchist concern. Largo Caballero was no friend of the CNT, and the mixed juries controversy had not been forgotten. But he alone among various contenders for the premiership—the others were Diego Martínez Barrio, the republican leader, and the socialists Indalecio Prieto and Juan Negrín—seriously sought to balance communism with anarchism in any permanent coalition. Too great a dependence upon the USSR, Largo Caballero said privately, might further weaken the international prestige of the Second Republic. This was why he offered two at-large places in his cabinet to CNT/FAI representatives on September 4 and 5, 1936.

Anarchists rejected his bid the next day and made a counterproposal. Six points stood out: reshaping of the Madrid government into a National Council of Defense (equal in power to the President of the Republic, so no vetoes could override its decisions); regional autonomy at all levels of government; creation of committees similar to the Anti-Fascist Militia Committee to run all ministries; establishment of a united popular militia; seizure of banks and Church property; and a new foreign policy that might draw upon anti-fascism rather than pro-communism.[36] These proposals exceeded earlier suggestions in their boldness. Nothing so concrete had been put forth by Spanish anarchists previously. One foreign anarchist called it their greatest achievement.[37]

Even so, the plan was ponderous and awkward. Essentially the CNT/FAI called for an expansion of the Anti-Fascist Militia Committee to national proportions. Communists were excluded entirely, with five seats each going to the UGT and CNT and four to the republicans. A fifteenth place went to the President of the Republic, who would chair the junta. State and local governments received similar types of councils. The executive nature of the proposed government was underscored by the loss of power and independence by the ministries, now reduced to the level of technical bureaus or service agencies under supervision of representatives appointed by the junta. The fifteen advisors watched one another to ensure that equity was maintained in all things.

This demand for equity contained a quality of desperation. A defense against takeover by communists dominated the proposal to the exclusion of more typically anarchist concerns. Syndicalism was almost completely missing. The only mention of a role for syndicates came in the discussion of a popular tribunal, whose judges would be nominated by the Council of Defense, syndicates, and anti-fascist groups. Even the call for seizing banks and Church properties appeared to be added as an afterthought, almost a visceral anarchist reflex unrelated to the plan itself. And the anarchist suggestion that plebiscites be used in the four largest republican cities (Madrid, Barcelona, Valencia, Malaga) for ratification of the plan within two weeks was simply impractical.

To the principal writers of the manifesto—Juan López (the moderate former *Solidaridad Obrera* editor), Federica Montseny, and Aurelio Fernández (the FAI activist)—these drawbacks did not detract from its main anti-communist point. The proposals represented an attack upon the PSUC, a declaration of war against "statist" Stalinism. The shifting sympathies of republicans outraged the plan's authors, who accused government ministers of adopting communism in a final attempt to hide their personal incapacity as politicians and statesmen in a counterrevolutionary plot.[38] Anarchists managed to combine shock, outrage, national pride, naiveté, and bluff in their statements. Privately, the CNT/FAI leaders feared the moment when they would have to reveal to their followers that the anarchist revolution faced liquidation. The counterproposal was a last vain effort to stave off subordination under the Popular Front.

During the next few weeks Francisco Largo Caballero refused to consider the anarchist proposal. While sympathetic to the position of the CNT/FAI, the Premier was nevertheless a realist when it came to practical matters. Point eight of the proposal was undoubtedly the least realistic; it demanded convocation of an interim conference of all anti-fascist elements to develop a new foreign policy. The implicit assumption was that the Comintern be abandoned as chief agency for mobilizing international public opinion, and this Largo Caballero could not do.

The reason for the Premier's dependency upon communist aid lay primarily in the weakness of international anarchism. Try as they might, anarchists could not hope to match communist activity abroad. The membership of the AIT stood at slightly less than a hundred thousand. It had been greatly diminished by loss of its chapters in

188

Germany, Italy, Portugal, and Argentina, where it was outlawed by dictatorships.[39] While the Popular Front stratagem made the period from 1935 to 1938 successful years for international communism, the AIT now represented only small circles of anarchists or minority factions within a few formerly syndicalist unions. None of these groups was very large, and few had much popular appeal. Anarchists might use such a respected libertarian as the American exile Emma Goldman to lead their foreign propaganda efforts or aid drives, but there were few like her. Rudolf Rocker was now a refugee in the United States, where he was unknown. Nestor Makhno had died in 1934, while Sébastien Faure was in poor health. Thus, Spanish Relief rallies in London had difficulty filling Royal Albert Hall under the sponsorship of the anarchists.[40] The Friends of Spanish Democracy and the Spanish Medical Aid Society, both communist in their sympathies, did much better in raising support. Anarchist volunteers in the Spanish Civil War declined, and none of the foreign anarchist groups could provide new military equipment.[41]

Francisco Largo Caballero did not mention this depressing reality when he rejected the CNT/FAI's proposal, but it was a major factor in his decision. He told the Spanish anarchists that a National Council of Defense was too similar to the loose coalition that ruled nationalist Spain from Burgos, General Franco's capital. The main point of the civil war was to resist the power of fascism by keeping Spanish democracy alive. The anarchist plan would only confuse international opinion and stop what aid was being sent. Someday, perhaps, the world would respond generously, once the issues of democracy and fascism had been clarified.[42] At the same time, Largo Caballero did not want to reject the anarchists entirely. He recognized a need to balance communists and anarchists, but doing so was not immediately possible.

The republican military continued to foster a sharp hostility towards the militia. Its leaders discussed plans for surprise attacks upon the anarchists, sometimes in conjunction with communists, sometimes not.[43] What this would accomplish was never clarified, but such plotting at least worked off tensions caused by a collapsing southern front in New Castile. Here, along the Tagus river, regular army units, communists, and anarchist militia columns from Madrid frequently quarreled and sometimes even exchanged shots. Regular army officers accused the militia of laxity, theft of munitions, and often a refusal to fight.[44] Bitterness grew as republican armies were pushed back along the Toledo road. Madrid politicians began pressuring Largo Caballero to abolish the Anti-Fascist Militia Committee

189

and to destroy the Popular Executive Committee in Valencia, a similar type of organization.[45]

The Valencia committee was the first to collapse, since it depended heavily upon Madrid for credits and assistance. The PSUC and UGT demanded submission to the government throughout late August, and on September 8, 1936, the Popular Executive Committee was dissolved. Juan López, the leading anarchist in Valencia, agreed with the decision and so became the first anarcho-syndicalist to abandon the position of no collaboration. His justification for this step was a refusal to condone a civil war within a civil war.[46]

Another anarchist setback occurred on September 11, when Luis Companys created his own Council on the Economy in Catalonia. It bureaucratized economic planning and removed input from the militia committee—the first reversal in the flow of power that had come to the anarchists since the start of the civil war. Hereafter, collectivized industries dealt with financial departments of the Catalan regional government for capital. The CNT, still embroiled in the defense council scheme, did not oppose Luis Companys strenuously when he implemented the plan, probably hoping that their acquiescence might improve the flow of necessary raw materials.[47] As a disillusioned anarchist observed, having proposed the creation of a new government, it was not a big step for the CNT/FAI to collaborate with an already existing one.[48] Since Francisco Largo Caballero refused to reconsider earlier proposals, anarchists had no options available. Communist success in recruiting and propagandizing pursued them no matter what they did.

The next period, September 12–25, 1936, proved to be equally traumatic. A few concessions had been made, but the supply situation did not significantly improve. Madrid had little to share; two months of fighting had depleted military stocks alarmingly. The anarchists, however, had no way of knowing this, since communications between Barcelona and Madrid were minimal. Without participation in the Popular Front cabinet, they were cut off, isolated, and about to lose control of their own revolution. A national plenum in Barcelona on September 15, called by the CNT, tried to negotiate ground rules for a CNT-UGT government. When this attempt failed, the CNT reiterated the proposals of September 6, evidently not realizing that Largo Caballero, a socialist, surely would be informed of their desperation.[49]

The second battle of Huesca, coming after these political reverses, proved to be a turning point. Once it was clear that Huesca would not fall, many leaders began to think only in terms of what

190

could be salvaged. Buenaventura Durruti seemed near despair, while Juan García Oliver and Federica Montseny privately called for negotiations with Francisco Largo Caballero.[50] A few believed that only a major transfusion of aid might salvage the campaign. The Congress of Syndicates talked about obtaining the gold reserves more than any item on their agenda, and Solidaridad Obrera featured daily editorials on the same theme. Some anarchists went from deep pessimism to wild enthusiasm over the possibility of seizing the gold, but amid this euphoria Luis Companys calmly proposed a total abolition of the militia committee.

The Catalan Premier's announced reason for this policy change was to free anarchist energies for the war in Aragon.[51] He simultaneously cajoled and threatened, persuaded and dictated, aware that his proposal called for major concessions from the CNT/FAI. His most telling argument portrayed the committee as too narrowly based politically to serve the needs of war. In its place he suggested an all-party cabinet of the Catalan regional government to coordinate and unify the militia army. This could broaden participation of socialists and communists in Catalan and Aragonese affairs and increase rapport with Madrid. Aragon would become a purely Catalan war, aided but not directed by Castile, utilizing a united front psychology that might unleash strong Catalan feelings.

His initiative could not have come at a worse time. Anarchists had expected anything but this, so caught up were they in their joint struggle against communism and fascism. There were rumblings from Solidaridad Obrera and great confusion among anarchist rank-and-file but no statement from the leadership. The Congress of Syndicates presented the only challenge, but the indecision of many speakers cancelled out the militancy of others. By September 26 the committee had been abolished and supplanted by an executive cabinet. Three ministries went to the Esquerra, one (agriculture) to the Rabassaires, two to the PSUC (labor and public services), the Ministry of Justice to the POUM's Andrés Nín, and three to the CNT/FAI—economy (Juan Fábregas), supply (Juan Domench), and health (Antonio Birlán). The first two anarchist positions had considerable power, but the Ministry of Health was far less useful than either of the PSUC's two ministries, putting the two groups on an equal footing in the cabinet, both certainly with less power than the Esquerra. The Council of Aragon assumed many functions of the militia committee, but a militarization decree on September 29 limited its prerogatives. This decree by Francisco Largo Caballero was a fait accompli that could not have proceeded so smoothly without the prior action of Luis Companys. No doubt the two Premiers coordinated their action to make sure all went well.

The dimensions of this double anarchist disaster became known in October. The anarchists had been forced to abandon revolutionary power to join a legitimate government not of their own making, all in the hope that by their doing so their military effort in Aragon would receive the material support it needed badly. But by the militarization decree the central militia committee merged with the War Department of the Generalitat, led by Colonel Díaz Sandino. Although he seems to have been a capable administrator, he experienced difficulties almost immediately, for the militarization decree centralized the war effort in the hands of the Ministry of Defense, now dominated by Colonel José Asensio Torrado, commander of the central front. Pessimistic and gloomy over Madrid's chances of survival, Asensio refused to countenance further arms shipments to Aragon. As quickly as Díaz Sandino requested new aid, Asensio rejected it, and as a result the supply situation did not improve. .

This failure embittered the CNT/FAI. Why had they capitulated on the militia committee and militarization if Madrid would not change its views on the supply crisis in Aragon? As October wore on and the situation remained unchanged, Juan García Oliver dropped his "possibilism" to protest the duplicity that had subordinated the revolution to the needs of the civil war.[52] To quiet his outburst, Luis Companys made García Oliver head of the new Popular Military School, subjecting him to regular military discipline. In other cases, bitterness gave way to panic. Mariano Vázquez, for example, accused Joaquín Ascaso of revolutionary infantilism for obligating the CNT to the Catalan regional government without gaining substantial benefits.[53] Durruti, lost in conflicting passions of anti-fascism and anti-communism, showed serious concern over the military situation. By the middle of the month this last factor dominated everyone's thoughts as General Franco's nationalist armies drove to the outskirts of Madrid. The impending battle for the capital developed so quickly that the mistakes of the past few weeks were dwarfed by this new crisis.

III. Madrid

The first major bombing attack upon Madrid came on the afternoon of October 23, a signal of the approaching nationalist offensive. Toledo fell on September 27, and remnants of the southern militia poured into Madrid, spreading panic and disorganization. They were a ragtag group, dispirited by losses to the Moors and the Spanish Foreign Legion and now clearly a liability to the Republic. Communists called these survivors "anarchists" and sought to identify them with Aragonese militiamen, when in fact most were anarchists only in the usual visceral southern way—a mixture of peasants and primitive rebels swept up or impressed into the civil war.* This propaganda campaign succeeded in persuading Largo Caballero to order an immediate adoption of "mixed brigades" modelled after the communist Fifth Regiment, which had the task of defending Madrid. The mixed brigade combined four battalions of infantry with artillery, communication squads, and supply and motor sections.[54] An idea imported to Spain from Russian civil war experience, it introduced flexibility and integration of functions into the republican army. Had the concept been introduced earlier, the militia army in Aragon might have avoided some of its difficulties, but now the reorganization opened up possibilities of large-scale intervention by the Ministry of Defense.

Other changes followed rapidly. Formation of a new Catalan army was announced on October 27. In time, it would totally absorb anarchist forces. A code of military justice was also introduced— much to Durruti's displeasure, since political activities henceforth could be punished as a breach of conduct. *Solidaridad Obrera* lamented that the old regular army was in the process of being resurrected under cover of a new crisis. Anarchists could not oppose it without appearing counterrevolutionary.[55]

Criticism of the republican and Catalan governments already had become difficult after the two cabinets agreed to nationalize all land under their control on October 15, 1936. Anarchists feared this act would lead to creation of state farms to threaten their own communes.[56] But popular response was very high, and the anarchists were ignored. The peak of Largo Caballero's popularity came soon after when new military accords were signed with the USSR, which now, alarmed at German and Italian assistance to the nationalists, abandoned participation in the Non-Intervention Committee to send military assistance to the Second Republic. Soviet tanks went into action on October 24, and Russian military advisors appeared on the Madrid front on October 29.

*Mundo Obrero, the Madrid communist newspaper, was filled with "anarchist" references during October and November 1936. In fact, the campaign in southern Castile had been run under the direction of the Ministry of Defense in Madrid and was not connected with Durruti or the military staff of the CNT/FAI.

These developments momentarily demoralized the anarchists. Many could only adopt "realism" or advocate a pallid sort of anti-fascism. The CNT/FAI went so far in the latter direction that it signed an anti-fascist pact with the PSUC-controlled UGT.[57] Some anarchist newspapers eulogized the Soviet Union, and the CNT actively participated in a commemorative mass meeting in Barcelona on November 7, 1936, celebrating the anniversary of the Bolshevik revolution.[58] Buenaventura Durruti sent a letter of friendship to the USSR on October 30 in appreciation for its aid to Spain.[59] Juan Peiró and Horacio Prieto demanded full anarchist participation in the republican government as the only effective way of fighting fascism.[60]

This new mood of cooperation increasingly forced anarchists to reconsider their earlier adamant refusals to join the Popular Front cabinet. The Premier had renewed his offer several times in the period after September 4, and now, at the end of October, as the battle of Madrid began, the anarchists were poised ready to enter the cabinet. What persuaded them to do so was the decision of Francisco Largo Caballero and his Finance Minister, Juan Negrín, to ship half the Spanish gold reserves to the Soviet Union in advance payment for Russian war materials. Any thought of running the civil war as a purely Spanish affair disappeared. Italy, Germany, Portugal, and Russia had all "openly flouted" the Non-Intervention Accords by this time, and most intelligent anarchists recognized the need of protection by a Great Power.[61]

In any case, news from Madrid seemed to indicate an imminent collapse of the government. President Manuel Azaña had already left Madrid for safety in Catalonia, and Largo Caballero prepared to move the rest of the government to Valencia. (Emma Goldman, who was in Spain at this time, commented: "Leave it to any government to run to cover at the first sign of danger."[62]) In their place, a new defense junta ran Madrid, led by General José Miaja, Caballero's favorite military leader.* He presided over a nine-man council, ostensibly balanced between communists and socialists but in fact effectively controlled by the former.[63]

Formation of this new junta convinced many anarchists that they should accelerate their entrance into the government. If Madrid was to become the most crucial battle of the Spanish Civil War,

---

*General Miaja had once been a member of the Unión Militar and in early July had been most unsympathetic towards the Republic. His lack of connection with the old Spanish Left, of course, was what recommended him to Francisco Largo Caballero. Cf. Burnett Bolloten, *The Grand Camouflage: The Spanish Civil War and Revolution, 1936–39* (London: Pall Mall Press, 1968), pp. 236–238, for further details.

then whoever played a leading role in saving the capital would dominate the military scene thereafter.[64] On the other hand, Rudolf
Rocker believed that the CNT/FAI accepted ministerial posts only to
gain supplies for the militia in Aragon, a point of view also shared by
Diego Abad de Santillán and Buenaventura Durruti.[65] Others explained the decision to collaborate as a desperate gamble to keep the
republican army away from communist control.[66] Juan García Oliver
said later that anarchists joined the Popular Front to save it from
dissolving in panic at the approach of General Franco.[67] The FAI
based its official explanation upon the exigencies of war:

> The complex problems of the war leave us no choice. These are mo-
> ments when the fate of the Spanish people, and the very existence of the
> CNT and FAI, depend upon the progress of the war against fascism.
> This fate hung on the decisions of the anarchists. They could not take
> any precipitate action, they could not allow themselves to be swayed by a
> desire for vengeance, they could not risk any daring innovations.[68]

But of all the explanations, perhaps only Federica Montseny's
caught the passion and drama of the moment.

> We were the only ones who kept the masses alive; the only ones who
> remained faithful to their revolutionary creed. Without our continued
> vigilance, Spain today [February 1937] would be very different. A timid
> democracy, a reformist socialism would have held back the masses. Our
> constancy, some might call it our madness, was necessary to wear down
> the oppressive forces of the old democracy which, in Spain, was a
> hundred years behind the times. . . . Although it had been our aim, to
> attempt a total conquest [in November] would have meant a broken
> front, and consequently, failure. The fact is that we were the first to
> modify our aspirations, the first to understand that the struggle against
> international fascism was in itself great enough.[69]

This last statement, if Emma Goldman was correct, concealed a
high degree of latent Spanish nationalism. The American, who had
argued with Federica Montseny for hours against collaboration, believed the anarchists had abandoned political principle to save Spain
from further foreign intervention.[70] Such a course was not surprising
in the context of Spanish history, but the real tragedy of the anarchists was that they were "pulled further and further into the mire of
compromise. . . . Even from the standpoint of joining the government
the CNT/FAI is permitting itself to be treated like children."[71] In a
later article, she wrote that "never before was a revolution and its
leading organization so scandalously sabotaged as in Spain."[72] Nationalism blinded the Spanish anarchists to what was actually occurring.

Diego Abad de Santillán, for one, disagreed with Emma Goldman. Asked what collaborating or not collaborating meant at the time, he wrote: "We wanted to establish in Spain a socialist economy and a regime of liberty for all, even our adversaries, . . . and in November 1936 this could only be done through the Popular Front cabinet. There were neither committees nor individuals in our circle with sufficient prestige and power to achieve this."[73] Anarchism had gone as far as it possibly could go alone. Collaboration was simply a recognition that the civil war had ramifications beyond social revolution. The international context of the conflict made all other principles obsolete.

At the time only a few libertarians were unalterably opposed to collaboration. Without a doubt, the most outspoken opponent was Camillo Berneri, the Italian anti-fascist resident of Barcelona who, beginning on October 24, wrote vitriolic articles in his *Guerra di Classes* demanding, among other things, development of an international revolutionary campaign as the prime defense of the Republic.[74] He also attacked the mood of anarchist collaboration. Difficulties in Aragon did not necessitate a total capitulation to the communists. Membership in the Popular Front cabinet, far from solving anything, would only put anarchists under extreme coercion to maintain unanimity in Madrid. All differences of ideology eventually would be extinguished and Stalinist statism imposed—a tragic end to a long anarchist tradition.[75]

George Orwell reacted in much the same way: communists were working "not to postpone the Spanish revolution till a more suitable time, but to make sure that it never happened."[76] Shortly after his return from Spain he added: "Communism is now a counter-revolutionary force; the communists everywhere are in alliance with bourgeois reformism and use the whole of their powerful machinery to crush or discredit any party that shows signs of revolutionary tendencies."[77] These two comments only illustrated the gulf between the principle for which foreigners were fighting in Spain and the reality that governed the decisions of Spanish anarchists. The civil war created difficulties that had never before been anticipated.

Finally, on November 4, 1936, the CNT/FAI entered the Popular Front cabinet. Four portfolios went to anarchist ministers, among them the new Minister of Health, Federica Montseny, the only Spanish woman ever to achieve cabinet rank. The most important office of the four, the Ministry of Justice, went to Juan García Oliver, although he strongly resisted the offer and expressed a preference to remain on the Aragon front. Juan López and Juan Peiró of the CNT became

Ministers of Commerce and Industry respectively. Both these positions previously had been held by a single person—an indication of their relative unimportance. As a matter of fact, none of the anarchist cabinet posts had any direct bearing on the war effort or much impact upon the problems that drove anarchists to join the cabinet in the first place. Undoubtedly Largo Caballero made these appointments to avoid conflict with the communists, but after anarchist demands for control of the Defense and Finance ministries were rejected, they made no further attempts to strengthen their numbers. Instead, they placed new faith in the list of conditions for participation which the four new ministers brought with them. Since the list was identical to the one of September 6, there was no reason to believe that a Council of Defense might be adopted. *Solidaridad Obrera* lamely explained that the presence of anarchist ministers in the cabinet surely would lead to the changes demanded for so long.[78]

In welcoming the new cabinet members, Francisco Largo Caballero merely indicated that a realignment of government might occur if the anarchists could convince the other members. This was unlikely with six socialists, two communists, several communist sympathizers (including Julio Álvarez del Vayo, the Foreign Minister), and five Left Republicans in the cabinet. And if this array of opponents were not enough, almost immediately after the anarchists joined the government, the battle for Madrid began, making any prolonged political debate impossible.

On November 7, nationalist Legionnaires attacked the southern flank of Madrid along the Casa de Campo, the royal park south of the Manzanares river. Key government personnel hurriedly left the city, while the Fifth Regiment and anarchist militias barely managed to push back waves of attackers. The first contingents of the International Brigades (recruited by communist parties on behalf of the Comintern after the USSR had abandoned the Non-Intervention Committee) reached the lines on November 8, 1936. A few Russian- and French-made planes fought Italian and German aircraft in the skies above the city.

The militia of Madrid in this "central epic" of the Spanish Civil War has received comparatively little attention from historians.[79] The dispirited troops of the early battles had been reformed, and they fought well in the battles of Sesena, Torrejon de Velasco, and Torrejon de la Calzada y Cubas in late October.[80] On November 4, however, they lost control of Getafe airport and Carabanchel Alto— defeats which allowed the nationalists to push through the outer defenses of Madrid to occupy a line close to the Manzanares river.

Their reputation as fighters fell so low that both Louis Fischer, the American correspondent, and André Malraux, the French writer, believed that the militia's loss of Carabanchel Alto had opened the way into Madrid for the nationalists.[81] Ill trained and badly armed, the militia, which had never been under anarchist leadership, faced the best of the Legionnaires and Moroccans, whom it could not possibly match in armaments or training.

Yet almost immediately thereafter the Madrid militia did improve. The turnabout was due to the return of Cipriano Mera from the Guadarrama front and a decision to place the militia under his leadership.[82] The former construction worker managed to coordinate and discipline the militia within a few days. Good equipment finally reached them after inordinate delays, and, even more important, the Madrid junta began employing "methods that the men of the CNT . . . had advocated . . . : arming the people, omnipotence of the Committees, action by the masses, and summary revolutionary justice."[83] The outpouring of popular support from the city was strong. *"No pasarán,"* "they shall not pass," became the motto of Madrid. Anarchists worked best in neighborhood groups, collecting and sharing food, erecting barricades on many streets, and preparing for urban guerrilla warfare. This revolutionary process created local leaders like Mauro Bajatierra, González Marín, Eduardo Val, and Pablo Verardini. Publications like *CNT* and *Frente Libertario* exhorted the citizens of Madrid to resist.

The end result was a fair improvement in the military performance of the militia troops. They still did not have the training or the supplies of the International Brigades, but at least one Brigade member, coming into contact with the anarchists for the first time, was not entirely unimpressed with their determination and their unity with the people.[84] However, others remained unconvinced of their reliability.[85] Perhaps this scorn was inevitable, for as one regular Spanish officer remarked, "the International Brigades were well-equipped and well-fed while the Spaniards starved and shivered in the cold."[86]

By November 8, when the battle for Madrid escalated, anarchists were scattered through the Arce and Mena, Cavada, Enciso, Alvarez Coque, and López-Tienda columns along the southern Madrid front.[87] A much larger number filled the ranks along the northern and northwestern Madrid front, particularly in the area from Hiendelaencina to Solodosos, where sizeable contingents of the Madrid construction syndicates had been fighting General Mola's troops since August. Cipriano Mera and his assistants (Teodoro Mora, Eustaquio Rodríguez, José Luis Ruiz, and Eusebio Sanz) operated as a miniature general staff to unify the militia forces. During this period they were successful in frustrating General Mola's drive towards Alcala de Henares, which confused the plan that would have linked the nationalists' northern and southern armies.[88] This holding action, one of the most effective republican battles of the entire war, was not as close to Madrid as the Casa de Campo or University City and so did not receive the same publicity.

Meanwhile, the struggle for Madrid was taking place along the river. Here, the Eleventh and Twelfth International Brigades, made up of the Thäelmann, André Marty, Garabaldi, and Edgar André battalions, held the crucial sections. Fighting with extraordinary bravery, they withstood a major nationalist onslaught in the Casa de Campo on November 8. The next day the battle shifted south to the Carabanchel Abajo-Villaverde sector. By November 10–11 the Valencia highway on the eastern side of Madrid was endangered. To protect it, the Eleventh International Brigade and four battalions of militia attempted to seize the monastery of Cerro de los Angeles, the highest point overlooking the road. Their frontal charge failed, but it forced the nationalist generals to slacken pressure on the center of the line in order to strengthen their eastern flank. Momentarily, the tempo of combat slowed, but both sides knew that the next few days would determine the outcome of the struggle.

IV. Durruti in Madrid

For some time preparations had been made to reinforce the army of Madrid from Aragon. Buenaventura Durruti and Francisco Largo Caballero had agreed at their famous meeting on October 2 that the militia army might be called upon for reinforcements if Madrid was threatened. The Premier first requested additional troops in mid-October against the wishes of the Defense Ministry and the central command, mainly staffed by communists or communist sympathizers. The requests were so hurried and imprecise that Barcelona did not take them seriously until late in the month, when Largo Caballero anxiously sent further queries. In reply, Juan García Oliver opposed any commitment of troops until basic anarchist demands were met.[89] It was a perfect time to settle the matter of the defense council. But Federica Montseny persuaded the CNT/FAI that no one should profit politically from the situation. Madrid was a crisis

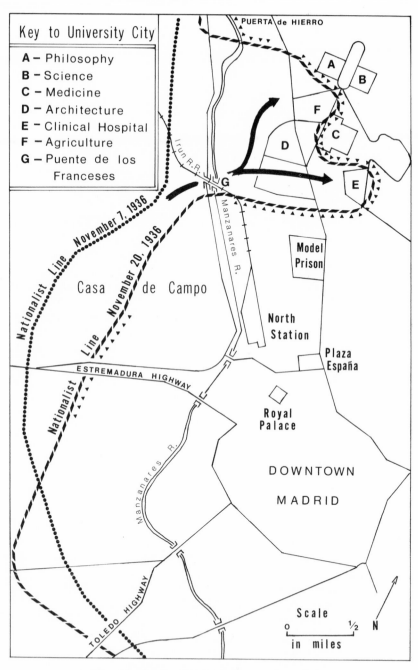

Key to University City

A – Philosophy
B – Science
C – Medicine
D – Architecture
E – Clinical Hospital
F – Agriculture
G – Puente de los
        Franceses

PUERTA de HIERRO

A
B
F
C
D
E

Model
Prison

North
Station

Plaza
España

Royal
Palace

DOWNTOWN

MADRID

Nationalist Line November 7, 1936
Line November 20, 1936
Nationalist

Irun R.R.

Manzanares R.

Casa   de   Campo

ESTREMADURA HIGHWAY

Manzanares R.

TOLEDO HIGHWAY

Scale
0   ½   N
in miles

The Battle for Madrid, November 1936

The arrows mark the nationalist advance, and the triangular symbols the
parts of the republican line held by anarchists.

of the people, and any sectarian gains were unthinkable.[90] Her argument cleared the way for the Madrid defense council to make the final decision, on the night of November 7–8, to bring Durruti and the Aragonese militia to the capital.

The initial request was for ten thousand men, but a lack of transport and strategic considerations in the North reduced that request to three thousand. The 26th Brigade, perhaps the best in the militia, was chosen to go. It incorporated elements of Rojo y Negro, Pachín, and the Aguiluchos, all experienced veterans of the war in Aragon.[91] While these groups withdrew from the lines and boarded a special train, Durruti flew to Valencia to meet with the four anarchist ministers, Largo Caballero, army commander José Miaja, and Colonel Vicente Rojo, the main strategist of the Madrid campaign. No one in Valencia had reliable intelligence information on the situation in Madrid, and Durruti left wondering if the government felt Madrid was indefensible.[92] Even after he had arrived in Madrid on November 12, his mood continued to be pessimistic, although he wired Largo Caballero that the city must be defended at all costs.[93] Soon afterwards he began to respond positively to the optimism of the hundreds of Madrid residents who gathered around his headquarters in the palace of the Duke of Sotomayer at Calle de Miguel Angel 27. By the late afternoon of November 13, after his troops arrived and were billeted in houses along the Calle de Granada, he was convinced that Madrid could be held and that revenge for his failure to take Saragossa was at hand.

Before more definite plans could be made, rumors reached the anarchists of a new nationalist night guerrilla raid on the Model Prison, where many important fascist prisoners were incarcerated. Miaja and Rojo demanded that Durruti put his men into action immediately, and the column moved out about 10 p.m. towards the prison and the Plaza de la Moncloa. The area lay to the south of University City, which faced the position of heaviest nationalist strength, since it was the easiest crossing point of the Manzanares river. Scattered fighting occurred all through the night, and despite the hurried organization of defenses, the nationalist raiding party was turned back.

At dawn of November 14, new orders sent the 26th Brigade into the lines just west of the river across from University City, on a line with the clinical hospital on the eastern side. The crucial events of this day long have been considered controversial. An account sympathetic to the International Brigades portrays Durruti as a vain, cocky figure who demanded and got the most difficult assignment on the front.[94] His adjutant, however, says that the 26th was ordered into the line by Rojo and General Emil Kléber (pseudonym of the Austrian communist Gregory Stern), commander of the International Brigades in Madrid.[95] By this time the 26th had fought through their first night in the city after several long months in Aragon and a hurried trip. The International Brigades, which had arrived in Madrid fresh five days previously, had fought up to the time of the militia's arrival, when many were relieved from front-line duty. The anarchist militia was no more fresh and rested than the other Madrid defenders.

An accusation of later origin was that Durruti demanded special aviation and artillery cover for his advance into the lines.[96] In fact, this sector near the clinical hospital was generally recognized as the most dangerous in the defense of Madrid. Air and artillery cover had been operative here for several days to prevent a breakthrough, and while they increased when the 26th went into the lines, it was not a great increase or one that exceeded the norm for a military maneuver of this type.

Instead, many of the military problems in this sector stemmed from communist placement of the anarchist militia. Rojo and Kléber put Durruti's forces on a line from the Puerta de Hierro north of the hospital to the Parque del Oeste above the North Railway Station.[97] Unfortunately, part of the militia was on the west side of the Manzanares river, well within range of nationalist artillery, where the troops could be supplied only at night. Intermingling of other units alongside the militia presented an additional difficulty, since the scattered units confused command and communications. Durruti established his main post in the Plaza de la Moncloa north of the station, but he had direct contact with only about half of his forces. No one knew the urban terrain, and there was little time to settle in. From the start heavy fighting went on all down the line, making it difficult to prepare positions. Most of November 14 was spent in erecting barricades and digging trenches. Russian arms, promised since the 26th Brigade arrived, did not reach it until late in the afternoon.

Unfortunately, the next day, November 15, had already been selected by the enemy for the launching of a major new thrust which Colonel José Varela, the nationalist commander of the sector directly across from the hospital, hoped would begin the most decisive battle of the civil war. The attack came at dawn and did not lift for three days. Approximately sixty percent of Durruti's men died during this period, including three of his most important *jefes de la columna*. Ammunition was exhausted several times before 10 a.m. on November 15, an indication of the chaotic state of Madrid's supply system, over which the anarchists had no control. A nationalist aviation group staged nonstop bombing raids on the area, while Colonel Juan Yägue, head of a new assault team, used massive artillery and tank attacks to drive the 26th Brigade back from the river. Rojo and Kléber were slow in sending reinforcements, and by 4 p.m., November 15, nationalists had established a permanent beachhead on the east side of the Manzanares.

It took another twenty-four hours for Yägue's troops to force their way into the ground floor of the hospital itself. More than eight hundred anarchists died at this stage of the battle, but there had been no mass flight, as sometimes has been suggested. Durruti was angry at being driven back, but it was a mixture of pride and unhappiness with Rojo and Kléber rather than embarrassment over the performance of his troops.[98] The last-ditch, mid-morning defense against nationalist tanks in the Plaza de la Moncloa on November 17 was largely the work of members of the 26th Brigade and indicated their determination to continue the battle long after some sources say they had collapsed.[99] Alleged apologies attributed to Durruti do not ring true in these circumstances.[100]

Fighting decreased on November 18. Both sides had exhausted their reserves and could not continue the tempo of battle without massive replacements. The Manzanares had been breached, but Madrid still remained unconquered. Anarchists believed that "Madrid was not saved on November 8 [by the arrival of the International Brigades], but on November 15 by the Durruti column."[101]

Durruti used the lull to consolidate and resupply his lines. Much of his energy, too, went into negotiations with Madrid officials to straighten out logistical problems. He also sought to improve particular points along the perimeter of the hospital in preparation for further fighting.

But Durruti never lived to return to battle. His statement upon receiving the orders to depart to the front—"I go to Madrid to win or die"—took on a prophetic irony when, at about 4 p.m. on November 19, on a short inspection trip, he had his car stop about a thousand meters (though probably less) away from the clinical hospital so that he could talk with several militiamen on guard there. There had been no action for some time, but as he got out of the car, two (or more) shots rang out from the third floor of the hospital. One bullet struck Durruti above the heart and wounded him seriously. Julio Graves, his assistant and driver, Miguel Yoldi, Sergeant Manzana, and several militiamen immediately rushed him to the former Ritz

Hotel, now a militia hospital.[102] There Durruti lingered near death while doctors operated to no avail. He died at 3 a.m. November 20.

Rumors spread that someone important had been shot. Mariano Vázquez ordered all who knew to say only that an anarchist leader had been wounded.[103] But the 26th Brigade soon learned that it was Durruti, and strong feelings provoked fights between anarchists and communists or republicans. In the late evening, anarchist units received an order from Kléber to stand down, and by the following day most had been removed from the lines.[104] More rumors speculating on the identity of Durruti's killers caused increasing bitterness and division within the republican army. In the ensuing years the events surrounding his death have remained as mysterious as they were at the time. An official government explanation tried to calm the atmosphere by contending that Durruti had accidentally shot himself while getting out of the car. No one believed this version because Durruti had been killed by a rifle bullet, while he himself usually carried only a pistol.[105]

Communists dismissed his shooting as the act of a disgruntled anarchist. This version drew considerable support later, much like the rumors that had circulated after Salvador Seguí's murder in 1923.[106] However, this presupposed a shot from close range by someone familiar to Durruti; in fact, the angle of entry into his body indicated that the bullet had come from a considerable height.[107] Furthermore, exhaustive interrogations at the time cleared all of Durruti's companions. None were found to be double agents.

Anarchists naturally suspected the communists of assassinating Durruti in order to remove the most important republican military figure. This rumor began in the Durruti column and was suppressed in anarchist publications only at the insistence of the four CNT/FAI ministers. Not until the spring of 1937 did a new libertarian paper, El Amigo del Pueblo, begin to hint at this possibility again.[108] Ironically, the paper was sponsored by a new anarchist group called the Amigos de Durruti (Friends of Durruti), who themselves have been suspected of complicity in the assassination, although from dubious evidence.* In the end no communist assassin was ever discovered,

*In an interesting review of James Joll's book, The Anarchists, a reviewer charged that the assassination indeed had been carried out by the Amigos de Durruti (The Times Literary Supplement, December 24, 1964, p. 743). Albert Meltzer (The Times Literary Supplement, January 7, 1965, p. 14) rebutted that the group was not formed until several months later. The reviewer answered that the nationalists did not hold the part of the hospital from which the bullet came (The Times Literary Supplement, February 2, 1965, p. 123). This is a good point, but one for which, unfortunately, no proof can be found one way or another, despite exhaustive examination of the material.

despite long searches and the interrogation of communist sympathizers and members of the International Brigades. Moreover, if there had been any truth to the story, the Franco regime surely would have publicized it from the voluminous materials the fascists inherited after the war.

Thus the only tenable assumption that can be made is that the nationalists were responsible for Durruti's death. Colonel Yägue had snipers scattered throughout the area, and their job was made easier by the close quarters and the many no-man's lands that the urban terrain offered. More important, Yägue had a two-fold reason for ordering snipers around the hospital. After all, the attack upon Madrid had been thwarted there, and the nationalist command was furious at his failure. Any blood which could be extracted at this spot might partly avenge the setback. Another reason for revenge existed in the fact that the head of the fascist Falange party, José Antonio Primo de Rivera, a prisoner of the Second Republic since the previous April, had been sentenced to death on November 17 for acts of treason.

Although Largo Caballero's cabinet was known to be reviewing the sentence, news of Durruti's death ironically may have hastened the decision to execute José Antonio. The Falangist leader was executed on November 20 in Alicante, a matter of hours after the death of Durruti. It is difficult to link the two incidents causally, but Durruti's killing certainly sealed José Antonio's fate. The two most typically "Spanish" leaders of the civil war died on the same day, an enormous loss to each side, as the legends and cults that grew up around both men showed.* Hereafter the war belonged more to international politics than to Spain.

---

*The Durruti legend, stemming from his mysterious death, continued to grow from this point onwards. Ernest Hemingway, in *For Whom the Bell Tolls* (New York: Scribners, 1940), p. 370, had Robert Jordan muse on the night before he died: "Durruti was good and his own people shot him there at the Puente de los Franceses. Shot him in the glorious discipline of indiscipline." As James Baldwin argued in *The Times Literary Supplement*, February 25, 1965, p. 147, "if Robert Jordan thought it, Ernest Hemingway believed it, because Robert was the man Ernest wanted to be." Likewise, the number of legends and cults which grew up around José Antonio were considerable. See Stanley Payne, *Falange: A History of Spanish Fascism* (Stanford: Stanford University Press, 1961), pp. 190–191.

CHAPTER NINE

Crisis and Collapse

I consider our comrade Durruti the very soul of the Spanish revolution.... [He] was Spain. He represented her strength, her gentleness, as well as her rugged harshness so little understood by people outside.... I found Buenaventura Durruti on the eve of an offensive surrounded by scores of people coming to him with their problems and their needs. To each he gave sympathetic understanding, comradely direction, and advice. Buenaventura had the capacity to put himself in the place of another, and to meet everyone on his own ground. I believe it was this which helped to create the inner discipline so extraordinary among the brave militias who were the pioneers of the anti-fascist struggle. [Emma Goldman in a draft of an obituary, undated, Archive of the International Institute of Social History, Amsterdam]

I. The Funeral

Buenaventura Durruti's body was sent to Barcelona only a few hours after his death. The hearse travelled unannounced to avoid ceremonies in villages along the way.[1] On Sunday, November 22, 1936, Durruti lay in state at the CNT/FAI headquarters while delegations of militia members and various political groups marched by. More than half a million people gathered to pay homage. Theaters and cafes closed for the day in Barcelona and Valencia, as did factories and military installations. The huge crowd, singing the anarchist hymn "Hijos del Pueblo," followed the cortege to the Columbus monument at the foot of the Ramblas. Here, speeches were given by the Russian consul general (who managed to avoid mention of Durruti's anarchism) and representatives of the POUM,

UGT, and Rabassaires. Juan García Oliver concluded the service with a eulogy.

A week later, Durruti's coffin was moved from a vault to its final grave. As a British correspondent described it,

> the cemetery of Barcelona is one of the most beautiful in the world. It lies on the western slope of the Montjuich, and to get there one has to skirt the gloomy fortress whose cells were so often full of Durruti's comrades and in whose trenches they were shot. The cemetery is laid out in rocky terraces planted with groves of cypress, pepper, and eucalyptus. On the extreme edge, overlooking the *huerta* and the sea, they had made a grave for Durruti and another for Ascaso, beside a third, that of the unfortunate Ferrer y Guardia, the old gentleman who was shot in 1909 for attempting to introduce secular education into Catalonia. This time there was a very small crowd; the sextons were incompetent at getting the huge coffin into the grave; they talked and asked advice, the others stood about smoking or watching the winter sunset. When it was finally in, a soldier put the anarchist flag over it and said, "We, the German soldiers serving in your column, will never forget you. Salud! Kamerad."[2]

Durruti's life had possessed epic qualities, so many that he seemed like a modern Odysseus. For nineteen years he lived the role of a political outlaw in Spain and abroad. Many of his exploits, when examined carefully, were hardly as pure or revolutionary as the legends portrayed. In particular, his Latin American adventures were filled with gangsterism and acts of bravado more typical of Butch Cassidy and the Sundance Kid than a serious political figure. One can construct wonderful romantic fantasies about his incredible flight, but the fact that Durruti's political reputation came in large part from this adventure says a great deal about the romantic inclinations of the Left in Spain and Western Europe.

Afterwards, forced into exile, he returned to Spain only at the start of the Second Republic, unprepared to deal constructively with reality. Old animosities played a large role in his opposition to the Second Republic. His attempts to overthrow the Republic were millenarian and impulsive, at a time when state policy was still in a formative stage. Even moderates in his own movement advised against such heedless action, but he went ahead without reservation.

If these criticisms are true, was Durruti simply a "noble gunman," as Eric Hobsbawm has called him?[3] After all, he left no writings, no political theory, and no social philosophy other than the events of his own life. Personally responsible for the deaths of half a

207

dozen men, he had planned even greater violence. Poorly educated, he showed some intellectual curiosity while in Paris working with Sébastien Faure, but this was frustrated by his imprisonment and extradition difficulties. Although the time he spent in Brussels from 1929 to 1931 gave him a brief respite, from the moment of his arrival back in Spain his life was one of constant violent action.

Yet Buenaventura Durruti had some great strengths. Like many active Spanish anarchists, he grew up in a village but spent his adult life in the city. He knew both worlds better than most Spaniards and combined rural and urban values in much that he did. The concept of village solidarity provided a springboard for his anarchist belief in a voluntary society, one governed by a multitude of non-authoritarian institutions. Durruti's role was charismatic: he sought to personify the best virtues of a long-delayed revolution and bring them to life. In an unusually backward, isolated society, he radiated hope and optimism. By his example Spaniards might themselves begin a serious reformation of their lives—an action which, in a socially disorganized society, was not easy to perform. He lived this philosophy and learned through his urban experiences to reach large numbers of people in a way that earlier leaders like Fermín Salvochea and Salvador Seguí never discovered. His adventures in Latin America, capricious though they were, nevertheless kept the spirit of Spanish anarchism alive during the difficult days of the dictatorship. Likewise, his furious campaign against the Second Republic brought mass attention to the lack of popular land reform and enlightened labor legislation. Many old Spanish anarchists still believe that this work was his greatest triumph.

All this is a long way for Eric Hobsbawm's assertion that Spanish anarchism was a disaster because it made no attempt to change the style of primitive revolt but, in fact, deliberately reinforced it.[4] The whole thrust of Durruti's violent career centered on a visionary attempt to mobilize anarchist masses from a society of isolation and backwardness. Perhaps he was too passionate and emotional, too rough and crude to bring the kind of change that would have been ideal; but for a man who had risen from nowhere, he forcefully conveyed a will to be free of those social institutions that in his lifetime had brought misery to Spaniards.

The Spanish anarchist movement itself, as Federica Montseny and Diego Abad de Santillán show, had already undergone an intellectual reawakening. Buenaventura Durruti accepted new ideas even while he played his role as the most proletarian European revolutionary leader, but it is this role alone that he is remembered for.

July 19, 1936: the battle begins.

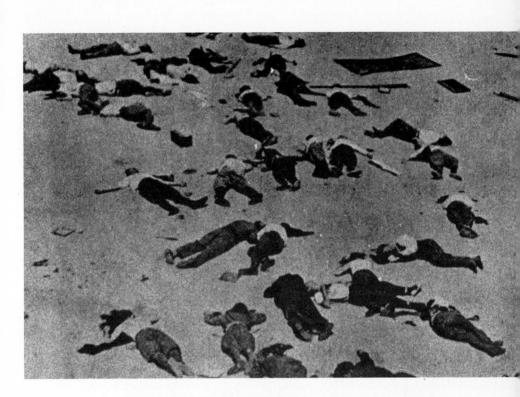

Formation of the militia. Standing at center above, wearing tie, is Diego Abad de Santillán.

The militia goes to the front.

*Above: Francisco Ascaso and
Federica Montseny.*

Federica Montseny.

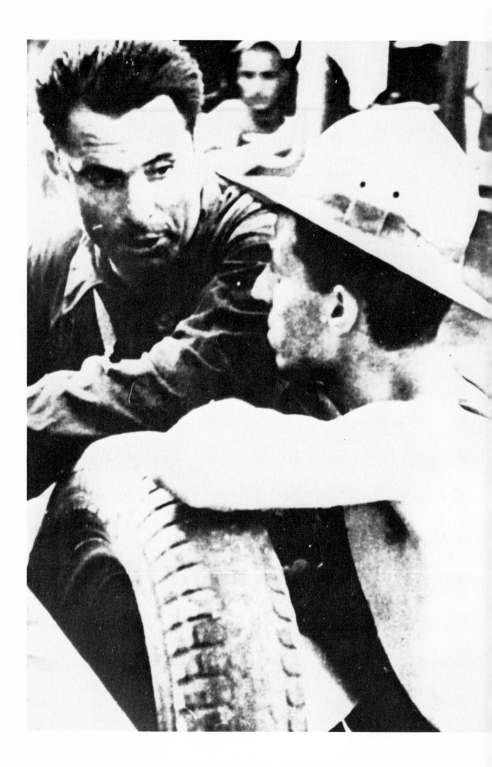

Buenaventura Durruti.

War scenes.

Slogans of the revolution; at top right, a publication on the first anniversary of Durruti's death.

RUTA

El individuo es tanto más perfecto cuanto más se emancipa del Estado.

ORGANO DE LAS JUVENTUDES LIBERTARIAS DE CATALUÑA

Año I — Núm. 3 — 15 cts.

Redacción de «Ruta» Cortes, 491 - Teléfono 30655
Administración de «Ruta» Unión, 7 - Teléf. 25655

Barcelona, 31 octubre 1936

Anarchist art.

Below and at bottom of facing page: obituaries of Ascaso and Durruti from the anarchist press.

el frente

C. N. T.   BOLETIN DE GUERRA DE LA 26 DIVISION · DURRUTI   F. A. I.

AÑO II   Bujaraloz, 28 de Junio de 1937.   NUM. 88

EL HOMBRE Y EL HEROE

FRANCISCO ASCASO

POR PEDRO PABLO PORTERO.

El célebre autor de «Fausto», gloria de la Alemania liberal y estudiosa (¡ay! cuyas cenizas inmortales aprietan hoy las botas ensangrentadas del megalómano Hitler) nos aconseja ser mesurados y discretos en el elogio. Es más: nos recomienda terminantemente no gastar pólvora literaria ni verbal de esa clase. Porque, nos dice, el que *reconoce* una superioridad, pone de manifiesto al mismo tiempo su talla de pigmeo, su inferioridad propia...

Nosotros, los anarquistas, siempre fuimos iconoclastas por principio y creo que principalmente por temperamento. El espíritu servil, sumiso, gregario, nos llena de indignación, a la vez que de profunda pena.

Queremos que el individuo lleve bien puesta la cabeza sobre los hombros, con un corazón rebosante de moral brava, higiénica, saludable; por humana, solidaria y fraterna.

Nuestro entrañable problema capital, manantial de todas nuestras inquietudes, lo constituye la personalidad humana, la cual deseamos verla siempre erguida, rebelde, apuesta, dueña de sí misma, como cultivada en los climas más vitalizadores de la Cultura... Deseamos verla, en resumen, libre de trabas externas, que tengan su origen en la tiranía o en la explotación, en el dolo o fraude. Completamente libre, sin perder por ello el buen sentido de cooperación y solidaridad sociales.

La personalidad de Francisco Ascaso, fuerte y culta, presenta esas perspectivas amables. En vida, fué un hombre, todo un hombre, porque fué sobre todo, alma bien templada y conducta ejemplar.

Por ser un hombre, todo un hombre, su vida entera fué un martirio permanente.

Su *verdad* fué la Libertad, y su libertad fué la Austeridad. Mirémonos en ese espejo, camaradas.

Como un nuevo Cristo, más sagaz, más humano y más bravo, dedicó su existencia llena de tormentos y de dolores, a la defensa de los oprimidos, de los explotados, de los parias del trabajo, de los ilotas aferrados a prejuicios y normas esclavizantes.

Su verdad, su evangelio, fué la Libertad, con la convivencia sana y recta, sincera, austera, alegre y fecunda.

Cuando dejó de ser hombre, con su muerte, con su asesinato por la tiranía, pasó a ser héroe, pasó a ser símbolo.

Es el hermano gemelo de Durruti, quizá superior a Durruti.

Pero los dos son espejos limpidos y luminosos (nos reflejan el porvenir anhelado) donde debemos mirarnos, camaradas, y a los cuales debemos imitarles como héroes de acción y del pensamiento libre, si en verdad deseamos exterminar a los nuevos bárbaros que asolan nuestra patria de origen (nuestra patria es el Mundo), a cara des-

Publication with Durruti's slogan: "Nothing less than victory."

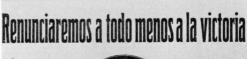

May 1937: another "Tragic Week" in Barcelona.

May 1937: the end of the anarchist struggle.

The militia accepted women alongside men in the front lines specifically at Durruti's urging, despite the extremely sexist nature of Spanish society. His speeches contained strong demands for massive public education, and the militia spent a great deal of time educating its members. He was not therefore a "noble gunman" or a barbarian outside the gates so much as a tough man who assumed political leadership in order to rouse his people to face the twentieth century. Although much more had to be done before Spain could truly change, Durruti took the first necessary steps away from primitivism.

His most remarkable quality, especially in a land of *caudillos* and *caciques* where bombastic politics were common, was his own lack of egotism. He was an altruist despite himself, a man alien to politics who did not think about his career in personal terms. Durruti never attempted to rule the CNT or FAI with an iron hand or construct an ideological empire. He did not castigate political opponents or always push sectarianism to the furthest limits. Other leaders were more hostile to the *treintistas* than he was, and he even dealt with communists without losing his perspective. Once elevated to command in the civil war, he did not turn his back on people. Individuals continued to approach him easily, and as Emma Goldman indicated, he listened to their problems. Like most Spaniards, he had a *tertulia* of friends in the Solidarios and Nosotros, but while they were close, they did not form a palace guard. Many others worked with him without encountering friction. His hope for the militia was that it would train thousands of Spaniards to make the Nosotros or FAI unnecessary.

What emerged from these various contradictions was an adventurer turned political leader, a man of simple but strong vision who sought to create an authority-free society with populist overtones. His basic commitment was not to modernization or some form of state socialism but to a freeing of the people. In this populist faith he was the prototype of Ché Guevara, not programmatic but undeniably a revolutionary leader. The civil war forced him away from pure voluntarism towards the role of an organizer. Where this might have led him is difficult to judge. Perhaps, like Fidel Castro, he would have eventually embraced a more systematic socialism as the crisis of the civil war mounted.[5] But the only evidence to support this supposition was his acceptance of militarization, which he fought until the supply crisis reached monumental proportions. The values of anarchism were deeply rooted in the consciousness of most Spanish libertarians. This set of values had existed far longer than the period during which Fidel Castro, for example, considered the possibilities of Marxist-Leninism. Moreover, Durruti knew that worker-dominated factory councils or large-scale agricultural communes made sense in a country where, under capitalism, productivity was low and technological efficiency still lacking, and where any radical or communist experiment in nationalization would risk major conflict with regionalism. Above all, the Spanish state remained more alien and more hated even than the Batista government before the Cuban revolution. Against this background, it is hard to see Durruti changing ideologies.

But now he was dead, and with him died the model, prototype, and inspiration for revolution. A voluntarist course of action demands great spiritual qualities, and no other anarchist possessed his charisma. Only Durruti had the stature to negotiate with Largo Caballero or to hold the militia together and keep its dissident elements from going off on their own tangents. Probably he alone might have halted the disastrous slide of anarchist fortunes after the cabinet recaptured political power. The heroic action of the 26th Brigade raised the possibility of an anarchist revival, but only dimly and certainly not after his death.

In the six months after Durruti's death, anarchist power continued to decline and communist control of the Second Republic to rise. Throughout the period—and long afterwards, in fact—the survivors were haunted by what might have happened if Buenaventura Durruti had not died in Madrid at the very apex of his career. This cult placed too much emphasis upon the "great man" theory, for anarchist power had ebbed even before he had arrived in Madrid. Still, the fact remains that the movement showed greater signs of disorientation, confusion, and divided leadership after his death than before. The growth of Soviet power in Spain was largely responsible for the ensuing disasters, but the loss of Durruti robbed anarchists of the inspiration to fight back.

II. The Militia Declines

The militia concept lasted until June 1937 in name, if not always in fact. Militarization made independence a thing of the past, with political control resting in Madrid and Barcelona. The CNT was permitted to name Durruti's successor, but the job now seemed so unattractive that Juan García Oliver, the first choice, decided to remain as Minister of Justice. A former assistant to Durruti, Ricardo

Sanz, finally filled the position. Under his guidance, the 26th was reorganized into a division composed of three mixed brigades—the 120th, 121st, and 199th. Other anarchist or Catalan forces were also altered, with the Macià-Companys column becoming the 30th Division, and the Ortíz column the 25th, while the Ascaso, Aguiluchos, Rojo y Negro, and others became the 28th.[6] Some fought again at the battle of Jarama east of Madrid in February 1937, but most returned to Aragon, where they reinforced the towns of Sietamo and Alcubierre.

The desire to avenge the death of Durruti dominated the thoughts of Madrid veterans so greatly that, four days before Christmas 1936, Ricardo Sanz called upon them to stage a daring night attack on Saragossa. A severe snow storm hampered the advance, and it took fourteen hours to reach the outskirts of the city. The delay isolated groups of anarchist saboteurs and insurrectionists who had already begun a small-scale rising. The nationalists executed more than a hundred on Christmas day, and twice that number died fighting in the streets. Only a few managed to link up with raiding parties from the 26th Division.[7] Together, they managed to hold several areas of the city until New Year's Day, when the last survivors fled back to the militia lines. Saragossa remained unconquered, and it was small comfort that more than two thousand anarchists managed to escape. A majority of them became the backbone of the Sur Ebro column.

Still another attack began in mid-January 1937. Small groups infiltrated nationalist lines and carefully photographed Falange barracks, Civil Guard headquarters, war industries, and artillery emplacements. These photographs were smuggled back to Alcubierre, where miners in the militia determined the exact amount of explosives necessary and began the long task of moving it into the city. Fuendetodos, the anarchist stronghold nearest to Saragossa, became the staging depot for a major attack scheduled to take place on January 24, 1937, after saboteurs had done their job. Then the entire 26th Division would be committed to battle from its bases in Fuendetodos and Torrero, while smaller offensives would begin in Zuera, Bujaraloz, and along the Huesca and Madrid highways—a front of more than a hundred kilometers.

More than seven hundred mules were collected at the front as transport, but the Defense Ministry in Madrid, convinced that the 26th did not have sufficient equipment, ordered the Catalan Council of Defense to cancel the offensive. Ricardo Sanz protested bitterly that more than five thousand guerrillas awaited the militia within

Saragossa, but the order stood and the attack never occurred.[8] Perhaps Durruti might have used his prestige and forcefulness to countermand this decision, but Sanz had none to use. The abandoned January offensive marked one of the last major anarchist offensives in Aragon. It was long remembered as the campaign Madrid did not want them to win.

This fiasco underscored the difficulties that were developing in Aragon. Ricardo Sanz found it increasingly hard to deal with PSUC regiments or military authorities in Madrid. Command staff meetings often deteriorated into acrimonious debate over sectarian political matters or over such questions as who would receive credit for military successes, few though they were.[9] Many anarchist veterans believed that PSUC protests to the Defense Ministry had been instrumental in cancelling the last attack upon Saragossa.[10] An additional difficulty stemmed from the Ministry's decision to send more communists to the Aragon front. Ricardo Sanz vetoed use of the International Brigades; they were "adventurers imposed upon the Spanish people against their will."[11] The flow of communists from training centers near Valencia and Alicante continued without interruption, however, since a number of regular army officers on the central and southern fronts convinced their brigades that they should accept communist discipline.

The AIT vainly tried to stem this flow by organizing foreign brigades of its own. Two *centurias* of foreigners joined the 26th Division, and two others drawn from youth groups were financed, but not recruited, by the AIT.[12] In addition, Durruti's death inspired a few libertarians to rush to Spain in order to fight in Aragon. One Bulgarian anarchist began hitchhiking to Barcelona as soon as he heard the news.[13] Unfortunately, this was hardly a match for the volume of communist recruitment. Anarchists had very thin international resources on which to rely.

This growing disparity of strength between the political forces encouraged the Madrid defense junta, communist sympathizers in the government, and the Defense Ministry to interfere increasingly in militia affairs. Communists actively controlled public order, supplies, and the Defense Ministry itself, while the Russian general Goriev worked closely with Miaja on all military matters.[14] The air force, tank corps, artillery, and anti-aircraft defenses were led by Soviet advisors, who could also be found in the Fifth Regiment and the International Brigades. The entire thrust of their influence after November 1936 was to diminish the importance of the militias. The first stage of militarization closed the possibility of organizing more columns representing political parties, while abolition of the Anti-Fascist Militia Committee removed the political arm of the Aragon army. In its place Madrid established the General Commissariat of War on October 15, 1936, to maintain loyalty, enforce discipline, and educate republican soldiers on a national scale. It quickly became a vehicle for further communist influence, mainly because Angel Pestaña, the CNT delegate, became seriously ill and was replaced by a communist sympathizer.[15]

This reversal was a crucial setback with serious ramifications. Almost at once the use of commissars increased. Anarchists could only look on while militia personnel and regular soldiers were pressured to join communist groups.[16] The climax came on December 24, 1936, when General Miaja announced a final reorganization of the republican army. In time, it was decreed, militias would be entirely absorbed into the regular army. Professional officers, commissars, and strict military discipline were now imposed upon all branches of the army. No political group could directly control units of the new model army except for the communists, whose services were considered indispensable. Moreover, the War Ministry assumed total control over all aspects of military opposition to fascism. The decree's tone made it quite clear that the anarchist revolution was over.

Anarchist anguish at this decision poured out bitterly and at great cost. The Madrid newspaper *CNT* was suspended for its criticism two days after the decree.[17] The FAI daily *Nosotros* of Valencia encountered the same trouble on February 27, 1937. The Basque government closed *CNT del Norte* on March 26, 1937, and *CNT* and *Castilla Libre* of Madrid received longer suspensions on April 11, 1937.[18] Perhaps the most adamant opposition came from the Iron Column stationed in Teruel. Its members refused to accept militarization and issued a set of counter-demands calling for a total disarming of all security police. In a touch reminiscent of anarchism's earlier days, they also demanded destruction of all archives and records of state and capitalist institutions.[19] Indignation continued to run so high in the column that the government finally agreed to appoint neither professional officers nor commissars. Eventually the Iron Column was purged and became the 83rd Brigade.

This pattern of anarchist protest occurred everywhere. *Ruta* protested on November 28, 1936, that "if we sail along with the authoritarian current . . . , nothing will remain of anarchist ideals," but when the number of professional officers sent to the Aragon front was increased, no further protest was heard. Camillo Berneri attacked militarization as sure to lead to state police activity, the normalization of middle-class life, and the dismantling of the revolution.[20] Juan Peiró criticized the other anarchist ministers for putting the war above the social revolution. Federica Montseny and Juan García Oliver answered him by pointing to the lack of effort and the bourgeois attitudes in the rearguard. They also criticized the transfer of Catalan security police (Moços d'Esquadra) to Luis Companys' control and the creation of a national state police agency (Consejo Nacional de Seguridad) in Madrid.[21]

Such confusion indicated how much Buenaventura Durruti was missed; anarchists now had no strong voice or influence. Judging from Diego Abad de Santillán's comments, Durruti had not altogether rejected the concept of a regular army and might have accepted staff and command changes if the militia itself had been left intact. But the actual militarization that was instituted led to a compound error. It cut off enthusiasm for the war, and it transformed a popular war into one monopolized by the state—"a war versus the will and the interests of a great mass of individuals."[22] Durruti, always extremely conscious of the popular will, undoubtedly would have revolted against the final militarization orders of December 24, 1936. His leadership could have brought a second revolution more interesting than the first, or so, at least, ran the logic of the ultra-radicals who appeared in the following months.

At the time, however, only Diego Abad de Santillán was outspoken on military matters. His new periodical *Timón* fought strenuously for the militias at every opportunity. Very anti-Russian, he argued that the Soviets opposed the militia because of their own experiences with Nestor Makhno during the Russian civil war. The republican government refused to consider irregular warfare led by anarchists, yet militarization meant only the imitation of a professional army that had largely gone over to General Franco. Suppression of guerrilla tactics, as exemplified by cancellation of the last attack upon Saragossa, hastened the defeat of the Second Republic. "It was done by a government which had no understanding of the people—a government without capacity or courage."[23] So much of Diego Abad de Santillán's venom was concentrated upon the Russians, in fact, that he remained silent on class issues and the flight of the middle class into the communist party. Nevertheless, he tried to fill the shoes of Buenaventura Durruti.

But no amount of criticism could prevent the communists from strengthening their power. The fall of Malaga on February 8, 1937, demonstrated their grip on the Madrid government. General Asensio, an anti-communist, received blame for the defeat and lost his position as Deputy War Minister. His replacement, Carlos de Baraíbar, nominated by the communists, was totally without military experience, having previously edited a socialist newspaper.[24] Rumors spread again of militia inefficiencies, and communists demanded immediate conscription, which began a few weeks later. The draft ended political recruiting and severed political parties from paramilitary operations. The communists, of course, relied upon the commissar system within the regular army to do their own work for them.

As the disastrous loss of Malaga showed, the communist military effort was often weaker and less dependable than the anarchists' own campaigns. Cayetano Bolívar, a communist and the political head of the Malaga defense junta, had been in charge of its military preparations. If allegations against him were correct, he spent more time on political matters than in organizing military resistance.[25] General Asensio believed the communists bore heavy responsibility for Malaga's collapse, and even Colonel Villalba, the able military commander appointed too late to reorganize the city's forces, mentioned the excessive political proselytizing the communists undertook.[26] As for the militia, the differences between its northern and southern contingents have already been noted. Many of these troops were not anarchists at all.

After Malaga, Ricardo Sanz perceived the fate of the militias all too clearly. In April 1937 he ordered two more attacks upon Saragossa and Huesca in the vain hope of salvaging a last victory that might postpone absorption of his anarchist militia. The 26th pushed forward in several places, but it faced an enemy now armed with superior German and Italian weapons. Handicapped by familiar supply problems, the campaign failed after ten days. In the ensuing weeks even the most militant anarchists lost faith that the elusive victory could ever be obtained.

III. The Anarchist Ministers

New power for the regular army was only one of many changes in republican Spain during this period. In Catalonia, Luis Companys quietly regained normal executive power by taking control of the security police. On October 11, 1936, he claimed the right to dissolve all local juntas that interfered with the regional government's free-

215

dom of action. In addition, he assumed reprieve power over decisions of the Popular Tribunals.

From its base in Lerida, the Trotskyist POUM loudly attacked these actions and was itself condemned as fascist by the Russian consul general, Vladimir Antonov-Ovseenko, on December 2, 1936.[27] The isolated POUM had been seeking an alliance with the CNT for some time, but in fact POUM "was liked by nobody, being overbearing and claiming with its small forces leadership over the old established mass organizations, both anarchist and socialist."[28] Trotskyists hated the PSUC for its Stalinism and rapid rise to power, while the PSUC detested the POUM for its anti-Stalinism in Russian affairs and its ultra-radical position on Spanish questions. Luis Companys listened to the Russians and on December 16, 1936, reshuffled the cabinet of his government to exclude the POUM. Andrés Nín lost the Ministry of Justice. In Madrid the POUM was also excluded from the defense junta, and its offices and newspapers were closed.

In national politics similar events took place. Francisco Largo Caballero's long-time socialist rival, Indalecio Prieto, led moderate socialists into an alliance with the communists. This coalition made explicit the moderates' rejection of class war in favor of a strict anti-fascism and, by implication, indicted the Premier for his toleration of political diversity in the midst of a civil war. The CNT countered by aligning with the Largo Caballero wing of the UGT and demanding an extension of collectivization to all regions of republican Spain, while also considering the possibility of converting the FAI into a genuine political party.[29] The Congress of Caspe, a national gathering of commune representatives, supported these moves and praised the Premier's growing unwillingness to dismantle the revolution.[30]

After the fall of Malaga, Largo Caballero's position daily became more difficult and, as a result, he moved closer to the anarchists. This surprising *rapprochement* enhanced the importance of the four anarchist ministers in his cabinet, for Largo Caballero rarely quarreled with them and usually gave blanket approval to their plans. This encouraged other anarchists to join the Madrid government at a time when they were being driven out of Catalan affairs. The libertarian José Alandi became Under-Secretary of State; Sigfrido Català, Director-General of Interior; Horacio Prieto, Director-General of Foreign Trade; Pedro Cané, Under-Secretary of Industry; and Mariano Roca, Under-Secretary of Justice. Anarchist aspirations were transferred *en bloc* from Barcelona to Madrid.

The impact of this transfer on government policy was mixed.

Juan López and Juan Peiró occupied such relatively minor offices that their only contribution was a protection of collectivized industries against communist plans for nationalization—a holding action without much positive force. On the other hand, Federica Montseny converted her modest portfolio at the Ministry of Sanitation and Public Works into a major position within the Madrid government. She began by firing bureaucratic personnel to bring in social activists. Whenever possible, councils with CNT and UGT delegates received broad responsibility to gather opinions on social services. The Council on Sanitation and Social Assistance generally set policy once public opinion was known.[31] Party representation in government was thus kept alive, but efforts to expand the scope of the councils eventually encountered opposition from the Treasury and the Ministry of Public Education.[32] Federica Montseny solved this problem by creating other bodies, such as the Council of Social Supplies, to purchase medical equipment, clothing, and food for the needy. A council on medicine attracted the participation of doctors in order to develop additional public health projects. Soon, too, a new Institute of Food Hygiene emerged from their work. Massive inoculation campaigns against infectious diseases operated effectively.

Montseny also attempted to achieve broad changes in social roles and welfare benefits. One of her symposia produced a proclamation on the rights of children which embodied a number of far-reaching and progressive ideas; another was held on the rights of women.[33] New homes for the blind and rehabilitation centers for former prostitutes were two other offshoots of this work.[34] She also made arrangements with French libertarians to send groups of Spanish orphans to France for safety. This led her to travel to Geneva, Switzerland, to address the International Health Committee of the League of Nations, where she defended the cause of the women and children caught behind nationalist lines.

She gave hundreds of speeches in Catalonia and Valencia, perhaps in a conscious attempt to assume Buenaventura Durruti's role as spiritual leader of the revolution. If so, she filled the role well, although it did take time away from her ministerial functions. Budgetary limitations and lack of adequate staff made some of her projects appear rudimentary and poorly executed.[35] Yet whatever deficiencies existed, no one worked harder to develop a workable anarchist program than the Minister herself.

As Minister of Justice, Juan García Oliver kept equally busy but was certainly more controversial in his job. In volume, the legal changes he sponsored matched Federica Montseny's projects. One of his first acts guaranteed the right of defendants to a lawyer's services, even if they were indigent.[36] On December 12, 1936, stringent new penalties for participation in the black market or other kinds of speculation were decreed. These were followed by a sweeping amnesty for those convicted of a variety of political crimes committed before July 19, 1936.[37]

Juan García Oliver also cooperated with Federica Montseny in altering many aspects of family law. Common-law marriages became legally binding, with both partners equally protected. Children of such alliances were no longer stigmatized as illegitimate. He, too, sponsored symposia on legal problems, including one on prison reform that developed guidelines based on the principles of enlightened penal practice. The Minister, a former prison inmate himself, must have taken considerable delight in these reforms, and he also used them adroitly to influence public opinion against communist security measures.

Without a doubt, Juan García Oliver's major effort went into amplification of legal precedents and procedures, based on the lessons of the revolution, to govern the work of the Popular Tribunals. By May 13, 1937, when this decree was finally published, the tide was running very strongly against the anarchists. Representing the last revolutionary project to outline aspects of a new libertarian society, it lowered the scale of punishments for major crimes, instructed tribunals to base their decisions upon the socioeconomic background of defendants (with vocational training in reformatories for lesser crimes and in case of extenuating circumstances), and generally followed the philosophy that human rights were of greater importance than property rights.[38]

Even while hearings were being held on the decree, the proposed revision outraged many persons, both moderates and communists. Juan García Oliver, of course, was no lawyer; he did not have the slightest legal training. This disturbed moderates so much that one Englishman who had some familiarity with Spanish law wrote a book in 1938 entitled *Revolutionary Justice in Spain*. He castigated García Oliver for allowing Popular Tribunals to revise decisions handed down before July 19, 1936, and to declare as fascist any act which directly or indirectly assisted the military rebellion.[39] The president and twelve jury members of a tribunal, he further charged, seldom had the legal training or general education to make informed judgments.

García Oliver disagreed vehemently:

Justice must be hot, justice must be alive, justice cannot be restricted within the bounds of a profession. It is not that we definitely despise books and procedure, but the fact is [that] there were too many lawyers. Justice must not be in doubt as to whether it is in the right or not; it must have an inflexibility which is above circumstances. Justice must be something more than popular—it must be primitive.[40]

In other words, justice had to be returned to the people. Its basis was the collective wisdom of a people's experience. Moreover, champions of revolutionary justice refused to accept professionalization for fear the law would once again become the personal property of an elite. Instinct, not abstract principles or elaborate codification, now governed Spanish justice, a disquieting prospect for all but the anarchists.

Communists reacted by bringing pressure to bear in Barcelona and Madrid to abolish the Popular Tribunals and to normalize judicial administration. When Largo Caballero refused, the communists organized their own system. A scandal resulted when it was discovered that José Cazorla, Commissar for Public Order in the Madrid defense junta, had created a secret political police, a *cheka*.[41] Defendants freed by the tribunals frequently experienced rearrest and imprisonment, until Cazorla himself went to jail. In the aftermath, Largo Caballero dissolved the junta and replaced it with a regular city council.

Despite this temporary victory, the deeper reality of increasing communist strength could not be denied. Even in the area of justice the communist control of republican police limited anarchist influence. In Catalonia, too, control patrols lost jurisdiction over crime control and found themselves rendered all but useless.[42] Voices within the CNT/FAI soon asked why the four ministers continued their apostasy by cooperating with the state in the face of such anti-revolutionary developments.

Federica Montseny answered for the ministers in February 1937, when she made a speech in Valencia. The retrograde nature of fascism demanded a new approach; this new form of totalitarianism represented statism at its worst. Anarchists in the cabinet were the first to understand that the struggle against fascism was of primary importance. "We think by [cooperating with Largo Caballero] we will avoid a repetition of the fate of the anarchist movements in other countries where communists assumed direction of the revolution. . . ."[43] Only an anti-fascist libertarian coalition could rid Spain of totalitarianism. But under no circumstances had the anarchist ministers abandoned a desire to change society. Ultimately, once

219

fascism was destroyed, each region of Spain would hold a plebiscite to determine its form of political and economic organization. Above all, Federica Montseny felt confident that a new federal Spain would emerge at the end of a victorious civil war. Experience in collectivization had unified workers and peasants, and their common effort gave them the confidence to develop a libertarian society and thereby realize the old dream of anarchism.

This speech by Federica Montseny was the last anarchist expression of optimism before renewed violence led to the final collapse of anarchist power. She and the other CNT/FAI members of the government, certain that their loyalty to Largo Caballero protected the movement and that the Premier remained strong, ignored new signs of sectarian schism. But, in fact, almost no one anticipated the suddenness of the May 1937 crisis.

In retrospect, it seems that the CNT/FAI entrance into the Popular Front in November 1936, by abandoning principle, may have exhausted the Spanish anarchist movement long before May 1937. Or perhaps anarchist leaders believed that their loyalty to the Popular Front now had been so amply demonstrated that anarchism could not be disturbed by shifts of power within the Republic. Whichever the case, the anarchist ministers of state were so consumed by work that it was very difficult for them to remain adequately informed about the current political situation. When the AIT and Camillo Berneri tried to warn them of approaching danger, their duties prevented them from squarely facing the problem.[44]

IV. Time of Assassins

The success of Federica Montseny and Juan García Oliver in Madrid threatened both the Catalan regionalists and the communists. What if the CNT/FAI created a political party? Rumors circulated that the FAI intended to contest the local elections that were scheduled to be held in a few months.[45] It seemed possible that an anarchist or anarcho-syndicalist political party might become a dominant force very quickly. Conservative Catalans were sufficiently alarmed at this specter to demand that Luis Companys take action to curb the anarchists. When he refused to go further in his campaign against the CNT/FAI, a *coup d'état* was staged. Its failure forced the flight of Juan Casanoves, President of the Catalan parliament, and the secret execution of Andreu Reverter, Commissioner of Public Order.[46]

Throughout 1937, Casanovas worked with others (Lluhi Vallescá, Xicota Sancho, and Ventura Gassol) in the exile party Estat Català to propagandize in favor of an autonomous and conservative Catalan republic severed entirely from Madrid. The group claimed to speak for outraged middle-class Catalans who would no longer put up with anarchist control of the Northeast. Estat Català's aversion to the CNT/FAI led to negotiations with Juan Comorera, the PSUC chairman, on April 20, 1937, or so AIT sources in Paris claimed.[47] Catalan anarchists believed that Estat Català and the communists made plans at this meeting for a concerted attack upon the CNT/FAI in Barcelona.

Communist reaction to anarchist successes had been equally negative. Indalecio Prieto's split with Francisco Largo Caballero destroyed the alignment of the Popular Front and hastened the possibility of communist cabinet control—if anarchist ministers could be driven from government. But before this could happen, a communist maneuver to end anarchist military influence backfired. In February 1937, military executions of militia leaders were ordered by the Defense Ministry. The case of Francisco Maroto, anarchist commander of Malaga, became a *cause célèbre*. Maroto, a scapegoat for the republican loss of Malaga, was given the death sentence by a military court dominated by communists. However, his sentence was commuted under pressure from the anarchist ministers and in the backlash from José Cazorla's *"cheka"* scandal.[48] For the first time in several months the communists found their power declining. In addition, continuing merger activity by the CNT and UGT syndicates presented a greater threat to communist power. Both the Russian political security (OGPU) chief, Arthur Stashevsky, and a leading Spanish communist sympathizer, Julio Álvarez del Vayo, were deeply concerned.

This background explains why such dissimilar allies as PSUC and Estat Català sought a common policy against the anarchists. Their collaboration was only one of a series of new offensives as the communists sought to regain the advantage. The most serious was a campaign begun by Artemio Ayguadé, Catalan Minister of Internal Security, and Eusebio Rodríguez Salas, Commissioner-General of Police (both either communist party members or sympathizers), against "uncontrollable elements." On March 12, 1937, they demanded that all parties and individuals surrender their weapons. CNT members of the Catalan government remained off work until April 16 (a walkout of thirty-five days duration), and when they returned, the PSUC insisted that a new oath of government loyalty be administered to the anarchists. Their refusal almost precipitated another walkout, and the Catalan government finally made the oath non-mandatory. CNT and FAI members vowed never to allow communists or regionalists another chance to take advantage of their political principles.

But the new communist hard line continued to cause violence. A battle had already raged in January 1937 between the PSUC and the FAI in the Catalan town of Fatarella. In April, after both sides had obtained more arms, gunfights occurred almost daily. On March 5, 1937, ten armored cars stolen by Catalan military officers were found hidden in a barn on the outskirts of Barcelona.[49] The sense of approaching battle became more real, and some anarchists reacted by readopting a maximalist revolutionary position.

The best example of this sharp sectarianism was the Amigos de Durruti (Friends of Durruti), a shadowy faction about which little has been known. Its origin lay partly in the expulsion of the POUM from the Catalan regional government in December 1936. A number of young Trotskyists, including Gregorio Munís and the group publishing the newspaper *La Voz Leninista*, began searching for a new, more effective organization to join. Their opportunity came in January 1937, after the national conference of the FAI, when radical *faístas*—Jaime Balius, Gregorio Jover, Juan Carreno, Pablo Ruiz, and Eleuterio Roig—challenged policies concerning anarchist participation in the Madrid and Barcelona governments. They lost, even though representatives of chapters in Lerida, Vich, Tortosa, Hostafranchs, and Tarragona supported their caucus.[50] In the weeks after the meeting, radical *faístas* and Trotskyists joined forces in Barcelona to create a new political action group, the Friends of Durruti, which began publishing a newspaper, *El Amigo del Pueblo*, choosing its title from Marat's broadsheet during the French revolution. Jaime Balius financed the paper and became its publisher, while Eleuterio Roig, Pablo Ruiz, and Domingo Paniagua wrote the editorials. Gregorio Jover, the old man of the group, had been in the Solidarios and the Nosotros and was a veteran of the exile days in France and Belgium, when he had been a close companion of Buenaventura Durruti and Francisco Ascaso. To the young members of the Amigos de Durruti, he seemed to be a link with the romantic libertarian past of the "action groups." Jover himself, deeply embittered by the deaths of both Durruti and Ascaso, had suicidal tendencies; and though he had spent seven months on the battlefront in Aragon, his capacity for fighting remained undiminished. Always a violent terrorist (the real assassin of Spanish anarchism), Jover now swore to find revenge. The Friends of Durruti provided a new opportunity.

El Amigo del Pueblo circulated secretly in April and early May 1937 and illegally thereafter until November 1937, when it was suppressed. The CNT never authorized its publication and in fact thoroughly disapproved of it.[51] In its first issue the paper denounced the CNT (for joining the Popular Front cabinet), Luis Companys' rule, middle classes, the government in Valencia, and of course the PSUC. It headlined its second issue: "The petite bourgeoisie has to be eliminated from ruling this country! This is the hour of the proletariat!"[52] The paper advocated complete direction of economic and social life by the syndicates, municipal assemblies run on the basis of direct democracy, abolition of all armed police, and re-creation of the Anti-Fascist Militia Committee.[53] Spain was envisaged as a work society, with forced syndicalization, work exchanges, equal wages, and the socialization of all means of production and finance. Bureaucracy and strict conformity to any official ideology would be eliminated to prevent elitism and political direction from abroad— i.e., from the USSR.

Jaime Balius was eventually arrested and executed along with four other members of the Friends of Durruti. During the summer of 1937, members of the group were arrested in Asco, Puigcerda, Seo de Urgel, and Barcelona.[54] Rumors were rampant that the paper was entirely a Trotskyist operation or that it was secretly funded by the PSUC to provoke the Catalan government into taking strenuous action against the CNT/FAI. Jaime Balius denied all these charges in *Fraga Social* and described himself as anti-middle class and anti-collaborationist—a revolutionary who used Buenaventura Durruti's life as a guide.[55] He felt that the CNT had been captured by *treintistas* content to concentrate on narrow syndicate issues to the exclusion of all political questions, which they left to the PSUC. Unless this policy ended immediately, there would be little choice except to capitulate to the communists.

It was unlikely that the PSUC secretly sponsored *Amigo del Pueblo*. It may have kept the Catalan government from closing the paper in order to have proof that "uncontrollable elements" did in fact exist in Catalonia, but this purpose was quickly served. Still, the paper struggled onward, propelled by the Trotskyists on the staff who, denied a forum elsewhere, continued to use anarchist assistance to seek an audience. Radical anarchists, hostile to participation of the CNT in government, welcomed the Trotskyists for their bitter anti-government attitude—a variant, they thought, of their own philosophy. The FAI crisis mentality knew no limits, and acceptance of strange political allies was natural at this moment.

The PSUC and other Catalan political groups were delighted to have such an outspoken but tiny opposition group facing them. New restrictive measures could now be justified, from purges of militia personnel in the regular army to house-to-house searches for personal arms in Barcelona. Anarchists reacted angrily as the tension raised frustrations to a new level. A few advocated an alliance with the POUM, but the majority wanted nothing to do with the Trotskyists. Some supported a complete halt to all CNT participation in state activities; Camillo Berneri attacked Federica Montseny for still believing that her presence in the government alone kept the revolution from being sidetracked.[56] Even Helmut Rüdiger and Augustin Souchy feuded bitterly over the dilemma. The AIT was unable to make sense out of the debate and unprepared to cope with the many facets of the situation. In the end the FAI persuaded the AIT to call an international anarchist congress in Barcelona during July to work out a compromise acceptable to all.[57] But the crisis would not wait for the summer, and in late April the situation took on violent overtones.

An area of extraordinary tension between political groups was the territory along the French border, where anarchists and communists clashed repeatedly in April 1937 over customs and passport control. Anarchists tried to stop communist volunteers and supplies for the International Brigades from coming into Spain, while communists facilitated their entry. Then, on April 25, in Molins de Llobregat, a PSUC member, Roldán Cortada, was assassinated. He had been a syndicalist and had in fact signed the *treintista* manifesto. Five years later, disenchanted by FAI adventurism, he had joined the PSUC, subsequently behaving, in the words of one observer, like the Calvo Sotelo of the PSUC. His murder caused the immediate arrest of many anarchists, among them Luis Cano, allegedly his assassin. Street battles in Puigcerda caused additional deaths, including that of Antonio Martín, the anarchist leader of the area and a smuggler of great repute.

On April 27 the PSUC paraded through the streets of Barcelona and held a large memorial service for Roldán Cortada. Fights broke out in many districts as anarchists and communists reacted to the tension. The same afternoon, General Sebastián Pozas, commander of the Army of the East, stationed new troops from Madrid on the main thoroughfares and reissued the order banning private arms. The ostensible reason was a threat of violence by the Friends of Durruti or the POUM, but on April 29 *Solidaridad Obrera* warned against cooperation. Many anarchists who marched in the May Day parade a few days later openly brandished pistols and rifles. Street fighting broke out again, with both sides using heavy weapons. The climax had been reached, and only a minor incident was needed to begin a civil war within the civil war.

V. *The May Crisis*

That incident occurred at the telephone building in Barcelona two days later, on May 3, 1937. ITT had lost control of its subsidiary at the start of the war, but in recent months the collective that ran it, controlled by the CNT but also containing UGT and government representatives, had come under criticism from moderate Catalans and communists alike, who demanded nationalization of the telephone company as a way of penalizing the anarchists. The CNT, forewarned, placed armed guards on the premises in April, an action that alarmed the regional government because the telephone building occupied a strategic corner overlooking the Plaza Cataluña in the center of the city. On May 3 the Commissioner-General of Police, Rodríguez Salas, decided that the presence of the guards constituted a threat to the stability of Barcelona. About 3 p.m. three truck-loads of police occupied the first floor of the building. Twelve armed workers seized the upper story and mounted a machine gun, which, after an exchange of shots, kept the police on the ground floor.

This stalemate lasted within the telephone building for the next four days. Internal Security Minister Ayguadé, supporting the police commissioner's contention that the anarchists were in rebellion against constituted authority, declared a state of emergency that sent armed police into every part of the city, despite the arrival at the telephone building of several CNT officials and the head of the control patrols, who were seeking a truce.[58] Police activity stopped these negotiations, and the CNT used its radio facilities to denounce Rodríguez Salas and Ayguadé and call for their resignations. Militants built barricades in the Sans and Hostafranchs districts, while the Barcelona bullring fell into the hands of some militiamen on leave. By late evening the conflict had spread as far away as Lerida.

Any hope for a peaceful settlement disappeared in the early

morning of May 4. Both sides began sniping in the center of the city, and police occupied the Palace of Justice and a few CNT/FAI centers. The CNT issued an appeal that read in part:

> It is necessary to come to a quick solution of this conflict. The incidents now taking place in the street are the result of a long and painful development aiming at the sacrifice of the CNT and its leaders after using their blood and strength to defeat the treacherous fascist. Don't let them betray you! You know very well, and you have proof of it, that the CNT/FAI is not against you, either as individuals or as a unit. You are, like ourselves, soldiers of the antifascist front. Offer your arms to the people and place yourselves on their side as you did on July 19.[59]

By afternoon, unfortunately, fighting had increased, and when Federica Montseny and Juan García Oliver arrived in Barcelona, they were advised by representatives of the Catalan regional government not to consult with President Companys or Premier Josep Tarradellas.

Catalan officials, in fact, were so enraged by the new battles that they refused to negotiate until all demonstrators left the streets. Instead, the PSUC began building a barricade some three hundred meters from the headquarters of the CNT/FAI on Vía Durruti. The ensuing fight heavily damaged the headquarters and killed more than thirty defenders. By 4 p.m. the situation had deteriorated so badly that the anarchist leadership sent Federica Montseny, Juan García Oliver, and Mariano Vázquez (CNT national secretary) to confer with Luis Companys. All they could agree upon was an appeal for a temporary cessation of hostilities. Notice of this agreement did not reach the Civil Guard in time to prevent attacks upon the Hide and Leather Workers syndicate (the medical station used by the anarchists) or the Libertarian Youth center. The PSUC did momentarily suspend its attack upon the CNT/FAI headquarters, but a blockade continued.

Leaders from both sides prolonged their conference through the night. By 9 a.m. on May 5 a CNT threat to bring the militia back from Aragon to defend anarchist centers in Barcelona forced the resignation of the two police officials, Rodríguez Salas and Ayguadé, and gave anarchists membership in a new provisional Catalan regional cabinet. At 11 a.m. the CNT and FAI held meetings all over the city to calm their followers, but anarchists in the district of Coll occupied a military installation. By 2 p.m. fierce street fighting had begun again in the center of Barcelona. Catalan soldiers joined the PSUC in the siege of the CNT/FAI headquarters. Around 5 p.m. an unidentified official ordered the militia in the bullring to attack the besiegers, and several hundred militiamen, accompanied by a few armored cars and tanks, joined the battle. The Catalans and the PSUC were soon reinforced, however, and the anarchist counter-attack was quickly repulsed.

The headquarters almost surrendered by 6 p.m., but Federica Montseny, in desperation, called for a new truce, with each side maintaining its positions while negotiation resumed. In the chaos her appeal went unanswered. With the anarchists losing, the PSUC and the Catalans did not want to discontinue hostilities until they achieved substantial gains. But in the evening of May 5, the old Solidarios activist Gregorio Jover, now a member of the Friends of Durruti, reached the headquarters with a small group of militiamen from Rojo y Negro and Aguiluchos. Jover established a regional defense committee to mobilize anarchist forces by calling upon armed FAI groups to reinforce central Barcelona. If need be, he was prepared to use the Aragon militia, and a series of communiqués went out to this effect. The Catalan cabinet, realizing the seriousness of the threat, began to order their forces to withdraw.

The defense committee rallied support during the night of May 5–6 by portraying the struggle as a simple defense of CNT inter-ests. Federica Montseny and Juan García Oliver kept revolutionary rhetoric out of their statements, but an anonymous pamphlet, per-haps published by the Friends of Durruti, appeared the same night, declaring that "a revolutionary junta has been constituted in Barce-lona. All those responsible for the putsch, maneuvering under the protection of the government, shall be executed. The POUM shall be a member of the revolutionary junta because they stood by the workers."[60]

Exactly who published this broadsheet is unknown. The anar-chists emphatically denied any responsibility, but so did the Friends of Durruti, even though they continued to call for a revolutionary junta long afterwards.[61] Jaime Balius was arrested and blamed for the incident, but the suspicion lingered that either the PSUC or the POUM was actually responsible. Trotskyists had lost heavily in the fighting and knew that the POUM would be outlawed if the PSUC won. By using the Friends of Durruti as cover, the Trotskyists may have expected to put pressure upon the anarchists to abandon the Popular Front and ally themselves with the POUM.

However, the PSUC possessed an even greater motive for issu-ing the anonymous pamphlet. If its authorship could be attributed to the anarchists or the POUM, the Catalan regional government

227

might not be so willing to negotiate with the CNT/FAI. The PSUC was pressuring the regionalists to use their military power in a final campaign against the anarchists and Trotskyists. With the headquarters of the CNT/FAI about to fall, victory was not far away, and destruction of the anarchists and Trotskyists would leave the PSUC without competition on the Left in Catalan politics.

This last explanation of the pamphlet is the most likely. As part of the overall plan, if we assume that one existed, squads of PSUC members took to the streets in the early morning hours of May 6 to assassinate leading anarchists. Efforts were made to locate Federica Montseny and Juan García Oliver, but they were too well protected. The chief victim of the death squads was Camillo Berneri, the anti-fascist, anti-Stalinist, Italian exile writer, who, with a friend, was arrested and then executed about 2 a.m. near Luis Companys' headquarters. Almost two hundred other anarchists were killed during this bloody night, about half of the five hundred CNT/FAI members who died during the crisis. Many of them were outspoken anti-communists.

In a later speech, Juan Comorera, the PSUC leader, put the events of May 6 in perspective by arguing that the anarchists had placed their revolution ahead of anti-fascism. If they were allowed to continue, the "prestige" of republican support abroad might erode, and the Second Republic would become isolated.[62] The attack upon the telephone building had been undertaken to ensure a continuation of telephone communications "without the indiscreet ear of the controller hearing it."[63] By ignoring the participation of other groups in the telephone collective, Juan Comorera provoked the destruction of Catalan anarchism, no doubt on Soviet orders. Counterfeiting of the Friends of Durruti pamphlet and the death of Camillo Berneri were probably part of the same PSUC plan.

But on the morning of May 6 the startling rapidity of the PSUC's offensive obscured these events. The FAI, shocked and indecisive, kept wavering towards negotiations. The violence of the previous night forced *faístas* to evacuate their workers from the telephone building at 3 p.m. on May 6. Luis Companys promised to remove the police, but at 4:30 p.m. PSUC members and Catalan officials occupied the entire building and brought in members of the UGT to run the telephone equipment.[64] Under Secretary of State Juanel Molina, a *faísta*, tried to get all political factions out of the building, but the PSUC refused and reinforced its elements in the area instead.

This action enraged the anarchists, but before they could take the offensive, the PSUC and some Catalan groups attacked the FAI units that held the northern railway station (Estación de Francia). As Federica Montseny sped off to protest this new incident at Companys' headquarters, her car came under fire. Mariano Vázquez and her secretary, Enrique Baruta, were wounded, and the party had to return to the railway station. Rumors reached the besieged force that large convoys of republican troops were converging upon Barcelona from Madrid and Jarama. The situation seemed extremely threatening, and another delegation was sent to Luis Companys to protest the afternoon's truce violations. "Neither the CNT nor the FAI attacked any police headquarters, nor any other institutions of state, nor the Catalan regional government," the message of the delegation read. "At no time, and at no place, did the first shot ever come from any responsible members of the CNT."[65] The message concluded with an appeal for unity of the CNT and the UGT and for a continued struggle against fascism.

Throughout the night of May 6–7, the anarchists waited while Luis Companys considered the situation. The PSUC urged rejection of the appeal, but the President feared open warfare between the militia and the regular army. In the end, he balanced an armistice with threatened prosecution of the Friends of Durruti and the POUM, but it was not until 5 a.m. on May 7 that the anarchists received word that the Catalan regional government had agreed to an armistice. All parties would leave the barricades, and all patrols or guards would return to their headquarters or place of residence. By noon on Friday, May 7, Barcelona was calm again.

When communications returned to normal and news from other areas could be received, the Catalan CNT/FAI saw that the crisis had not been a local affair. Violence against anarchists had occurred in Montesquieu, Lafarga, Bisaura, La Cenia, Tortosa, Villadalan, Amposta, and Beija.[66] Headquarters were occupied, militants disarmed, and their leaders either arrested or shot. In Tarragona the Esquerra and the police burned down anarchist centers and executed nine leaders. Lesser violence took place in Lerida, Gerona, and other towns. Moreover, it did not always stop with the signing of the truce. Communes continued to be suppressed around Tortosa and on May 11 in Sardanola the bodies of twelve members of an anarchist youth group were dumped near a cemetery.[67] Thousands remained in jail, and the deaths of some anarchists, like Domingo Ascaso, were discovered only weeks afterwards.

VI. Consequences and Decline

A few days after the end of fighting, George Orwell saw "the Spanish Republican flag ... flying all over Barcelona—the first time I had seen it, I think, except over a Fascist trench."[68] The English writer believed the Barcelona struggle gave the Valencia government a long-awaited excuse to assume fuller control over Catalonia. The belief "in the revolution and the future, a feeling of having emerged into an era of equality and freedom," now disappeared from his life.[69] Sought by communists because he had fought for the POUM and sympathized with the anarchists, Orwell fled a hospital bed and hid in Barcelona for a time before he managed to escape to England.

Emma Goldman watched the May crisis from London. Although she would return to Spain for a short stay in the fall of 1937, the events of May struck her as the greatest tragedy of her life. Anarchism as a "philosophy of new social order based upon liberty unrestricted by man-made law" now lay in ruins.[70] The CNT, caught between fascism and communism, was "plunging to its death" and could not escape total destruction. Tragically, the century-long anarchist movement collapsed with it, since only a handful of anarchists remained in Europe, South America, and the United States. A comrade wrote: "The movement seems to have failed—*but not the ideas*," and this fitted her own feelings.[71] The rise of mass totalitarian movements paralyzed international anarchism and caused it to lose resolve.

Other partisan observers of the crisis bitterly sought scapegoats. Alexander Shapiro wrote: "Anarchists in government will and *must* act like all officials and ministers."[72] His criticism was aimed at Federica Montseny and Juan García Oliver, who became the subject of an extraordinary AIT congress held in Paris on December 7, 1937.[73] Neither could explain aspects of their participation in the Popular Front to the foreign anarchists, and a deep schism appeared in the relations between the AIT and the CNT/FAI. Spanish anarchists were now abandoned by foreign members of their own movement, and a mood of bitterness settled over the CNT/FAI.

The May crisis had many long-term consequences. Almost as soon as the shooting stopped, the Catalan regional government completely disarmed the anarchists and Trotskyists, while allowing the PSUC to keep their weapons. On June 15, 1937, the Friends of Durruti and the POUM were classified as illegal organizations. Dragnets rounded up members of both groups, and they were arraigned as counterrevolutionaries. The PSUC quickly attacked Francisco Largo Caballero for having permitted the continued political participation of these groups in various aspects of government for so long.

Initially, perhaps, the PSUC expected only to pry away the Premier's other portfolio as Defense Minister. Largo Caballero refused to consider this step for fear of giving the communists total control of the Second Republic. But the PSUC insisted that there was no alternative: the persistent struggle for power disrupted the war against the nationalists. When the Premier challenged this assertion, the communists increased their attacks upon anarchists and Trotskyists and called Largo Caballero a friend of provocateurs and "social fascists" who were unworthy of representation in the Popular Front.

Finally, on May 15, 1937, the Premier clashed with two communists in the cabinet, Vicente Uribe (Minister of Agriculture) and Jesús Hernández (Minister of Information), on a proposal to outlaw the POUM formally. When Federica Montseny attempted to prove the complicity of the PSUC in the May crisis, tensions within the national cabinet became very high, and the discussion grew so violent that Uribe and Hernández walked out. Communists threatened to cut off all aid to the government unless Largo Caballero resigned, and the Premier did so on May 16. The four anarchist cabinet members handed in their resignations in protest.

Francisco Largo Caballero's successor was Juan Negrín, a socialist willing to work closely with the communists. He and Indalecio Prieto aligned the moderate wing of the UGT with the PSUC, as did Luis Companys and the Catalan regional government, much to the delight of the middle class in the Northeast. Most anarchists resigned their positions in Catalonia, and the two governments were devoid of anarchists in major positions until the summer of 1938, when communist influence in republican Spain began to wane as the Soviet Union became increasingly preoccupied with the approach of World War II.[74]

Between the summers of 1937 and 1938 loss of political power crippled many anarchist institutions and activities. In Aragon, Enrique Lister and the 11th Division, composed mainly of International Brigade survivors, moved to the front beside Ricardo Sanz and the 26th Division. Tension between them rose when the 11th Division began harassing communes and attacking CNT offices, in one case merely to destroy a portrait of Durruti.[75] The two units spent much of the summer skirmishing with one another until finally the 26th was scattered in the new Army of the East commanded by General Sebastián Pozas. Obviously not a CNT sympathizer, the general curbed the CNT/FAI in the area by abolishing the Council of Aragon and appointing a new governor, José Ignacio Mantecón, whom Sanz described as a *señorito* from a "good" family in Saragossa. Under Mantecón's auspices, the communes, now run by political commissars from the PSUC, were forced to produce large quotas of produce for the government at fixed prices. Their connections with the CNT and the FAI became a thing of the past.

Juan Negrín's new Minister of Defense, Indalecio Prieto, a long-time opponent of the anarchist movement, delighted in giving the communists support. In the late summer of 1937 he ordered a massive concentration of forces for a new attack upon Saragossa. Vicente Rojo and General Kléber joined the staff, and supplies long withheld flowed to the front. The offensive began on August 24 with attacks upon Quinto, Codo, and Belchite, which fell on September 6. The southern approaches to Saragossa were momentarily threatened, and republican lines moved fifteen kilometers northwest, but the advance was too costly to continue. By mid-September the nationalists counterattacked at Teruel and Jaca, ending Indalecio Prieto's dream that he, not Buenaventura Durruti, would be the ultimate victor in Aragon. Fighting was renewed at Teruel on December 15, 1937, and lasted until February 20, 1938, turning the dream into a nightmare. More than ten thousand republicans died at Teruel, and fifteen thousand surrendered, many of them veterans of the earlier columns and militia.[76]

Behind the lines life was equally bad. Juan Negrín's cabinet, never popular, made so many enemies that it had to rely upon strong police tactics. Secret communist prisons multiplied; Diego Abad de Santillán mentioned Santa Ursula in Valencia as the worst.[77] More than three hundred former members of Durruti's army were imprisoned in the first few months after Largo Caballero's resignation.[78] Gregorio Jover and Miguel Vivancos, both veterans of the Solidarios and the Nosotros, died under mysterious circumstances after being arrested for "military crimes." The former had been a marked man since his exploits in the May crisis, but other anarchists found themselves in equally difficult straits. Abad de Santillán had to go into hiding several times as the result of his criticism of Juan Negrín in *Timón*. Lesser known militants disappeared into *cheka* prisons.

Police control gave the cabinet power to tamper with the anarchist revolution. In September 1937 collectivized farms needed to show proof of ownership for their confiscated lands. If they had none, the land came under cabinet control on October 27, 1937. The decree provided very complicated rules for legalization; some

160 communes, in fact, did not qualify.[79] Villages no longer were permitted to start new collectives, and the government sometimes denied existing collectives the necessary resources for survival. Vicente Uribe, the communist Minister of Agriculture, stepped in to take control of communes in the name of the cabinet, the PSUC, or previous owners. He also helped organize the Federación Campesina to compete with CNT and UGT agricultural unions. Merger of the latter two groups partially met this challenge; but the anarchists steadily lost ground to the communists in rural affairs.

A similar decline took place in union and industrial affairs. The shop floor became a battleground as the cabinet prohibited strikes, altered existing labor agreements, and broke up industrial collectives, returning plants to their previous owners—this latter step as an inducement to Catalan industrialists to support the new regime.[80] Confiscated foreign industrial property fell under a new nationalization decree of August 11, 1938, which established a series of government-controlled basic industries. Juan Negrín also got far-reaching powers to develop a war economy. The FAI vigorously opposed nationalization by advocating noncooperation.[81] This appeal barely skirted the limits of treason, and many FAI members soon found themselves in Catalan jails again.

Such setbacks divided anarchists even more deeply. A minority continued to react in the old way: an underground newspaper, *Libertad*, published urgent appeals in August 1937 for the start of an anti-communist campaign and a new Nosotros-type of terrorist band, Grupo Ácrata, tried to keep the example of Durruti alive, without much success.[82] Foreign anarchists applauded these acts and told the CNT to go back to first principles. However, the FAI and the CNT refused to return to the past. Buenaventura Durruti's own acceptance of organization and discipline in the militia made a return to the tactics and psychology of terrorism impossible.

Hereafter the FAI changed very rapidly. It dropped affinity groups in favor of *agrupación*, more like traditional cells. After Juan Negrín, seeking to make his regime more palatable, announced the reopening of parliament, the CNT refashioned the FAI into a political arm of the libertarian movement. It became a basic premise that the movement had to remain political—and that the FAI was best prepared to be its political branch.[83] When the parliament reopened in October 1937, FAI representatives worked aggressively in it without embarrassment.[84]

Many people had a hand in developing this new policy: Federica Montseny, Juan García Oliver, Angel Pestaña (who died in Decem-

233

ber 1937), Pedro Herrera, and Horacio Prieto—the latter a middle-rank CNT official and former associate of Valeriano Orobón Fernández, who was familiar with the concept of a workers' alliance, the former policy perhaps closest to the current line. Their attitudes towards the conversion of the FAI into a political party summarized the later history of Spanish anarchism.

The CNT leadership believed that anarchist policy had generally been successful. Anti-monarchical and anti-clerical militancy had purged Spanish society of the king and priesthood. More recently, the Second Republic, under strong pressure from Buenaventura Durruti, had evolved towards the ideal of a workers' republic. Only the May crisis had been a failure for the movement. Communism had dislodged anarchism from a position of revolutionary power, beginning a reversion towards re-creation of the bureaucratic state. Internal division had weakened the CNT/FAI when it needed to maintain maximum strength. The reasons could be traced to the initial unwillingness to join the Popular Front, the lack of awareness of the tasks necessary to support the militia, and the bitter criticism of anarchist cabinet ministers. All were caused by a reliance upon excessive principle, the product of an earlier, pre-industrial time when privileged elites controlled the state and were anathematized by classical anarchists like Pierre-Joseph Proudhon and Peter Kropotkin.

The Russian revolution had changed the principles of anarchism. Nations were now conquered by popular causes. No longer did peasants and workers live in isolation without power; they had become their own masters. But many anarchists continued to see themselves as isolated rebels in the manner of Proudhon or Kropotkin at a time when only Michael Bakunin's motto made sense: "Let us revolt to make the revolution."[85] Opportunity existed to create the "future" society today; struggle for its own sake was obsolete. Anarchist ideas had been put into practice in July 1936 and had worked, at least insofar as they had been allowed to work. Buenaventura Durruti's spontaneous voluntarism lifted Spaniards to the threshold of radical change—and beyond, as Catalan society changed into one dominated by factory committees and communal organizations.

Unfortunately, the military crisis of the civil war left the fate of the Second Republic uncertain. There had been no time for anarchists to develop a clear revolutionary consciousness that acknowledged the changed circumstances of the situation or the new goals sought by the CNT/FAI. Militants continued to reject authority at the very moment when they should have been seeking to consolidate power behind the anarchist revolution of the Northeast. But the memory of the *faísta-treintista* schism, personal disputes, and a lack of coordination within the movement led to defeat. In this sense, the May crisis had been a product of internal anarchist weakness.

To avoid a similar collapse in the future, the leadership created the Comité Ejecutivo del Movimiento Libertario (CEML)—an upper-level body incorporating all Spanish anarchist organizations. If the nationalist victory of General Franco had been delayed, the CEML might have created the anarchist party of the future. The spectrum of its values included federalism, collectivism, and participation in the activities of the state. The CEML influenced the FAI to designate itself as a revolutionary labor party and to demand reinclusion in the Popular Front. Together, the CEML and the FAI represented an amazing turnabout in anarchist thought.

By April 1938, when the transformation of the FAI was complete, the collapsing military situation of the Second Republic limited the anarchists' new program to a careful adherence to anti-fascist principles and a strong brand of anti-communism.[86] A few anarchists, like Mariano Vázquez, refused to work with the CEML and the FAI (although Vázquez was discredited by his continued cooperation with Juan Negrín), while others, like Diego Abad de Santillán and the AIT, maintained relations with the CEML/FAI without accepting the idea of a political party. Even the right wing of the socialist UGT worked with the CEML/FAI after Indalecio Prieto ended his collaboration with the PSUC.

But unity came too late. The Basque provinces fell to General Franco in the summer of 1937. In Aragon, after the fall of Teruel, a retreat eastward began in March 1938. Nationalist forces reached the Mediterranean in April, cutting the Second Republic in two. The last republican offensive, the brave but abortive Ebro campaign, (October 30–November 16, 1938), failed to do more than momentarily raise the hopes of its supporters—at a cost of seventy thousand casualties. The CEML/FAI plotted to depose Juan Negrín as Premier or to replace him with Manuel Azaña, the silent President, but in the end did nothing because the end of the Republic was now only a matter of time. The invasion of Catalonia started on December 23, 1938, with the nationalists capturing Barcelona on January 26, 1939, and reaching the French border on February 10. Madrid held out until late March 1939, but by this time most prominent anarchists in Catalonia had long since fled in the mass migration of refugees north to France and exile. The time for revolution was over.

PART FOUR

Conclusion

CHAPTER TEN

Beyond the Dream

Men make their own history, but they do not make it just
as they please; they do not make it under circumstances
chosen by themselves, but under circumstances directly encountered, given, and transmitted from the past. [Karl
Marx, *The Eighteenth Brumaire of Louis Napoleon*]

I. Analyzing the Revolution

After a quarter of a century Spanish anarchists finally found the
opportunity to stage their revolution, though it did not take place
under circumstances they chose. The vitality of the movement en-
abled them to defeat the monarchy, the Church, and economic oppressors. In the end, however, the past returned to haunt the CNT/
FAI, when a revived middle class, once seemingly consigned to obliv-
ion, used regionalism, communism, and an odd type of anti-fascism
to dismantle the anarchist revolution. The libertarian society so long
in the making disappeared almost overnight.

Since 1937 the nature of this revolution has become increasingly difficult to understand. So few nonpartisan observers existed
in Spain before and during the civil war that sources pertaining to
anarchism are not trustworthy. The historian uses objective material to correct bias whenever he can. In this case, unfortunately,
there is almost none. And when anarchist material is used, the
policies of the CNT/FAI are hidden by a clash of personalities,
sects, and opposing factions. Even so long after the war's end it is
difficult to determine events accurately. Yet there is much of great
interest worth discussing.

A point of contemporary fascination is the factory councils of

239

Catalonia. Unfortunately, few first-hand accounts of these organizations exist.[1] Without an oral history project to interview former workers in Catalan industry, it is difficult to estimate how effectively workers' control operated. Augustin Souchy argued that it usually came as a prelude to expropriation.[2] Industrial unions, through the National Federations of Industry, integrated all affiliated phases of production into local collectives just prior to the full collectivization of a particular industry. If Diego Abad de Santillán's observation is correct, after full collectivization, workers' self-management became no more than a simple responsibility for purely local questions. All other management tasks thereafter were performed by the industrial councils. While each individual factory council was represented, it did not have the right to veto decisions made by the industrial council.

Despite the centralism that this arrangement caused, some anarchists hoped the result would allow worker solidarity to eliminate speed-ups, labor exploitation, and other labor-intensive techniques, while improving productivity. Each plant would contribute suggestions for handling the flow of raw materials and finished products, obviating a need for elite managerial methods, whether capitalist or state socialist. By tapping the collective knowledge of workers about their jobs, self-management might destroy inefficient procedures and recombine the steps of industrial work into more effective patterns.

As it happened, there was no time to effect this kind of reconstruction. Baking, shoemaking, and a few other labor-intensive areas were collectivized in July 1936, but heavy industry in Catalonia, with some exceptions, had to be content with shadow collectives. The need for war materials was too great to permit free experimentation with full workers' control. In October 1936 the Catalan regional government assumed management of most industries, set work norms and production standards, and created managerial policies through the Council of the Economy. The abrupt end of economic revolution truncated full development of a collectivized economy before it had operated long enough to develop distinct characteristics.

Even Souchy admitted that little had really changed in Spanish industry. Wages, for example, were "still not at a standard sufficient for men's needs."[3] Technical guidance was lacking, some syndicates were more backward than others, and inflation made direct exchange of goods among industries extremely difficult. "The economic difficulties pile up," he commented sadly.[4] Even if collectivization had proceeded normally, a dearth of technical expertise and managerial experience would have placed obstacles in the path of the anarchist revolution.

Only the enthusiasm of workers gave the councils strength. One council of a potash mine in Sallent wrote:

> We all earn the same wage, we all have the same rights and duties, without having to keep parasites. With regard to technicians we have left two specialized overseers and an engineer sent to us from Barcelona. As regards the work, we are carrying it out under perfect conditions. There are no more accidents. Moreover, we hold the enterprise under conditions which will produce an income of one hundred and fifty percent more than before the 19th of July.[5]

In short, the revolution fulfilled the expectations of some militant individuals. Workers were willing to labor for lower wages and longer hours. A psychology of intense personal pride affected many of the collectives. Perhaps this would have been enough to allow the revolution to go on, but it is doubtful. Not all Spaniards were anarchists, and not all workers were so favorably disposed towards the revolution.

Collectivization, of course, did exist at other levels. The agricultural communes collectivized whole villages and rural districts. Emma Goldman, visiting Albalate de Cinca in the province of Huesca, described the mood of the commune as one of having adopted a new life. Land had been confiscated and was now worked in common. A new threshing machine and several plows were collectively purchased, while the means of livelihood had been apportioned according to the size of each family.[6] However, even she admitted that the efforts of the villagers were taking place at a very unusual time, when most of the able-bodied workers were away fighting at the front. The leader of the commune, a seventy-year-old man, seemed to indicate that some of the arrangements for agricultural production were temporary, a set of wartime measures.

Whether communes would have continued their collectivization and libertarian communism if the Second Republic had survived is a difficult question. José Peirats, the first historian of Spanish anarchism, answered in the affirmative. His picture of the collectivized villages was a very positive one. All villagers between the ages of fourteen and sixty were expected to work, although women might be excused for family care if the need arose. Surplus commodities were exchanged through district and regional councils or bartered directly with other villages. Village assemblies usually established the labor value that a person earned, payable in standard commodities. A careful accounting of goods taken from the collective's storehouse was then credited against labor contributed.[7] In other cases, vouchers issued by the commune served as substitute money, while a minority of villages lived purely by barter. None of these systems was satisfactory as a model for the national economy.

Complicated accounting was minimized wherever possible by the development of collective institutions. Many towns had municipal dining halls to feed their populations. Savings in food costs and clothing manufacture, another common activity, could be used to improve medical or educational facilities, although a conscious effort to improve education or medical services could not compensate entirely for a severe lack of trained personnel or provide the considerable investment necessary to solve the existing problems. Nonetheless, if war had not intervened, real progress might have been made in education and medicine.

Even discounting the wartime psychology that popularized the communes and the threat of violence that drove some people into them, many villagers did possess a deep-seated commitment to live communally and to share in common. Opposition to communal agriculture in Catalonia probably would not have dissuaded a majority of rural Spaniards from following the communal path if the peasants had had a free choice. Many villages faced extreme difficulty in modernizing even by following the communal route, but rural life during the past century had been so depressed that the illusion of freedom was enough to raise millenarian expectations. Republican failure to solve land problems between 1931 and 1933 made villagers ready to complete the long arduous process of reform themselves.

Yet, as this study demonstrates, the anarchists' ties with the countryside were not as close as they thought. How well they might have coordinated and controlled the communes if the movement had not fallen from power in 1937 is questionable. Perhaps rural Spain was heading for another cantonal movement similar to the one in 1873, when Andalusian towns declared themselves autonomous city-states.

On the other hand, the Congress of Caspe in February 1937 did much to unify communes and prevent extreme isolation. The peasant federation of the Levante, organized by the CNT, performed the same tasks at a regional level.[8] Whether these agencies could have offset particularism to bring change to the rural areas depended largely upon the national success of anarchism. The CNT/

FAI would have had to enlarge its operations and incorporate peasants into the organizational structure more fundamentally than ever before. In the interval, other political groups, such as the UGT and PSUC, would have had an equal opportunity to organize the villages and to entice communes. Many Andalusian anarchists had already become communists by May 1937, and others might have followed suit if the CNT failed to demonstrate more concern for rural matters. There is no assurance that anarchism would have eventually triumphed in the countryside, even if the movement had not encountered such great political difficulties.

The same was true of the concilar form of government the anarchists proposed. Drawn from federalist ideas of Francisco Pi y Margall, this form of government was embodied in the Council of Aragon—the only such government institution, including the short-lived Anti-Fascist Militia Committee, to operate for at least a year. More study needs to be done on this agency before firm conclusions can be reached. Mariano Vázquez defended the council for the apolitical quality of its efforts to meet the economic and social needs of the region and for its refusal to engage in political posturing.[9] He overlooked the fact that the presence of the militia army considerably simplified its tasks. Durruti's soldiers assumed responsibility for police administration, public works, and many aspects of planning.

Whether the council could have improved socioeconomic conditions or even survived the pressure of the central government is dubious. After all, in 1898 Joaquín Costa had attempted a similar program throughout Aragon with his Unión Nacional but failed to dislodge either the politicians or the parties there.[10] The same thing happened to the Council of Aragon. On July 7, 1937, council representatives failed to convince the central government of the council's usefulness, and it was consistently outmaneuvered thereafter until its abolition in September 1937. The struggle between anarchism and communism had a great deal to do with these maneuvers, but the failure of the council to survive illustrates the difficulties any such group would have had in fending off normal political opposition. Even in the civil war, free of many tasks normally a part of governmental activity, the Council of Aragon was not able to defend itself adequately. The council form of government probably would not have operated more skillfully under more routine circumstances.

In the end, the anarchist revolution faced many difficulties that threatened to alter its program or force a change of format. Anarchists had been so far from power that their program was makeshift

243

and temporary. That so much was accomplished in a short time was a real triumph of improvisation, but it was not enough to save the revolution.

II. Analyzing the Movement

Despite its shortcomings, the Spanish anarchist movement came to maturity during the civil war. It emerged from the rural backlands and districts at the edge of northern industrial cities to participate in Spanish political life in a way unthinkable even five or six years earlier. Light years separated anarchist attitudes of 1911 from anarchist beliefs and practices in 1937. A Canadian socialist, travelling in Catalonia during the latter year, observed:

> It is the anarchists who are mainly in control of all industry, of education, of transport, and of the distribution of food supplies to the people. These are no light tasks and require a high order of constructive ability.... They have a hand in more activities in Catalonia than any other political group. In a new school which they were organizing, some English visitors were astounded to find a number of religious books which had been left by the monks who had previously run a school there. "Yes," [the anarchists] said "we are going to keep those books in our library because they are good books."[11]

A small incident, but starkly different from the portrayal of drunken militiamen so often found in other writings about anarchists.

Increasingly, younger anarchists were second- or third-generation city dwellers, not the same type as their parents. While anarchism, with its workers' clubs and organizations, still provided a simple haven for some, it educated others to a level that few common people in Spain had reached. The "surly proletarians" of Salvador Seguí's time became better educated, less uncomfortable in the city, and more willing to experiment with the content of anarchism.

This, in part, explains the *treintista* controversy. Between 1931 and 1934 the movement experienced violent growing pains as it debated the issues of unionism versus terrorism. The unionists lost, but only temporarily. The failure of three putsches against the Second Republic finally convinced even the Nosotros that a new reasonableness was more appropriate. Efforts by the CNT and the FAI to participate in the affairs of state during the civil war stemmed from this realization.

The tragedy was that Francisco Largo Caballero did not accept the anarchists as full partners in his cabinet before January 1937, when he did finally turn to them for aid and support. Unfortunately, the movement's reputation preceded it and made Largo Caballero wary, as anyone would have been. Anarchists lacked both the tradition of negotiation and compromise and expertise in these activities. One difficulty in remaining apart from political life was that anarchists did not develop adequate political instincts, as they found out in the spring of 1937. Militants in the movement also obstructed every step that took the anarchists closer to normal political life, making it impossible for them to achieve a consensus. If time and pressure from General Franco and the USSR had not been so strong, the CNT/FAI might have made the transition successfully, but circumstances called for immediate decisions. Few open organizations could then have moved more quickly than the anarchists did. As it happened, the union between Largo Caballero and the anarchists proved powerless to stop the drift of events in the civil war, although greater unity in September 1936, when Largo Caballero first approached the movement, might at least have curbed the Catalan separatists in their attack upon revolutionary institutions.

The breach with the Catalans ended several decades of simultaneous activity, if not close cooperation, between anarchists and the regionalist movement. The two groups shared a belief in federalism and a disgust with Madrid that allowed them to cooperate on many occasions. The political explosions and other crises caused by this joint action are too numerous to recount; unity finally collapsed in 1936 when the Madrid government was dangerously weakened by the generals' revolt. Each movement went its own way, the anarchists towards social revolution, the Catalans towards autonomy.

Now that the opportunity existed to accomplish long-sought goals, the Catalans, fearing that competition between anarchists and communists might complicate life in autonomous Catalonia, attacked the social revolution in Barcelona. They openly sympathized with the communists and undoubtedly facilitated the development and growth of the PSUC, hoping to split the radicals into two camps. Many times in the past, anarchists had overshadowed Catalan protest with their own violence, and government oppression had jailed Catalan and anarchist alike. Luis Companys refused to let this happen again, especially with many of his followers coming from the middle class. It served Catalan purposes to accept the communist argument that anti-fascism came before revolution. As a result, Catalan separatist participation in the May crisis of 1937 was decisive in

245

forming a new alignment of forces that toppled the CNT/FAI from power.

And so the anarchists, despite their concessions to political reality, found themselves even more isolated than before, at least until late 1938, when the civil war was almost over. They had changed drastically since 1911. Once undisciplined and uneducated, with primitive political values, Spanish anarchism grew into a unique mass movement. Its activity ranged from social banditry to the development of a popular press that stressed nineteenth century scientific and political ideas and values, the influence of which had been delayed by the slow modernization of Spain. As a movement, anarchism held together despite exaggerated individualism and excessive violence, gradually learning, slowly modernizing itself. By July 1936 the Spanish anarchists had moved into the political mainstream. Only the direct intervention of the fascist powers and of the Russians at the height of the successful Popular Front period destroyed the anarchists' bid for power, although a lingering suspicion remains in the minds of many old anarchists that the real cause of defeat was the abandonment of traditional libertarian values.

After 1939 the movement waged a series of small guerrilla wars against General Franco and formed various parties and groups in exile to carry on in opposition.[12] The passage of time scattered the leaders of the movement: Montseny to France, García Oliver to Mexico, and Abad de Santillán to Argentina.[13] Did the scattering of the anarchists mean that the struggle had been in vain?

In one sense, the answer is no. To the militant who had been willing to risk all in the struggle, anarchism represented an end to alienation and promised a measure of freedom until then unknown in Spain. It symbolized a great collective task whose fulfillment would establish a firm and courageous human solidarity under which all would be possible. The means used to attain this goal sometimes were at great variance with the ideal, but despite these imperfections, the dreams fostered by the anarchists became an important part of daily life. Spaniards who resisted General Franco's repression of political and social life from 1939 to 1975 did so with courage at least in part generated by memories of the anarchist ideals. Since Franco's death, the rapid rise of neighborhood associations seems to manifest some of the old libertarian qualities.[14]

But in another sense the answer to any question about the long-term future of Spanish anarchism must be pessimistic. Contemporary Spain is more modern than is generally supposed. Urbanization is almost complete, and even the clientele of the neighborhood associations may decline. Concerns of a mass society dominate Spain today; public education, inflation, and job security have replaced millenarianism and revolution. Basques and Catalans still hunger for autonomy, but they certainly are not potential leaders of a new upsurge of anarchism, since both regions today are even more prosperous than they were forty years ago. And while assassinations, riots, and deep political unrest in Spain still make headlines, those involved are radical democrats, regionalists, socialists, or communists. Anarchism died a violent death during the Spanish Civil War, and the great social and economic changes since that era severely curtail any possibility of a new outburst of anarchist politics.

Appendixes, Notes, and Bibliography

Statutes of the FAI

Resolution I: Of the Organization and Its Purpose*

ARTICLE 1. These bylaws constitute the principles ... of the Federación Anarquista Ibérica, with headquarters in Valencia, and must be accepted by all the individuals who believe in the ideas and programs reflected in these statutes and the norms of conduct which have been established by the plenos and congresses which have written them.

ARTICLE 2. The fundamental objectives which the FAI resolves to attain are:

a) The nullification of the exploitation of man by man, by socializing all the means of production and distribution.
b) To make impossible all dictatorship of estate or party which tries to impose political and totalitarian processes on the Iberian Peninsula, and to establish, on the other hand, the cordial collaboration of every socio-political sector that concurs in the fundamental points necessary for the creation of a society without classes and privileges.
c) The free federation of all the towns of Spain, respecting the maximum autonomy of the municipality, area, or region, as long as it does not jeopardize the full development of the whole.
d) To put aside the prejudices of Race and Patriotism which tend to establish differences among similar beings in order to establish true brotherhood among the Peoples of the World.
e) To propel the free development of the sciences and the arts in such a manner that human thought may attain its most elevated concretions; for which it is necessary that education, from the primary grades to the upper levels, be completely free and oriented in opposition to all dogma which damages the formation of children, within the framework recognized as the rights of the child.

**The material in this Appendix is translated from *Estatutos de la FAI* (Valencia: Empresa Colectivizada T. G. Hostench, 1937).*

251

  f) To maintain cordial relations with the organizations which tend to seek the total or partial realization of this purpose and especially the Confederación Nacional de Trabajo.

Resolution II: Concerning the Affiliates

ARTICLE 3. Those persons who may be affiliates of the FAI are all manual and intellectual workers of both sexes who, accepting fully the aspirations outlined in the previous resolution, are ready to cooperate in order to realize them, abiding by resolutions which the Organization may accept to this effect.

ARTICLE 4. To join the Federation, the aspirant must send his/her application, endorsed by two fully affiliated members, to the local or district group existing in the area where he/she lives. Membership will be granted, if the result of the information previously communicated is satisfactory.

ARTICLE 5. Persons who will be full affiliates, possessing all rights, are:

  a) Those who were included in the anarchist movement before August 1931 [later changed to July 1936 and then to July 1937].
  b) Those who, on request, document having been active as militants in syndical, cultural, or other Organizations related to anarchism, previous to August 1931.

ARTICLE 6. Once admitted, the affiliates who do not fulfill the conditions noted in the previous article may not hold office or serve as representatives until six months after their admittance. If it were considered necessary to make any exception, it would be necessary, in order to grant it, to consult the Regional Federation of Groups.

ARTICLE 7. In order for the Federation to be able to meet the economic necessities which its maintenance establishes, all affiliates ought to punctually pay in full the established monthly dues.

ARTICLE 8. Each affiliate ought to be provided, through the intercession of the corresponding Local Group, with a book of identification papers issued by the Peninsular Committee.

  This book of identification papers will contain, besides the personal description and social background of each affiliate, the sheet recording dues payment, where the coupons attesting to having paid in full the corresponding dues shall be placed.

ARTICLE 9. No affiliate may belong to two Groups at the same time; neither one of the general area nor one of a different town. Nor may he/she belong to the anarchist Group of a place different from that one where he/she has maintained residence for a maximum of three months.

ARTICLE 10.   When an affiliate has changed localities, he/she is obliged to obtain from the group committee a resume of activities and behavior, which will be attached to the membership card. Without meeting this requirement the affiliate will not be allowed to enter the Group in the new locality in which he/she resides.

ARTICLE 11.   Affiliates of the FAI shall be obligated to respond to the call of their respective Committees to discharge the functions which are entrusted to them by those committees and which are in agreement with the general line of conduct that the Federation may outline.

Resolution III: Structure of the Federation

ARTICLE 12.   The Federación Anarquista Ibérica, in its new structure, shall be articulated in the following associations:

a) *District Group*, subdivision of the Local Group in towns or cities of more than 60,000 inhabitants, whose organic development allows it.
b) *Local Group*, genuine representative body of the affiliates in every town.
c) *Regional Federations*, formed by all the Local Groups existing in the region.
d) *Territorial Federations*, if it be deemed convenient, but without reducing the powers of the Local Groups. Regional Federations will be subdivided into Territorial Federations.

Resolution IV: Concerning the Local Associations

ARTICLE 13.   All the affiliates resident in a municipal district itself shall join the Local Anarchist Group. They shall be governed by their own statutes based on the ones presented here and in which the absolute acceptance of the General Statutes of the FAI is clearly recorded.

ARTICLE 14.   The Local Group will be administered and ruled by a Committee composed of the following members: Secretary, Treasurer, Auditor, Vice-Secretary, and five voting members. All will be named by the general assembly of the Group.

ARTICLE 15.   When the town where the Local Group is constituted has more than seventy thousand inhabitants and the organic possibilities allow it, Groups of the District shall be created, which among themselves will form the Local Group, this body having absolute competence in the representation of the Groups of the District in the administrative order, and correspondence, and general operations in the Federation.

253

ARTICLE 16. There shall be created in every Group a Commission, named in general assembly, called the Admissions Commission that, in contact with the Committee, but answering before the assembly that elected it, shall be responsible for:

a) Receiving the adherences of the aspirants to affiliation.
b) Communicating the information that each one requires.
c) Granting admission to those deserving of it.

ARTICLE 17. It shall remain the job of the Local Committee to name special technical Commissions for the development and good functioning of the Organization. These commissions shall be limited to being efficient auxiliaries of the Committee upon whom the direct responsibility before the affiliates falls.

ARTICLE 18. The Local Committee must obligatorily meet in plenary session once a week and extraordinarily as often as may be necessary.

ARTICLE 19. When the Local Group is formed by district groups, the naming and composition of the Committee shall be concluded in the following way: Secretary, Vice-Secretary, Auditor, and Treasurer will be named by the Plenary Session of District Groups bringing to the Plenary Session the opinion of their affiliates and as Voting Members acting as a direct representative body of each District Group.

ARTICLE 20. The District Group will be made up of the affiliates living in the district of the urban division where it is constituted. When, in the judgment of the Local Committees it is found that there is an insufficient number of affiliates to the FAI living in a district to form a Group, they will belong to the closest Group of those existing in the city.

ARTICLE 21. The District Group will consider itself obligated to send a replacement for the delegate it sent to the Local Committee, if this delegate be considered incompatible with the majority of the members of said committee.

Resolution V: Concerning the Regional and Peninsular Associations

ARTICLE 22. The Regional Federations formed by the existing Local Groups in the geographic region that embraces each one of them will be as many as the regions that exist in the actual configuration of Spain, including Portugal, which will constitute one more region.

ARTICLE 23. Each Regional Federation will be represented by a Committee made up of: Secretary, Auditor, and Treasurer, named in Plenary Sessions or Regional Congresses of Local Groups and by five Voting Members named in the Local Group where the Regional Committee resides.

ARTICLE 24. It shall name from among its own members or with affiliates not serving on the Committee, if it is believed necessary, strictly controlled technical-advisory Commissions to study and express opinions about fundamental problems that may be presented: about the political order, economic order, etc. As the auxiliary associations created in the local Groups respond only to their respective Committees (the Regional in this case), it is this Committee which assumes responsibility before the section of the Organization which it represents and before the Peninsular Committee as well.

ARTICLE 25. The total representation of the Federación Anarquista Ibérica will be the responsibility of its Peninsular Committee, which will maintain a constant and direct relationship with the regional associations and, by means of these, with the Local Associations.

ARTICLE 26. The Peninsular Committee will be composed of the following positions: Secretary, Treasurer, and Auditor, named in Congresses or Peninsular Plenary Sessions, in whose order of the day the election for positions figures. As many Voting Members as the members of the secretariat deem appropriate, elected from within or outside the place of residence, will aid in the work of the Committee, forming part of it, with the agreement of the Organization.

ARTICLE 27. The residence of the Peninsular Committee will be determined by each ordinary Congress of the Federation, or, if special circumstances demand it, by a Peninsular Plenary Session of Regional Associations convoked for that purpose.

Resolution VI: Concerning the Offices

ARTICLE 28. The duration in the exercise of the offices of the different Committees of the Federation will be one year, being renewed periodically and by half of the members of each Committee, in conditions which the Assemblies and Plenary Sessions determine. Those comrades who, in the judgment of the Assembly or Plenary Session which named them, are considered worthy of it may be re-elected to continue filling their offices.

ARTICLE 29. All comrades who fill offices within the Federation shall be personally responsible for their actions and behavior, in addition to the collective responsibility which pertains to them as an integral part of the association in which they work.

ARTICLE 30. The delegates whom the FAI may have in public offices remain under the obligation to deliver accounts of their expenses and action to the Committees by whom they were named, maintaining close contact with them at all times.

ARTICLE 31. Every affiliate of the FAI who fulfills any public office whatsoever, and whatever his/her character, may, if his/her conduct is bad, have his/her power taken away and will cease exercising the office as soon as the appropriate associations of the Federation determine it.

Resolution VII: Concerning the Assemblies, Plenary Sessions, and Congresses

ARTICLE 32. The most authoritative expression of the organized anarchist movement in each locality resides in the General Assemblies of the Local Anarchist Groups. All affiliates may freely speak their minds in the Assemblies, but only full members may vote.

ARTICLE 33. General Assemblies shall be held periodically and regularly, as many times as is determined in the Statutes of the Group and whenever, advised by circumstances or petition on the part of affiliates, the Committees convoke extraordinary assemblies.

ARTICLE 34. The sense of the Federation shall be declared regionally by means of the Regional Congresses of the Anarchist Groups, these Groups being present at such Congresses with direct representatives and resolutions for settlement dealing with the various problems which the Order of the Day establishes.

ARTICLE 35. The Regional Congresses of an ordinary nature shall take place once every six months and must be definitively convoked by the Regional Committee at least one month prior to the date of their being held.

ARTICLE 36. An Extraordinary Regional Congress may be held whenever, in the judgment of the Regional Committee, circumstances warrant it and whenever it is so resolved by resolutions of the Regional Plenary Session.

ARTICLE 37. In order to guide the progress of the movement in accordance with the general sense of the Organization, even in those questions of procedure or general questions which do not require a Congress in order to be dealt with or which cannot await the meeting of the next ordinary session, the representatives of the Committee of Local Groups shall meet regularly every two months in a Regional Plenary Session.

ARTICLE 38. The Peninsular Committee shall be invited to all these Assemblies, Plenary Sessions, and Congresses of a regional nature in order that it may be present with a direct delegation. Its attendance is optional at the Plenary Sessions, but mandatory at the Congresses.

ARTICLE 39. The Federación Anarquista Ibérica shall meet in a Peninsular Congress once a year. The Local Groups of the Peninsula shall be present with direct delegations at this Assembly, the principal demonstration of the full power of the Federation. The presence of the Regional Committees shall be mandatory, but their delegations will be only of an informative character.

ARTICLE 40. At each of the Congresses of those cited in the previous article, it shall be mandatory that there be included in the Order of the Day: a rendering of accounts and explanation of the various aspects of their management by the Peninsular Committee; nomination for the positions that have regularly been vacated and for those vacant because of resignation or various causes; assigning the place of residence of the Peninsular Committee and establishing the position on as many fundamental problems as interest the movement in order to designate the standards of future conduct.

ARTICLE 41.   The Congress ought to be convened normally, with the Peninsular Committee sending to the Groups, a month and a half prior to the Congress, the Order of the Day and the corresponding suggestions and reports.

ARTICLE 42.   An Extraordinary Peninsular Congress may be held at the demand of more than two Regional Federations and by agreement of a Peninsular Plenary Session of the time. In these assemblies, only those questions which have been specified in the letter of convocation will be dealt with.

ARTICLE 43.   Every three months, a Peninsular Plenary Session of Regional Federations ought to be convened which will serve to establish collaboration with the Peninsular Committee in the orientation of the Organization for resolution of those problems of procedure which do not have the importance claimed by those that ought to be dealt with in Congresses, and to solve as many problems of an urgent and important nature as may present themselves. Besides these trimestrial Plenary Sessions, there should be convened as many as the Peninsular Committee deems it pertinent to convoke.

ARTICLE 44.   The representational groups of the Regional Committees or the Regional Plenary Sessions, as may be designated by them, shall be present as delegates at the aforementioned Plenary Sessions.

Resolution VIII: Concerning Responsibilities

ARTICLE 45.   The conduct of the affiliates in that group which affects the moral and material interests of the Federation may and ought to be examined by the Anarchist Groups. In cases of irregularity in behavior, the Committee of the Group shall propose the appropriate sanction to the General Assembly which shall establish it definitively.

ARTICLE 46.   Whenever the said affiliate is not in agreement with the sanction which has been imposed, by reason of considering it unjust, he/she shall be able to apply, in demand of review, to the Association immediately superior to the one which applied the sanction; and while it is being definitively resolved, he/she shall respect the order of the Assembly which pronounced the judgement.

ARTICLE 47.   The affiliate who levels accusations against another comrade of the organization, whether occupying a position of responsibility or not, and who does not prove the truth of them, when he/she is investigated for it within the Organization, shall be relentlessly sanctioned, in proportion to the gravity of the slander hurled against the comrade, being subject, by reason of this inclination, to expulsion.

ARTICLE 48. The Committees of the various Organizations that make up the Federation shall be able to request an accounting of the behavior, in the course of discharging the duties of offices, of those comrades whom they have named to office, and apply the convenient sanction, the interested party being able to appeal to the Peninsular Committee against the decision.

Resolution IX: Concerning the Dissolution of the Federation

ARTICLE 49. The Federación Anarquista Ibérica shall not be able to dissolve itself so long as there remains any Group which wishes to continue belonging to it.

ARTICLE 50. In event of dissolution, the furniture, valuable moveable and non-moveable goods, and valuables in current account or cash in hand shall pass under control of the Cultural and Social Assistance entities which, existing in the country, have as their basis of existence and standard of conduct the principles most analogous to anarchism.

Regional Communes in Spain, 1936-1937

Regions*	No. of Towns	Members	Communes
ARAGON			
Alcaniz	6	596	6
Alcorisa	3	10,000	13
Albalate de Cinca	2	4,068	16
Angues		6,201	36
Caspe		2,197	5
Ejulve	3	3,807	8
Escucha		400	6
Granen			12
Lercera	2	2,045	9
Monzon			35
Sastago		478	4
Puebla de Hejar		7,146	9
Pina de Ebro		2,924	6
Torrente			3
Valderrobres	4	11,449	18
Mas de las Matas	19	7,930	14
Muniesa		2,254	11
Mora de Rubielor		3,782	21
Ainsa			
Alfambra		502	6

*Each region or town named is one in which communes are known to have existed. The blank spaces indicate instances for which the figures are unavailable or unreliable. Sources for the calculations are: Diego Abad de Santillán, *Por qué perdimos la guerra* (Buenos Aires: Iman, 1940), pp. 94–96; Gaston Leval, *Espagne libertaire: 1936–1939* (Paris: Editions du Cercle, 1971), *passim*; and the periodicals *Solidaridad Obrera*, *Spain and the World*, and *Timón*.

Regions	No. of Towns	Members	Communes
Benabarre		407	6
Barbastro		7,983	31
Pancrudo		215	4
Graus	43	4,600	15
Fraga		8,000	51
Binefar	38	7,000	58
Andorra		3,337	6
Esplus	1	1,100	1

THE LEVANTE

Adamuz			
Alborache			
Carcagente	27	18,000	16
Catarroja			
Chella			
Foyos			
Gandia			
Jarafuel			
Jativa		17,000	17
Moncada			
Onteniente			
Paterna			
Puerto Sagunto			
Requena			
Sagunto			
Utiel			
Villar del Arzobispo			
Sueca			
Villamarchante			
Alcantara del Jucar			
Titaguas			
Ombay			

MURCIA

Caravaca
Cartagena
Vieza
Lorca
Mazarron
Mula
Pacheco
Eleche de la Sierra
Hellin

Regions	No. of Towns	Members	Communes
ALICANTE			
Alicante			
Alcoy			
Almansa			
Elda			
Elche			
La Nucia			
Orihuela			
Villayoyosa			
Villena			
CASTELLON DE LA PLANA			
Castellon			
Albocacer			
Alcora			
Morella			
Nules			
Onda			
Segorbe	1	7,000	3
Vinaroz			
Jerica			
Soneja			
Benicarlo	22		16
ALBACETE			
Albacete			
Alcarraz			
La Roda			
Casas Ibanez			
CASTILE			
Miralcampo			6
Manzanares		25,000	9
Alcazar de Cervantes	12	14,000	10
CATALONIA			
Colonia Montseny			
Colonia Durruti			
Colonia Ascaso			

Notes

Introduction

1. Gabriel Jackson, *The Second Republic and the Spanish Civil War* (Princeton: Princeton University Press, 1965).

2. Noam Chomsky, *American Power and the New Mandarins* (New York: Random House, 1969), pp. 74–124.

3. Burnett Bolloten, *The Grand Camouflage* (London: Pall Mall, 1968).

4. José Peirats, *La CNT en la revolución española,* 3 vols. (Toulouse: Ediciones CNT, 1951–1953).

5. Gaston Leval, *Espagne libertaire 1936–1939* (Paris: Editions du Cercle, 1971), and Abel Paz (pseud. Diego Camacho), *Durruti: le peuple en armes* (Paris: Editions de la Tête de Feuilles, 1972).

6. César Lorenzo, *Les anarchistes espagnols et la pouvoir 1868–1969* (Paris: Editions du Seuil, 1969), and Stephan John Brademas, "Revolution and Counter-Revolution in Spain: A Contribution to the History of the Anarcho-Syndicalist Movement in Spain, 1930–1937" (unpublished Ph.D. dissertation, Brasenose College, Oxford University, 1953). Brademas' later revision, somewhat less useful for this study, has come out as *Anarco-sindicalismo y revolución en España 1930–1937* (Madrid: Ariel, 1974). References throughout are to the dissertation.

7. Maximiano García Venero, *Historia de las Internacionales en España,* 3 vols. (Madrid: Ediciones del Movimiento, 1956), and *Historia de los movimientos sindicalistas españolas* (Madrid: Ediciones del Movimiento, 1961). Also see Eduardo Comín Colomer, *Historia del anarquismo español (1836–1948)* (Madrid: RADAR, n.d.).

8. Murray Bookchin has recently written *The Spanish Anarchists: The Heroic Years, 1868–1936* (New York: Free Life Editions, 1977), which was published too late to be used as a major reference in this study. The other sources mentioned are: George Woodcock, *Anarchism: A History of Libertarian Ideas and Movements* (New York: Meridian, 1962); James Joll, *The Anarchists* (New York: Grosset and Dunlap, 1964); and Daniel Guérin, *Anarchism* (New York: Monthly Review Press, 1970).

9. The biography is Paz's *Durruti,* and the novel, by Hans Magnus Enzensberger, is *Der kurze Sommer der Anarchie: Buenaventura Durrutis Leben und Tod* (Frankfurt am Main: Suhrkamp, 1972).

10. Emma Goldman, draft of speech, October 8, 1936, Internationaal Instituut voor Sociale Geschiedenis (Amsterdam), Rudolf Rocker Collection, Goldman file. [The Institute shall hereafter be abbreviated as IISG.]

11. Eric Hobsbawm, *Primitive Rebels* (New York: Vintage, 1959), p. 5.

12. Joaquín Maurín, *Hacia la segunda revolución* (Barcelona: Gráficos Alfa, 1935), p. 91.

13. V. I. Lenin, "On Provisional Revolutionary Government," in *Anarchism and Anarcho-Syndicalism* (Moscow: International Publishers, 1972), pp. 187–196. Leon Trotsky is quoted in Maurín, *Hacia la segunda revolución,* p. 83.

14. Guérin, *Anarchism,* pp. 127–128.

15. Woodcock, *Anarchism,* p. 398.

16. Chomsky, *American Power,* p. 123.

17. Stanley Payne, *The Spanish Revolution* (New York: Norton, 1970), p. 374.

18. David C. Rapoport, *Assassination and Terrorism* (Toronto: CBC, 1971), p. 48.

19. Payne, *The Spanish Revolution;* Richard A. H. Robinson, *The Origins of Franco's Spain: The Right, the Republic and the Revolution, 1931–1936* (Newton Abbot: David and Charles, 1970); Edward Malefakis, *Agrarian Reform and Peasant Revolution in Spain* (New Haven: Yale University Press, 1970); and Gerald Brenan, *The Spanish Labyrinth* (London: Cambridge University Press, 1942).

20. Particularly inside the movement; e.g., Vernon Richards, *Lessons of the Spanish Revolution* (London: Freedom Press, 1953).

Chapter One

1. One of the best traveller's reports is G. H. B. Ward, *The Truth about Spain* (London: Cassell, 1911).

2. Frank Deakin, *Spain To-day* (London: Labour Publishing Co., 1924), p. vi.

3. Joaquín Costa, "Manifiesto de la Cámara del Alto-Aragón," in Costa, ed., *Reconstitución y europeización de España* (Madrid: San Francisco de Sales, 1900), pp. 3–4.

4. Robert W. Kern, *Liberals, Reformers and Caciques in Restoration Spain* (Albuquerque: University of New Mexico Press, 1974), pp. 14–18.

5. Jaime Vicens Vives, *An Economic History of Spain* (Princeton: Princeton University Press, 1969), p. 639.

6. Diego Abad de Santillán, *El organismo económico de la revolución* (Barcelona: Ediciones Tierra y Libertad, 1937), p. 43.

7. Laurie Lee, *As I Walked Out One Midsummer Morning* (London: Pen-

guin, 1969), is an English poet's fascinating remembrance of a walking tour through Spain in 1934–1936 and of the isolation of the small villages.

8. C. A. M. Hennessy, *The Federal Republic of Spain, 1868–1875* (Oxford: Clarendon Press, 1962), pp. 196–220.

9. The main work on cantonalism is Julian de Zugasti, *El bandolerismo,* 8 vols. (Madrid: Fortanet, 1874–1878).

10. Eric Hobsbawm, *Primitive Rebels* (New York: Vintage, 1959), p. 78.

11. Clara Lida, "Agrarian Anarchism in Andalusia," *International Review of Social History,* XIV (1969), part 3, pp. 315–352. This has been expanded into *Anarquismo y revolución en la España del siglo XIX* (Madrid: Siglo Veintiuno de España, 1972).

12. Abad de Santillán, *El organismo económico,* p. 25.

13. Edward Malefakis, *Agrarian Reform and Peasant Revolution in Spain* (New Haven: Yale University Press, 1970), pp. 103–104.

14. *Ibid.,* p. 100.

15. Abad de Santillán, *El organismo económico,* p. 26.

16. *Ibid.*

17. Gerald Brenan, *The Spanish Labyrinth* (Cambridge: Cambridge University Press, 1943), pp. 92–93.

18. Raymond Carr, *Modern Spain, 1808–1939* (Oxford: Clarendon Press, 1967), p. 420.

19. Several anthropological studies have looked at the flight of peasants from the villages. Susan Tax Freeman, *Neighbors: The Social Contract in a Castilian Hamlet* (Chicago: University of Chicago Press, 1970), pp. 157–174, and Carmelo Lison-Toledana, *Belmonte de los Caballeros: A Sociological Study of a Spanish Town* (Oxford: Clarendon Press, 1966), are two examples.

20. Carr, *Modern Spain,* pp. 264–266, 406–407.

21. It should be noted that by no means all these newcomers to Barcelona were Andalusians. Jaime Alaina Caules, "Investigación analítica sobre la evolución demográfica de Cataluña," *Cuadernos de Información Económica y Sociológica* (Barcelona), June 1955, pp. 28–34, shows that emigrants from rural Catalonia, Valencia, and Aragon came to Barcelona in much larger numbers than the Andalusians, whom he calculates as only about 2.82 percent of the work force in the early twentieth century. However, there are many variables that do not enter into his figures. Some peasants from the South made their way to Barcelona slowly, with many stops along the way. Valencia particularly served as a way station, as did Madrid. In all likelihood, the real figure was much higher.

22. José Peirats, *Los anarquistas en la crisis política española* (Buenos Aires: Editorial Alfa, 1964), p. 127.

23. Alberto Balcells, *El sindicalismo en Barcelona 1916–1923* (Barcelona: Editorial Nova Terra, 1965), p. 13.

24. Joan Connelly Ullman, *The Tragic Week* (Cambridge: Harvard University, 1967), pp. 68–72.

25. The allegations were expressed most vividly in Francisco Tarrida del Marmol, *Les Inquisiteurs de l'Espagne* (Paris, 1897). Also see Manuel Bue-

nacasa, *El movimiento obrero español 1886–1926* (Barcelona: Impresos Costa, 1928), pp. 39–43.

26. José Boix, "Sindicalismo católico: su actuación en Barcelona," *Revista Social Hispano-Americano* (Barcelona), March 1911, pp. 209–219. At this time Barcelona had a population of 587,411 (1910 figures).

27. Ullman, *The Tragic Week*, p. 167.

28. The earliest anarchist notables included López Rodrigo, Teresa Claramunt, Tomás Cano Ruiz, José Sánchez Rosa, Sebastián Oliva, Galo Díez, Juan Beraza, and Manuel Fandiño. Buenacasa, *El movimiento obrero*, pp. 23–24.

29. Biographies of Bakunin include E. H. Carr, *Michael Bakunin* (New York: Vintage, 1961), and G. P. Maximoff (with chapters by Rudolf Rocker and Max Nettlau), *The Political Philosophy of Bakunin* (New York: Free Press, 1953). A good selection of Bakunin's writings can be found in Sam Dolgoff, ed. and trans., *Bakunin on Anarchy* (New York: Vintage, 1971). Max Nettlau's *Michael Bakunin*, 3 vols. (London, 1899), is no longer available, except for Clara Lida's edited version, published by Iberama (Madrid) in 1971.

30. Friedrich Engels, "The Bakuninists at Work," in Karl Marx and Friedrich Engels, *Anarchism and Anarcho-Syndicalism* (Moscow: International Publishers, 1971), pp. 128–146. Engels felt that the Spanish anarchists in 1873 relied too heavily upon bourgeois elements. Industrialism, Engels predicted prematurely, would wipe out the movement entirely: "The Workingmen of Europe in 1877," *ibid.*, p. 162. Lenin later characterized the revolution of 1873 as petit bourgeois in its failure to organize from above: "On Provisional Revolutionary Government," *ibid.*, pp. 187–196. For the best general summary of these controversies and the various ideas of the nineteenth-century Spanish anarchists, see José Alvarez Junco, *La ideología política del anarquismo español (1868–1910)* (Madrid: Siglo Veintiuno de España, 1976).

31. Eugene Pyziur, *The Doctrine of Anarchism of Michael A. Bakunin* (Milwaukee: Marquette University Press, 1955), p. 101.

32. Michael Bakunin, "Revolutionary Catechism," in Dolgoff, *Bakunin on Anarchy*, p. 76.

33. *Ibid.*, pp. 78–79.

34. *Ibid.*, p. 80.

35. *Ibid.*, p. 92.

36. Joaquín Costa, Francisco Giner de los Ríos, and José María Pantoja, eds., *Derecho consuetudinario y económico popular de España*, 2 vols. (Barcelona: M. Sole, 1885), discussed examples of collective agrarian and social practices. Some were related to the medieval *fueros*, which were grants of autonomy that once had regulated many aspects of local life. The decline of this tradition began in the fifteenth and sixteenth centuries. The first Carlist war (1834–1839), a conservative revolt, ended with the abolition of all special local and regional privileges.

37. Bakunin, "Federalism, Socialism and Anti-Theologism," in Dolgoff, *Bakunin on Anarchy*, p. 134.

38. Bakunin, "The Franco-Prussian War and the Paris Commune," *ibid.*, p. 202.

39. Bakunin, "The Program of the International Brotherhood," *ibid.*, p. 155.

40. Bakunin, "Letter to Albert Richard," *ibid.*, pp. 180–181. For the limitations he placed upon the revolutionaries, see Max Nettlau, ed., *Gesammelte Werke Bakunin* (Berlin: n.p., 1921), II, 62.

41. According to Max Nomad (pseud. Max Nacht), "The Anarchist Tradition and Other Essays," IISG, Nomad Collection, file 4, p. 5, the "invisible dictatorship" would last even after the revolution had succeeded, bringing such a conflict with libertarian elements that a new struggle for power would occur.

42. Buenacasa, *El movimiento obrero,* pp. 36–44, gives membership figures and an account of this time. One might also consult two works of Max Nettlau, *Anarchisten und Social-Revolutionäre die historische Entwicklung des Anarchismus in der Jahren 1880–86* (Berlin, 1886) and *La Première Internationale en Espagne* (1868–1888) (Dordrecht: Reidel, 1969). In addition, there is Clara Lida, *Anarquismo y revolución en la España del siglo XIX.*

43. Malefakis, *Agrarian Reform and Peasant Revolution,* p. 140.

44. Anselmo Lorenzo, *El proletariado militante: memorias de un internacional* (Mexico City: Ediciones Vertice, 1943), I, 62–65.

45. Bakunin, "Revolutionary Catechism," in Doigoff, *Bakunin on Anarchy,* pp. 95–97.

46. Daniel Guérin, *Anarchism* (New York: Monthly Review Press, 1970), pp. 74–75.

47. Nazario González, *El anarquismo en la historia de España contemporánea* (Barcelona: Universidad de Barcelona Facultad de Filosofía y Letras, 1970), p. 43. Urales' real name was Juan Montseny, and he was the father of Federica Montseny, later one of the most important anarchist theorists and an editor, with her father, of *La Revista Blanca.*

48. See particularly Ashley Montagu's foreword in Peter Kropotkin, *Mutual Aid* (Boston: Porter Sargent, n.d.). Woodcock, *Anarchism,* pp. 184–221, also has an excellent essay on Kropotkin.

49. Ullman, *The Tragic Week,* pp. 93–102, is the most recent treatment of Ferrer.

50. The French anarchist Paul Brousse, who had spent some time in Catalonia, became a reformist member of the Paris Municipal Council and founder of the "Possibilist" party after his break with anarchism. David Stafford, *From Anarchism to Reformism* (Toronto: University of Toronto Press, 1971), pp. 199–241. The Italian anarchist Carlo Cafiero went mad in 1882 over difficulties facing the anarchist movement as it moved into its "propaganda of the deed" phase. Richard Hostetter, *The Italian Socialist Movement. Vol. I: Origins 1860–1882* (Princeton: Princeton University Press, 1971), p. 431.

51. George Woodcock, *Anarchism: A History of Libertarian Ideas and Movements* (New York: Meridian, 1962), p. 334.

52. César Lorenzo, *Les anarchistes espagnols et la pouvoir 1868–1969* (Paris: Editions du Seuil, 1969), pp. 40–41. Ricardo Mella and José Prat wrote *La barbarie gubernamental en España* (Barcelona, 1897), which drew European attention to the social war between terrorists and the Civil Guard in Barcelona.

53. Ullman, *The Tragic Week,* pp. 118–126.

54. An example of the protests against the execution of Ferrer can be found in Emma Goldman, "Francisco Ferrer: The Modern School," in Goldman's *Anarchism and Other Essays* (New York: Mother Earth, 1911), pp. 151–172.

55. Sylvain Humbert, *Le mouvement syndical* (Paris: M. Rivière et Cie., 1912), p. 100.

56. Buenacasa, *El movimiento obrero,* p. 34.

57. Early anarchist newspapers in the North, such as *El Corsario, El Productor, La Emancipación,* and *Bandera Roja,* did exist in considerable numbers. Corunna, where there had been large strikes in 1901 and 1909, was a center of labor activity in Galicia; leaders there were Constancio Romero and Juan No. In Leon and Asturias strong CNT support came from the mines and the city of Gijon, where the Sindicato Minero Asturiano, led by Eleuterio Quintanilla and José María Martínez, supported a workers' school, the Ateneo Obrero de Gijón, and strongly leaned towards syndicalism. *Ibid.,* pp. 246, 254.

58. *Ibid.,* pp. 173, 186, 190, and Lorenzo, *Les anarchistes espagnols,* p. 63.

59. Montseny's *La Revista Blanca* published sporadically after 1899, and his *Tierra y Libertad,* begun in Madrid in 1903, was forced to stop publishing in 1905. After the Tragic Week, the only anarchist publishing effort was Francisco Sempere's collection of Bakunin, Proudhon, Kropotkin, Reclus, Lorenzo, and others. Peirats, *Los anarquistas en la crisis política española,* p. 275.

60. Buenacasa, *El movimiento obrero,* pp. 48–49.

61. José Peirats, *La CNT en la revolución española* (Toulouse: Ediciones CNT, 1951–1953), I, 3.

62. Malefakis, *Agrarian Reform and Peasant Revolution,* p. 144.

63. José Martín Blázquez, *I Helped to Build an Army* (London: Secker and Warburg, 1939), p. 212.

64. Francisco Bernis, *Consecuencias económicas de la guerra* (Madrid: E. Maestre, 1923), p. 52.

65. Ministerio de Trabajo, *Boletín,* March 1931, pp. 234–235.

66. Instituto de Reformas Sociales, *Estadística de huelgas* (Madrid, 1918), ix.

67. Victor Serge, *Memoirs of a Revolutionary* (Oxford: Clarendon Press, 1963), p. 53.

68. F. D. Sola Cañizares, *Salvador Seguí: su vida, su obra* (Barcelona: n.p., 1960), p. 156.

69. Serge, *Memoirs,* pp. 55–56.

70. *Solidaridad Obrera,* June 17, 1917, p. 1.

71. Abel Paz (pseud. Diego Camacho), *Durruti: le peuple en armes* (Paris: Editions de la Tête de Feuilles, 1972), pp. 25–26.

72. For the socialist leaders, see Francisco Largo Caballero, *Mis recuerdos* (Mexico City: Ediciones "Alianza," 1941), and Juan José Morato, *Pablo Iglesias, educador de muchadumbres* (Madrid: Espasa-Calpe, 1931). The major work is Gerald H. Meaker, *The Revolutionary Left in Spain 1914–1923* (Stanford: Stanford University Press, 1974), pp. 77, 79, and *passim*.

73. Rudolf Rocker, *Revolución y regresión* (Buenos Aires: Editorial Tupac, 1952), p. 172. Meaker, *The Revolutionary Left in Spain*, pp. 62–95, covers the strike in full.

74. Abad de Santillán had already written *Discurso sobre los grandes hombres y sobre la existencia de un redentor de España* (Madrid: Victoriano Suárez, 1914), and *El derecho de España a la revolución* (Madrid: Fortanet, 1916). His *Psicología del pueblo español* (Madrid: F. Peña Cruz, 1917) was dedicated to Joaquín Sánchez de Toca, an old Conservative party reformer.

75. Abad de Santillán's writings on the FORA include *La FORA: ideología y trayectoria del movimiento obrero revolucionario en la Argentina* (Buenos Aires: Editorial Proyección, 1971). Also see Sebastian Marotta, *El movimiento sindical argentino*, 3 vols. (Buenos Aires: Ediciones "Lacio," 1961).

76. Quoted in Malefakis, *Agrarian Reform and Peasant Revolution*, p. 147.

77. CNT, *Memoria del Congreso celebrado en el Teatro de la Comedia de Madrid, los días 10 al 18 de diciembre de 1919* (Barcelona: CNT, 1932), p. 34.

78. Lorenzo, *Les anarchistes espagnols*, p. 56.

79. Max Nomad uses the same term in "The Anarchist Tradition," p. 47.

80. Part of the influence was indirect, through the work of the French Conférence Nationale des Fédérations de Unions et des Bourses du Travail, held at Clermont-Ferrand in 1917 as a positive response to the Russian revolution and in expectation that syndicalism would associate with the Third International. See François Maspero, ed., *Syndicalisme revolutionnaire et communisme: les archives de Pierre Monatte* (Paris: n.p., 1968), p. 252.

81. Rudolf Rocker, "Verhaftung des Genossen Carbó," IISG, Rocker Collection, file 1, folder 7.

82. Nomad, "The Anarchist Tradition," p. 143.

83. Juan Díaz del Moral, *Historia de las agitaciones campesinas andaluzas* (Madrid: Revista de Derecho Privado, 1929), pp. 275–384.

84. Quoted in Arthur H. Hardinge to the Earl of Curzon, February 11, 1919, British Record Office, *Calendar of State Papers Relating to Western and Southern Europe*, FO 371, file 4119, no. 2550. [Cited hereafter as *Calendar.*]

85. Lorenzo, *Les anarchistes espagnols*, pp. 45–46.

86. Serge, *Memoirs*, p. 58.

87. Edward Banfield, *The Moral Basis of a Backward Society* (New York: Free Press, 1958), pp. 83–101, postulates a concept of "amoral familialism" that can be usefully applied to any sectarian group in Spanish society.

Chapter Two

1. Report of C. N. Sterling, May 25, 1933, *Calendar*, FO 371, file 4491, no. 17435, W 3809.

2. *Ibid.*

3. Ricardo Sanz, *El sindicalismo y la política: los "Solidarios" y "Nosotros"* (Toulouse: Imprimerie Dulaurier, 1966), p. 34.

4. *Solidaridad Obrera*, February 10, 1919, pp. 1–2.

5. Alberto Barcells, *El sindicalismo en Barcelona 1916–1923* (Barcelona: Editorial Nova Terra, 1965), pp. 114–116.

6. Manuel Buenacasa, *El movimiento obrero español 1886–1926* (Barcelona: Impresas Costa, 1928), pp. 78–79; Angel Pestaña, *Lo que aprendí en la vida* (Madrid: M. Aguilar, 1934), p. 163.

7. *Solidaridad Obrera*, March 14, 1919, p. 2.

8. Buenacasa, *El movimiento obrero*, p. 96, hints at this. The best information comes from Sanz, *El sindicalismo*, pp. 25, 53.

9. Barcells, *El sindicalismo en Barcelona*, p. 89.

10. Sanz, *El sindicalismo*, p. 53.

11. According to Federica Montseny, *El anarquismo militante y la realidad española* (Barcelona: CNT, 1937). A slightly different version is her *La commune de Paris y la revolución española* (Barcelona: Oficina de Información, Propaganda y Prensa del Comité Nacional CNT-FAI, 1937).

12. Buenacasa, *El movimiento obrero*, pp. 296–297, and Ramón Plá y Armengol, *Impresiones de la huelga general de Barcelona, del 24 de marzo al 7 de abril de 1919* (Barcelona: n.p., 1930), pp. 95–96.

13. The passage on rural conditions in the South is from Gerald Brenan, *The Spanish Labyrinth* (Cambridge: Cambridge University Press, 1943), pp. 179–183.

14. See the report in *Calendar*, FO 371, file 4120, no. 2550, pp. 4–5.

15. Juan Díaz del Moral, *Historia de las agitaciones campesinas andaluzas* (Madrid: Revista de Derecho Privado, 1929), pp. 570–572.

16. *Ibid.,* p. 335, and Edward Malefakis, *Agrarian Reform and Peasant Revolution in Spain* (New Haven: Yale University Press, 1970), p. 151.

17. CNT, *Memoria del Congreso celebrado en el Teatro de la Comedia de Madrid, los días 10 al 18 de diciembre de 1919* (Barcelona: CNT, 1932), pp. 46–47.

18. Letter of Sir Esme Howard to Lord Curzon, October 25, 1920, *Calendar*, FO 371, file 249, no. 5497, p. 152.

19. *The Times* (London), December 24, 1920, p. 9.

20 *El Imparcial*, May 14, 1919, pp. 1, 3.

21. Letter of Talbot Dawes to Sir William Tyrrell, November 8, 1920, *Calendar*, FO 371, file 5459, no. 2509, pp. 9–10.

22. *El Imparcial*, May 14, 1919, p. 1.

23. Malefakis, *Agrarian Reform*, p. 148; Abel Paz (pseud. Diego Camacho), *Durruti: le peuple en armes* (Paris: Editions de Tête de Feuilles, 1972), pp. 30–31.

24. Buenacasa, *El movimiento obrero*, p. 246.

25. Barcells, *El sindicalismo en Barcelona*, p. 111.

26. Koenig's real name may have been Colmann or Köhlmann. See Augustin Souchy, *Anarcho-Syndikalisten über Bürger-Krieg und Revolution in*

Spanien (Darmstadt: Marz Verlag, 1969), p. 39, and Jorge Subirato Centura, "La verdadero personalidad del 'Baron de Koenig,' " *Cuadernos de Historia Económica de Cataluña*, V (1971), pp. 103–118.

27. *La Tribuna* (Madrid), August 1, 1929, p. 4. Gerald H. Meaker, *The Revolutionary Left in Spain 1914–1923* (Stanford: Stanford University Press, 1974), pp. 312–322, has an excellent discussion of the situation.

28. Sanz, *El sindicalismo*, p. 69.

29. For a picture of life in Barcelona during 1919 and 1920, see Angel Pestaña, *El terrorismo en Barcelona* (Barcelona: Solidaridad Obrera, 1920).

30. Barcells, *El sindicalismo en Barcelona*, p. 121.

31. Letter of Arthur H. Hardinge to the Earl of Curzon, November 5, 1919, *Calendar*, FO 371, file 4120, no. 2550, p. 1.

32. Letter of Sir Esme Howard to the Earl of Curzon, December 30, 1919, *Calendar*, FO 371, file 4120, no. 2981, p. 2.

33. *El Liberal* (Barcelona), January 5, 1920, p. 1.

34. *Heraldo de Madrid*, January 12, 1920, pp. 1–2.

35. Sanz, *El sindicalismo*, p. 68.

36. Letter of Arthur L. Rowley to Sir Esme Howard, January 25, 1920, *Calendar*, FO 371, file 1134, no. 171385.

37. Letter of Arthur L. Rowley to Sir Esme Howard, January 10, 1920, *Calendar*, FO 371, file 1134, no. 170033.

38. Juan Gómez Casas, *Historia del anarchosindicalismo español* (Madrid: Editorial ZYX, 1968), p. 124, breaks down membership and delegate totals of the CNT as follows: Catalonia, 427,000 and 128; Valencia, 132,000 and 71; Andalusia (including Estremadura), 90,000 and 73.

39. For the socialists in 1919–1920, see Stanley Payne, *The Spanish Revolution* (New York: Norton, 1970), pp. 62–75, and Meaker, *The Revolutionary Left in Spain*, pp. 226–233.

40. CNT, *Memoria del Congreso*, p. 41.

41. Gómez Casas, *Historia del anarchosindicalismo*, pp. 126–127.

42. CNT, *Memoria del Congreso*, p. 42.

43. *Ibid.* Also see Meaker, *The Revolutionary Left in Spain*, pp. 233–248.

44. Gómez Casas, *Historia del anarchosindicalismo*, p. 129.

45. The term "libertarian possibilism" was used in Helmut Rüdiger, "Rapport du Secretariat de Barcelone pour la Congrès de l'AIT à Paris, le 7 décembre 1937," IISG, Rocker Collection, file 2, folder 3, p. 14.

46. Angel Pestaña, *Setenta días en Rusia: lo que yo ví* (Barcelona: n.p., 1924), p. 197.

47. According to Joaquín Maurín, "Sur la communisme en Espagne," quoted in Branko Lazitch and Milorad Drachkovitch, *Lenin and the Comintern* (Stanford: Hoover Library Press, 1972), I, 315.

48. See Souchy, *Anarcho-Syndikalisten*, p. 124. Makhno's legendary career is covered by Paul Avrich, *The Russian Anarchists* (Princeton: Princeton University Press, 1967), pp. 209–222. Alexander Shapiro, a follower of Peter Kropotkin, worked for the Commissariat of Foreign Affairs in the

Soviet Union during 1919 and 1920 before breaking with the communists and returning to Germany.

49. Emma Goldman, *Living My Life* (New York: Scribner, 1932), II, 799.

50. CNT, "Memoria del Congreso Regional Celebrado en Zaragoza, los días 8–10 de mayo de 1922," Archivo de CNT/FAI, Toulouse, France.

51. *Ibid.*

52. Joaquín Maurín, *Revolución y contrarrevolución en España* (Paris: Ruedo Ibérico, 1966), p. 248.

53. See Lenin, *Left-Wing Communism, an Infantile Disorder* (Moscow: International, 1931), pp. 62–71.

54. Rudolf Rocker, *Revolución y regresión* (Buenos Aires: Editorial Tupac, 1952), p. 138.

55. *Ibid.*, pp. 140–142.

56. Augustin Souchy, Rudolf Rocker, and Alexander Shapiro had all joined Kropotkin in his English exile. Rocker, a German, remained there until after World War I, while Shapiro, a Russian, followed Kropotkin back to the USSR after the Russian revolution. Both Souchy and Rocker had close ties with Max Nettlau, a major figure in twentieth-century European anarchism. Rocker, *Revolución y regresión,* gives frequent glimpses of Nettlau's life and influence.

57. Letter of Sir Esme Howard to the Earl of Curzon, March 1, 1920, *Calendar,* FO 371, file 2550, no. 4121.

58. *Ibid.*

59. *La Correspondencia de España* (Madrid), March 24, 1920, p. 1.

60. Sanz, *El sindicalismo,* p. 53.

61. *La Tarde* (Barcelona), September 10, 1920, p. 2.

62. *El Día Gráfica* (Barcelona), September 10, 1920, p. 1.

63. Political Report, October 10, 1920, *Calendar,* FO 371, file 2509, no. 5495.

64. Payne, *The Spanish Revolution,* p. 55, and Meaker, *The Revolutionary Left in Spain,* pp. 338–345.

65. Sanz, *El sindicalismo,* p. 110.

66. The *somatén* had been a volunteer militia in Catalonia during the Napoleonic wars. Rocker, *Revolución y regresión,* p. 184.

67. A municipal strike won recognition of syndicates in Saragossa when the civil governor could find no one to replace the workers in September 1921. A month later all syndicates were abolished after unemployed men had been imported from the South. This led to a large protest movement which radicalized part of the city. Paz, *Durruti,* p. 42.

68. Payne, *The Spanish Revolution,* p. 76.

69. Paz, *Durruti,* pp. 44–45.

70. Sanz, *El sindicalismo,* p. 78.

71. See *The Times* (London), March 28, 1932, p. 6.

72. Sanz, *El sindicalismo,* p. 58.

73. *Ibid.*, p. 109.

74. Raymond Carr, *Modern Spain, 1808–1939* (Oxford: Clarendon Press, 1967), pp. 516–517, calls Annual "the most discreditable defeat in the military annals of Spain."

75. Gómez Casas, *Historia del anarchosindicalismo*, p. 189.

76. Francisco Ascaso edited *Cristol* and headed the group, which included Buenaventura Durruti, from Leon; Juan García Oliver, Barcelona; Aurelio Fernández, Austurias and Saragossa; Ricardo Sanz, Valencia; Gregorio Suberviela, Navarre; Miguel García Vivancos, Murcia; and Manuel Campos, Castile. Cf. César Lorenzo, *Les anarchistes espagnols et la pouvoir 1868–1969* (Paris: Editions du Seuil, 1969), p. 59.

77. *Cristol,* January 14, 1923, n.p.

78. The executive committee of the Relaciones Anarquistas group was all from Solidarios: Ricardo Sanz, Aurelio Fernández, Antonio Perra, and Sebastián Clará. Sanz, *El sindicalismo*, p. 101.

79. *Cristol,* February 19, 1923, n.p.

80. Sanz, *El sindicalismo*, p. 106.

81. Paz, *Durruti*, p. 71.

82. Sanz, *El sindicalismo*, p. 114.

83. Political Report, September 4, 1922, *Calendar,* FO 371, file 2589, no. 8309, p. 5.

84. *El Socialista,* February 18, 1922, p. 1.

85. Speech of Count Romanones, April 17, 1922, Congreso de los Diputados, *Diario del Congreso de los Diputados,* XXIV, no. 9 (1920 series), p. 99.

86. Letter of Sir Esme Howard to the Earl of Curzon, October 21, 1922, *Calendar*, FO 371, file 2589, no. 8389.

87. *Gaceta de Madrid,* January 24, 1923, pp. 4–11.

88. Letter of Sir Esme Howard to the Earl of Curzon, March 16, 1923, *Calendar,* FO 371, file 576, no. W 2100. Howard went on: "According to one of the labor papers of Barcelona [Seguí] had been working actively in the cause of pacification, and on this account had lately received several threatening letters from extreme anarchists."

89. See Sanz, *El sindicalismo*, p. 129.

90. Carr, *Modern Spain*, p. 523.

Chapter Three

1. José Peirats, *La CNT en la revolución española* (Toulouse: Ediciones CNT, 1951–1953), I, 9.

2. Ricardo Sanz, *El sindicalismo y la política: los "Solidarios" y "Nosotros"* (Toulouse: Imprimie Dulaurier, 1966), p. 127.

3. *Ibid.*, p. 141.

4. Abel Paz (pseud. Diego Camacho), *Durruti: le peuple en armes* (Paris: Editions de la Tête de Feuilles, 1972), p. 9. This book has now been trans-

lated by Nancy Macdonald: *Durruti, the People Armed* (New York: Free Life Editions, 1977).

5. Association Internationale des Travailleurs, "Rapport por Alexandre Shapiro sur l'activité de la Confédération National du Travail d'Espagne," October 1933, in IISG, AIT Collection, file 3, folder 4.

6. A good source on UGT history in the Twenties is Enrique Santiago, *La Unión General Trabajadores ante la revolución* (Madrid: Sáez Hermanos 1932), pp. 52–71.

7. "Ley de Provincias," *Gaceta de Madrid,* April 8, 1925, p. 4.

8. Stephan John Brademas, "Revolution and Counter-Revolution in Spain: A Contribution to the History of the Anarcho-Syndicalist Movement in Spain, 1930–1937" (unpublished Ph.D. dissertation, Brasenose College, Oxford University, 1953), p. 27.

9. CNT, *Memoria del Congreso extraordinaria celebrado en Madrid, los días 11 al 16 de junio de 1931* (Barcelona: CNT, 1931), p. 67.

10. Interview with Miguel Jiménez, in Brademas, "Revolution and Counter-Revolution," pp. 41–42.

11. Sanz, *El sindicalismo,* p. 147.

12. Letter of the Marques of Crewe to Sir Austin Chamberlain, January 27, 1927, *Calendar,* FO 371, file 2597, no. 10595, p. 17.

13. Stanley Payne, *Politics and the Military in Modern Spain* (Stanford: Stanford University Press, 1966), pp. 228–229.

14. *El Amigo del Pueblo* (Barcelona, Valencia), June 27, 1936, p. 3.

15. Rudolf Rocker, *Revolución y regresión* (Buenos Aires: Editorial Tupac, 1952), pp. 176–178.

16. Hem Day (pseud. M. Dieu), *Sébastien Faure, le pacifiste* (Brussels: n.p., 1961), p. 9.

17. Nestor Makhno, born in the Ukraine in 1889, became a participant in the revolution of 1905. For the rest of his life, see Voline (pseud. Vsevolod Mikhailovitch Eichenbawm), *The Unknown Revolution: Kronstadt 1921, Ukraine 1918–1921* (London: Freedom Press, 1955). Voline's book is particularly interesting because it was originally written in 1941, just after the end of the Spanish Civil War. A comparison of the Russian and Spanish anarchist experiences is implicit in the study.

18. Nestor Makhno, "Las consecuencias de la guerra revolucionaria," *Tierra y Libertad,* April 27, 1934, p. 2.

19. The glorification of Durruti and Ascaso began with Valentín de Roi, *Ascaso, Durruti, Jover: su obra de militantes, su vida de perseguidos* (Buenos Aires: Antorcha, 1927); grew during the Civil War, as in Gilberto Gilabert, *Durruti, un héroe del pueblo* (Buenos Aires: Ediciones Nervio, 1937), or FAI, *Homenaje del comité de la FAI* (Barcelona: FAI, 1937); continued to grow with Ricardo Sanz, *Figuras de la revolución española: Buenaventura Durruti* (Toulouse: Ediciones El Frente, 1945), and S. Cánovas Cervantes, *Durruti y Ascaso y la revolución de julio* (Toulouse: Paginas Libres, n.d.); and has come to fruition, rather inexactly, with Hans Magnus Enzensberger, *Der kurze Sommer der Anarchie: Buenaventura Durrutis Leben und Tod* (Frankfort am Main:

Suhrkamp, 1972), and Peter Newell, *The Forgotten Heroes: Makhno and Durruti* (London: Freedom Press, 1969), as well as, of course, Abel Paz.

20. Paz, *Durruti*, p. 99.

21. *Ibid.*, pp. 101–102.

22. *Ibid.*, p. 106.

23. Abad de Santillán's writings include one publication, *Los anarquistas y la reacción contemporánea* (Mexico City: Grupo Cultural Ricardo Flores Magón, 1925), which the Spanish exiles may have helped get published. It is also likely that Abad de Santillán was in Mexico City at the same time Durruti was.

24. Cánovas Cervantes, *Durruti y Ascaso*, p. 11.

25. Paz, *Durruti*, p. 109.

26. See *Le Populaire* (Paris), November 22, 1926, p. 1.

27. *La Vanguardia* (Madrid), November 10, 1926, pp. 1, 4.

28. See particularly *Le Quotidien, L'Oeuvre*, and *Le Populaire* throughout 1926 and 1927 for Paris news coverage of the trial.

29. Sébastien Faure, "L'affaire Durruti," *Iberión*, March 1, 1927, pp. 1–2.

30. *Tiempos Nuevos* (Paris), February 19, 1927, p. 3.

31. Paz, *Durruti*, pp. 120–121.

32. Rocker, *Revolución y regresión*, pp. 179–180. As a journalist, Erich Mühsam had collaborated with Gustav Landauer, later a Premier of the Munich Soviet in 1919, on the pre-World War I newspaper *Sozialist*, one of the first and most important attempts to reconcile socialism and anarchism. After the Munich uprising, Mühsam fled to the USSR but later left in disgust in the aftermath of Kronstadt and the realization of Bolshevik one-party government. In 1928 he became a successful playwright; his political drama *Staatsräson* dealt with the trial of Sacco and Vanzetti, two figures he strongly identified with Durruti and Ascaso. Cf. Richard Grunberger, *Red Rising in Bavaria* (London: Barker, 1973), pp. 27–28 and *passim*, for additional biographical material on Mühsam.

33. Sanz, *El sindicalismo*, p. 153.

34. *La Voz de Libertaria* was actually a supplement to a Belgian anarchist newspaper, *La Voix Libertarie*.

35. Sanz, *El sindicalismo*, pp. 170–171.

36. Elisée Reclus, "El hombre y la tierra," *La Revista Blanca*, IV, nos. 79–82 (September 1926–March 1927), *passim*.

37. *Ibid.*, IV, no. 79 (September 1, 1926), p. 10.

38. *Ibid.*, IV, no. 80 (September 15, 1926), p. 42.

39. Max Nettlau, "Comunismo autoritario y comunismo libertario," *ibid.*, VI, nos. 113–114 (February 1 and 15, 1928), pp. 513–517, 545–550, and no. 115 (March 1, 1928), pp. 578–579. The discussion can be found in "Para preparar la sociedad futura," beginning in V, no. 81 (January 1, 1927), pp. 475–477, and continuing intermittently thereafter.

40. A complete bibliography of Federica Montseny's novels is in Shirley Fredricks, "Social and Political Thought of Federica Montseny, Spanish Anarchist, 1923–1937" (unpublished dissertation, University of New Mexico, 1972), pp. 199–201.

41. For a good examination of the early life and ideas of Federica Montseny, see *ibid.*, p. 22 and *passim*.

42. Letter of Emma Goldman to Mariano Vázquez, October 11, 1937, IISG, Goldman Collection, file 28 B. A general discussion of this theme can be found in Temma Kaplan, "Spanish Anarchism and Women's Liberation," *Journal of Contemporary History*, VI, no. 2 (1971), pp. 101–110.

43. Montseny, "La tragedia de la emancipación femenina," *La Revista Blanca*, II, no. 39 (December 15, 1924), p. 520.

44. Montseny, *El problema de los sexos* (Toulouse: n.p., 1943), pp. 15–16.

45. *Ibid.*

46. Montseny, "Feminismo y humanismo," *La Revista Blanca*, II, no. 35 (October 1, 1924), p. 484.

47. Montseny, "La mujeres de Aragón," *ibid.*, IV, no. 68 (July 15, 1926), p. 102.

48. Montseny, "La mujer nueva," *ibid.*, IV, no. 96 (August 1, 1927), p. 105.

49. Cf. Fredricks, "Social and Political Thought," p. 33n.

50. *Ibid.*, pp. 38–40, and Montseny, "Eliseo Reclus o una vida estetica," *La Revista Blanca*, VII, no. 127 (October 15, 1929), pp. 225–229, and "Mi individualismo," *ibid.*, VII, no. 100 (December 15, 1927), pp. 426–427. Elisée Reclus, along with his brother, Elie, became involved with Pierre-Joseph Proudhon, and by the late 1860s they were the leading Bakuninists in France, playing important roles in the Paris commune in 1871. Elisée Reclus fled afterwards to Italy, where he spent a great deal of time with Bakunin until the Russian anarchist died in 1876. Much of Reclus' later life was spent in Switzerland, working on the anarchist newspaper *Le Travailleur*. He also wrote a number of geographic studies, an interest he picked up from Bakunin.

51. Federica Montseny, "Concepto heroico de la vida," *La Revista Blanca*, VI, no. 119 (June 15, 1929), pp. 40–42, or "Juan Wolfgang Goethe," *ibid.*, VII, no. 143 (June 15, 1930), p. 617.

52. Sanz, *El sindicalismo*, p. 171; Rocker, *Revolución y regresión*, p. 212.

53. Cf. April Carter, *The Political Theory of Anarchism* (London: Routledge and Kegan Paul, 1971), pp. 74–77.

54. Federica Montseny, "Por la fuerza, la unidad, y el prestigio del anarquismo ibérico," *La Revista Blanca*, X, no. 398 (February 1, 1934), p. 181.

55. Montseny, "Miguel Bakunin," *ibid.*, IV, no. 67 (July 1, 1926), pp. 76–78.

56. Montseny, *La incorporación de las masas populares a la historia. La Comune: primera revolución consciente* (Barcelona: n.p., n.d.), p. 14.

57. Fredricks, "Social and Political Thought of Federica Montseny," p. 60.

58. Federica Montseny, "Hacia una nueva aurora social," *La Revista Blanca*, VIII, no. 214 (February 15, 1932), pp. 556–559.

59. Montseny, "Sindicalismo revolucionario y comunismo anarquista," *ibid.*, VIII, no. 235 (November 1, 1932), p. 331.

60. Montseny, "La defensa del ideal," *ibid.*, V, no. 109 (December 15, 1928), pp. 389–393; V, no. 110 (January 1, 1929), pp. 422–426, and VI, no. 111 (January 15, 1929), pp. 458–461.

61. Montseny, "Sindicalismo revolucionario," p. 332.

62. Montseny, *Los precursores: Anselmo Lorenzo, el hombre y la obra* (Barcelona: CNT/FAI, 1938), p. 20, and "El último romántico de la política burguesa," *La Revista Blanca*, IV, no. 55 (December 15, 1926), p. 399.

63. Montseny, "Plataformismo o reformismo libertaria," *La Revista Blanca*, V, no. 108 (December 1, 1928), pp. 364–366.

64. This resulted in Nettlau's *La Première Internationale en Espagne (1868–1888)*, although it was not published in its final form until 1969. Max Nettlau (1865–1944), born in Vienna, university-trained as a philologist, became an early political activist and in the 1890s spent a number of years in England, where he worked with Kropotkin. During this period he wrote the three volumes of *Michael Bakunin* (London, 1896–1900), which was in fact a lifelong project, now incorporated in Arthur Lehring (ed.), *Archives Bakounine*, 4 vols. (Leiden: Reidel, 1961–1965). Unknown to the public, Nettlau was important to the international anarchist movement, since his work of chronicling anarchist activities put him in contact with its most diverse elements. His impact on Federica Montseny was particularly strong; she served as his informant on Spain and helped him gather material, assisted by her mother, Soledad Gustavo. One of Montseny's pamphlets, *Los desheredados* (Barcelona: n.p., n.d.), provided documentary materials on nineteenth-century Spanish anarchism very much imitative of Nettlau's own style.

65. Raymond Carr, *Modern Spain, 1808–1939* (Oxford: Clarendon Press, 1967), p. 573.

66. Sanz, *El sindicalismo*, p. 157.

67. Letter of Harold Sarall to Horace Rumbolt, April 8, 1926, *Calendar*, FO 371, file 59, no. W 3028.

68. The only good source at present on the Confederação Geral do Travalho is Manuel Joaquim de Sousa, *O sindicalismo em Portugal* (Lisbon: Edição da Comissâo Escolar e Propaganda do Sindicalo do Possoal de Câmaras de Marinha Mercante Portuguesa, 1931), which was confiscated by the Salazar government before it could be distributed. Most of the copies were destroyed except for a handful smuggled out of the country. Otherwise, there are very few studies of the Portuguese Left. Poor exceptions are provided by César Nogueira, who has written numerous monographs on the topic, including *Notas para a história de socialismo em Portugal* (Lisbon: Portugália Editora, n.d.). There is also Vicente de Bragança Cunha, *Revolutionary Portugal* (London: J. Clarke, 1938), and recently Antonio de Figueiredo, *Portugal: Fifty Years of Dictatorship* (London: Penguin, 1975).

69. Rocker, *Revolución y regresión*, p. 140.

70. On the Portuguese republic see Jesús Pabón, *La republica portuguesa*, 2 vols. (Madrid: Espasa-Calpe, 1941–1945).

71. Anonymous interview.

72. Anonymous interview.

276

73. Manuel Buenacasa, *La CNT, los Treinta y la FAI* (Barcelona: Alfa, 1933), pp. 10–13.

74. Brademas, "Revolution and Counter-Revolution," p. 43. This work contains a long interview on the origins of the FAI.

75. FAI, "Memoria del Pleno Peninsular de Regionales de FAI celebrado en Madrid, los días 28, 29, y 30 de octubre de 1933," IISG, Rocker Collection, pp. 1–3.

76. Cf. the interview with Miguel Jiménez in Brademas, "Revolution and Counter-Revolution," p. 46.

77. Anonymous interview.

78. César Lorenzo, *Les anarchistes espagnols et la pouvoir 1868–1969* (Paris: Editions du Seuil, 1969), p. 67.

79. Buenacasa, *La CNT*, p. 9.

80. CNT, "Informe general de administración al finalizar el mes de enero de 1937," IISG, Rocker Collection, p. 36.

81. Sousa, *O sindicalismo,* pp. 72–77; Cunha, *Revolutionary Portugal,* pp. 109–110.

82. Anonymous interview.

83. According to Angel Pestaña, *Sindicalismo y unidad sindical* (Valencia: n.p., 1933), p. 113.

84. Cf. Alexander Shapiro, "Rapport sur l'activité de la Confédération National du Travail d'Espagne, 16 décembre 1932–26 février 1933," IISG, AIT Collection, file 9, p. 28.

85. Brademas, "Revolution and Counter-Revolution," p. 46.

86. See *¡Despertad!,* March 15 and May 1, 1929, for the FAI's position at this time.

87. Cf. A. Ramos Oliveira, *Politics, Economics and Men of Modern Spain 1808–1946* (London: Victor Gollancz, 1946), pp. 197–198.

88. Bernardo Bou and Ricardo Magríña, *Un año de conspiración* (Barcelona: Solidaridad Obrera, 1933), pp. 65–68.

89. Angel Pestaña, "Situemos," *¡Despertad!,* May 16, 1928, p. 1.

90. Peirats, *La CNT en la revolución española,* pp. 24–25.

91. *¡Despertad!,* April 26, 1930; *Acción Social Obrera,* November 1, 1930; and Bou and Magríña, *Un año de conspiración,* p. 28. These events are covered closely in Brademas, "Revolution and Counter-Revolution," pp. 49–53.

92. José Peirats, *Los anarquistas in la crisis política española* (Buenos Aires: Editorial Alfa, 1964), p. 56; Juan Gómez Casas, *Historia del anarchosindicalismo español* (Madrid: Editorial ZYX, 1968), p. 150.

93. Brademas, "Revolution and Counter-Revolution," p. 57.

94. CNT, *Memoria del Congreso . . . de 1931,* pp. 68–72, discusses the position of the CNT/FAI on the action committees and other issues at the end of the dictatorship.

95. Sanz, *El sindicalismo,* p. 225.

96. Cf. General Emílio Mola Vidal, *Memorias* (Valladolid: Libreria Santaren, 1940), pp. 283–284.

97. Gómez Casas, *Historia del anarchosindicalismo,* pp. 151–152.

98. CNT, *Memoria del Congreso . . . de 1931,* pp. 75–76.
99. See Carr, *Modern Spain,* p. 596, for the Jaca insurrection.

Chapter Four

1. Rudolf Rocker, *Revolución y regresión* (Buenos Aires: Editorial Tupac, 1952), p. 177.
2. Letter of Federica Montseny to Max Nettlau, December 12, 1931, IISG, Montseny Collection, file 3, folder 2.
3. Helmut Rüdiger, "Rapport du Secretariat de Barcelone pour la Congrès de l'AIT à Paris, le 7 décembre 1937," IISG, Rocker Collection, file 2, folder 3.
4. *Tierra y Libertad,* May 4, 1931, p. 4.
5. The number of exiles is the estimate of General Emilio Mola Vidal, *Memorias* (Valladolid: Libreria Santaren, 1940), p. 207.
6. The only memoir of Durruti by Emilienne Morin can be found in Gilberto Gilabert, *Durruti, un héroe del pueblo* (Buenos Aires: Ediciones Nervio, 1937), pp. 44–45.
7. For the composition of Alcalá Zamora's provisional government, cf. Manuel Ramíerez Jiménez, *Los grupos de presión en la Segunda República española* (Madrid: Editorial Tecnos, 1969), p. 30.
8. Joaquín Arraras, *Historia de la segunda republica española* (Madrid: Editora Nacional, 1964), I, 28.
9. Cf. *Solidaridad Obrera,* May 2, 1931, p. 1.
10. Abel Paz (pseud. Diego Camacho), *Durruti: le peuple en armes* (Paris: Editions de la Tête de Feuilles, 1972), p. 153, gives a description of these meetings. Also see Gilabert, *Durruti, un héroe del pueblo,* p. 17.
11. *Solidaridad Obrera,* May 2, 1931, p. 1.
12. Largo Caballero decreed the mixed juries on May 7, 1931. See "El Ministro del Trabajo, de los Comités Paritarios y nuestra continuidad en la oposición y protesta," *Solidaridad Obrera,* May 17, 1931, p. 2.
13. Nazario González, *El anarquismo en la historia de España contemporánea* (Barcelona: Universidad de Barcelona Facultad de Filosofía y Letras, 1970), p. 94, follows this interpretation, but César Lorenzo, *Les anarchistes espagnols et la pouvoir 1868–1969* (Paris: Editions du Seuil, 1969), p. 65, disagrees. According to Lorenzo's argument, the 29 percent absenteeism rate in the April elections showed that few anarchist went to the polls.
14. José Peirats, *La CNT en la revolución española* (Toulouse: Ediciones CNT, 1951–1953), I, 23.
15. Quoted in Diego Abad de Santillán, "Buenaventura Durruti," *Timón,* November 1938, p. 16.
16. Gilabert, *Durruti, un héroe del pueblo,* p. 48.
17. *Solidaridad Obrera,* April 19, 1931, p. 1.
18. E. Allison Peers, *Catalonia Infelix* (London: Methuen, 1937), pp. 190–198.

19. Raymond Carr, *Modern Spain, 1808–1939* (Oxford: Clarendon Press, 1967), p. 623.

20. *Solidaridad Obrera,* May 14, 1931, p. 3.

21. Ricardo Sanz, *El sindicalismo y la política: los "Solidarios" y "Nosotros"* (Toulouse: Imprimie Dulaurier, 1966), p. 208.

22. *Ibid.,* p. 202.

23. Joaquín Maurín, *Hacia la segunda revolución* (Barcelona: Gráficos Alfa, 1935), p. 90.

24. *Ibid.,* p. 92.

25. González, *El anarquismo,* p. 96.

26. Francisco Largo Caballero, *Mis recuerdos* (Mexico City: Ediciones "Alianza," 1941), p. 153.

27. Stephan John Brademas, "Revolution and Counter-Revolution in Spain: A Contribution to the History of the Anarcho-Syndicalist Movement in Spain, 1930–1937" (unpublished Ph.D. dissertation, Brasenose College, Oxford University, 1953), pp. 102–103.

28. Sanz, *El sindicalismo,* p. 199.

29. Paz, *Durruti,* p. 165, and *Solidaridad Obrera,* August 1 and 16–20, 1931.

30. Sanz, *El sindicalismo,* p. 199.

31. Some of these groups came and went, although all were active at the beginning of the Second Republic. After 1933 the flow of members tended to be out of the Nosotros into other groups. Lorenzo, *Les anarchistes espagnols,* p. 70, lists Jacinto Toryho, Abelardo Iglesias, and Ricardo Sanz as leaders of Group A, Diego Abad de Santillán and Pedro Herrera as the central figures in the Nervio group.

32. Rüdiger, "Rapport," p. 24, indicates that communist infiltration and control extended to a number of syndicates as well. For the communists and their history, see Eduardo Comín Colomer, *Historia del Partido Comunista de España* (Madrid: Editora Nacional, 1965).

33. See the interview with Federica Montseny in *España Libre,* June 10, 1951, p. 3, and her article in *El Luchador,* September 18, 1931, pp. 43–44.

34. FAI, *Estatutos de la FAI* (Valencia: Empresa Colectivizada T.G. Hostench, 1937), p. 3.

35. *Ibid.,* p. 5.

36. Helmut Rüdiger, "Buenaventura Durruti," in *Durruti* (Barcelona: Deutschen Informationsdienst der CNT-FAI, 1936), p. 5.

37. Anonymous interview.

38. Letter of Juan García Oliver, March 9, 1953, in Brademas, "Revolution and Counter-Revolution," p. 118.

39. Maurín, *Hacia la segunda revolución,* p. 90. However, Max Nomad, in *Dreamers, Dynamiters, and Demagogues* (New York: Walden Press, 1964), p. 194, suggests that the FAI members were actually behaving in the purest possible way as Bakuninists to form revolutionary cells within larger organizations (in this case, the CNT). Nomad says that this strategy was very much like that of the Revolutionary Brotherhood within the Social Democratic

Alliance. The cells would then provide the "invisible collective dictatorship" that the revolution needed.

40. Manuel Buenacasa, *La CNT, los Treinta y la FAI* (Barcelona: Alfa, 1933), pp. 51–53.

41. "La Confederación Nacional del Trabajo ante el momento actual," *Solidaridad Obrera,* May 14, 1931, p. 3.

42. Lorenzo, *Les anarchistes espagnols,* pp. 68–69.

43. CNT, *Memoria del Congreso extraordinaria celebrada en Madrid, los días 11 al 16 de junio de 1931* (Barcelona: CNT, 1931), p. 25. Fragments of the Rocker speech can be found in the Rocker Collection, IISG, folder 2, file 7. Also see Rudolf Rocker, *Revolución y regresión* (Buenos Aires: Editorial Tupac, 1952), pp. 260–264, which gives an interesting description (but shows none of the tension) of the Congress. Max Nettlau and Augustin Souchy, another AIT official, also attended the sessions and lent a foreign note to its activities. Above all, the CNT felt strengthened by outside support for the first time, and this became a factor in the CNT resistance to the FAI.

44. CNT, *Memoria del Congreso . . . de 1931,* p. 187.

45. *Ibid.,* p. 209.

46. Speech of Juan Peiró, *ibid.,* p. 208. Also see his *Problemas del sindicalismo y del anarquismo* (Toulouse: Ediciones Movimiento Libertario Español, 1945).

47. CNT, *Memoria del Congreso . . . de 1931,* p. 121.

48. *Ibid.,* p. 123.

49. *Ibid.,* p. 147.

50. Civil War institutions included not only the National Federations themselves but also the Council of Aragon (in part), the Consejo de Económico de Cataluña, and the Comité de Empresa del Colectivizaciones. José Peirats, *Los anarquistas en la crisis política española* (Buenos Aires: Editorial Alfa, 1964), p. 118. One reason the FAI came to be more closely identified with the national federation concept was the writings of Diego Abad de Santillán, especially his *El organismo económico de la revolución: cómo vivimos ·y cómo podríamos vivir en España* (Barcelona: Ediciones Tierra y Libertad, 1935).

51. For Angel Pestaña's position at the Congress, see the CNT, *Memoria del Congreso . . . de 1931,* pp. 10–12. His later ideas were summarized in *El sindicalismo: que quiere y adónde va* (Barcelona: Biblioteca Selección, 1933) and *Lo que aprendí en la vida.*

52. Sanz, *El sindicalismo,* p. 199.

53. Mariano Vázquez, a steelworker, became national secretary of the CNT in 1936. His activist stance during the earlier years led to six arrests and twenty-nine months in jail. Such notoriety got him the job. Cf. AIT, "La actividad del Secretariado de la AIT en Barcelona," July 11, 1937, IISG, AIT Collection, file 5, pp. 18–19. But Emma Goldman, the American anarchist who made two trips to Spain during the civil war as part of her propaganda effort on behalf of the CNT/FAI in Great Britain, felt that Vázquez, despite his record, was still a moderate. Letter of Emma Goldman [hereafter EG] to Pedro Herrera, August 31, 1938, IISG, Goldman Collection, file 29.

54. Anonymous interview.

55. Brademas, "Revolution and Counter-Revolution," pp. 91–92.

56. Cf. *ibid.*, p. 115, quoting Juan López.

57. "Confederacíon Nacional del Trabajo a todos los sindicatos," *Solidaridad Obrera,* August 16, 1931, p. 4. "El anarquismo y el movimiento actual," *ibid.*, August 25, 1931, p. 14.

58. Gilberto Gilabert, *La CNT, la FAI, y la revolución española* (Barcelona: Biblioteca Tierra y Libertad, 1932), p. 14.

59. "El anarquismo y el movimiento actual," p. 14.

60. "Manifiesto de la Treinte," *El Combate Sindicalista,* September 5, 1931, pp. 1–3.

61. Lorenzo, *Les anarchistes espagnols,* p. 70.

62. Juan López, "Recordatorio: la historia no debe repetirse," *Material de la discusión para los militantes de la Confederación Nacional del Trabajo de España* (Milford Haven, England: n.p., 1945), p. 17.

63. Alexander Shapiro, "Rapport sur l'activité de la Confédération National du Travail d'Espagne, 16 décembre 1932–26 février 1933," IISG, AIT Collection, p. 41.

64. *Ibid.*

65. Maurín, *Hacia la segunda revolución,* pp. 90–91.

66. For commentary on the Constitution of 1931 see Gabriel Jackson, *The Spanish Republic and the Civil War* (Princeton: Princeton University Press, 1965), p. 45 and *passim.*

67. Labor relations in fascist Portugal and Italy are discussed in Vicente de Bragança Cunha, *Revolutionary Portugal* (London: J. Clarke, 1938), p. 189, and Benito Mussolini, *Four Speeches on the Corporate State* (Rome: "Laboremus," 1935).

68. Edward Malefakis, *Agrarian Reform and Peasant Revolution in Spain* (New Haven: Yale University Press, 1970), pp. 162–185.

69. Federica Montseny, "Martirio," *La Revista Blanca,* IV, no. 77 (August 1, 1926), p. 145.

70. Federica Montseny, "Voces en el gran desierto: hablan los hombres," *La Revista Blanca,* V, no. 94 (June 15, 1927), p. 37.

Chapter Five

1. Manuel Buenacasa, *La CNT, los Treinta y la FAI* (Barcelona: Alfa, 1933), pp. 51–53.

2. Gabriel Jackson, *The Spanish Republic and the Civil War* (Princeton: Princeton University Press, 1965), p. 52.

3. Miguel Maura, *Así cayó Alfonso XIII* (Madrid: Ariel, 1968), p. 289.

4. Technical writings on the mixed juries are scarce, but newspapers of the time were full of accounts. Cf. *El Sol* during September 1931.

5. Federica Montseny, "La crisis interna y externa de la Confederación," *El Luchador,* September 18, 1931, p. 1.

6. *Ibid.*

7. Juan García Oliver, "El fascismo y las dictaduras," *Tierra y Libertad,* January 2, 1932, p. 1.

8. Cf. Jackson, *The Spanish Republic and the Civil War,* pp. 69–70.

9. Juan Gómez Casas, *Historia del anarcosindicalismo español* (Madrid: Editorial ZYX, 1968), p. 169.

10. Abel Paz (pseud. Diego Camacho), *Durruti: le peuple en armes* (Paris: Editions de la Tête de Feuilles, 1972), p. 173.

11. Gilberto Gilabert, *Durruti, un héroe del pueblo* (Buenos Aires: Ediciones Nervio, 1937), p. 21.

12. Anonymous interview.

13. "Manifiesto de la FAI," *Solidaridad Obrera,* July 2, 1932, p. 5.

14. *Ibid.*

15. Letter of Sir G. Grahame to Sir John Simon, June 8, 1932, *Calendar,* FO 371, W 6810, no. 16505.

16. Gómez Casas, *Historia del anarcosindicalismo,* p. 171.

17. Stephan John Brademas, "Revolution and Counter-Revolution in Spain: A Contribution to the History of the Anarcho-Syndicalist Movement in Spain, 1930–1937" (unpublished Ph.D. dissertation, Brasenose College, Oxford University, 1953), p. 134.

18. Alexander Shapiro, "Rapport sur l'activité de la Confédération National du Travail d'Espagne, 16 décembre 1932–26 février 1933," IISG, AIT Collection, file 9, pp. 33–38, gives considerable detail on the controversy with the Sabadell syndicates.

19. Gómez Casas, *Historia del anarcosindicalismo,* p. 172. Actually, the confusion at this particular moment was very great. In an article entitled "Al pueblo en general y a los trabajadores catalanes en particular," in the CNT/ FAI publication "Conferencia Regional del Trabajo de Aragón, Rioja y Navarra," IISG, Rocker Collection, some CNT members argued that it was the duty of the syndicates to maintain an apolitical attitude towards *all* factions. They pointed out that the *treintistas* claimed these regional groups when in fact the groups were simply trying to follow an apolitical course.

20. "Juventudes dinamismo," *Tierra y Libertad,* August 19, 1932, p. 4.

21. For a detailed description of the Agrarian Reform Law of September 1932, see Edward Malefakis, *Agrarian Reform and Peasant Revolution in Spain* (New Haven: Yale University Press, 1970), pp. 204–35.

22. Cf. *ibid.,* pp. 243–250.

23. On the almost nonexistent ties between anarchists and peasants, consult the CNT "Sindicato de campesinos y oficios varios de Morón de la Frontera," IISG, Rocker Collection, and Malefakis, *Agrarian Reform and Peasant Revolution,* pp. 294–316.

24. *Ibid.,* pp. 290–291. For rural unrest, see pp. 305–307. The FNTT staged 925 strikes between 1930–1932.

25. *Ibid.,* pp. 317–342.

26. Cf. *El Sol,* July 2, 1932, pp. 1–3. Also see *El Sol* for May 17, 19, 21–24, 26–29, and June 1–4, 11, 14, 18, 22, 28, for extensive accounts of anarchist reaction.

27. Horacio Prieto, *Marxismo y socialismo libertario* (Rennes: Imprimeries Réunies, 1945), pp. 31–33.

28. Durruti did travel to Andalusia on several occasions, and he was one of the few CNT/FAI leaders to stress the importance of close ties with rural areas. Gilabert, *Durruti, un héroe del pueblo,* p. 47.

29. Helmut Rüdiger, "Rapport du Secretariat de Barcelone pour la Congrès de l'AIT à Paris, le 7 décembre 1937," IISG, Rocker Collection, file 2, folder 3. Rüdiger went to Spain in 1932 and became an official representative of the AIT. A German, he had been editor of the *Syndikalist* in Berlin during the Weimar period.

30. José Peirats, *Los anarquistas en la crisis política española* (Buenos Aires: Editorial Alfa, 1964), p. 89.

31. Jackson, *The Spanish Republic and the Civil War,* p. 83.

32. Gilabert, *Durruti, un héroe del pueblo,* p. 83.

33. Federica Montseny wrote letters to *La Prensa de Madrid,* on January 11, 1933, and to *La Tierra* on January 12. Juan García Oliver smuggled a letter of his own out of prison, and this was also forwarded to the press. It was later reprinted in Federico Urales, *España, 1933: la barbarie gubernamental* (Barcelona: Ediciones de "El Luchador," 1933), pp. 33–56.

34. *Ibid.,* pp. 101–104.

35. *Ibid.,* pp. 131–139.

36. Manuel García Ceballos, *Casas Viejas* (Madrid: Fermín Uriarte, 1965), p. 63. Also see "Casas Viejas," *El Sol,* January 13, 1933, p. 1.

37. These towns included Utrera, Dehenes, La Rinconada, Sanlucar de Barrameda, Medina Sidonia, and many smaller villages. Urales, *España, 1933,* pp. 178–238.

38. García Ceballos, *Casas Viejas,* p. 161.

39. Another critic of Azaña in the parliament was Diego Martínez Barrio. *Ibid.,* p. 277. A vote of censure failed by forty-three votes.

40. *Ibid.,* p. 225. Manuel Azaña discusses Casas Viejas in his *Memorias íntimas de Azaña* (Madrid: Ediciones Españolas, 1939), p. 189.

41. This is the thesis of Carlos Seco Serrano, *La crisis de Casas Viejas* (Madrid: Atlas, 1964), p. 10.

42. Cf. Frank E. Manuel, *The Politics of Modern Spain* (New York: McGraw-Hill, 1938), pp. 119–120.

43. Unpublished article of Helmut Rüdiger, "Bermerkungen zur Haltung der CNT in der spanischen Oktoberbewegung," January 1935, IISG, Rocker Collection, file 1, folder 7, p. 1.

44. For the AIT point of view on January 1933, see the letter of Alexander Shapiro to EG, March 20, 1937, IISG, Goldman Collection, file 29.

45. Buenacasa, *La CNT, los Treinta, y la FAI,* p. 101.

46. CNT, "Memoria de Pleno Regional de la CNT/FAI de Cataluña, de marzo 1933," IISG, Rocker Collection.

47. "Del pleno regional," *Sindicalismo,* March 31, 1933, p. 4.

48. Brademas, "Revolution and Counter-Revolution," p. 142, cites the

metal, transport, and dock workers' syndicates of Valencia, and the fabric and textile unions of Alcoy as strong units in the syndicates of opposition.

49. "Ateneo Sindicalista Libertario," *El Combate Sindicalista*, May 27, 1933, p. 3, and "Los sindicatos de la oposición adoptan una resolución firme: '¡ni un paso atrás frente al faísmo!'" *Sindicalismo*, June 9, 1933, p. 1.

50. "Una tragedia más," *Cultura Libertaria*, January 19, 1933, p. 1.

51. "Ni frases ni tópicos: realidades," *Sindicalismo*, November 3, 1933, p. 4.

52. For Angel Pestaña's political views see his *Por qué se constituyó el Partido Sindicalista* (Barcelona: n.p., 1936?).

53. "Una trayectoria revolucionaria," *Sindicalismo*, November 3, 1933, p. 1.

54. See *El Combate Sindicalista*, April 29, 1933, p. 4.

55. The figure is in Jackson, *The Spanish Republic and the Civil War*, p. 96.

56. "El Treintismo y la escisión," *Sindicalismo*, September 5, 1933, p. 4.

57. "La Federación de Anarquistas Portugueses," *Tierra y Libertad*, May 27, 1932, p. 3, and "Crónica de Portugal," *ibid.*, October 13, 1933, p. 6.

58. Among the Portuguese anarchists arrested by the Salazar regime were Francisco Quintal, G. de Sousa, L. Larenjeira, Emilio Santana, J.A. de Castro, Manuel Joaquim de Sousa, and Alfonso Simões Januário. Ernesto Gil, one of the most important writers and intellectuals in the movement, and also a member of the FAI, was given life imprisonment. *Ibid.*, October 13, 1933, p. 6.

59. For a general political background to the rise of Salazar and Portuguese corporativism in this period, see Hugh Kay, *Salazar and Modern Portugal* (New York: Hawthorn, 1970).

60. The prison study groups are discussed in Helmut Rüdiger, "Informe para el Congreso extraordinario de la AIT el día 6/12/37," IISG, AIT Collection, file 8, p. 19.

61. E. Allison Peers, *The Spanish Tragedy 1930–1937: Dictatorship, Republic, Chaos, Rebellion, War* (London: Methuen, 1937), pp. 138–139.

62. "Frente al Fascismo," *Sindicalismo*, October 13, 1933, p. 1.

63. Brademas, "Revolution and Counter-Revolution," pp. 188–189.

64. "Frente al Fascismo," *Sindicalismo*, October 13, 1933, p. 1.

65. "La CNT en la entraña del proletariado del pueblo," *Solidaridad Obrera*, November 7, 1933, p. 1.

66. Ricardo Sanz, *El sindicalismo y la política: los "Solidarios" y "Nosotros"* (Toulouse: Imprimie Dulaurier, 1966), p. 247.

67. Anarchists claimed that up to 50 percent of the electorate failed to vote. "Lo que dice y lo que calla la prensa," *Solidaridad Obrera*, November 29, 1933, p. 2.

68. Manuel, *The Politics of Modern Spain*, pp. 122–125.

69. See Stanley Payne, *The Falange: A History of Spanish Fascism* (Stanford: Stanford University Press, 1961), for the rise of this movement.

70. Anonymous interview.

71. Quoted in *El Sol*, November 26, 1933, p. 3.

72. Gilabert, *Durruti, un héroe del pueblo,* p. 24.

73. The demand for revolution after the elections is discussed in "¿Qué hacer ahora?," *Sindicalismo,* December 1, 1933, p. 4.

74. Miguel González Inestal, *Cipriano Mera, revolucionario* (Havana: Editorial Atalaya, 1943). Isaac Puente served as the conduit for many libertarian ideas later used in the development of Argaonese communes. See his "The Political and Economic Organization of Society," in Sam Dolgoff, ed., *The Anarchist Collectives: Workers' Self-Management in the Spanish Revolution 1936–1939* (New York: Free Life Editions, 1974), pp. 28–33. He was killed in the fighting at Alava early in the civil war.

75. Letter of Sir G. Grahame to Sir John Simon, December 12, 1933, *Calendar,* FO 371/17427, W 2725.

76. Letter of Norman King to Sir G. Grahame, December 12, 1933, *ibid.,* FO 371/17432, W 2725.

77. *Ibid.*

78. "Enseñanzas del último movimiento," *Sindicalismo,* December 19, 1933, p. 2.

79. *Ibid.*

80. Jackson, *The Spanish Republic and the Civil War,* p. 122.

81. Payne, *The Falange,* p. 47.

82. Cf. "El momento ibérico," *Tierra y Libertad,* March 16, 1934, p. 2.

83. "La revolución española, sus errores y posibles correciones," *ibid.,* May 4, 1934, p. 2.

84. "Movimiento anarquista," *ibid.,* May 19, 1934, p. 3.

85. Brademas, "Revolution and Counter-Revolution," p. 180.

86. José Peirats, *La CNT en la revolución española* (Toulouse: Ediciones CNT, 1951–1953), II, 70–78.

87. *Ibid.,* p. 69.

88. Cf. Stanley Payne, *The Spanish Revolution* (New York: Norton, 1970), pp. 140–142.

89. "Discurso de Largo Caballero," *Claridad,* May 26, 1934, p. 2.

90. "Nuestro anarquismo," *Tierra y Libertad,* February 23, 1934, p. 1.

91. "El problema de la tierra," *ibid.,* June 23, 1934, p. 4.

92. "¿Quién es Trotzky? El nuevo judío errante," *ibid.,* April 27, 1934, p. 3.

93. "El socialismo en España: un partido que no quiere perecer," *Solidaridad Obrera,* July 14, 1934, p. 1.

94. Letter of EG to Alexander Shapiro, February 23, 1937, IISG, Goldman Collection, file 29.

95. Diego Abad de Santillán, *Los anarquistas españoles y la insurrección de octubre* (Detroit: Grupo Comunismo Libertario, 1936), p. 14.

96. Abad de Santillán estimated that as many as 15,000 CNT/FAI members were still in jail by August 1934. *Ibid.,* p. 5.

97. *Ibid.,* p. 9.

98. Cf. Payne, *The Spanish Revolution,* pp. 127–128, 151–152, for background on Dencàs.

99. Brademas, "Revolution and Counter-Revolution," pp. 235–236, and Gerald Brenan, *The Spanish Labyrinth* (Cambridge: Cambridge University Press, 1943), pp. 263–264.

100. Anonymous interview.

101. Abad de Santillán, *Los anarquistas españoles y la insurrección de octubre*, p. 21.

102. This is the assertion of Jackson, *The Spanish Republic and the Civil War*, p. 157, although there is not much evidence on this point.

103. According to Payne, *The Spanish Revolution*, p. 156.

Chapter Six

1. For the complicated relationship between CEDA and Lerroux, see Richard A. H. Robinson, *The Origins of Franco's Spain: The Right, the Republic and the Revolution, 1931–1936.* (Newton Abbot: David and Charles, 1970), pp. 193–237.

2. Stanley Payne, *The Spanish Revolution* (New York: Norton, 1970), pp. 157–158.

3. *Tierra y Libertad*, December 3, 1935, p. 1; December 10, 1935, p. 1; December 17, 1935, pp. 1–2; and December 24, 1935, p. 1.

4. "He aquí un relato de lo ocurrido en el penal de Duesco," *Tierra y Libertad*, May 8, 1936, p. 3.

5. Francisco Ascaso, "El estado," in *Homenaje del Comité Peninsular de la FAI a F. Ascaso* (Barcelona: Tierra y Libertad, 1938), p. 13. This was an article first printed in 1935, one of the few of Ascaso's to be published.

6. Ascaso, "Nuestro anarquismo," *ibid.*, p. 9.

7. Cf. Edward Malefakis, *Agrarian Reform and Peasant Revolution in Spain* (New Haven: Yale University Press, 1970), pp. 347–363, particularly on the work of the CEDA Minister of Agriculture, Manuel Jiménez Fernández, who favored a conversion of the agrarian reform into a strengthening of small independent farmers.

8. A history of the POUM is provided by Pierre Broué, *Trotsky y la guerra civil española* (Buenos Aires: J. Alvarez, 1966).

9. IISG, Rocker Collection, file 1, folder 7, miscellaneous notes.

10. Payne, *The Spanish Revolution*, p. 167.

11. The manifesto of the communists is discussed in Enrique Matorrás, *El comunismo en España* (Madrid: n.p., 1935), pp. 121–122 and *passim.*

12. Anonymous interview.

13. Alexander Shapiro, "Rapport sur l'activité de la Confédération National du Travail d'Espagne, 16 décembre 1932–26 février 1933," IISG, AIT Collection, file 9, p. 12.

14. *Ibid.*, pp. 19–20.

15. Cf. Robert W. Kern, *Liberals, Reformers and Caciques of Restoration Spain* (Albuquerque: University of New Mexico Press, 1974), pp. 101–110.

16. "Sobre la detención de D. A. de Santillán," *Tierra y Libertad,* October 15, 1935, p. 3.

17. Diego Abad de Santillán, *Psicología del pueblo español* (Madrid: n.p., 1917), pp. 18–26.

18. Peter Kropotkin, *Mutual Aid* (New York: McClure, Phillips and Co., 1902), and *The Conquest of Bread* (London: Chapman and Hall, 1906).

19. Diego Abad de Santillán, *El organismo económico de la revolución: cómo vivimos y cómo podríamos vivir en España* (Barcelona: Ediciones Tierra y Libertad, 1935), p. 16. There is also an English translation, *After the Revolution* (New York: Greenberg, 1937).

20. Abad de Santillán, *El organismo económico,* p. 28.

21. *Ibid.,* p. 31.

22. *Ibid.,* p. 30.

23. *Ibid.,* pp. 34–38.

24. For Antonio Gramsci's ideas on factory councils, see John M. Cammett, *Antonio Gramsci and the Origins of Italian Communism* (Stanford: Stanford University Press, 1967), pp. 77–95.

25. Abad de Santillán, *El organismo económico,* p. 50.

26. *Ibid.,* p. 87.

27. Examples of Krausismo literature abound: Joaquín Costa, *Crisis política de España* (Madrid: Fortanet, 1901); *Reconstitución y europeización de España* (Madrid: Succ. de Rivadeneyra, 1900); and, ed., *Oligarquía y caciquismo como la forma actual de gobierno en España* (Madrid: M. G. Hernández, 1902). Gumersindo Azcárate wrote *El régimen parlamentario en la práctica* (Madrid: Minuesa de los Ríos, 1885) and *El self-government y la monarquía doctrinaria* (Madrid: San Martín, 1877). Damián Isern, *Del desastre nacional y sus causas* (Madrid: Minuesa de los Ríos, 1899), Ricardo Macías Picavia, *El problema nacional* (Madrid: Victoriano Suárez, 1900), and Joaquín Lucas Mallada, *Los males de la patria* (Barcelona: Delgado, 1891), were other writings in this school.

28. Joaquín Costa, Francisco Giner de los Ríos, and José María Pantoja, eds., *Derecho consuetudinario y económico popular de España* (Barcelona: M. Soler, 1885), and Rafael Altamira y Crevea, *Historia de la civilización española* (Madrid: Espasa-Calpe, 1935).

29. Malefakis, *Agrarian Reform and Peasant Revolution,* p. 358.

30. Gabriel Jackson, *The Spanish Republic and the Civil War* (Princeton: Princeton University Press, 1965), pp. 176–177.

31. Abad de Santillán, *El organismo económico,* p. 61.

32. Diego Abad de Santillán, *Por qué perdimos la guerra* (Buenos Aires: Iman, 1940), p. 42.

33. Payne, *The Spanish Revolution,* pp. 127–128, 150–152.

34. José Peirats, *La CNT en la revolución española* (Toulouse: Ediciones CNT, 1951–1953), I, 97–103.

35. Quoted by Helmut Rüdiger in Deutschen Informationdienst, *Buenaventura Durruti* (Barcelona: CNT, 1937), p. 27.

36. *Solidaridad Obrera,* February 23, 1936, p. 2, and Jackson, *The Spanish Republic and the Civil War,* p. 193.

37. Emma Goldman disagreed that the participation of the anarchists in the elections did not affect their psychology and political goals afterwards. She felt it was the start of anarchism "becoming just another political party." EG to Alexander Shapiro, February 23, 1937, IISG, Goldman Collection, folder 29.

38. Letter of Ogilvie Forbes to Foreign Office, April 19, 1936, *Calendar*, FO 371, file 62, W 8994.

39. Abad de Santillán, *Por qué perdimos la guerra*, p. 42.

40. "Conflictos del ramo del agua y transporte," *Solidaridad Obrera*, March 6, 1936, p. 1.

41. "Discurso del Casares de Quiroga," *El Sol*, March 18, 1936, p. 3.

42. Erich Mühsam died in a Nazi prison camp in 1934, one of the victims of Hitler. The entire German anarcho-syndicalist movement was prohibited, and members fortunate enough to escape took refuge in Spain. At least two thousand of them fought in the anarchist militia during the Spanish Civil War.

43. Ricardo Sanz, *El sindicalismo y la política: los "Solidarios" y "Nosotros"* (Toulouse: Imprimie Dulaurier, 1966), p. 267.

44. "¡Arriba la revolución!," *Solidaridad Obrera*, May 14, 1936, p. 4.

45. No final report of the Saragossa Congress was ever produced because of the civil war. The only accounts can be found in *Solidaridad Obrera*, May 1–24, 1936.

46. On Francisco Largo Caballero, see his *Mis recuerdos* (Mexico City: Ediciones "Alianza," 1941), pp. 213–215.

47. On the PSUC and JSU, see Payne, *The Spanish Revolution*, pp. 283–285 and 291–293.

48. Richard A. Barrett, *Benabarre: The Modernization of a Spanish Village* (New York: Holt, Rinehart and Winston, 1973), pp. 36–38.

49. No accurate report of the political fighting in the spring of 1936 can be made, but see *El Sol* for these months. Political journalism, especially in this newspaper, began to come of age in Spain, and the accounts make fascinating reading. Also see Stanley Payne, "The Ominous Spring of 1936," in his edited work, *Politics and Society in Twentieth-Century Spain* (New York: New Viewpoints, 1976), pp. 120–142.

50. "Programme of Unity of Action between the UGT and the CNT," *Spain and the World*, April 8, 1937, p. 3.

51. "Huelga de construcción," *El Sol*, July 6, 1936, p. 2.

Chapter Seven

1. On military aspects of the civil war, see Hugh Thomas, *The Spanish Civil War* (London: Eyre and Spottiswoode, 1961). For anarchists in the Spanish navy, see Diego Abad de Santillán, *Por qué perdimos la guerra* (Buenos Aires: Iman, 1940), pp. 192–194.

2. The best account of the fighting given by a participant is Juan

García Oliver, "19 July 1936 in Barcelona: Pages of Working Class History," *Spain and the World,* August 26, 1938, pp. 2–3.

3. *Ibid.,* and also see Abel Paz (pseud. Diego Camacho), *Paradigma de una revolución (19 de julio 1936, en Barcelona)* (Toulouse: Ediciones AIT, 1967).

4. However, Ascaso had recently purchased a considerable number of weapons in France. Most of them were destined for the militia training center but had not yet been shipped.

5. García Oliver, "19 July 1936," *Spain and the World,* p. 3.

6. Ricardo Sanz, *Los que fuimos a Madrid: Columna Durruti 26 División* (Toulouse: Imprimerie Dulaurier, 1969), p. 51.

7. Paz, *Paradigma de una revolución,* pp. 65–77.

8. "Duelo nacional e internacional," *Solidaridad Obrera,* November 22, 1936, p. 3.

9. César Lorenzo, *Les anarchistes españols et le pouvoir 1868–1969* (Paris: Editions du Seuil, 1969), p. 96.

10. Abad de Santillán, *Por qué perdimos la guerra,* p. 43.

11. Anonymous interview.

12. Cf. Pierre Broué and Emile Témime, *The Revolution and the Civil War in Spain* (Cambridge: MIT Press, 1972), pp. 117–118.

13. Abad de Santillán, *Por qué perdimos la guerra,* minimizes the quarrel. Emma Goldman dwells on it at some length: EG to Alexander Shapiro, October 19, 1937, IISG, Goldman Collection, file 23.

14. "Origenes del Comité Antifascista," *El Amigo del Pueblo,* July 20, 1937, p. 2.

15. For criticism of this decision from within the anarchist movement, see Vernon Richards, *Lessons of the Spanish Revolution* (London: Freedom Press, 1953), pp. 28–29 and *passim.*

16. Abad de Santillán, *Por qué perdimos la guerra,* pp. 56–57.

17. Helmut Rüdiger to Rudolf Rocker, July 29, 1936, IISG, Rocker Collection, folder 4, p. 3.

18. *Homenaje del Comité Peninsular de la FAI a F. Ascaso* (Barcelona: Tierra y Libertad, 1938), p. 12.

19. Abad de Santillán, *Por qué perdimos la guerra,* p. 63.

20. *Ibid.,* p. 65.

21. Cf. Franz Borkenau, *The Spanish Cockpit* (Ann Arbor: University of Michigan Press, 1963), pp. 97–98; and Gabriel Jackson, *The Spanish Republic and the Civil War* (Princeton: Princeton University Press, 1965), p. 292n.

22. *Guerra di Classes* is difficult to obtain, but a collection of Berneri's work was published shortly after his death: Camillo Berneri, *Guerre de classes en Espagne* (Montpellier: Les Cahiers de Terre Libre, 1938). One might also consult Rudolf Rocker, *Revolución y regresión* (Buenos Aires: Editorial Tupac, 1952), p. 390, and "The Tragic End of an Anarchist Fighter," *Spain and the World,* June 11, 1937, p. 3.

23. George Orwell, *Homage to Catalonia* (New York: Harcourt, Brace and World, 1952), *passim.*

24. "Las chekas del partido comunista," IISG, Rocker Collection, box 2, folder 1, no. 64.

25. Olay (which was not his real name) was born in Oviedo in 1893 but as a young man emigrated to Cuba and then to Tampa. He taught Spanish at several schools in the United States before beginning the publication of a newspaper in Chicago. He supported the FAI strongly and in 1933 wrote a short pamphlet, *Spain Swings to the Left* (Chicago: Red and Black, 1933).

26. The only aviation study of the Spanish Civil War is Colonel José Gomá, *La guerra en la aire* (Barcelona: n.p., 1958).

27. Abad de Santillán, *Por qué perdimos la guerra,* p. 66.

28. Ricardo Sanz, *El sindicalismo y la política: los "Solidarios" y "Nosotros"* (Toulouse: Imprimerie Dulaurier, 1966), p. 272.

29. For life in nationalist Saragossa see Eduardo Fuembuerra, *Guerra en Aragón* (Saragossa: Maestes, 1938).

30. Quoted by Alexander Shapiro, "Durruti," *El Combata Syndicalista,* September 2, 1936, p. 1.

31. Anonymous interviews given by brigade members still living in Spain.

32. José Martín Blázquez, *I Helped to Build an Army* (London: Secker and Warburg, 1939), pp. 89–91.

33. Rocker, "Memoria: una brigada heroica," undated, IISG, Rocker Collection, box 2, folder 3.

34. Sanz, *El sindicalismo,* p. 271.

35. EG to Helmut Rüdiger, June 3, 1938, IISG, Goldman Collection, file 27 B.

36. Abad de Santillán, "Buenaventura Durruti," *Timón,* November 25, 1937, p. 302.

37. Nazario González, *El anarquismo en la historia de España contemporánea* (Barcelona: Universidad de Barcelona Facultad de Filosofía y Letras, 1970), p. 124.

38. Rocker, "JJEL et femmes libres," undated, IISG, Rocker Collection, file 1, folder 2, pp. 2–9.

39. Federica Montseny, "Discurso en el Teatro Olympia," *Solidaridad Obrera,* August 11, 1936, p. 3.

40. For other civil war organizations, see José Peirats, *Los anarquistas en la crisis política española* (Buenos Aires: Editorial Alfa, 1964), pp. 118–119.

41. Abad de Santillán, *Por qué perdimos la guerra,* p. 70.

42. Peirats, *Los anarquistas en la crisis política española,* p. 282.

43. *Ibid.,* p. 284.

44. Helmut Rüdiger to Rudolf Rocker, July 29, 1936, IISG, Rocker Collection, folder 4, p. 2.

45. "Rapport du Plenum," July 28, 1936, IISG, Rocker Collection, file 1, folder 3, p. 17.

46. Stephan John Brademas, "Revolution and Counter-Revolution in Spain: A Contribution to the History of the Anarcho-Syndicalist Movement

in Spain, 1930–1937" (unpublished Ph.D. dissertation, Brasenose College, Oxford University, 1953), p. 373.

47. "Sobre el Comité Nacional de Militicias," *Solidaridad Obrera,* August 28, 1936, p. 2.

48. "Pages in Working Class History," *Spain and the World,* August 26, 1938, p. 3.

49. "Notes on the AIT Secretariat," undated, IISG, Rocker Collection, file 1, folder 3.

50. E. Allison Peers, *The Spanish Tragedy 1930–1937: Dictatorship, Republic, Chaos, Rebellion, War* (London: Methuen, 1937), p. 193.

51. Juan Maragall, *Obras completas de Juan Maragall* (Barcelona: Sala Parés, 1930), II, 144.

52. Peirats, *Los anarquistas en la crisis política española,* p. 185.

53. EG to Rudolf Rocker, October 1, 1936, IISG, Rocker Collection, Goldman file.

54. Emma Goldman would write in early November that Federica Montseny "has gone to the Right and she has a great influence here." EG to Rudolf Rocker, *ibid.* In August Montseny supported anarchist participation in the Anti-Fascist Militia Committee.

55. Diego Abad de Santillán, *Mensaja circa de la situación actual del movimiento libertario español* (Buenos Aires: Subdelegación de la CNT en la Argentina, 1946), pp. 16–23.

56. "AIT Congrès Extraordinaire, Paris, 6 Dec. 1937, Minutes," IISG, Rocker Collection, file 1, folder 3.

57. *Ibid.*

58. Peirats, *Los anarquistas en la crisis política española,* p. 208.

59. J. G. Martin, *Political and Social Changes in Catalonia during the Revolution* (Barcelona: Generalitat, 1937), p. 18.

60. Brademas, "Revolution and Counter-Revolution," p. 286, and "Le rôle du Comité Central des Milices Antifascistes," *La Révolution Espagnol,* no. 2 (September 10, 1936), pp. 3–4.

61. "Consejo de Aragón," *Boletín de Información CNT/AIT/FAI,* September 18, 1936, p. 1.

62. Background on Aragonese self-government ideas can be found in Robert W. Kern, *Liberals, Reformers, and Caciques in Restoration Spain* (Albuquerque: University of New Mexico Press, 1974), pp. 90–92.

63. José Peirats, *La CNT en la revolución española* (Toulouse: Ediciones CNT, 1951–1953), I, 215; Peirats, *Los anarquistas en la crisis política española,* pp. 123–124.

64. André Jean, *Economic Transformation in Catalonia* (Barcelona: Generalitat, 1938), p. 19.

65. The Catalan Regional of the CNT/FAI voted on August 1, 1936, to support full collectivization. Peirats, *Los anarquistas en la crisis política española,* p. 128.

66. Abad de Santillán, *Por qué perdimos la guerra,* p. 79.

67. *Ibid.*, p. 103. Also, see in particular Josep Maria Brincall, *Política económica de la Generalitat (1936–1939): evolució i formes de la producció industrial* (Barcelona: Edicions 62, 1970). This is a valuable book for any student of the Catalan situation.

68. At least eighty foreign firms were confiscated and collectivized. Peirats, *Los anarquistas en la crisis política española,* pp. 125–126. Also see "The Socialized Oil Industry," *Spain and the World,* January 22, 1937, p. 3; the economic material in another of Abad de Santillán's periodicals, *Timón;* and *Síntesis de Orientación Política Social,* first series, nos. 1–6 (July–December 1938), Barcelona, and second series, nos. 1–6, (November 1939–March 1940), Buenos Aires.

69. Antonio Fontana to R. Palmer, August 18, 1936, *Calendar,* FO 371, file 62, 20535, W 9656.

70. Abad de Santillán, *Por qué perdimos la guerra,* pp. 85, 120.

71. Norman King to Foreign Office, January 21, 1938, *Calendar,* FO 371, file 25, 22620, W 900.

72. Martín Blázquez, *I Helped to Build an Army,* pp. 267–270.

73. Abad de Santillán, *Por qué perdimos la guerra,* pp. 114–115.

74. *Ibid.,* p. 70.

75. F. Fraser Lawton to H. Malcomb Hubbard, August 24, 1936, *Calendar,* FO 371, file 25, 20535, W 9657, p. 159; Martín Blázquez, *I Helped to Build an Army,* pp. 266–267.

76. Montseny, "Discurso en el Teatro Olympia," p. 3.

77. Abad de Santillán, *Por qué perdimos la guerra,* p. 72.

78. Peirats, *La CNT en la revolución española,* I, 197–198.

79. "Le rôle du Comité Central des Milices Antifascistes," p. 3.

80. The control patrols operated in the following districts: Casco Viejo, Este-Norte, Barceloneta, Pueblo Seco-Casa Antunez, Seins-Hostafranchs, Bonanova-Pedralbes, Grau-San Gevasio, Clot-Poblet, Horta-Carmelo-Gunardo, San Andres, and Pueblo Nuevo.

81. Jean Raynaud, *En Espagne "Rouge"* (Paris: Editiones du Cerf, 1937), p. 677.

82. Clara Campoamor, *La Révolution Espagnol: vue par une républicain* (Paris: Librairie Plon, 1937), p. 137.

83. Borkenau, *The Spanish Cockpit,* p. 253; E. Allison Peers, *Catalonia Infelix* (London: Methuen, 1937), p. 260.

84. F. Fraser Lawton to H. Malcomb Hubbard, August 24, 1936, *Calendar,* FO 371, file 25, 20535, W 9657, p. 160.

85. Cf. Edward Malefakis, *Agrarian Reform and Peasant Revolution in Spain* (New Haven: Yale University Press, 1970), especially pp. 50–64.

86. Cf. Joaquín Costa, Francisco Giner de los Ríos, and José María Pantoja, eds., *Derecho consuetudinario y económico popular de España* (Barcelona: M. Soler, 1885), for details of the *fueros* thought to contain prior collectivist practices.

87. Barrett, *Bennabarre: The Modernization of a Spanish Village* (New York: Holt, Rinehart and Winston, 1973), pp. 23–38.

88. See especially Gaston Leval (pseud. Pedro Piller), *Né Franco né Stalin: le collettività anarchiche spagnole nella lotta contro Franco e la reazione staliniana* (Milan: Instituto Editoriale Italiano, 1955), and his more recent *Espagne libertaire: 1936–1939* (Paris: Editions du Cercle, 1971). A useful set of translations on the collectivization process can be found in Sam Dolgoff, ed., *The Anarchist Collectives: Workers' Self-Management in the Spanish Revolution 1936–1939* (New York: Free Life Editions, 1974), pp. 111–164.

89. Pierre Broué and Emile Témine, *The Revolution and the Civil War in Spain* (Cambridge: MIT Press, 1972), p. 159; Peirats, *Los anarquistas en la crisis política española,* p. 145; and Leval, *Espagne libertaire,* p. 80.

Chapter Eight

1. Interview with H. L. Mitchell, co-founder of the Southern Tenant Farmers Union, April 12, 1975.

2. Ricardo Sanz, *Los que fuimos a Madrid: Columna Durruti 26 División* (Toulouse: Imprimerie Dulaurier, 1969), p. 77.

3. Franz Borkenau, *The Spanish Cockpit* (London: Faber and Faber, 1937), pp. 109–110.

4. Diego Abad de Santillán, *Por qué perdimos la guerra* (Buenos Aires: Iman, 1940), p. 69.

5. Juan Peiró, *Peril a la retaguardia* (Mataró: Editiones Llibertat, n.d.), pp. 102–103. Also see Burnett Bolloten, *The Grand Camouflage: The Spanish Civil War and Revolution, 1936–39* (London: Pall Mall Press, 1968), p. 74.

6. Jesús Hernández, *Paris Midi,* August 8, 1936, quoted in Borkenau, *The Spanish Cockpit,* p. 111.

7. "La ansiada victoria se vislumbra," *Solidaridad Obrera,* September 2, 1936, p. 1.

8. Cf. Bolloten, *The Grand Camouflage,* pp. 221–225, and Robert G. Colodny, *The Struggle for Madrid: The Central Epic in the Spanish Conflict* (New York: Payne-Whitman, 1958), pp. 19–20.

9. Jesús Pérez Salas, *Guerra en España* (Mexico City: Gráficos, 1947), pp. 124–135.

10. Quoted in Federico Urales, "Armas y letras: por los frentes de combate," *Solidaridad Obrera,* October 6, 1936, p. 3. Also see Abad de Santillán, *Por qué perdimos la guerra,* p. 161.

11. Henry Buckley, *Life and Death of the Spanish Republic* (London: Hamish Hamilton, 1940), p. 354.

12. Gilberto Gilabert, *Durruti, un héroe del pueblo* (Buenos Aires: Ediciones Nervio, 1937), pp. 32–34.

13. Ricardo Sanz, *Figuras del la revolucion española: Buenaventura Durruti* (Toulouse: Ediciones El Frente, 1945), pp. 11–13.

14. "Regla de la milicia," *Boletín de Información CNT/AIT/FAI,* October 5, 1936, p. 6.

15. Cited in José Peirats, *Los anarquistas en la crisis política española* (Buenos Aires: Editorial Alfa, 1964), p. 181.

16. Jacinto Toryho, *La independencia de España* (Valencia: n.p., 1935?), pp. 239–242.

17. Gabriel Jackson, *The Spanish Republic and the Civil War* (Princeton: Princeton University Press, 1965), p. 318.

18. "Congreso de sindicatos," *Solidaridad Obrera,* September 25, 1936, p. 3.

19. Abel Paz (pseud. Diego Camacho), *Durruti: le peuple en armes* (Paris: Editiones de la Tête de Feuilles, 1972), p. 387.

20. *Ibid.,* p. 389.

21. Pierre Broué and Emile Témime, *The Revolution and the Civil War in Spain* (Cambridge: MIT Press, 1972), p. 219.

22. José Peirats, *La CNT en la revolución española* (Toulouse: Ediciones CNT, 1951–1953), p. 225.

23. Juan Mauro Bajatierra, "Durruti," *CNT,* October 6, 1936, p. 1.

24. See especially "Abajo el militar," *Frente Libertario,* October 27, 1936, p. 1.

25. Peiró, *Peril a la retaguardia,* pp. 134–137.

26. Borkenau, *The Spanish Cockpit,* p. 119.

27. EG to Rudolf Rocker, November 18, 1936, IISG, Rocker Collection, Goldman file.

28. Rudolf Rocker, "Die Tragödie spaniens," IISG, Rocker Collection, box 4, folder 4, p. 18.

29. "La CNT y la revolución," *Mundo Obrero* (Madrid), September 17, 1936, p. 3.

30. Rocker, "Die Tragödie spaniens," p. 23.

31. Stanley Payne, *The Spanish Revolution* (New York: Norton, 1970), pp. 284, 287.

32. A. Ramos Oliveira, *Politics, Economics and Men of Modern Spain, 1808–1946* (London: Victor Gollancz, 1946),· p. 599.

33. The dissenting newspapers were *Acracia* of Lerida, *Ideas* of Hospitalet, and *Nosotros* of Valencia. Stephan John Brademas, "Revolution and Counter-Revolution in Spain: A Contribution to the History of the Anarcho-Syndicalist Movement in Spain, 1930–1937" (unpublished Ph.D. dissertation, Brasenose College, Oxford University, 1953), p. 362.

34. "Giral," *Solidaridad Obrera,* August 28, 1936, p. 1.

35. Abad de Santillán, *Por qué perdimos la guerra,* p. 116.

36. "La CNT y el nuevo gobierno," *CNT,* September 6, 1936, p. 3.

37. Rudolf Rocker, miscellaneous materials, IISG, Rocker Collection, file 1, folder 1.

38. "La CNT y el nuevo gobierno," p. 3.

39. Rudolf Rocker, *Revolución y regresión* (Buenos Aires: Editorial Tupac, 1952), p. 140.

40. EG to Margaret Silver, May 24, 1937, IISG, Goldman Collection, file 27 D.

41. According to "Extranjeros y España," *Solidaridad Obrera*, March 14, 1938, p. 4.

42. Francisco Largo Caballero, *Mis recuerdos* (Mexico City: Ediciones "Alianza," 1954), p. 173.

43. José Martín Blázquez, *I Helped to Build an Army* (London: Secker and Warburg, 1939), p. 215.

44. *Ibid.*, pp. 209–210.

45. "Discurso del Ministerio Juan López," *Solidaridad Obrera*, February 11, 1937, p. 5.

46. *Ibid.*

47. Felix Morrow, *Revolution and Counter-Revolution in Spain* (New York: Pioneer Publishers, 1938), p. 40, called the collectivized industries producers' collectives which had no real financial power. The CNT thus simply recognized reality in permitting the Council on the Economy to be formed.

48. Brademas, "Revolution and Counter-Revolution," p. 372.

49. Peirats, *Los anarquistas en la crisis política española*, p. 208.

50. Federico Urales, "Armas y letras," p. 4.

51. Abad de Santillán, *Por qué perdimos la guerra*, pp. 115–116.

52. "Hablando García Oliver," *Solidaridad Obrera*, October 14, 1936, p. 2.

53. "La CNT y el Generalitat," *ibid.*, October 22, 1936, p. 3.

54. Colonel Segismundo Casado, *The Last Days of Madrid* (London: Peter Davies, 1939), p. 59.

55. "¡Resurrección del viejo ejército, no!," *Solidaridad Obrera*, October 31, 1936, p. 3.

56. Federico Urales, "Las dificultades económicas del nuevo order social," *Solidaridad Obrera*, October 13, 1936, p. 2.

57. "Regla de la milicia," p. 6.

58. EG to Rudolf Rocker, November 3, 1936, IISG, Rocker Collection, Goldman file.

59. Buenaventura Durruti, "Letra a Rusia," *Solidaridad Obrera*, October 30, 1936, p. 1.

60. Juan Peiró, "La revolución y la guerra," *Solidaridad Obrera*, October 28, 1936, p. 10.

61. Jackson, *The Spanish Republic and the Civil War*, p. 316.

62. EG to John Haynes Holmes, January 5, 1937, IISG, Goldman Collection, file 27 D.

63. Bolloten, *The Grand Camouflage*, pp. 236–238 n. 54, and Arturo Barea, *The Forging of a Rebel* (New York: Hitchcock, 1946), p. 579.

64. Abad de Santillán, *Por qué perdimos la guerra*, p. 118.

65. Rocker, *Revolución y regresión*, p. 390.

66. *Ruta*, November 28, 1936, p. 2.

67. Juan García Oliver, *Mi gestión al frente del Ministerio de Justicia* (Valencia: Información de CNT/AIT/FAI, 1937), pp. 6–7.

68. "The Spanish Anarchists Explain—," *Spain and the World*, September 30, 1938, p. 2.

69. Federica Montseny, "Militant Anarchism and the Reality in Spain," *Spain and the World,* February 19, 1937, p. 2.

70. EG to Alexander Shapiro, May 2, 1937, IISG, Goldman Collection, file 26.

71. EG to Rudolf Rocker, November 3, 1936, IISG, Rocker Collection, Goldman file.

72. "Emma Goldman Appeals," *Spain and the World,* February 5, 1937, p. 2.

73. Diego Abad de Santillán, *Mensaje acerca de la situación actual del Movimiento Libertario Español* (Buenos Aires: Subdelegación de la CNT en la Argentina, 1946), p. 19.

74. Camillo Berneri, "Que faire?" *Guerre de classes en Espagne* (Montpellier: Les Cahiers de Terre Libre, 1938), pp. 34–35.

75. Berneri, "Attention, tournant dangereux!," *ibid.,* pp. 15–19.

76. George Orwell, *Homage to Catalonia* (New York: Harcourt, Brace and World, 1952), p. 70.

77. George Orwell, *The Collected Essays, Journalism and Letters,* ed. Sonia Orwell and Ian Angus (New York: Harcourt, Brace and World, 1968), I, 270.

78. "¡Madrid!," *Solidaridad Obrera,* November 2, 1936, p. 1.

79. Particularly from Colodny, *The Struggle for Madrid,* who makes only thirteen references to anarchism in his book.

80. "El fascismo se derrumba," *Solidaridad Obrera,* October 30, 1936, p. 1.

81. Louis Fischer, *Men and Politics* (New York: Duell, Sloan and Pearce, 1941), p. 385.

82. Miguel González Inestal, *Cipriano Mera, revolucionario* (Havana: Editorial Atalaya), p. 31.

83. Broué and Témime, *The Revolution and the Civil War in Spain,* p. 247.

84. Ludwig Renn (pseud. Vieth van Golssenan), *Der spanische Krieg* (Berlin: Aufbau Verlag, 1956), p. 211.

85. Tom Wintringham, *English Captain* (London: Faber and Faber, 1939), p. 128 and *passim.*

86. Casado, *The Last Days of Madrid,* p. 96.

87. Adapted from José Manuel Martínez Bande, *La lucha en torno a Madrid* (Madrid: Libreria Editorial San Martín, 1968), p. 32.

88. González Inestal, *Cipriano Mera, revolucionario,* p. 36.

89. "García Oliver, ami intime de Durruti, nous parle du héros," *Durruti: sa vie—sa mort* (Paris: Editions du Bureau d'Information et de Presse, 1938), p. 55.

90. "Recuerdo póstumo de Federica Montseny al camarada Durruti, desde el micrófono del ministerio de la guerra," *Solidaridad Obrera,* November 22, 1936, p. 6.

91. Sanz, *Los que fuimos a Madrid,* p. 109.

92. *Ibid.*

93. *Ibid.,* p. 113.

94. Colodny, *The Struggle for Madrid,* pp. 74–75.

95. Sanz, *Los que fuimos a Madrid,* p. 114.

96. Colodny, *The Struggle for Madrid,* p. 75.

97. Sanz, *Los que fuimos a Madrid,* p. 114.

98. "El compañero Durruti ha dicho . . . ," *Solidaridad Obrera,* November 17, 1936, p. 1.

99. Sanz, *Los que fuimos a Madrid,* p. 117.

100. The most exaggerated portrayal of the events of November 15–17 is in Colodny, *The Struggle for Madrid,* pp. 74–79. Jackson, in *The Spanish Republic and the Civil War,* pp. 329–30, develops the thesis about Varela's fortuitous timing of his attack, but he does not discuss the militia in action after November 15 and has Durruti apologizing for alleged misdeeds of his troops. Fischer, *Men and Politics,* p. 395, may be the source of these allegations, but he gets many details wrong. Fischer clearly did not visit this section of the front during the battle, although he was in Madrid at the time.

101. Sanz, *Los que fuimos a Madrid,* p. 114.

102. The primary account of Durruti's death is found in Joan Llarch, *La muerte de Durruti* (Barcelona: Ediciones Aura, 1973), p. 17. Llarch has collected all known versions of the assassination. Some witnesses place the shooting on the Plaza de la Moncloa or in front of the Model Prison. The number of persons allegedly present also varies enormously.

103. Ángel Montoto, "La discutida muerte de Durruti," *La Actualidad Española,* March 17, 1971, p. 46.

104. Sanz, *Los que fuimos a Madrid,* p. 121.

105. Llarch, *La muerte de Durruti,* pp. 107, 207.

106. "Durruti," *Mundo Obrero,* November 23, 1936, p. 2, carries the original allegation that an anarchist killed Durruti. Foreign journalists like Cyril Connolly, "Barcelona," *The New Statesman and Nation,* December 19, 1936, pp. 1020–1021, picked it up, as did Fischer, in *Men and Politics,* pp. 395–396. Montoto, in "La discutida," p. 47, also uses this theme (although he speculates as well that Durruti may have accidentally shot himself). Eduardo Comín Colomer, in *Historia del anarquismo español 1836–1948* (Madrid: RADAR, n.d.), pp. 393–397, is another who accepts the anarchist identity of Durruti's killer. The most recent discussion of Durruti's death is "Cómo asesinaron a Durruti," *Posible,* July 1976, pp. 18–21.

107. Llarch, *La muerte de Durruti,* p. 139.

108. "¿No somos provocadores?," *El Amigo del Pueblo,* March 16, 1937, p. 1.

Chapter Nine

1. Cyril Connolly, "Barcelona," *The New Statesman and Nation,* December 19, 1936, p. 1020.

2. *Ibid.*

3. Eric Hobsbawm, *Revolutionaries* (London: Weidenfeld and Nicolson, 1973), p. 76.

4. *Ibid.,* p. 75.

5. Hobsbawm believes he had in fact made this change before his death. *Ibid.,* p. 76.

6. Ricardo Sanz, *Los que fuimos a Madrid: Columna Durruti 26 División* (Toulouse: Imprimerie Dulaurier, 1969), p. 127.

7. Diego Abad de Santillán, *Por qué perdimos la guerra* (Buenos Aires: Iman, 1940), p. 154.

8. *Ibid.,* p. 158.

9. Cf. Luis Romero Solano, *Vísperas de la guerra de España* (Mexico City: El Libro Perfecto, 1947), pp. 102–103.

10. Anonymous interview.

11. Abad de Santillán, *Por qué perdimos la guerra,* p. 176.

12. AIT (Delegación Permanente de la AIT en España), "Acta de la reunión del día 29 de abril 1937," IISG, Rocker Collection, file 1, folder 5.

13. Anonymous interview.

14. Burnett Bolloten, *The Grand Camouflage: The Spanish Civil War and Revolution, 1936–39* (London: Pall Mall Press, 1968), pp. 238–239.

15. *Ibid.,* p. 228.

16. Jesús Pérez Salas, *Guerra en España* (Mexico, D.F.: Graficos, 1947), p. 144.

17. José Peirats, *La CNT en la revolución española* (Toulouse: Ediciones CNT, 1951–1953), I, 247–248.

18. Felix Morrow, *Revolution and Counter-Revolution in Spain* (New York: Pioneer Publishers, 1938), p. 61.

19. "Manifiesto," *Nosotros,* February 16, 1937, pp. 1–3.

20. Camillo Berneri, "Attention, tournant dangereux!," *Guerre de classes en Espagne* (Montpellier: Les Cahiers de Terre Libre, 1938), pp. 15–19.

21. Peirats, *La CNT en la revolución española,* I, 252.

22. Abad de Santillán, *Por qué perdimos la guerra,* p. 170.

23. *Ibid.,* p. 159.

24. In fact, Baraíbar remained loyal to Largo Caballero and sometimes frustrated communist military plans, although at other times he was simply a passive observer.

25. Bolloten, *The Grand Camouflage,* p. 269.

26. General José Asensio, *El General Asensio: su lealtad a la república* (Barcelona: Artes Gráficas CNT, 1938), pp. 91–93.

27. Cf. *Manchester Guardian,* December 22, 1936, p. 5.

28. Franz Borkenau, *The Spanish Cockpit* (London: Faber and Faber, 1937), p. 182.

29. CNT/FAI, "Informe general de administración al finalizar el mes de enero de 1937," January 19, 1937, IISG, Rocker Collection, pp. 25–40.

30. Peirats, *La CNT en la revolución española,* I, 340–342.

31. Federica Montseny, "El paso de Federica Montseny, como Ministro de Salubridad en el Gobierno de Valencia," *Boletín de Informacion CNT/AIT/FAI,* April 30, 1937, p. 33.

32. *Ibid.,* p. 38.

33. *Ibid.,* pp. 41–43.

34. *Ibid.,* pp. 48–53.

35. EG to Mariano Vázquez, October 11, 1937, IISG, EG Collection, file 27 B.

36. Juan García Oliver, *Me gestión al frente del Ministerio de Justicia* (Valencia: Información de CNT/AIT/FAI, 1937), p. 10.

37. Another amnesty came on January 25, 1937. *Ibid.,* p. 11.

38. *Ibid.,* pp. 18–21.

39. Richard Berryer, *Revolutionary Justice in Spain* (London: Oates and Washbourne, 1938), p. 14.

40. *Diario Oficial,* October 13, 1936, p. 11.

41. Pierre Broué and Emile Témime, *The Revolution and the Civil War in Spain* (Cambridge: MIT Press, 1972), p. 273.

42. Cf. Bolloten in Raymond Carr, ed., *The Republic and the Spanish Civil War* (Oxford: Clarendon Press, 1971), pp. 140–142.

43. Federica Montseny, *Militant Anarchism and the Reality in Spain* (London: Spanish Relief Committee, 1937), p. 6.

44. Abe Bluestein to EG, January 4, 1938, IISG, Goldman Collection, file 28. In addition, foreign anarchists were disturbed by a quarrel between the old libertarian Voline and the CNT over an article he had written that was critical of anarchist policy in Spain. The closing of *El Frente Libertario* for offending official FAI policy also worsened relations, but the largest single issue was an FAI decision to establish the Solidaridad Internacional Antifascista, a propaganda group that ignored ideological boundaries in collecting money and aid for the Spanish war.

45. CNT to EG, April 27, 1937, IISG, Goldman Collection, file 27 D.

46. Stanley Payne, *The Spanish Revolution* (New York: Norton, 1970), p. 286, and Augustin Souchy, *The Tragic Week in May* (Barcelona: Ediciónes de la Oficina de Información Exterior de la CNT y FAI, 1938), p. 44.

47. *Ibid.,* p. 45.

48. José Peirats, *Los anarquistas en la crisis política española* (Buenos Aires: Editorial Alfa, 1964), p. 234.

49. Souchy, *The Tragic Week in May,* p. 8.

50. CNT/FAI, "Informe general de administración," pp. 23–25, and Nazario González, *El anarquismo en la historia de España contemporánea* (Barcelona: Universidad de Barcelona Facultad de Filosofía y Letras, 1970), pp. 151–152.

51. *El Amigo del Pueblo,* May 26, 1937, p. 2.

52. *Ibid.,* p. 3.

53. *Ibid.,* June 22, 1937, p. 1.

54. *Ibid.,* p. 2, and July 20, 1937, p. 3.

55. *Fraga Social,* June 2, 1937, p. 2.

56. Camillo Berneri, *Guerra di Classes,* April 14, 1937, quoted in "Open Letter to Federica Montseny," *Spain and the World,* June 4, 1937, pp. 1–3.

57. Comité Peninsular to EG, April 6, 1937, IISG, Goldman Collection, file 27 D.

58. Souchy, *The Tragic Week in May*, p. 10.

59. *Ibid.*, p. 12.

60. Quoted in *ibid.*, p. 16.

61. *El Amigo del Pueblo*, August 12, 1937, p. 1.

62. Speech of Juan Comorera in J. R. Campbell, *Spain Organizes for Victory* (London: Communist Party of Great Britain, 1937), n.p.

63. Quoted in "Catalonia—An Answer to Comorera," *Spain and the World*, September 8, 1937, p. 2.

64. Souchy, *The Tragic Week in May*, p. 22.

65. Quoted in *ibid.*, p. 25.

66. *Ibid.*, pp. 30–31.

67. Peirats, *Los anarquistas en la crisis política española*, p. 251.

68. George Orwell, *Homage to Catalonia* (New York: Harcourt, Brace and World, 1952), p. 144.

69. *Ibid.*, p. 6.

70. Emma Goldman, *Anarchism and Other Essays* (New York: Mother Earth, 1911), p. 50.

71. Abe Bluestein to EG, January 4, 1938, EG Collection, file 28E.

72. Quoted in EG to Rudolf Rocker, June 10, 1937, IISG, Rocker Collection, Goldman file.

73. Helmut Rüdiger, "Rapport du Secretariat de Barcelone pour la Congrès de l'AIT à Paris, le 7 décembre 1937," IISG, Rocker Collection, file 2, folder 3, pp. 15–34.

74. Segundo Blanco of the CNT became Minister of Education in the summer of 1938. The Ministry of Health was also staffed by some CNT members.

75. Sanz, *Los que fuimos a Madrid*, p. 153.

76. Cf. Hugh Thomas, *The Spanish Civil War* (London: Eyre and Spottiswoode, 1961), p. 475.

77. Abad de Santillán, *Por qué perdimos la guerra*, p. 186.

78. EG to Rudolf Rocker, November 19, 1937, IISG, Rocker Collection, Goldman file. "La chekas en Valencia," *ibid.*, box 2, folder 1, document 85.

79. Peirats, *Los anarquistas en la crisis política española*, p. 168.

80. Abad de Santillán, *Por qué perdimos la guerra*, pp. 200–201.

81. Movimiento Libertario, *Sobre la necesidad de reafirmar nuestra personalidad revolucionaria y de negar nuestro concurso a una obra de Gobierno necesariamente fatal para la guerra y para la revolución* (Barcelona: Comité Peninsular de FAI, September 1938), p. 12.

82. Cf. Grupo Ácrata, *Durruti* (Barcelona: n.p., n.d.).

83. "Posición de la FAI ante la declaración del Gobierno, de los trece puntos," IISG, Rocker Collection, box 2, folder 1, document 53.

84. "FAI Comment on Spanish Parliamentary Policy," *Spain and the World*, March 18, 1938, p. 3.

85. "Acuerdos del movimiento libertaria," October 22, 1938, IISG, Rocker Collection, box 1, folder 2, document 18.

86. The FAI's anti-fascism prompted the Comité Nacional de la CNT

to publish *El Nazismo al desnudo* (Barcelona: Imprenta y Editorial "Centro de Administración Municipal," 1938). The *faísta* critique of Juan Negrín was contained in Movimiento Libertario, *Sobre la necesidad de reafirmar nuestra personalidad revolucionaria*, pp. 18–23. Much of *Frente a la contrarrevolución: la CNT y la conciencia de España* (Barcelona: FAI, 1938) was also drawn from the work of the FAI.

Chapter Ten

1. The best work on the anarchist economic system in Catalonia is by Albert Pérez Baró, *Trenta mesos de collectivisme a Catalunya (1936–1939)* (Barcelona: Ariel, 1970).

2. Augustin Souchy, "Workers' Self-Management in Industry," in Sam Dolgoff, ed., *The Anarchist Collectives: Workers' Self-Management in the Spanish Revolution 1936–1939* (New York: Free Life Editions, 1974), p. 82.

3. Augustin Souchy, "The Economic Council of Workers," *Spain and the World*, March 18, 1938, p. 3.

4. *Ibid.*

5. "Revolutionary Achievements of the Proletariat," *ibid.*, April 16, 1937, p. 1.

6. Emma Goldman, "A Long Cherished Dream," *ibid.*, March 5, 1937, p. 3.

7. José Peirats, *Los anarquistas en la crisis política española* (Buenos Aires: Editorial Alfa, 1964), p. 153.

8. José Peirats, *La CNT en la revolución española* (Toulouse: Ediciones CNT, 1951–1953), I, 340–342; Gaston Leval, *Né Franco né Stalin: le colletività anarchiche spagnole netta lotta contra Franco e la reazione staliniana* (Milan: Instituto Editoriale Italiano, 1955), pp. 143–152.

9. Mariano Vásquez, "The Work of the Aragon Council Defended," *Spain and the World*, September 22, 1937, p. 2.

10. Robert W. Kern, *Liberals, Reformers, and Caciques in Restoration Spain* (Albuquerque: University of New Mexico Press, 1974), pp. 96–97.

11. Harold Metcalfe, "A Canadian Socialist's Views," *Spain and the World*, May 19, 1937, p. 2.

12. Cf. César Lorenzo, *Les anarchistes espagnols et le pouvoir 1868–1969* (Paris: Editions du Seuil, 1969), pp. 370–402, or Max Gallo, *Spain Under Franco* (New York: E. P. Dutton, 1969), p. 151 and *passim*. Barbara Probst Solomon's memoir, *Arriving Where We Started* (New York: Harper and Row, 1972), catches the mood of the exile period beautifully.

13. Diego Abad de Santillán has recently published a book in Spain, *Historia del movimiento obrero español* (Madrid: Editorial ZYX, 1968), a compilation of some of his earlier writings.

14. See Henry Giniger, "Neighborhood Units Gain Power in Spain," *New York Times*, October 24, 1976, p. 5.

Bibliography

I. Newspapers

Acción Social Obrera (Madrid, Barcelona). 1930.
Amigo del Pueblo, El (Barcelona, Valencia). 1936.
Claridad (Madrid). 1934.
CNT (Madrid, Barcelona). 1936–1937.
Combate Sindicalista, El (Valencia). 1931–1936.
Correspondencia de España, La (Madrid). 1920.
Cristol (Barcelona). 1921–1923.
¡Despertad! (Vigo, Blanes, Barcelona). 1928–1930.
Día Gráfica, El (Barcelona). 1920.
Fraga Social (Barcelona). 1936–1937.
Frente Libertario, El (Aragon, Barcelona, Valencia). 1936–1937.
Gaceta de Madrid. 1918–1923.
Heraldo de Madrid. 1919–1921.
Iberión (Paris, Brussels, Barcelona). 1927–1929.
Imparcial, El (Madrid). 1919.
Liberal, El (Barcelona). 1920.
Mundo Obrero (Madrid). 1936–1937.
New York Times. 1976.
Oeuvre, L' (Paris). 1927.
Populaire, Le (Paris). 1926–1928.
Prensa de Madrid, La. 1933.
Quotidien, Le (Paris). 1926–1927.
Révolution Espagnol, La (Paris). 1936.
Sindicalismo (Valencia). 1933–1934.
Socialista, El (Madrid). 1922–1923.
Sol, El (Madrid). 1923–1936.
Solidaridad Obrera (Barcelona). 1918–1937.
Spain and the World (London). 1936–1939.
Tarde, La (Barcelona). 1920.

Tierra y Libertad (Madrid, Barcelona). 1931–1937.
Times, The (London). 1920–1932.
Tribuna, La (Madrid). 1920.
Vanguardia, La (Madrid). 1926–1936.

II. Journals

Boletín de Información CNT/AIT/FAI (Barcelona). 1936–1937.
Cultura Libertaria (Barcelona, Paris, Brussels). 1933.
España Libre (Toulouse, Paris). 1953.
Luchador, El (Madrid, Barcelona). 1932–1936.
Revista Blanca, La (Barcelona). 1923–1934.
Tiempos Nuevos (Paris). 1924–1927.
Tierra, La (Barcelona). 1933.
Timón (Barcelona). 1935–1939.

III. Unpublished Sources

Association Internationale des Travailleurs. [Delegación Permanente de la AIT en España.] "Acta de la reunión del día 29 de abril 1937." Internationaal Instituut voor Sociale Geschiedenis, Amsterdam. [Hereafter IISG.] Rocker Collection.
———. "La actividad del Secretariado de la AIT en Barcelona." July 11, 1937. IISG. AIT Collection.
———. "Rapport par Alexandre Shapiro sur l'activité de la Confédération National du Travail d'Espagne." Report presented in October 1933. IISG. AIT Collection.
———. Various minutes, conference reports, correspondence, and memorandums. IISG. AIT Collection.
Brademas, Stephan John. "Revolution and Counter-Revolution in Spain: A Contribution to the History of the Anarcho-Syndicalist Movement in Spain, 1930–1937." Ph.D. dissertation, Brasenose College, Oxford University, 1953. Recently published in revised form as *Anarcho-sindicalismo y revolución en España 1930–1937* (Madrid: Ariel, 1974).
Confederación Nacional del Trabajo. "Memoria del Congreso Regional celebrado en Zaragoza, los días 8–10 de mayo de 1922." Archivo de CNT/FAI, Toulouse, France.
———. "Memoria de Pleno Regional de la CNT/FAI de Cataluña, de marzo 1933." IISG. Rocker Collection.
———. "Sindicato de campesinos y oficios varios de Morón de la Frontera." IISG. Rocker Collection.
Confederación Nacional del Trabajo and Federación Anarquista Ibérica. "Conferencia Regional del Trabajo de Aragón, Rioja y Navarra." IISG. Rocker Collection.

————. "Informe general de administración al finalizar el mes de enero de 1937." IISG. Rocker Collection.

Federación Anarquista Ibérica. "Memoria del Pleno Peninsular de Regionales de FAI celebrado en Madrid, los días 28, 29, y 30 de octubre de 1933." IISG. Rocker Collection.

Fredericks, Shirley. "Social and Political Thought of Federica Montseny, Spanish Anarchist, 1923–1937." Ph.D. dissertation, University of New Mexico, 1972.

Goldman, Emma. Various letters, drafts of articles, and personal writings. IISG. Goldman Collection.

Nomad, Max (pseud. Max Nacht). "The Anarchist Tradition and Other Essays." IISG. Nomad Collection.

Rocker, Rudolf. "JJEL et femmes libres." IISG. Rocker Collection.

————. "Memoria: una brigada heroica." IISG. Rocker Collection.

————. "Die Tragödie spaniens." IISG. Rocker Collection.

————. Various letters, notes, drafts of articles, and personal writings. IISG. Rocker Collection.

————. "Verhaftung des Genossen Carbó." IISG. Rocker Collection.

Rüdiger, Helmut. "Bermerkungen zur Haltung der CNT in der spanischen Oktoberbewegung." IISG. Rocker Collection.

————. "Informe para el Congreso extraordinario de la AIT el día 6/12/37." IISG. AIT Collection.

————. "Rapport du Secretariat de Barcelone pour la Congrès de l'AIT à Paris, le 7 décembre 1937." IISG. Rocker Collection.

Shapiro, Alexander. "Rapport sur l'activité de la Confédération National du Travail d'Espagne, 16 décembre 1932–26 février 1933." IISG. AIT Collection.

IV. Printed Documents

British Record Office. *Calendar of State Papers Relating to Western and Southern Europe.* British Record Office.

Confederación Nacional del Trabajo. *Memoria del Congreso celebrado en el Teatro de la Comedia de Madrid, los días 10 al 18 de diciembre de 1919.* Barcelona: CNT, 1932.

————. *Memoria del Congreso extraordinaria celebrado en Madrid, los días 11 al 16 de junio de 1931.* Barcelona: CNT, 1931.

Congreso de los Diputados. *Diario del Congreso de los Diputados.* XXIV, no. 9 (1920 series).

Federación Anarquista Ibérica. *Frente a la contrarrevolución: la CNT y la conciencia de España.* Barcelona: FAI, 1938.

Instituto de Reformas Sociales. *Estadística de huelgas.* Madrid: Instituto de Reformas Sociales, 1921.

López, Juan. "Recordatorio: la historia no debe repetirse." In *Material de la discusión para los militantes de la Confederación Nacional de Trabajo de España.* Milford Haven, England: n.p., 1945.

Movimiento Libertario. *Sobre la necesidad de reafirmar nuestra personalidad revolucionaria y de negar nuestro concurso a una obra de Gobierno necesariamente fatal para la guerra y para la revolución.* Barcelona: Comité Peninsular de FAI, 1938.

V. Anthologies, Collected Works, Speeches

Azaña, Manuel. *Obras completas.* 4 vols. Mexico, D.F.: Ediciones Oasis, 1966–1968.

Lehring, Arthur, ed. *Archives Bakounine.* 4 vols. Leiden: Reidel, 1961–1965.

Orwell, George. *The Collected Essays, Journalism and Letters.* Ed. Sonia Orwell and Ian Angus. New York: Harcourt, Brace and World, 1968.

Maragall, Juan. *Obras completas de Juan Maragall.* 7 vols. Barcelona: Sala Parés, 1930.

Maspero, François, ed. *Syndicalisme révolutionnaire et communisme: les archives de Pierre Monatte.* Paris: author, 1968.

VI. European Politics and Labor: Theory and Practice of Anarchism, Socialism, and Communism

Avrich, Paul. *The Russian Anarchists.* Princeton: Princeton University Press, 1967.

Bakunin, Michael. "Federalism, Socialism and Anti-Theologism." "Letter to Albert Richard." "The Program of the International Brotherhood." "Revolutionary Catechism." In Dolgoff, Sam, ed. and trans., *Bakunin on Anarchy.* New York: Vintage, 1971.

Bragança Cunha, Vicente de. *Revolutionary Portugal.* London: Clark, 1938.

Carr, Edward H. *Michael Bakunin.* New York: Vintage, 1961.

Carter, April. *The Political Theory of Anarchism.* London: Routledge and Kegan Paul, 1971.

Engels, Friedrich. "The Bakuninists at Work." In Marx, Karl, and Engels, Friedrich, *Anarchism and Anarcho-Syndicalism.* Moscow: International Publishers, 1971.

———. "The Workingmen of Europe in 1877." *Ibid.*

Figueiredo, Antonio de. *Portugal: Fifty Years of Dictatorship.* London: Penguin, 1975.

Goldman, Emma. *Anarchism and Other Essays.* New York: Mother Earth, 1911.

Grunberger, Richard. *Red Rising in Bavaria.* London: Barker, 1973.

Guérin, Daniel. *Anarchism.* New York: Monthly Review Press, 1970.

Hostetter, Richard. *The Italian Socialist Movement. Vol. I: Origins 1860–1882.* Princeton: Princeton University Press, 1971.

Humbert, Sylvain. *Le mouvement syndical*. Paris: M. Rivière et Cie., 1912.

Kropotkin, Peter. *The Conquest of Bread*. London: Chapman and Hall, 1906.

———. *Mutual Aid*. New York: McClure, Phillips and Co., 1902.

Lazitch, Branko, and Drachkovitch, Milorad. *Lenin and the Comintern*. Vol. I. Stanford: Hoover Library Press, 1972.

Lenin, V. I. *Left-Wing Communism, an Infantile Disorder*. Moscow: International Publishers, 1931.

Marotta, Sebastián. *El movimiento sindical argentino*. 3 vols. Buenos Aires: Ediciones "Lacio," 1961.

Marx, Karl, and Engels, Friedrich. *Anarchism and Anarcho-Syndicalism*. Moscow: International Publishers, 1971.

Maximoff, Gregor Petrovich. *The Political Philosophy of Bakunin*. New York: Free Press, 1953.

Nettlau, Max. *Anarchisten and Social-Revolutionäre die historische Entwicklung des Anarchismus in der Jahren 1880–86*. Berlin, 1886.

Nogueira, César. *Notas para a Historia de Socialismo em Portugal*. Lisbon: Portugália Editôra, n.d.

Pabón, Jesús. *La república portuguesa*. 2 vols. Madrid: Espasa-Calpe, 1941–1945.

Pyziur, Eugene. *The Doctrine of Anarchism of Michael A. Bakunin*. Milwaukee: Marquette University Press, 1955.

Rocker, Rudolf. *Revolución y regresión*. Buenos Aires: Editorial Tupac, 1952.

Sousa, Manuel Joaquim de. *O sindicalismo em Portugal*. Lisbon: Ediçâo da Comissão Escolar e Propaganda do Sindicalo do Possoal de Câmaras de Marinha Mercante Portuguesa, 1931.

Stafford, David. *From Anarchism to Reformism*. Toronto: University of Toronto Press, 1971.

Voline (pseud. Vsevolod Mikhailovitch Eichenbawm). *The Unknown Revolution: Kronstadt 1921, Ukraine 1918–1921*. London: Freedom Press, 1955.

Woodcock, George. *Anarchism: A History of Libertarian Ideas and Movements*. New York: Meridian, 1962.

VII. General Memoirs, Biographies, Eyewitness Accounts

Azaña, Manuel. *Memorias íntimas de Azaña*. Madrid: Ediciones Españolas, 1939.

Barea, Arturo. *The Forging of a Rebel*. New York: Hitchcock, 1946.

Campoamor, Clara. *La Révolution Espagnol vue par une républicaino*. Paris: Librairie Plon, 1937.

Day, Hem (pseud. M. Dieu). *Sébastien Faure, le pacifiste*. Brussels: author, 1961.

García Oliver, Juan. *Mi gestión al frente del Ministerio de Justicia*. Valencia: Información de CNT/AIT/FAI, 1937.

Goldman, Emma. *Living My Life*. New York: Scribner, 1932.

González Inestal, Miguel. *Cipriano Mera, revolucionario.* Havana: Editorial Atalaya, 1943.

Largo Caballero, Francisco. *Mis recuerdos.* Mexico, D.F.: Ediciones "Alianza," 1954.

Lorenzo, Anselmo. *El proletariado militante: memorias de un internacional.* 2 vols. Mexico, D.F.: Ediciones Vertice, 1942.

Martín Blázquez, José. *I Helped to Build an Army.* London: Secker and Warburg, 1939.

Mola Vidal, General Emilio. *Memorias: lo que yo supe.* Vallodolid: Libreria Santaren, 1940.

Morato, Juan José. *Pablo Iglesias, educator de muchadumbres.* Madrid: Espasa-Calpe, 1931.

Pérez Baró, Albert. *Trenta mesos de collectivisme a Catalunya (1936–1939).* Barcelona: Ariel, 1970.

Pestaña, Angel. *Lo que aprendí en la vida.* Madrid: M. Aguilar, 1934.

———. *Setenta días en Rusia: lo que yo ví.* Barcelona: n.p., 1925.

———. "Situemos." *¡Despertad!* May 11, 1928.

Reclus, Elisée. "El hombre y la tierra." *La Revista Blanca.* September 15, 1926.

Serge, Victor. *Memoirs of a Revolutionary.* Oxford: Clarendon Press, 1963.

Sola y Cañizares, Ferdinand. *Salvador Seguí: su vida, su obra.* Barcelona: n.p., 1960.

Wintringham, Tom. *English Captain.* London: Faber and Faber, 1939.

VIII. Durruti, Montseny, Abad de Santillán: Lives and Writings

A. DURRUTI

Cánovas Cervantes, Salvador. *Durruti y Ascaso y la revolución de julio.* Toulouse: Páginas Libres, n.d.

Connolly, Cyril. "Barcelona." *The New Statesman and Nation.* December 19, 1936.

Durruti: sa vie—sa mort. Paris: Editions du Bureau d'Information et de Presse, 1938.

Enzensberger, Hans Magnus. *Der kurze Sommer der Anarchie: Buenaventura Durrutis Leben und Tod.* Frankfort am Main: Suhrkamp, 1972.

Faure, Sébastien. "L'affaire Durruti." *Iberión.* March 1927.

Federación Anarquista Ibérica. *Homenaje del Comité de la FAI.* Barcelona: FAI, 1937.

Gilabert, Gilberto. *Durruti, un héroe del pueblo.* Buenos Aires: Ediciones Nervio, 1937.

Llarch, Joan. *La muerte de Durruti.* Barcelona: Ediciones Aura, 1973.

Montoto, Ángel. "La discutida muerte de Durruti." *La Actualidad Española.* March 17, 1971.

Montseny, Federica. "Recuerdo postumo de Federica Montseny al camarada

Durruti, desde el microfonó del ministerio de la guerra." *Solidaridad Obrera.* November 22, 1936.

Newell, Peter. *The Forgotten Heroes: Makhno and Durruti.* London: Freedom Press, 1969.

Paz, Abel (pseud. Diego Camacho). *Durruti: le peuple en armes.* Paris: Editiones de la Tête de Feuilles, 1972. Now translated by Nancy Macdonald, *Durruti: The People in Arms.* New York: Free Life Editions, 1977.

Roi, Valentin de. *Ascaso, Durruti, Jover: su obra de militantes, su vida de perseguidos.* Buenos Aires: Antorcha, 1927.

Sanz, Ricardo. *Figuras de la revolución española: Buenaventura Durruti.* Toulouse: Ediciones El Frente, 1945.

B. MONTSENY

Fredricks, Shirley. "Social and Political Thought of Federica Montseny, Spanish Anarchist, 1923–1937." Unpublished Ph.D. dissertation, University of New Mexico, 1972.

Montseny, Federica. *El anarquismo militante y la realidad española.* Barcelona: CNT, 1937.

———. *La commune de Paris y la revolución española.* Barcelona: Oficina de Información, Propaganda y Prensa del Comité Nacional CNT/FAI, 1937.

———. "Concepto heroico de la vida." *La Revista Blanca.* June 15, 1929.

———. "La crisis interna y externa de la Confederación." *El Luchador.* September 18, 1931.

———. "La defensa del ideal." *La Revista Blanca.* December 15, 1928.

———. *Los desheredados.* Barcelona: n.p., n.d.

———. "Discurso en el Teatro Olympia." *Solidaridad Obrera.* August 11, 1936.

———. "Eliseo Reclus o una vida estética." *La Revista Blanca.* October 15, 1929.

———. "Feminismo y humanismo." *La Revista Blanca.* October 1, 1924.

———. "Por la fuerza, la unidad, y el prestigio del anarquismo ibérico." *La Revista Blanca.* February 1, 1934.

———. "Hacia una nueva aurora social." *La Revista Blanca.* February 15, 1932.

———. *La incorporación de las masas populares a la historia. La Comune: primera revolución consciente.* Barcelona: n.p., n.d.

———. "Juan Wolfgang Goethe." *La Revista Blanca.* June 15, 1930.

———. "Martirio." *La Revista Blanca.* August 1, 1926.

———. "Miguel Bakunin." *La Revista Blanca.* July 1, 1926.

———. "Mi individualismo." *La Revista Blanca.* December 15, 1927.

———. "Militant Anarchism and the Reality in Spain." *Spain and the World.* February 19, 1937.

———. "La mujeres de Aragón." *La Revista Blanca.* July 15, 1926.

———. "La mujer nueva." *La Revista Blanca.* August 1, 1927.

———. "Plataformismo o reformismo libertario." *La Revista Blanca*. December 1, 1928.

———. *Los precursores: Anselmo Lorenzo, el hombre y la obra*. Barcelona: CNT/FAI, 1938.

———. *El problema de los sexos*. Toulouse: n.p., 1943.

———. "Sindicalismo revolucionario y comunismo anarquista." *La Revista Blanca*. November 1, 1932.

———. "La tragedia de la emancipación femenina." *La Revista Blanca*. December 15, 1924.

———. "El último romántico de la política burguesa." *La Revista Blanca*. December 15, 1926.

———. "Voces en el gran desierto: hablan los hombres." *La Revista Blanca*. June 15, 1927.

C. ABAD DE SANTILLÁN

Abad de Santillán, Diego. *After the Revolution*. New York: Greenberg, 1937.

———. *Los anarquistas españoles y la insurrección de octubre*. Detroit: Grupo Comunismo Libertario, 1936.

———. *Los anarquistas y la reacción contemporánea*. Mexico, D.F.: Grupo Cultural Ricardo Flores Magon, 1925.

———. *El derecho de España a la revolución*. Madrid: Fortanet, 1916.

———. *Discurso sobre los grandes hombres y sobre la existencia de un redentor de España*. Madrid: Victoriano Suárez, 1914.

———. *La FORA: ideología y trayectoria del movimiento obrero revolucionario en la Argentina*. Buenos Aires: Editorial Proyección, 1971.

———. *Historia del movimiento obrero español*. Madrid: Editorial ZYX, 1968.

———. *Mensaje cerca de la situación actual del movimiento libertario español*. Buenos Aires: Subdelegación de la CNT en la Argentina, 1946.

———. *El organismo económico de la revolución: cómo vivimos y como podríamos vivir en España*. Barcelona: Ediciones Terra y Libertad, 1935.

———. *Por qué perdimos la guerra*. Buenos Aires: Iman, 1940.

———. *Psicología del pueblo español*. Madrid: F. Peña Cruz, 1917.

IX. Spanish Histories

A. PRE-REPUBLIC

Alaina Caules, Jaime. "Investigación analítica sobre la evolución demográfica de Cataluña." *Cuadernos de Información Económica y Sociológica*. June 1955. Barcelona.

Azcárate, Gumersindo. *El régimen parlamentario en la práctica*. Madrid: Minuesa de los Ríos, 1885.

———. *El self-government y la monarquía doctrinaria*. Madrid: San Martín, 1877.

Bernis y Carrasco, Francisco. *Consecuencias económicas de la guerra.* Madrid: E. Maestre, 1923.

Boix, José. "Sindicalismo católico: su actuación en Barcelona," *Revista Social Hispano-Americano,* II (March 1911). Barcelona.

Costa, Joaquín. *Crisis política de España.* Madrid: Fortanet, 1900.

————. "Manifiesto de la Cámara del Alto-Aragón." In Costa, ed., *Reconstitución y europeización de España.* Madrid: San Francisco de Sales, 1900.

————. *Oligarquía y caciquismo como la forma actual de gobierno en España.* Madrid: M. G. Hernández, 1902.

Costa, Joaquín; Giner de los Ríos, Francisco; and Pantoja, José María, eds. *Derecho consuetudinario y económico popular de España.* Barcelona: M. Soler, 1885.

Deakin, Frank. *Spain To-Day.* London: Labour Publishing Co., 1923.

Hamilton, Bernice. *Spanish Political Thought in the Sixteenth Century.* London: Clarendon Press, 1963.

Hennessy, C. A. M. *The Federal Republic of Spain, 1868–1875.* Oxford: Clarendon Press, 1962.

Isern, Damían. *Del desastre nacional y sus causas.* Madrid: Minuesa de los Ríos, 1899.

Junco, José Alvarez. *La ideología política del anarquismo español (1868–1910).* Madrid: Siglo Veintiuno de España, 1976.

Kern, Robert W. *Liberals, Reformers and Caciques in Restoration Spain.* Albuquerque: University of New Mexico Press, 1974.

Lee, Laurie. *As I Walked Out One Midsummer Morning.* London: Penguin, 1969.

Macías Picavia, Ricardo. *El problema nacional.* Madrid: Victoriano Suárez, 1900.

Mallada, Joaquín Lucas. *Los males de la patria.* Barcelona: Delgado, 1891.

Maura, Miguel. *Así cayó Alfonso XIII.* Madrid: Ariel, 1968.

Mella y Cea, Ricardo, and Prat, José. *La barbarie gubernamental en España.* Barcelona, 1897.

Subirato Centura, Jorge. "La verdadero personalidad del 'Baron de Koenig,'" *Cuadernos de Historia Económica de Cataluña,* V (1971), pp. 103–118.

Ward, G. H. B. *The Truth about Spain.* London: Cassell, 1911.

Zugasti, Julian de. *El bandolerismo.* 8 vols. Madrid: Fortanet, 1874–1878.

B. REPUBLIC AND CIVIL WAR

Alba, Victor. *Histoire des républiques espagnoles.* Tr. Louis Parrot. Epilogue by Mario Aguilar. Vincennes: Nord-Sud, 1948.

Arraras, Joaquín. *Historia de la segunda republica española.* 2 vols. Madrid: Editora Nacional, 1964.

Berneri, Camillo. *Guerre de classes en Espagne.* Montpellier: Les Cahiers de Terre Libre, 1938.

Bolloten, Burnett. *The Grand Camouflage: The Spanish Civil War and Revolution, 1936–39.* London: Pall Mall Press, 1968.

Borkenau, Franz. *The Spanish Cockpit*. London: Faber and Faber, 1937.
Brademas, John. *Anarcho-sindicalismo y revolución en España*. Madrid: Ariel, 1974.
Brenan, Gerald. *The Spanish Labyrinth*. Cambridge: Cambridge University Press, 1943.
Broué, Pierre. *Trotsky y la guerra civil española*. Buenos Aires: J. Alvarez, 1966.
Broué, Pierre, and Témime, Emile. *The Revolution and the Civil War in Spain*. Cambridge: MIT Press, 1972.
Buckley, Henry. *Life and Death of the Spanish Republic*. London: Hamish Hamilton, 1940.
Carr, Raymond. *Modern Spain 1808–1939*. Oxford: Clarendon Press, 1967.
Casado, Segismundo. *The Last Days of Madrid*. London: Peter Davies, 1939.
Cierva, Ricardo de la. *Historia de la guerra civil española*. 2 vols. Madrid: Libreria Editorial San Martín, 1969.
Colodny, Robert G. *The Struggle for Madrid: The Central Epic in the Spanish Conflict*. New York: Payne-Whitman, 1958.
Comín Colomer, Eduardo. *Historia del partido comunista de España*. 2nd ed. Madrid: Editora Nacional, 1967.
Fischer, Louis. *Men and Politics*. New York: Duell, Sloan and Pearce, 1941.
Jackson, Gabriel. *The Second Republic and the Spanish Civil War*. Princeton: Princeton University Press, 1965.
Kern, Robert W. "Anarchist Principles and Spanish Reality: Emma Goldman as a Participant in the Civil War, 1936–1939." *Journal of Contemporary History*, XI (July 1976).
Manuel, Frank E. *The Politics of Modern Spain*. New York: McGraw-Hill, 1938.
Martínez Bande, José Manuel. *La lucha en torno a Madrid*. Madrid: Libreria Editorial San Martín, 1968.
Matorrás, Enrique. *El comunismo en España*. Madrid: n.p., 1935.
Maurín, Joaquín, *Hacia la segunda revolución*. Barcelona: Gráficos Alfa, 1935.
———. *Revolución y contrarrevolución en España*. Paris: Ruedo Ibérico, 1966.
Meaker, Gerald H. *The Revolutionary Left in Spain 1914–1923*. Stanford: Stanford University Press, 1974.
Morrow, Felix. *Revolution and Counter-Revolution in Spain*. New York: Pioneer Publishers, 1938.
Olay, Maximiliano. *Spain Swings to the Left*. Chicago: Red and Black, 1933.
Payne, Stanley. *Falange: A History of Spanish Fascism*. Stanford: Stanford University Press, 1961.
———. *Politics and the Military in Modern Spain*. Stanford: Stanford University Press, 1966.
———. *The Spanish Revolution*. New York: Norton, 1970.
Peers, E. Allison. *The Spanish Tragedy 1930–1937: Dictatorship, Republic, Chaos, Rebellion, War*. London: Methuen, 1937.
Peiró, Juan. *Peril a la retaguardia*. Mataró: Editiones Llibertat, n.d.
Pérez Salas, Jesús. *Guerra en España*. Mexico, D.F.: Gráficos, 1947.

Ramos Oliveira, Antonio. *Politics, Economics and Men of Modern Spain 1808–1946*. London: Victor Gollancz, 1946.
Raynaud, Jean. *En Espagne "Rouge."* Paris: Editiones du Cerf, 1937.
Renn, Ludwig (pseud. Vieth van Golssenan). *Der spanische Krieg*. Berlin: Aufbau Verlag, 1956.
Richards, Vernon. *Lessons of the Spanish Revolution*. London: Freedom Press, 1953.
Seco Serrano, Carlos. *La crisis de Casas Viejas*. Madrid: Atlas, 1964.
Thomas, Hugh. *The Spanish Civil War*. New York: Harper, 1961.
Toryho, Jacinto. *La independencia de España*. Barcelona: n.p., 1936.
Urales, Federico. *España, 1933: la barbarie gubernamental*. Barcelona: Ediciones de "El Luchador," 1933.

X. Anarchism and Labor in Spain

Bookchin, Murray. *The Spanish Anarchists: The Heroic Years 1868–1936*. New York: Free Life Editions, 1976.
Buenacasa, Manuel. *La CNT, los Treinta y la FAI*. Barcelona: Gráficos Alfa, 1933.
———. *El movimiento obrero español 1886–1926*. Barcelona: Impresos Costa, 1928.
Comín Colomer, Eduardo. *Historia del anarquismo español (1836–1948)*. Madrid: RADAR, n.d.
Díaz del Moral, Juan. *Historia de las agitaciones campesinas andaluzas*. Madrid: Revista de Derecho Privado, 1929.
García Ceballos, Manuel. *Casas Viejas*. Madrid: Fermín Uriate, 1965.
García Venero, Maximiliano. *Historia de las Internacionales en España*. 3 vols. Madrid: Ediciones del Movimiento, 1956.
———. *Historia de los movimientos sindicalistas españoles*. Madrid: Ediciones del Movimiento, 1961.
Gilabert, Gilberto. *La CNT, la FAI, y la revolucíon española*. Barcelona: Biblioteca Tierra y Libertad, 1932.
Gómez Casas, Juan. *Historia del anarchosindicalismo español*. Madrid: Editorial ZYX, 1968.
González, Nazario. *El anarquismo en la historia de España contemporánea*. Barcelona: Universidad de Barcelona Facultad de Filosofía y Letras, 1970.
Hobsbawm, Eric. *Primitive Rebels*. New York: Vintage, 1959.
———. *Revolutionaries*. London: Weidenfeld and Nicolson, 1973.
Joll, James. *The Anarchists*. New York: Grosset and Dunlap, 1964.
Leval, Gaston (pseud. Pedro Piller). *Espagne libertaire: 1936–1939*. Paris: Editions du Cercle, 1971.
———. *Né Franco né Stalin: le colletività anarchiche spagnole nella lotta contro Franco e la reazione staliniana*. Milan: Instituto Editoriale Italiano, 1955.
Lida, Clara. *Anarquismo y revolución en la España del siglo XIX*. Madrid: Siglo Veintiuno de España, 1972.

————. *Antecedentes y desarrollo del movimiento obrero español, 1835–1888: textos y documentos.* Madrid: Siglo Veintiuno de España, 1973.

Nettlau, Max. "Comunismo autoritario y comunismo libertario." *La Revista Blanca.* February 1, 1928.

————. *La Première Internationale en Espagne (1868–1888).* Dordrecht: Reidel, 1969.

————. "Para preparar la sociedad futura." *La Revista Blanca.* January 15, 1927.

Nomad, Max (pseud. Max Nacht). *Dreamers, Dynamiters, and Demagogues.* New York: Waldon Press, 1964.

Lorenzo, César. *Les anarchistes espagnols et le pouvoir 1868–1969.* Paris: Editions du Seuil, 1969.

Peirats, José. *Los anarquistas en la crisis política española.* Buenos Aires: Editorial Alfa, 1964.

————. *La CNT en la revolución española.* Toulouse: Ediciones CNT, 1951–1953.

Peiró, Juan. *Problemas del sindicalismo y del anarchismo.* Toulouse: Ediciones Movimiento Libertario Español, 1945.

Pestaña, Angel. *Porque se constituyó el partido sindicalista.* Barcelona: n.p., 1936.

————. *El sindicalismo, qué quiere y adónde va.* Barcelona: Biblioteca selección, 1933.

————. *Sindicalismo y unidad sindical.* Valencia: n.p., 1933.

Prieto, Horacio. *Marxismo y socialismo libertario.* Rennes: Imprimeries Réunies, 1945.

Santiago, Enrique. *La Unión General de Trabajadores ante la revolución.* Madrid: Sáez Hermanos, 1932.

Sanz, Ricardo. *El sindicalismo y la política: los "Solidarios" y "Nosotros."* Toulouse: Imprimerie Dulaurier, 1966.

Souchy, Augustin. *Anarcho-Syndikalisten über Bürger-Krieg und Revolution in Spanien.* Darmstadt: Marz Verlag, 1969.

XI. Anarchism, Politics, and Labor in Catalonia

Ascaso, Francisco. "El estado" and "Nuestro anarquismo." In *Homenaje del Comité Peninsular de la FAI a F. Ascaso.* Barcelona: Tierra y Libertad, 1938.

Barcells, Alberto. *El sindicalismo en Barcelona 1916–1923.* Barcelona: Editorial Nova Terra, 1965.

Bou, Bernardo, and Magríña, Ricardo. *Un año de conspiración.* Barcelona: Solidaridad Obrera, 1933.

Brincall, Josep Maria. *Política económica de la Generalitat (1936–1939): evolució i formes de la producció industrial.* Barcelona: Ediciones 62, 1970.

Dolgoff, Sam, ed. and trans. *The Anarchist Collectives: Workers' Self-Management in the Spanish Revolution 1936–1939.* New York: Free Life Editions, 1974.

Jean, André. *Economic Transformation in Catalonia.* Barcelona: Generalitat, 1938.

Martin, J. G. *Political and Social Changes in Catalonia during the Revolution.* Barcelona: Generalitat, 1937.

Orwell, George. *Homage to Catalonia.* New York: Harcourt, Brace and World, 1952.

Paz, Abel (pseud. Diego Camacho). *Paradigma de una revolución (19 de julio 1936, en Barcelona).* Toulouse: Ediciones AIT, 1967.

Peers, E. Allison. *Catalonia Infelix.* London: Methuen, 1937.

Pestaña, Angel. *El terrorismo en Barcelona.* Barcelona: Solidaridad Obrera, 1920.

Plá y Armengol, Ramón. *Impresiones de la huelga general de Barcelona, del 24 de marzo al 7 de abril de 1919.* Barcelona: n.p., 1930.

Sanz, Ricardo. *Los que fuimos a Madrid: Columna Durruti 26 División.* Toulouse: Imprimerie Dulaurier, 1969.

Ullman, Joan Connelly. *The Tragic Week.* Cambridge: Harvard University Press, 1967.

XII. General

Banfield, Edward. *The Moral Basis of a Backward Society.* New York: Free Press, 1958.

Barrett, Richard A. *Benabarre: The Modernization of a Spanish Village.* New York: Holt, Rinehart and Winston, 1973.

Chomsky, Noam. *American Power and the New Mandarins.* New York: Random House, 1969.

Freeman, Susan Tax. *Neighbors: The Social Contract in a Castilian Village.* Chicago: University of Chicago Press, 1970.

Lison-Toledana, Carmelo. *Belmonte de los Caballeros: A Sociological Study of a Spanish Town.* Oxford: Clarendon Press, 1966.

Malefakis, Edward. *Agrarian Reform and Peasant Revolution in Spain.* New Haven: Yale University Press, 1970.

Moore, Jr., Barrington. *The Social Origins of Dictatorship and Democracy.* Boston: Beacon, 1967.

Rapoport, David C. *Assassination and Terrorism.* Toronto: CBC, 1971.

Solomon, Barbara Probst. *Arriving Where We Started.* New York: Harper and Row, 1972.

Index

315

1 2 3 4 5 6 7 8 9 10 11 12 13 14 15   88 87 86 85 84 83 82 81 80 79 78